D1415986

THE WORLD AROUND US

NORTH CAROLINA

This Tar Heel quilt was created by the students, their parents, and the staff of the Clinton City Schools in North Carolina. It hangs in the Butler Avenue School. This beautiful work of art honors the symbols and products that are a part of the rich heritage of our state. From the top left to right are shown: peanuts, corn, Wright brothers' airplane, cotton, squirrel, Cape Hatteras Lighthouse, tar heel, rainbow trout, eagle, regions of North Carolina, cardinal, emerald, dogwood, longleaf pine, Scotch Bonnet, Blue Ridge Mountains, sweet potato, hog, and tobacco.

WILLIAM IMPERATORE LINDA SCHER

MACMILLAN/McGRAW-HILL SCHOOL PUBLISHING COMPANY
NEW YORK CHICAGO COLUMBUS

AUTHORS

William Imperatore is a Professor of Geography at Appalachian State University, where he teaches courses on the geography of the United States and Canada, world regional geography, and weather and climate. As Co-Coordinator of the North Carolina Geographic Alliance, Dr. Imperatore works closely with elementary and secondary social studies teachers on the teaching of geography.

Linda Scher is a native North Carolinian with 25 years of experience in book writing and editing. She has served as a curriculum consultant for North Carolina's Department of Public Instruction. Ms. Scher has also developed a program on the Holocaust for use in North Carolina schools. She lives in Raleigh, where her children attend the Wake County public schools.

PROGRAM AUTHORS

Dr. James A. Banks
Professor of Education and Director of the Center for Multicultural Education
University of Washington
Seattle, Washington

Dr. Barry K. Beyer
Professor of Education and American Studies
George Mason University
Fairfax, Virginia

Dr. Gloria Contreras
Professor of Education and Director of the Office of Multicultural Affairs
University of North Texas
Denton, Texas

Jean Craven
District Coordinator of Curriculum Development
Albuquerque Schools
Albuquerque, New Mexico

Dr. Gloria Ladson-Billings
Assistant Professor of Education
University of Wisconsin
Madison, Wisconsin

Dr. Mary McFarland
Director of Staff Development and Instructional Coordinator of Social Studies, K-12
Parkway School District
Chesterfield, Missouri

Dr. Walter C. Parker
Associate Professor of Social Studies Education and Director of the Center for the Study of Civic Intelligence
University of Washington
Seattle, Washington

CONTENT CONSULTANTS

Dr. Donald C. Bohlen
Social Studies Curriculum Specialist
Greensboro Public Schools
Greensboro, North Carolina

Alice Eley Jones
Instructor of History
North Carolina Central University
Durham, North Carolina

Dr. Melton McLaurin
Professor of History
University of North Carolina at Wilmington
Wilmington, North Carolina

Jacqueline Sherrod
Social Studies Supervisor
Public Schools of Robeson County
Lumberton, North Carolina

Dr. Karen Wood
Professor of Education
University of North Carolina at Charlotte
Charlotte, North Carolina

GRADE-LEVEL CONSULTANTS

Mary B. Johnson
Fourth Grade Teacher
Myers Park Traditional Elementary School
Charlotte, North Carolina

Glenna B. Kluttz
Fourth Grade Teacher
Black Mountain Primary School
Black Mountain, North Carolina

Frances Lowry
Fourth Grade Teacher
Foust Elementary School
Greensboro, North Carolina

Cassandra McMillion
Fourth Grade Teacher
Morganton Elementary School
Fayetteville, North Carolina

Sharon C. Roetger
Third/Fourth Grade Teacher
College Park Elementary School
Wilmington, North Carolina

Bonnie Torgerson
Fourth Grade Teacher
Penny Road School
Raleigh, North Carolina

Tami Weaver
Fourth Grade Teacher
Merrick-Moore Elementary School
Durham, North Carolina

TRADITIONS WRITERS

Eric Kimmel **Lila Summer**
Carole Marsh **Clifford E. Trafzer**

ACKNOWLEDGMENTS

The publisher gratefully acknowledges permission to reprint the following copyrighted material: Excerpt from THE OUTER BANKS by Anthony Bailey. Copyright © 1987, 1989 by Anthony Bailey. Reprinted by permission of Farrar, Straus & Giroux, Inc. Excerpt from GRAVEYARD OF THE ATLANTIC by David Stick. Published by The University of North Carolina Press, 1952. Holiday House, Inc. for excerpts from THE WRIGHT BROTHERS: HOW THEY INVENTED THE AIRPLANE by Russell Freedman, Copyright © 1991 by Holiday House, Inc. Reprinted by permission of the publisher. *Carolina in the Morning* by Walter Donaldson and Gus Kahn. © 1922 Copyright renewed 1949 Donaldson Publishing Co. and Gilbert Keyes Music Co. Used by permission. *Quail Dance Song* from WHERE THE RAVENS ROOST. © 1991 Western Carolina University. Used by permission of the Mountain Heritage Center at Western Carolina University. Excerpts from the Tar Heel Junior Historian, Fall 1987. Published by the Tar Heel Junior Historian Association. Reprinted by permission. Farrar, Straus & Giroux, Inc. for excerpt from "The Last American Hero" by Tom Wolfe in THE KANDY-KOLORED TANGERINE FLAKE STREAMLINE BABY. Copyright © 1965 by Tom Wolfe. Excerpt from CHARLOTTE: SPIRIT OF THE NEW SOUTH by Mary Norton Kratt. Continental Heritage Press, 1980. Excerpt from NORTH CAROLINA: PEOPLE AND ENVIRONMENTS by O. Gade and H.D. Stillwell. GEO-APP Publishing Company, 1986. National Geographic Society for excerpt from "Home to North Carolina," March 1980. Reprinted by permission of the publisher. Excerpt from YOUNG READER'S PICTUREBOOK OF TAR HEEL AUTHORS by Richard Walser and Mary Reynolds Peacock. Published by the North Carolina Department of Cultural Resources, Division of Archives and History, 1981. Harcourt Brace Jovanovich, Inc. for "Window" by Carl Sandburg from THE COMPLETE POEMS, Copyright © 1950 by Carl Sandburg. Reprinted by permission of the publisher. *Old Joe Clark* collected and adapted by John A. Lomax and Alan Lomax. TRO—© Copyright 1934 (renewed) Ludlow Music, Inc., New York, New York. Used by permission. "Bubbles" from THE COMPLETE POEMS OF CARL SANDBURG. Revised and Expanded Edition, copyright 1950 by Carl Sandburg and renewed 1978 by Margaret Sandburg, Helga Sandburg Crile, and Janet Sandburg. Reprinted by permission of Harcourt Brace Jovanovich, Inc. Excerpt from NORTH CAROLINA: OFF THE BEATEN PATH by Sara Pitzer. The Globe Pequot Press, 1990. Excerpt from COASTWATCH, May/June 1991. Excerpt from THE STATE, March 1990. National Geographic Society for excerpt from "Home to North Carolina," March 1980. Reprinted by permission of the publisher. National Geographic Society for excerpt from "Home to North Carolina," March 1980. Reprinted by permission of the publisher. New York Times Co. for quotation by Marshal Logan in "Southern Blacks Go Home Again" by Ronald Smothers. Reprinted by permission.

Macmillan/McGraw-Hill School Division
10 Union Square East
New York, New York 10003

Printed in the United States of America
ISBN 0-02-146006-X
7 8 9 RAI 99 98 97 96

CONTENTS

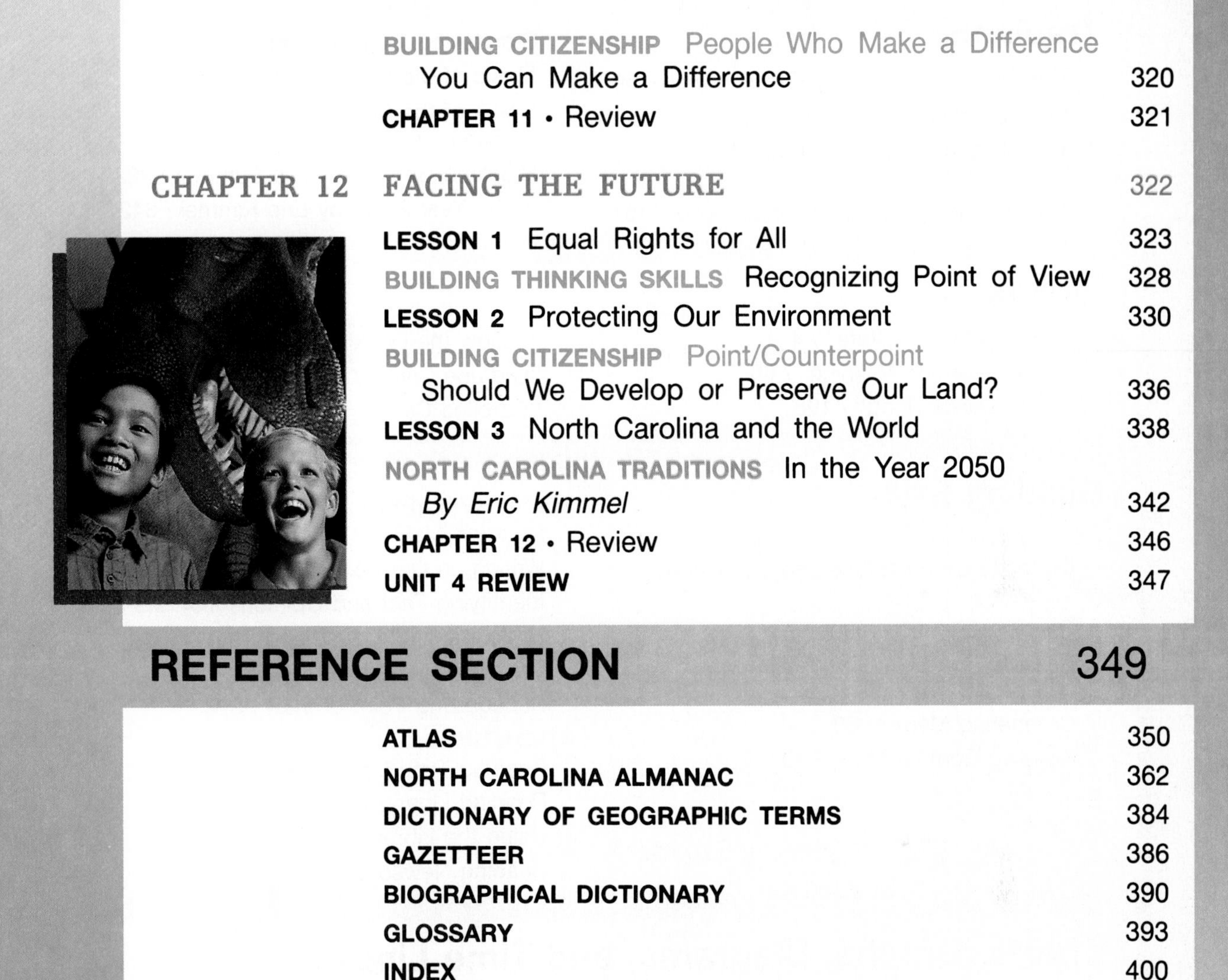

REFERENCE SECTION 349

Building Citizenship

Traditions

Songs

Building Skills

GEOGRAPHY

THINKING/READING

STUDY/TIME

Charts, Graphs, Diagrams, and Time Lines

Maps

Jenny Voysey
Robert Cocke & Family
Sharhonda Mayes
Madinah Hamidullah
Andrea WalkingStick & Grandfather
Julius Santiago & Grandparents
Loren Aldridge & Dad
Yina Maldonado
Chuom Prak & Friend
Janna and Shanna Reno
Nathan Katzin

WHAT IS A TAR HEEL?

Dear Students,

Look at the photographs on these pages. These students go to different schools and live in different parts of our state. However, they have one thing in common. Like you, they are *Tar Heels*—North Carolinians.

No one knows for sure where the name *Tar Heel* comes from. Some say North Carolina is called the Tar Heel State because of the tar that was made from the state's many pine trees during the 1700s. As workers gathered the sticky liquid from the trees, which they made into tar, some of it spilled on the ground and stuck to their feet. Others say that we are called Tar Heels because of the bravery of North Carolina's soldiers during the Civil War. These soldiers showed their courage by sticking at their posts during a fierce battle, as if they had tar on their heels. They kept fighting while soldiers from a nearby state fled.

As you read this book, you will have a chance to decide for yourself what it means to be a Tar Heel. As you will see, being a Tar Heel can mean living in the mountains or near the ocean, in a large city or a small town. As you learn about the geography of our state, you will see that each area of the state has its own history and celebrations that make it special.

You will also see that our state is made up of special people. This book will help you to understand how people have changed the land and found new uses for the resources of our state.

When you finish this book, you will know more about the part of North Carolina in which you live and about other parts of the state as well. You will see why as North Carolinians we are proud to call ourselves Tar Heels.

Sincerely,

William Imperatore

Linda Scher

Chad O'Neal

The Old North State

William Gaston

Collected and arranged by Mrs. E. E. Randolph

With spirit

The Old North State Words by William Gaston, collected and arranged by Mrs. E. E. Randolph. Extensive research failed to locate the author and/or copyright holder of this work.

USING YOUR TEXTBOOK

Your textbook contains many features that will help you read, understand, and remember the geography and people of the regions of North Carolina

TABLE OF CONTENTS
Lists all parts of your book and tells you where to find them

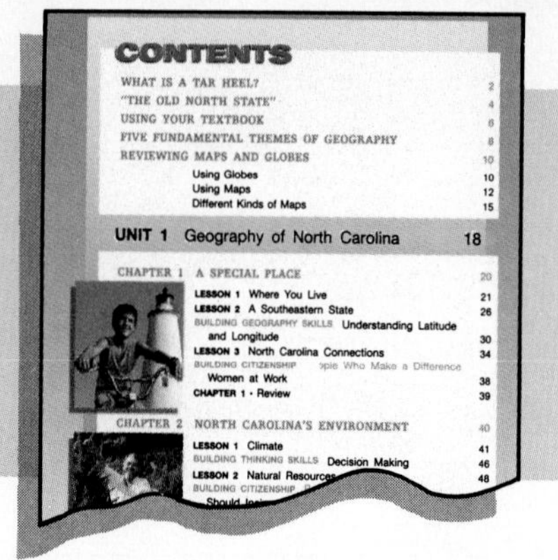
CONTENTS

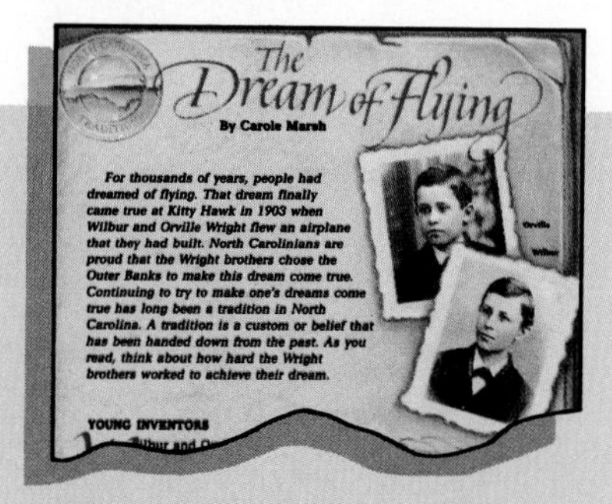
The Dream of Flying

By Carole Marsh

For thousands of years, people had dreamed of flying. That dream finally came true at Kitty Hawk in 1903 when Wilbur and Orville Wright flew an airplane that they had built. North Carolinians are proud that the Wright brothers chose the Outer Banks to make this dream come true. Continuing to try to make one's dreams come true has long been a tradition in North Carolina. A tradition is a custom or belief that has been handed down from the past. As you read, think about how hard the Wright brothers worked to achieve their dream.

YOUNG INVENTORS

REVIEWING MAPS AND GLOBES
Reviews skills that will help you use the maps in your book

TRADITIONS
Lessons that give you a deeper understanding of the cultures of the regions you are studying

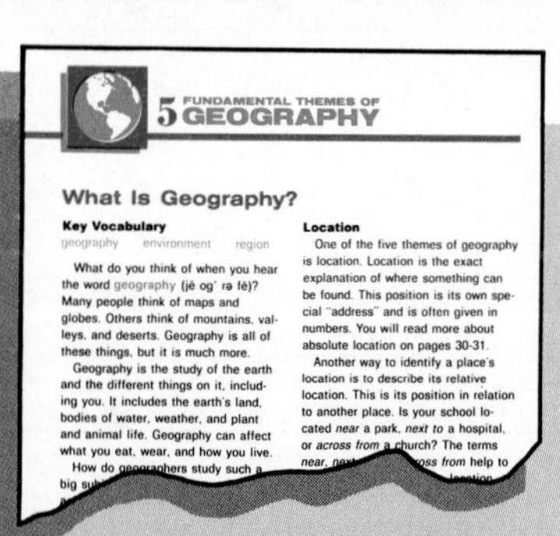
5 FUNDAMENTAL THEMES OF GEOGRAPHY

What Is Geography?

Key Vocabulary
geography environment region

What do you think of when you hear the word geography (jē og' rə fē)? Many people think of maps and globes. Others think of mountains, valleys, and deserts. Geography is all of these things, but it is much more.

Geography is the study of the earth and the different things on it, including you. It includes the earth's land, bodies of water, weather, and plant and animal life. Geography can affect what you eat, wear, and how you live.

How do geographers study such a

Location

One of the five themes of geography is location. Location is the exact explanation of where something can be found. This position is its own special "address" and is often given in numbers. You will read more about absolute location on pages 30-31.

Another way to identify a place's location is to describe its relative location. This is its position in relation to another place. Is your school located *near* a park, *next to* a hospital, or *across from* a church? The terms

FIVE FUNDAMENTAL THEMES OF GEOGRAPHY
Introduces important themes of geography that will help you to compare, to contrast, and to understand the land, regions, and people of North Carolina you are studying

LESSON OPENER

Important vocabulary, people, and places introduced in the lesson

Lesson introduction

Asks you to think about what you already know from previous lessons or your own experience

Question you should keep in mind as you read the lesson

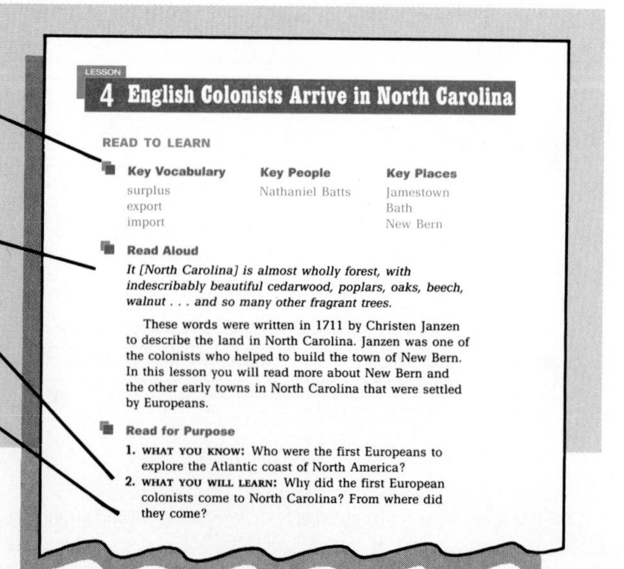
LESSON 4 English Colonists Arrive in North Carolina

READ TO LEARN

Key Vocabulary	Key People	Key Places
surplus	Nathaniel Batts	Jamestown
export		Bath
import		New Bern

Read Aloud

It [North Carolina] is almost wholly forest, with indescribably beautiful cedarwood, poplars, oaks, beech, walnut . . . and so many other fragrant trees.

These words were written in 1711 by Christen Janzen to describe the land in North Carolina. Janzen was one of the colonists who helped to build the town of New Bern. In this lesson you will read more about New Bern and the other early towns in North Carolina that were settled by Europeans.

Read for Purpose

1. WHAT YOU KNOW: Who were the first Europeans to explore the Atlantic coast of North America?
2. WHAT YOU WILL LEARN: Why did the first European colonists come to North Carolina? From where did they come?

REFERENCE SECTION

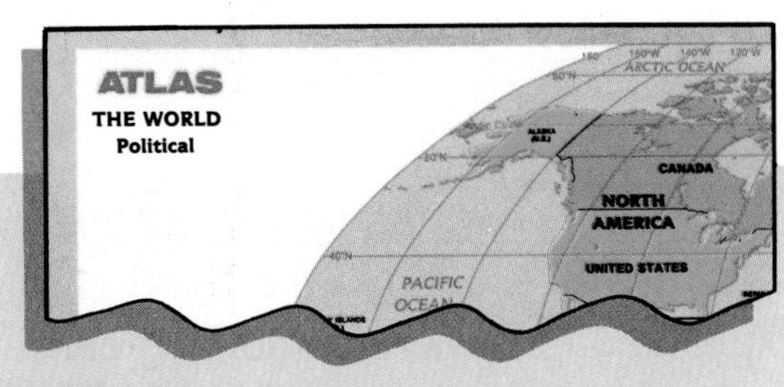

ATLAS

Maps of the world, the United States, and North Carolina

NORTH CAROLINA ALMANAC

Important and interesting facts about North Carolina

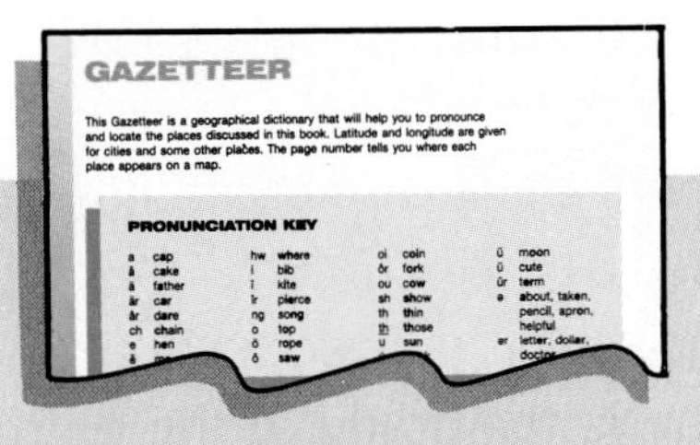

GAZETTEER

Location and pronunciation of all key places and the first page where each is shown on a map

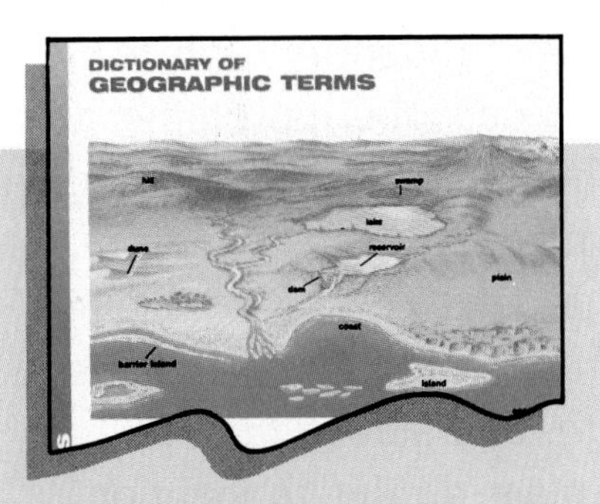

DICTIONARY OF GEOGRAPHIC TERMS

Definition and pronunciation of important geographic features

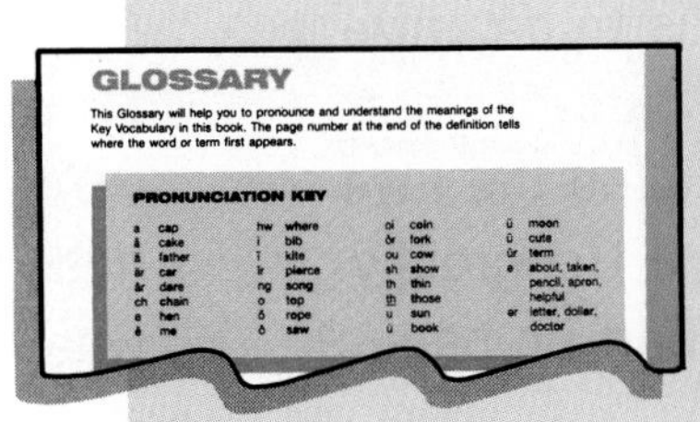

GLOSSARY

Definition and pronunciation of key vocabulary and the first page where each is found

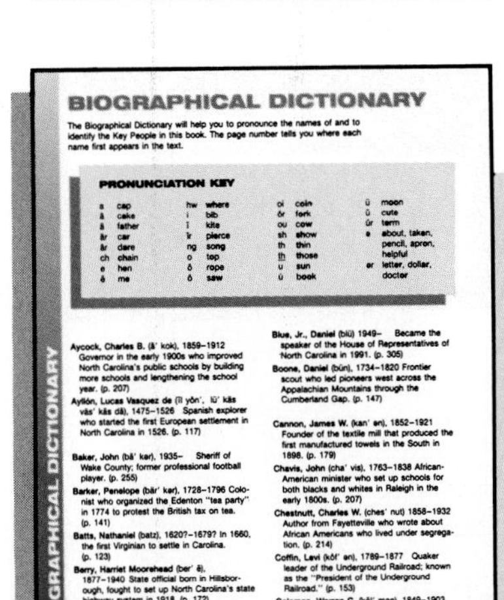

BIOGRAPHICAL DICTIONARY

Identification and pronunciation of names of key people discussed in your book and lists the first page where each is found

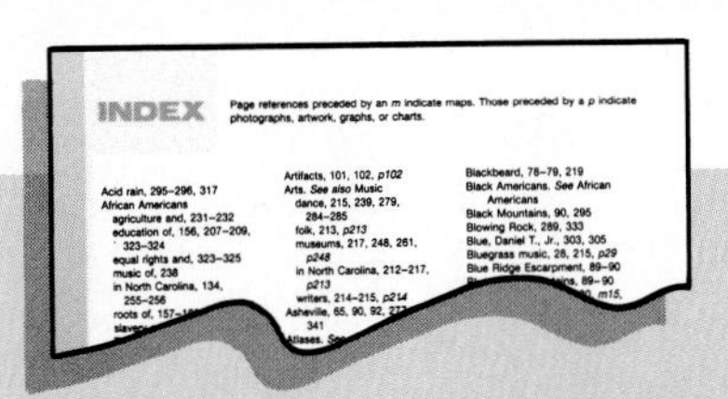

INDEX

Alphabetical list of important people and subjects in your book and the pages where information is found

5 FUNDAMENTAL THEMES OF GEOGRAPHY

What Is Geography?

Key Vocabulary

geography environment region

What do you think of when you hear the word **geography** (jē og′ rə fē)? Many people think of maps and globes. Others think of mountains, valleys, and deserts. Geography is all of these things, but it is much more.

Geography is the study of the earth and the different things on it, including you. It includes the earth's land, bodies of water, weather, and plant and animal life. Geography can affect what you eat, wear, and how you live.

How do geographers study such a big subject? One way is to organize it according to five important ideas in geography. They are called the Five Fundamental Themes of Geography and are listed in the chart on page 9.

Location

One of the five themes of geography is location. Location is the exact explanation of where something can be found. This position is its own special "address" and is often given in numbers. You will read more about absolute location on pages 30-31.

Another way to identify a place's location is to describe its relative location. This is its position in relation to another place. Is your school located *near* a park, *next to* a hospital, or *across from* a church? The terms *near*, *next to*, and *across from* help to describe a place's relative location.

Description of Place

A second theme of geography is description of place. Place explains what an area is like. Now look at the

5 FUNDAMENTAL THEMES OF GEOGRAPHY

THEME	
Location	• Where is a place located? What is it near? What direction is it from another place?
Description of Place	• What is a place like? What features does it have?
People and Their Environment	• How are people's lives shaped by the place where they live? How has a place been shaped by people?
Movement	• How do people and things move from one place to another? Why do they make these movements?
Regions	• Why are some places similar to others? What makes these places different from others?

photograph on page 8. How would you describe its features?

Geographers try to show what makes one place different from another one. Does the place have many mountains or farms?

People and Their Environment

A third theme of geography is people and their **environment**. The environment is the surroundings in which people, plants, and animals live. The environment shapes the ways in which people live. North Carolinians work in pine forests. Parts of our state have the right environment for these forests. But people also shape their environment. They cut down trees to make farms. Geographers study the connections between people and their environment.

Movement

Another theme of geography is the movement of people, goods, and ideas around the world. News moves into our lives through television. Goods from other countries move to our stores. Geographers study how movement affects people and their communities.

Regions

A fifth theme of geography is **Regions**. A region is an area with common land features that set it apart from other areas. A region can also be defined by a common language or ways of living.

Geographers divide the world into regions in order to study the earth and its people more closely. This year you will be reading about the regions of North Carolina. You will find out what makes them special.

1. What is geography?
2. Use each of the Five Fundamental Themes of Geography to describe the community in which you live.

Using Globes

Key Vocabulary

continent   hemisphere
ocean   equator

In social studies this year you will learn about our state, North Carolina. You will come to understand North Carolina's relationship with its neighboring states, with the rest of the United States, and with the world.

The students in this picture are using a globe to learn about North Carolina's place on the earth. As you study our state, you too will find that maps and globes can be very useful.

Maps and globes can show at a glance what would take a great deal of space to describe in writing. They can be thought of as special tools. Let's review how to use them.

Continents and Oceans

You have probably built or played with model trains or cars. A globe is also a model. It is a small copy of the earth. Like the earth, it is shaped like a ball. Another name for a round body is *sphere* (sfîr).

Globes show the earth's seven **continents** and four **oceans**. A continent is a very large body of land. An ocean is a very large body of salt water. The students in the picture learned that North Carolina is located on the continent of North America, and it borders on the Atlantic Ocean. The globe helped them understand where North Carolina is in relation to the earth's continents and oceans.

Hemispheres

No matter which way you turn a globe or how you position yourself to look at it, you can see only half of it at one time. Since a globe is a sphere, what you see is half a sphere. Another word for half a sphere is **hemisphere**. *Hemi* means "half."

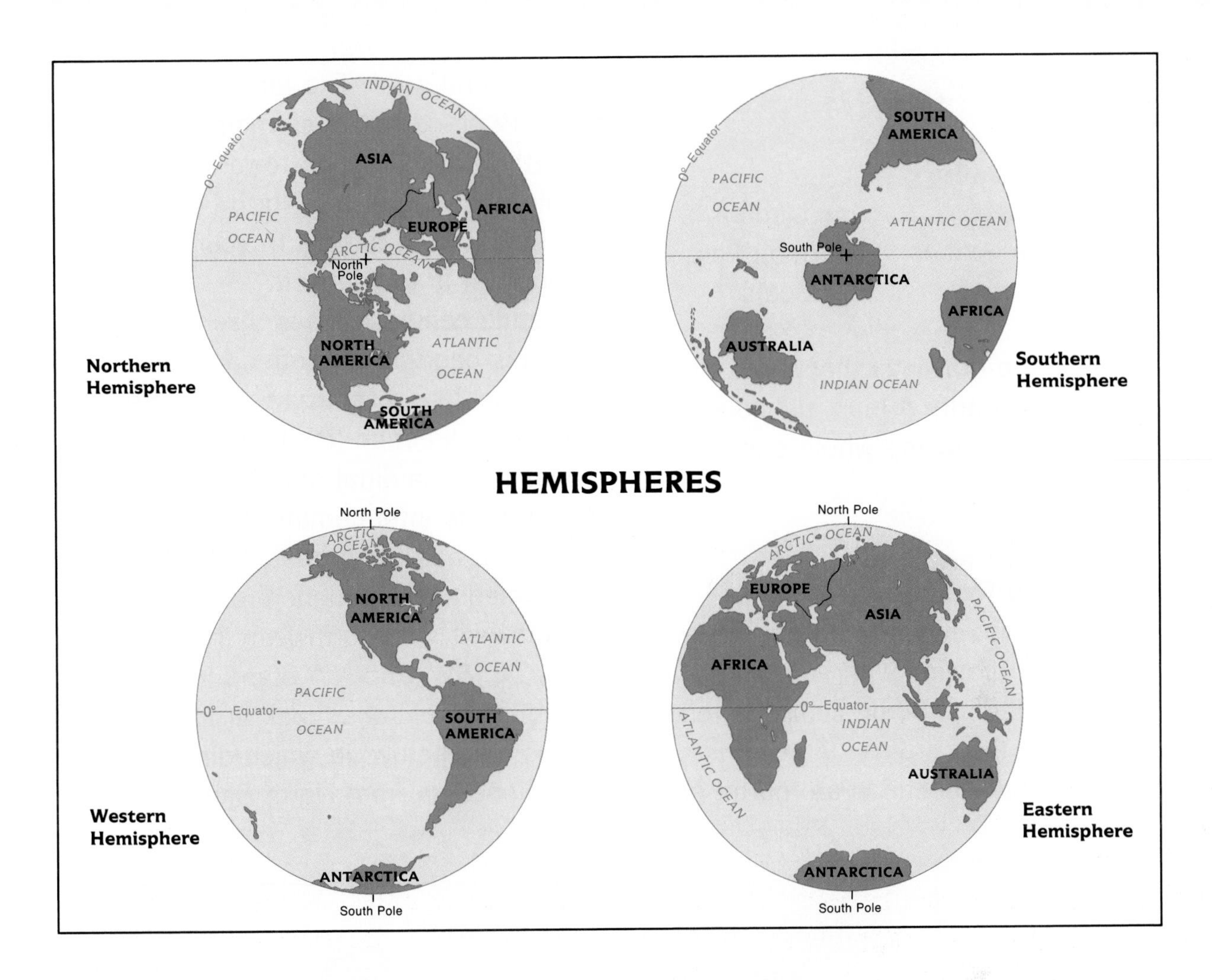

The maps on this page show that the earth can be divided into different hemispheres. Each map shows half of the earth. You can also see these different hemispheres by looking at a globe.

The northern half of the earth is divided from the southern half by the **equator**. The equator is an imaginary line that lies halfway between the North Pole and the South Pole. The equator divides the earth into the Northern Hemisphere and the Southern Hemisphere.

How many continents are found in the Northern Hemisphere? How many continents are found in the Southern Hemisphere?

The earth is also divided into the Eastern Hemisphere and the Western Hemisphere. The hemispheres are separated by other imaginary lines, which you will read about on pages 30–31.

1. What can you learn about the earth from looking at a globe?
2. What is a continent?
3. What does the word *hemisphere* mean?
4. What is the equator?
5. In which two hemispheres is North America located?

Using Maps

Key Vocabulary

compass rose
cardinal directions
intermediate directions
symbol
map key
scale

Maps are drawings that show all or part of the earth. A map, unlike a globe, can show the whole earth at once.

Directions and the Compass Rose

Many maps have a **compass rose**, or a small drawing with lines that show directions. Some compass roses show only the **cardinal directions**. The cardinal directions are north, east, south, and west. The letters *N*, *E*, *S*, and *W* stand for these main directions. North is the direction toward the North Pole. If you face the North Pole, south is behind you, east is to your right, and west is to your left.

Some compass roses, like the one on this page, show both cardinal and **intermediate directions**. Each intermediate direction lies halfway between two cardinal directions. Northeast is the intermediate direction between north and east. The other intermediate directions are southeast, southwest, and northwest. The letters *NE, SE, SW,* and *NW* stand for intermediate directions. Look at the compass rose below. In which direction is Minnesota from North Carolina?

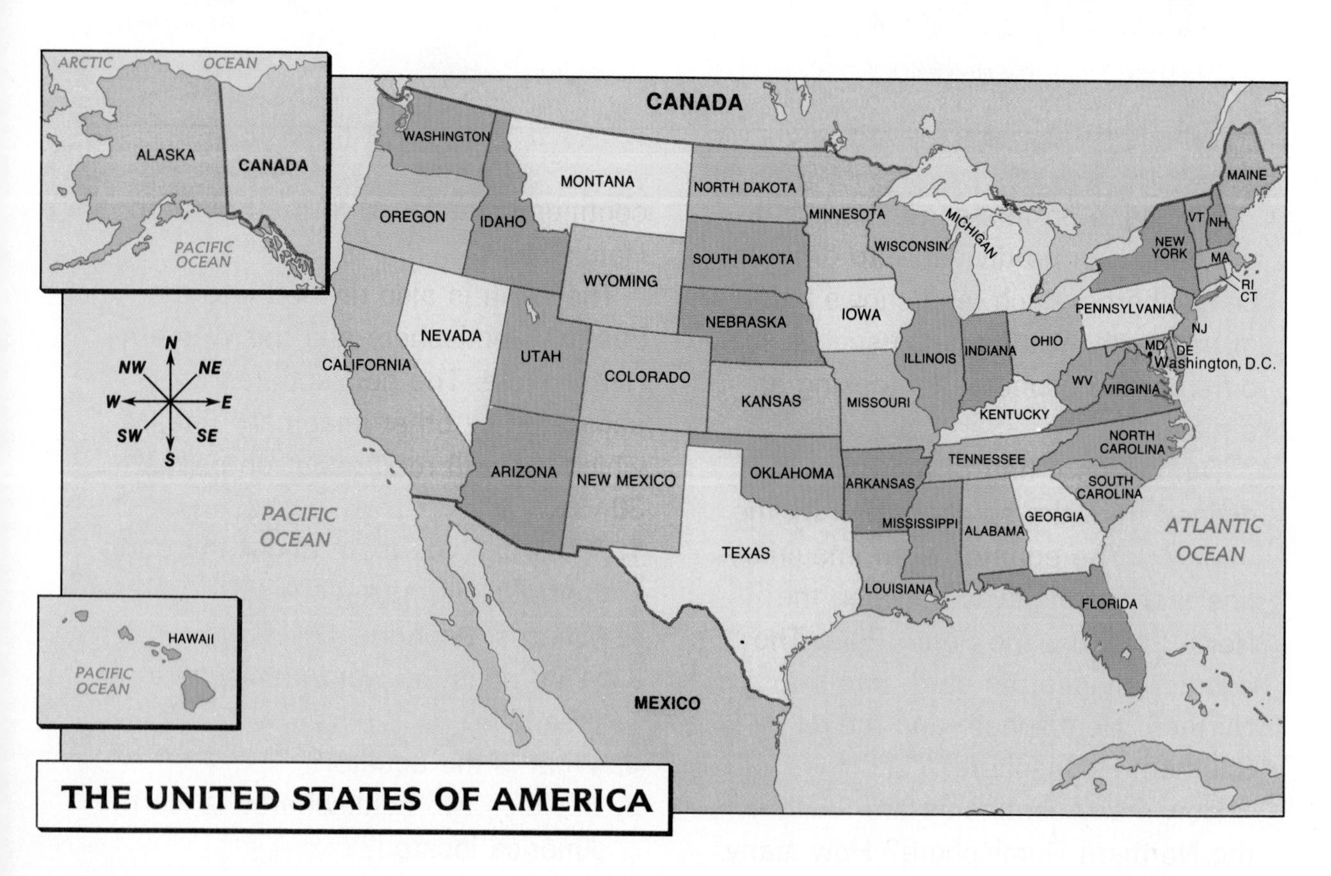

THE UNITED STATES OF AMERICA

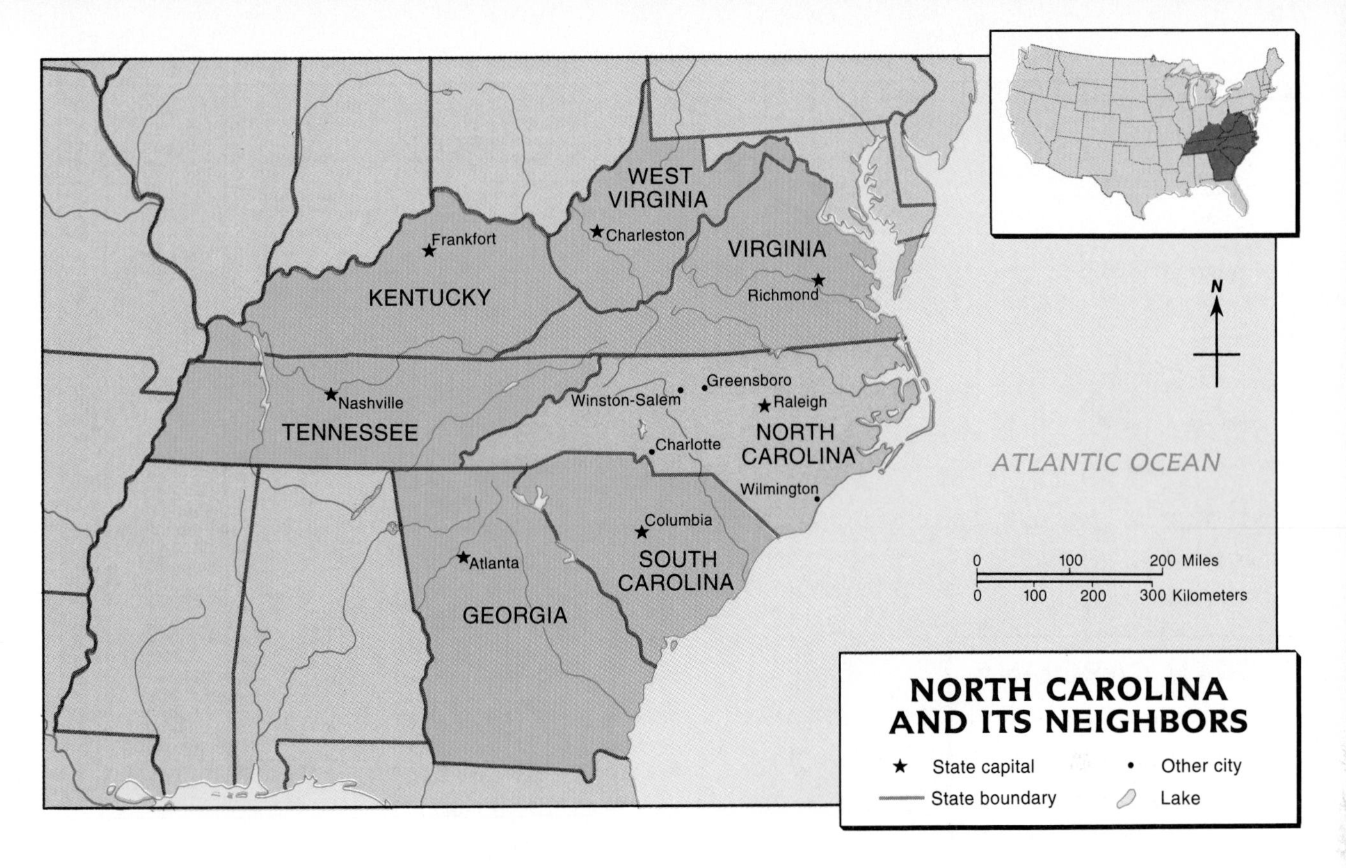

Not all maps have a compass rose. Instead, they have a north pointer. A north pointer is an arrow that shows which direction is north. If you know where north is, you can easily find the other directions. The map above has a north pointer. Use the north pointer on this map to name the states that are found to the west and the northwest of North Carolina.

Symbols and Map Keys

Symbols are used to give information on maps. A symbol is something that stands for, or represents, something else. Symbols are often small drawings of the things they represent. A drawing of an airplane is often used to represent an airport. Dots are often used to indicate cities and towns. Color is also a symbol. You probably know that the color blue often stands for water.

To understand, or "read," a map, you must know what the symbols used on the map represent. Most maps have a **map key**. The map key explains the meaning of each symbol used on the map.

Some symbols have the same meaning on different maps. For example, state boundaries are usually represented by lines. Some symbols mean different things on different maps. You should always check the map key to find out what the symbols used on that map stand for.

Look at the map key of the map "North Carolina and Its Neighbors" on this page. What does the star stand for? What does the blue symbol in the key stand for?

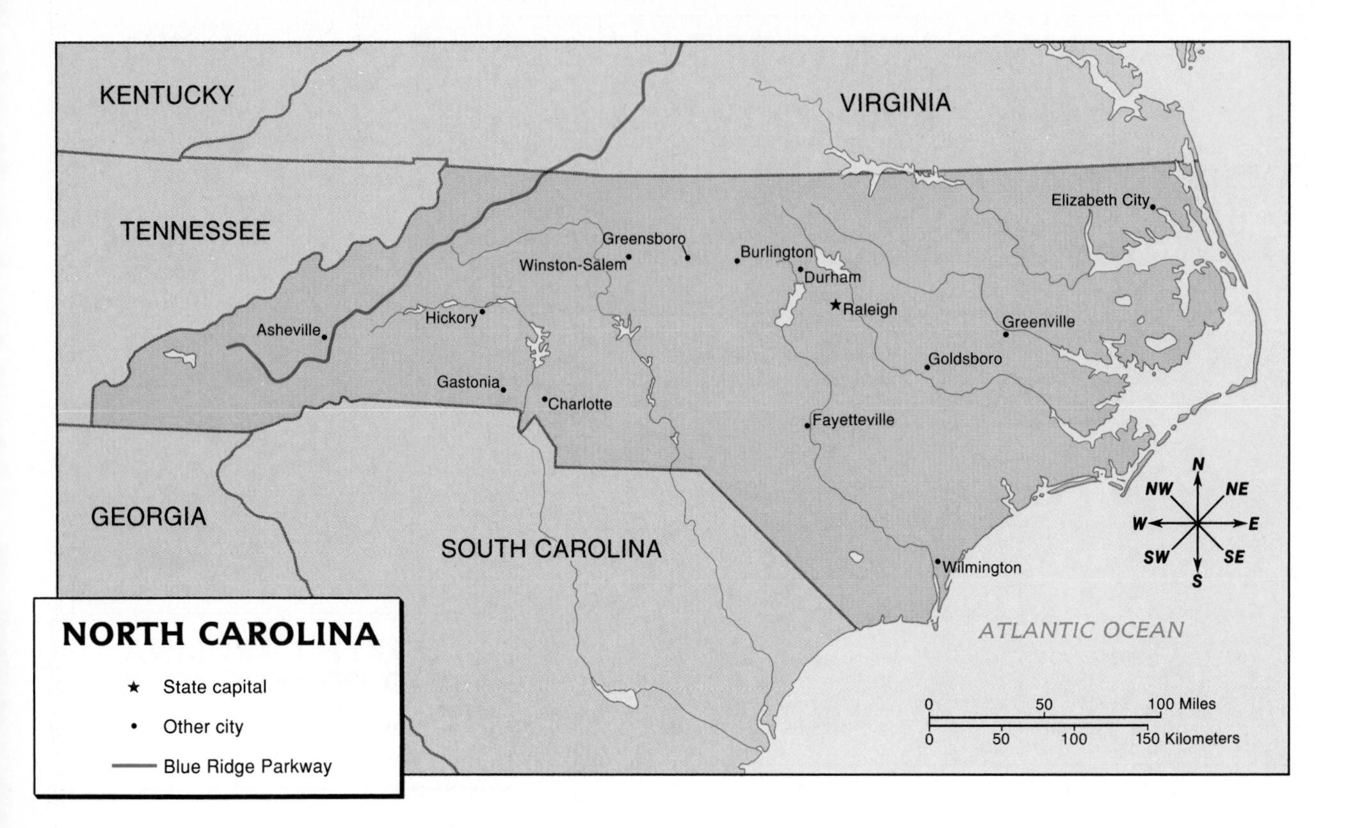

Scale

Maps are not the same size as the areas they show. Imagine what a map of North Carolina would look like if it were as big as our state! Just as a globe is a small copy of the earth, a map is a small copy of a drawing of a *part* of the earth.

However, maps can give a very accurate idea of size and distance. They do this by using small measurements, such as inches or centimeters, to represent much larger measurements, such as miles or kilometers. **Scale** is the relationship between the distances shown on the map and the actual distances on the earth.

In this book map scale is shown by two lines. The top line represents miles and the bottom line represents kilometers. The scale on the map above shows that 1 inch on the map represents 80 miles. The scale also shows that 2 centimeters on the map represent 100 kilometers.

One way to measure the distance between places on a map is to use a ruler. Look at the scale on the map of North Carolina on this page. Use it to measure the distance between Asheville and Greensboro. How many miles apart are these two cities?

1. Why is a compass rose useful?
2. Draw a compass rose and label the cardinal and intermediate directions.
3. What might a map key show?
4. What kind of information do map scales give?
5. Use the map scale on this page to find out how many kilometers it is from Wilmington to Fayetteville.

Different Kinds of Maps

Key Vocabulary

grid map
product map
transportation map

There are many different kinds of maps. Some maps show continents, oceans, countries, or states. Other kinds of maps can help travelers find their way. There are also maps that show where certain products are made. Each kind of map is useful in a different way.

When using a map, look at the map title. The title tells you what is shown on the map.

Grid Maps

Grids make it easier to find places on a map. A **grid map** is made up of two sets of lines that cross each other, often to form squares. One set of lines crosses the map from left to right. The spaces between these lines are labeled with letters. The other set of lines crosses the map from top to bottom. The spaces between these lines are labeled with numbers. Each square on the map can be identified by combining its letter with its number. This makes it easy to find places on the map and to give their locations.

Look at the grid map of the Blue Ridge Parkway. You can find Crabtree Meadows easily if you know that it is located in square F–2. In which square is Cumberland Knob?

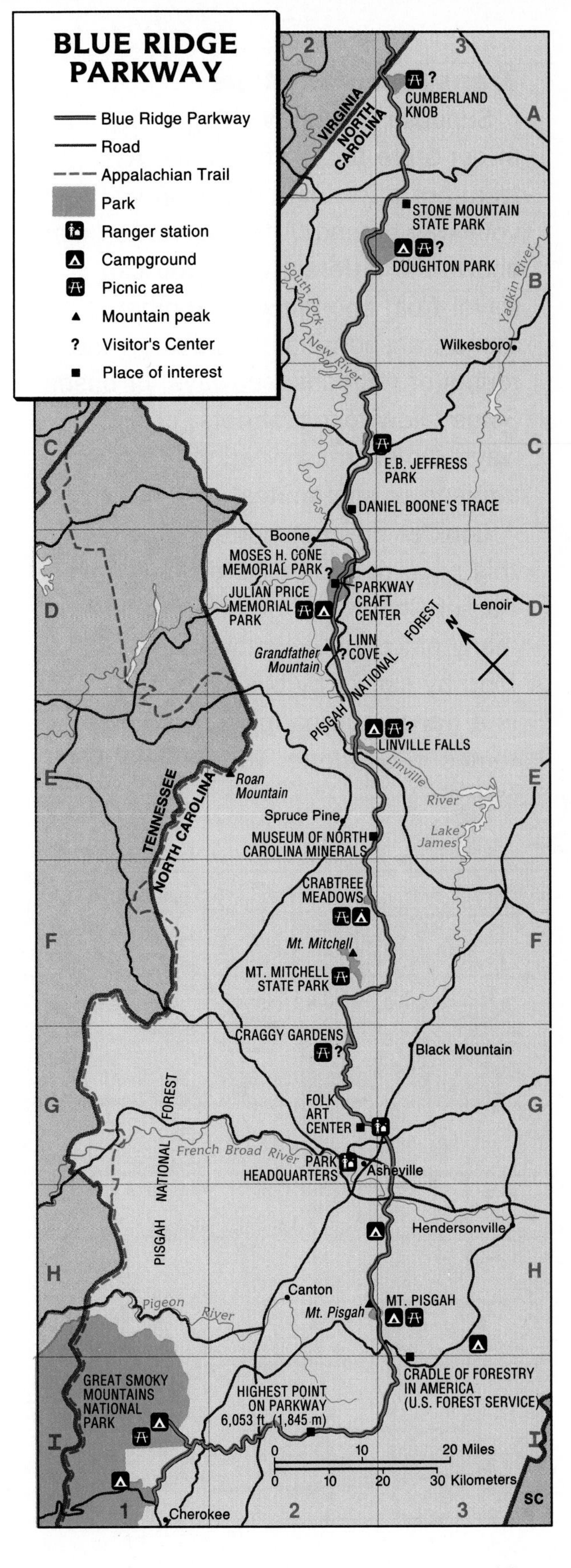

Transportation Maps

Suppose you are visiting a city in our state for the first time. A **transportation map** can help you find your way around. A transportation map shows the different ways you can travel from one place to another. Some transportation maps show the routes of railroads, subways, or buses. Some show roads, streets, or highways. Other transportation maps show airplane or ship routes.

Look at the transportation map on this page. It shows the downtown section of Charlotte. You can visit the many places in downtown Charlotte on foot, by car, or by bus. The map below is a transportation map of the bus routes in Charlotte. To find your way around Charlotte by bus, you would use a map like this one.

You can see that this map has colored lines on it. The map key tells you what the colored lines stand for. The red line is the express route and the green line is the local route. Use the map below to answer the following questions: Would you take a local or an express route to get to the corner of Davidson Street and 3rd Street? Would you take a local bus to go from Church Street and 5th Street to the Post Office on McDowell Street?

Many visitors to Charlotte like to go to the Spirit Square Arts Center at 7th and Tryon Streets. Which bus route goes there, an express route or a local one?

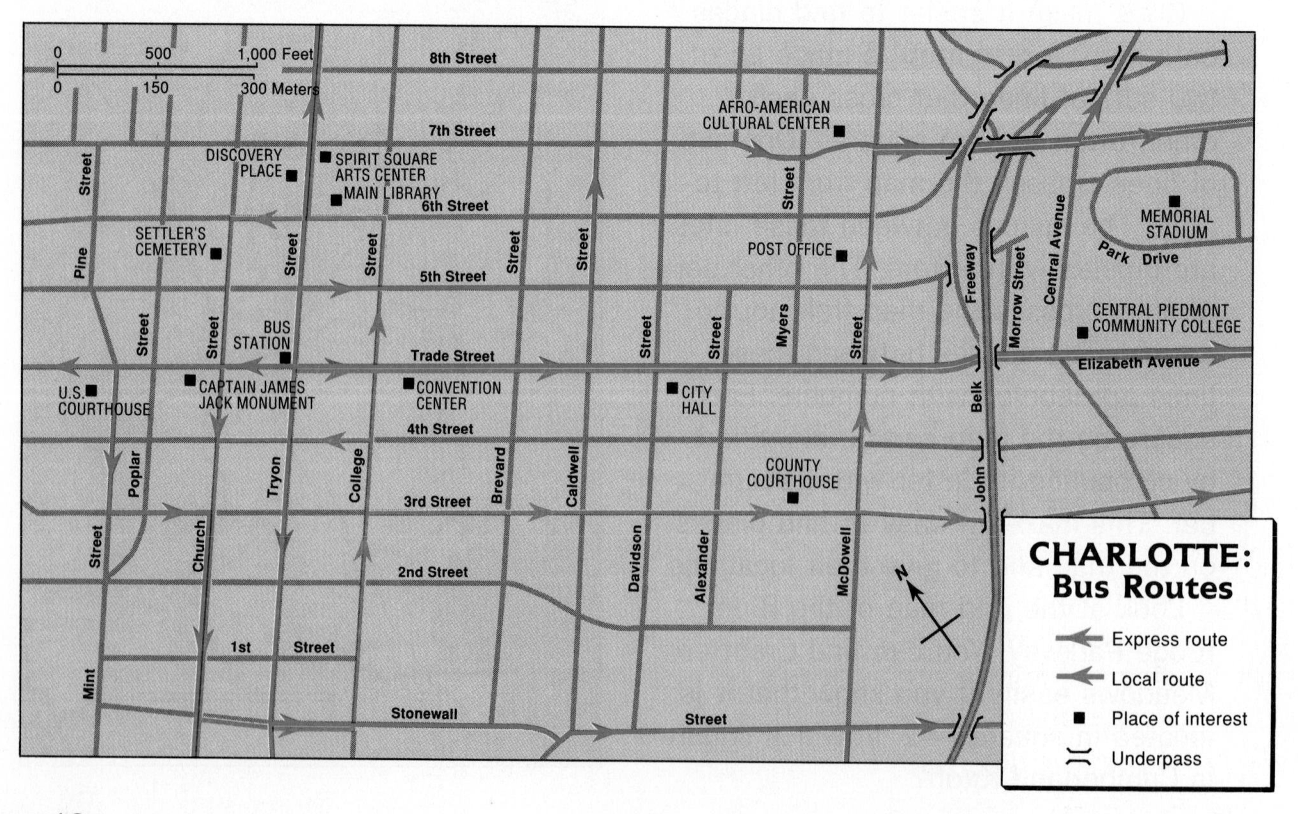

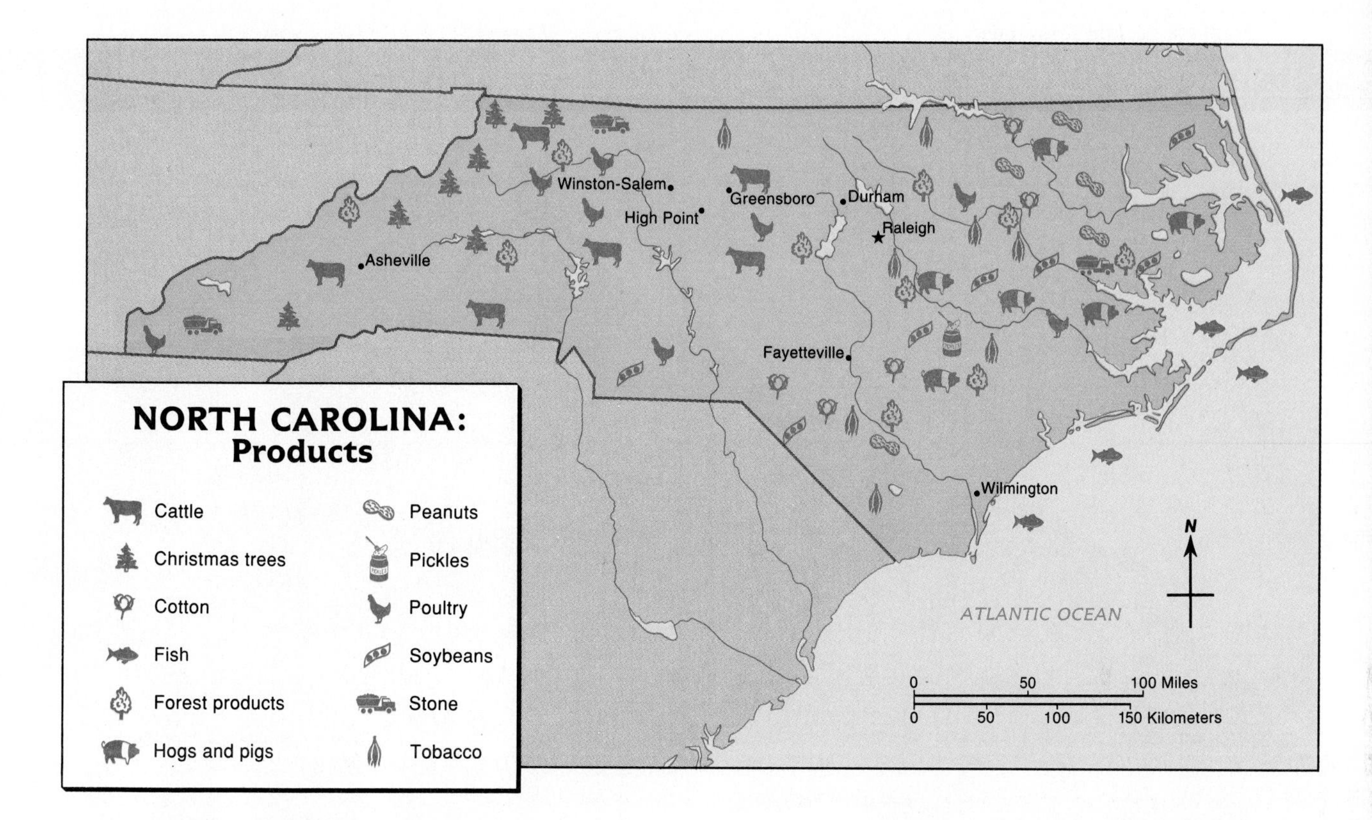

Product Maps

Suppose you want to find out where a certain product is made or grown. Some maps can give you this information at a glance. They are called **product maps**. Product maps show the kinds of things that are made or grown in a specific area.

The product map above shows some of the many products that are made or grown in our state. Look at the map key. It shows the symbol that represents each product. What is the symbol for tobacco? In which areas of the state are Christmas trees grown, according to the map? Which animals are raised in North Carolina?

Look at the map to find the peanut symbol in the northeastern part of the state. It tells you that peanuts are grown here. Which other products are grown in the northeastern part of the state? Which products are found in the western part?

By looking at the symbols on the map, you can tell that the southwest is an area where mining is important. You can also tell that fish are found off the coast.

1. What are some of the different kinds of maps people use?
2. Look at the grid map on page 15. In which square is Roan Mountain?
3. Name two kinds of transportation maps.
4. What can you learn by reading the title of a map?
5. If you were taking a trip through North Carolina, which kinds of maps might you use and why?

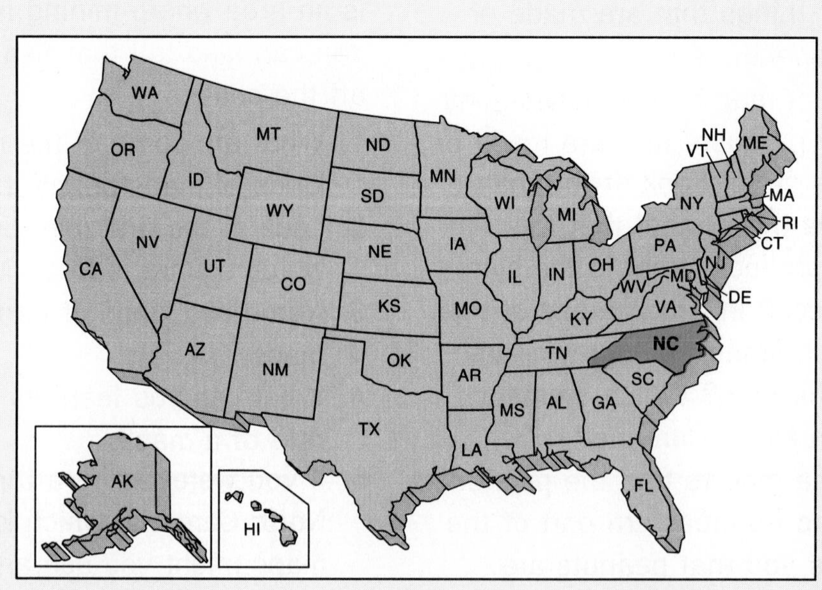

WA
OR
CA
ID
NV
MT
WY
UT
AZ
CO
NM
ND
SD
NE
KS
OK
TX
MN
IA
MO
AR
LA
WI
IL
MI
IN
OH
KY
TN
MS
AL
GA
FL
SC
NC
VA
WV
MD
DE
PA
NJ
NY
CT
RI
MA
VT
NH
ME
AK
HI

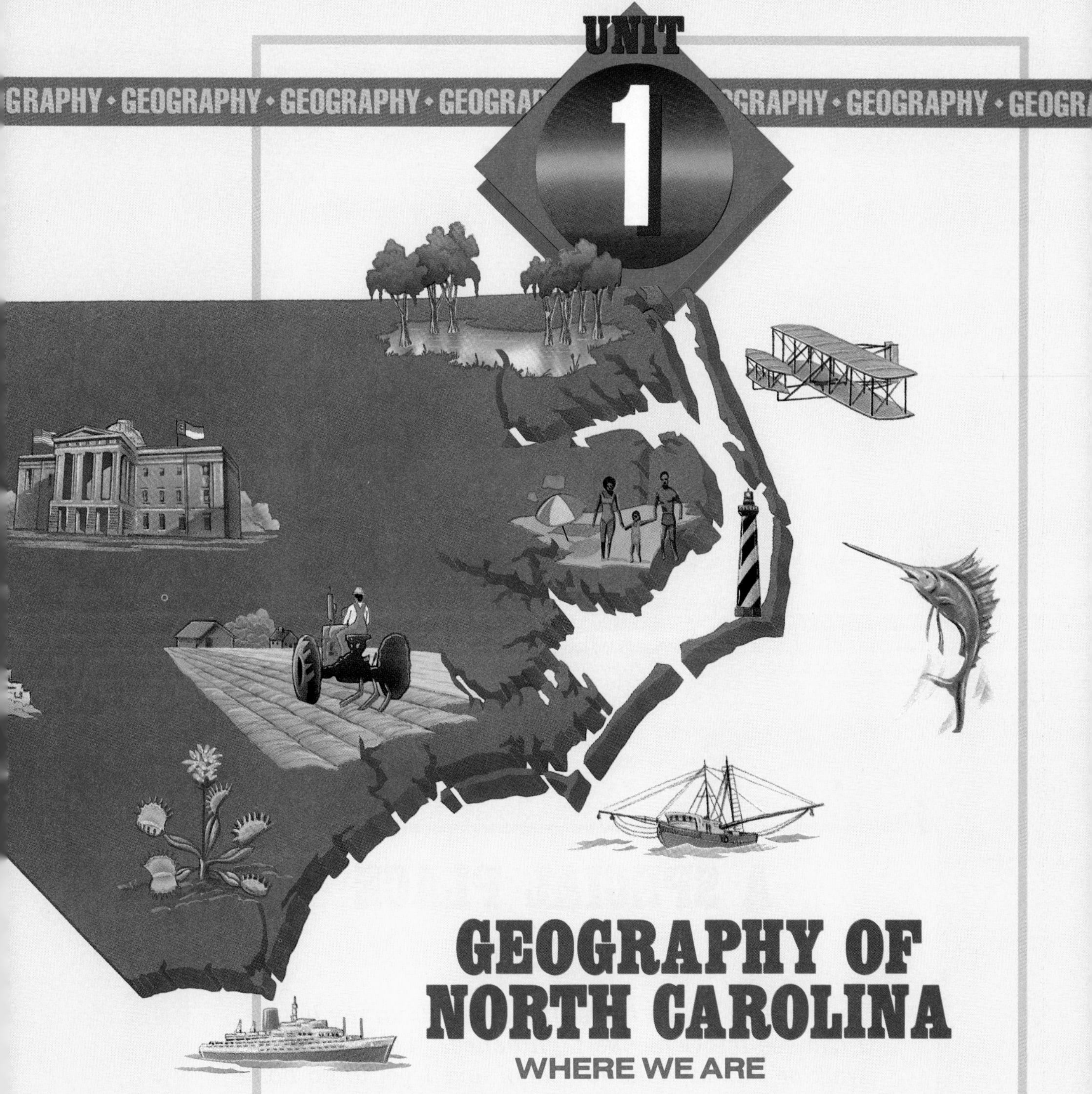

GEOGRAPHY OF NORTH CAROLINA

WHERE WE ARE

The state that we call home is in the part of the United States known as the Southeast. In our state you can go to the beach, sail in Lake Norman, or go skiing in the mountains. Or you can see where history was made at places like the Wright Brothers Memorial at Kitty Hawk. Let's find out about North Carolina—its land, its regions, and its people.

CHAPTER 1

A SPECIAL PLACE

FOCUS

I really like where I live. It's quiet. From my house I can see the Ocracoke Lighthouse. I can easily walk or ride my bike to school and I get to go home every day for lunch. I can swim in the ocean any-time it's warm or go fishing with my father.

Chad O'Neal lives on Ocracoke Island off the coast of North Carolina. One of Chad's favorite places is the lighthouse on the beach. What is special about the place in which you live?

LESSON

1 Where You Live

READ TO LEARN

Key Vocabulary

geography
county

Key Places

Cherokee
Ocracoke
Ocracoke Island

Read Aloud

Nothing could be finer than to be in Carolina in the morning.

These words from a song written by Gus Kahn to the music of Walter Donaldson describe how the people of North Carolina feel about our state. What is it about our state that makes North Carolinians happy to be living here? Maybe it is the many interesting places that you can find in North Carolina.

Read for Purpose

1. **WHAT YOU KNOW:** What is the land like in the place in which you live?
2. **WHAT YOU WILL LEARN:** How does learning about places help us to understand our state's geography?

PLACES ARE DIFFERENT

Suppose that you wanted to learn about a place that you had never visited. What could you do to find out about that place? You might start by writing to a pen pal who lives there. Having a pen pal is a good way to learn about different kinds of places. You read on page 8 that place is one of the five themes of geography. Every place has something special about it. In this lesson you will read about two pen pals who learned what makes the places they live in different.

The two pen pals, John Cornsilk and Susan Carter, both live in North Carolina. John is nine years old and lives in **Cherokee**, a town in the western part of the state.

John's new pen pal, Susan, is also nine years old. Susan lives in **Ocracoke** (ō′ krə kōk), a town on **Ocracoke Island** off the east coast.

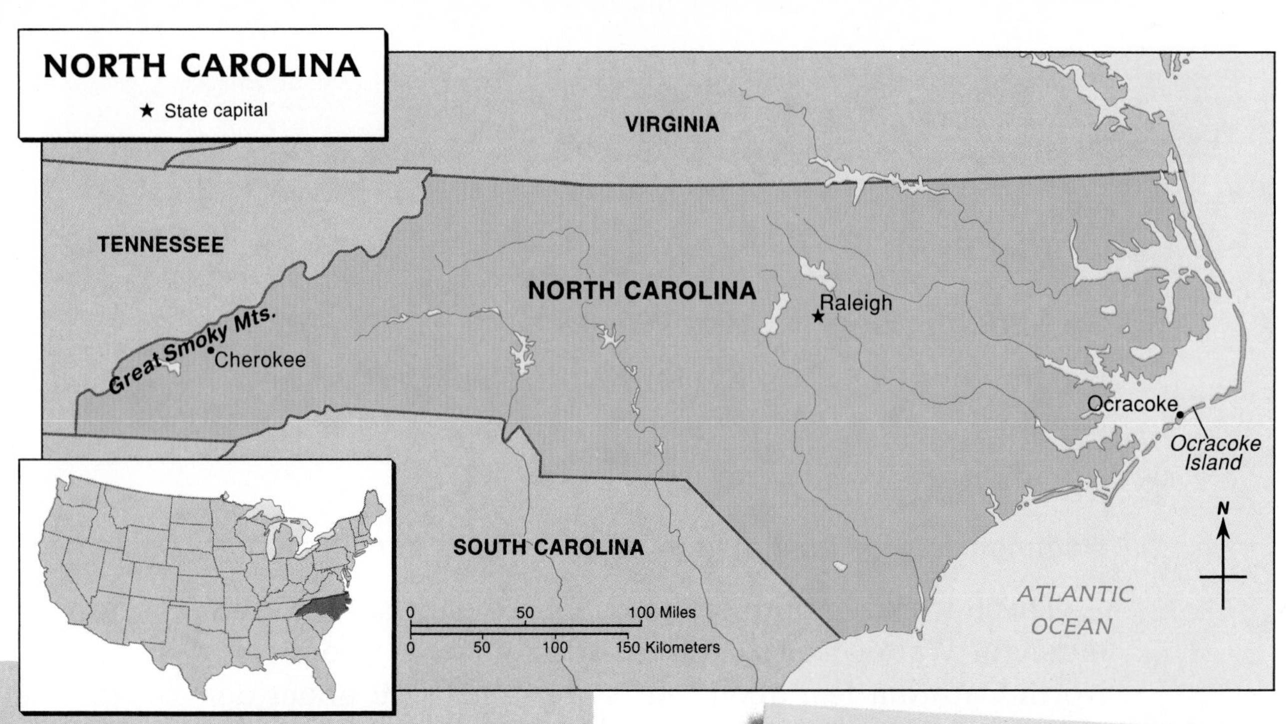

MAP SKILL: Which mountains are near John's hometown? What does John's letter *(below)* tell you about these mountains?

Dear Susan,

My name is John Cornsilk. I live in the mountains in a small town named Cherokee. The land here is steep, with narrow valleys between the mountains. The mountains are covered with tall trees.

In the summer it is always cool in the mountains. People come here to hike on the trails in the woods. There are streams and waterfalls in the mountains.

I love to go fishing in the streams. I am sending you some pictures of my friends and me at one of my favorite waterfalls.

Please write soon. Tell me what it is like where you live. Be sure to send some pictures.

Your pen pal,

John

Dear John,

Thank you for your letter and the interesting pictures. You seem to like living in the mountains.

Ocracoke is also a small town. But the land here on Ocracoke Island is very different from the land where you live. Here the land is very flat. I can see the Atlantic Ocean from nearly every place on the island.

We have sandy beaches all around us here. It is warm most of the time, even during the winter. My favorite time is summer, when I can spend the whole day at the beach. Last summer I learned how to fish, and now I go fishing on most weekends.

I hope that you enjoy the pictures I am sending you. Please write again soon.

Your pen pal,

Susan

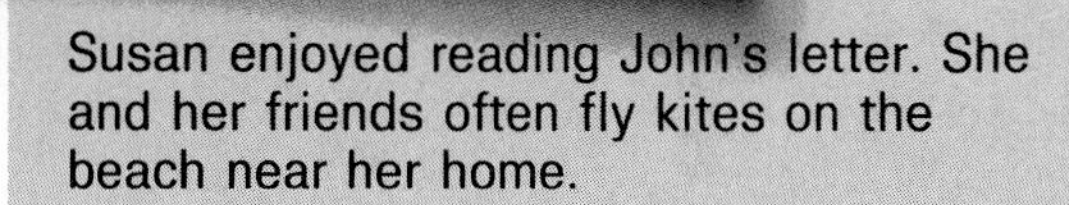

Susan enjoyed reading John's letter. She and her friends often fly kites on the beach near her home.

John's and Susan's letters appear on these two pages. They describe the places in which they live.

LEARNING ABOUT GEOGRAPHY

When John and Susan described the places in which they live, they were talking about **geography**. As you read on page 8, geography is the study of the earth's land, water, plants, animals, and people. In their letters, John and Susan wrote about the different kinds of land and weather in the places where they live. They also wrote about what people do for fun in the places where they live. All of these things are part of geography.

COMMUNITIES AND COUNTIES

Both John and Susan live in small communities. Find Cherokee and Ocracoke on the map on page 22. Each one has fewer than 1,000 people. The sizes of communities vary. The community in which you live might be smaller or larger than

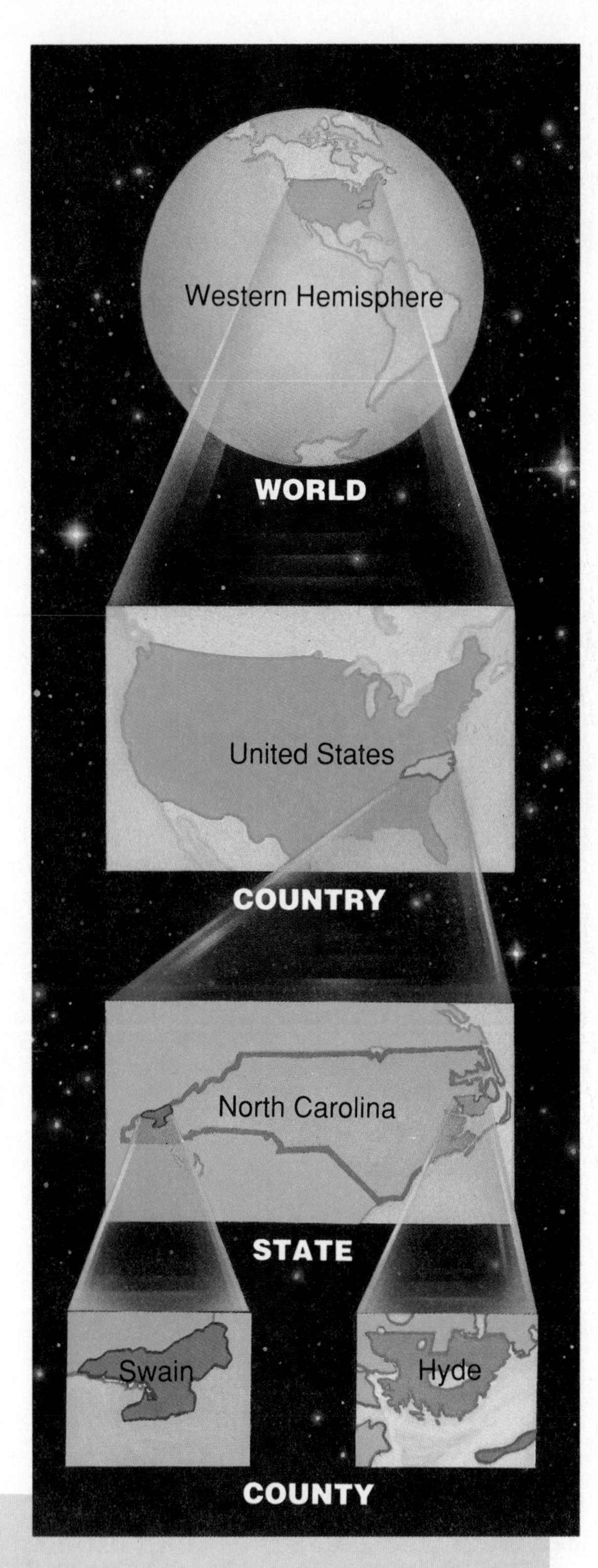

DIAGRAM SKILL: Of which larger areas is North Carolina a part? Which smaller areas fit into North Carolina?

Cherokee and Ocracoke are. What is the name of your community?

Several communities together form a **county**. A county is one of the sections into which a state is divided. North Carolina is divided into 100 counties. The town of Cherokee is part of Swain County, and the town of Ocracoke is part of Hyde County. Your community is also part of a county. What is the name of the county in which you live?

All places are part of larger areas. To help you see how this works, find Swain County on the diagram on this page. Swain and other counties are made up of many small communities, such as Cherokee. Swain and Hyde counties are shown at the bottom of the diagram. The larger area that counties form is shown above the counties. What is the name of this area? What is the largest area that is shown at the top of the diagram called?

THE STATE OF NORTH CAROLINA

Find North Carolina on the diagram. Our state is 1 of the 50 states that make up our country, the United States. Look at the Atlas map on pages 354 and 355 to see all of the states. Can you find North Carolina? One way to spot our state is to look for its special shape.

Another way to find our state is to study its location, or where it is found on a map. As you have read,

North Carolinians who live on the coast can watch the sun rise over the ocean.

location is also one of the five themes of geography. Look at the map on page 355 again. North Carolina is located north of South Carolina and east of Tennessee. It is also located along the Atlantic Ocean, in the southeastern part of the United States. What are some other ways in which you could describe the location of North Carolina?

PUTTING IT ALL TOGETHER

The diagram on page 24 shows some of the different kinds of places you have read about in this lesson and how these places fit together. As you have seen, the world has many countries. North Carolina is 1 of the 50 states that make up our country, the United States. Each of these states is made up of counties. For example, North Carolina has 100 counties. Each county has many smaller communities in it, such as Cherokee and Ocracoke.

As you read each chapter in this book, you will learn much more about our state and its geography. You will read about some of the many special places that make people say, "Nothing could be finer than to be in Carolina in the morning."

Check Your Reading

1. Identify two facts that describe Cherokee.
2. How is a community different from a county?
3. How does learning about places help us to understand North Carolina's geography?
4. **GEOGRAPHY SKILL:** Imagine that you are explaining the diagram on page 24 to a third grader. What might you say?
5. **THINKING SKILL:** Compare Cherokee with Ocracoke. How are the two communities different? How are they the same?

LESSON

2 A Southeastern State

READ TO LEARN

Key Vocabulary

region
culture
custom
Sunbelt

Key Places

Atlantic Ocean
Gulf of Mexico
Appalachian Mountains
Great Smoky Mountains

Read Aloud

No, it'll not do just to read the old tales out of a book. You've got to tell 'em to make 'em go right.

These are the words of Tom Hunt, a storyteller from North Carolina. People in North Carolina like to tell stories to one another. As this storyteller says, the best way to tell stories is to tell them aloud. In this lesson you will read about some other ways in which North Carolinians share their way of life with one another and with their neighbors.

Read for Purpose

1. **WHAT YOU KNOW:** How would you describe the location of North Carolina?
2. **WHAT YOU WILL LEARN:** What is a region? To which region does North Carolina belong?

WHAT IS A REGION?

In Lesson 1 you read about the pen pals, Susan and John. Each lives in a different place in North Carolina. Although their towns of Ocracoke and Cherokee are far apart, the two places still have many things in common. For example, both of the towns are located in North Carolina.

The towns of Ocracoke and Cherokee also have things in common because they are both part of a **region** of our country called the Southeast. A region is a large geographic area with common features that set it apart from other areas. Region is one of the five themes of geography. You can recognize a region by studying its features.

North Carolina is part of the Southeast. North Carolina's neighbors—Virginia, South Carolina, Tennessee, and Georgia—also are part of the Southeast. The other states of the Southeast are West Virginia, Kentucky, Florida, Alabama, Mississippi, Arkansas, and Louisiana. You can find all of these states on the map below.

A region is a little like a family. Each of the members in the region is different from the other members. However, all the members of the region share certain things. Let's look at some of the features that the states of the Southeast share.

A SHARED GEOGRAPHY

The seacoast along which Susan lives and the mountains in which John lives are two different kinds of land that are found in North Carolina. Some of the other states in the Southeast also share these types of

MAP SKILL: There are 12 states in the Southeast Region. Which states border North Carolina?

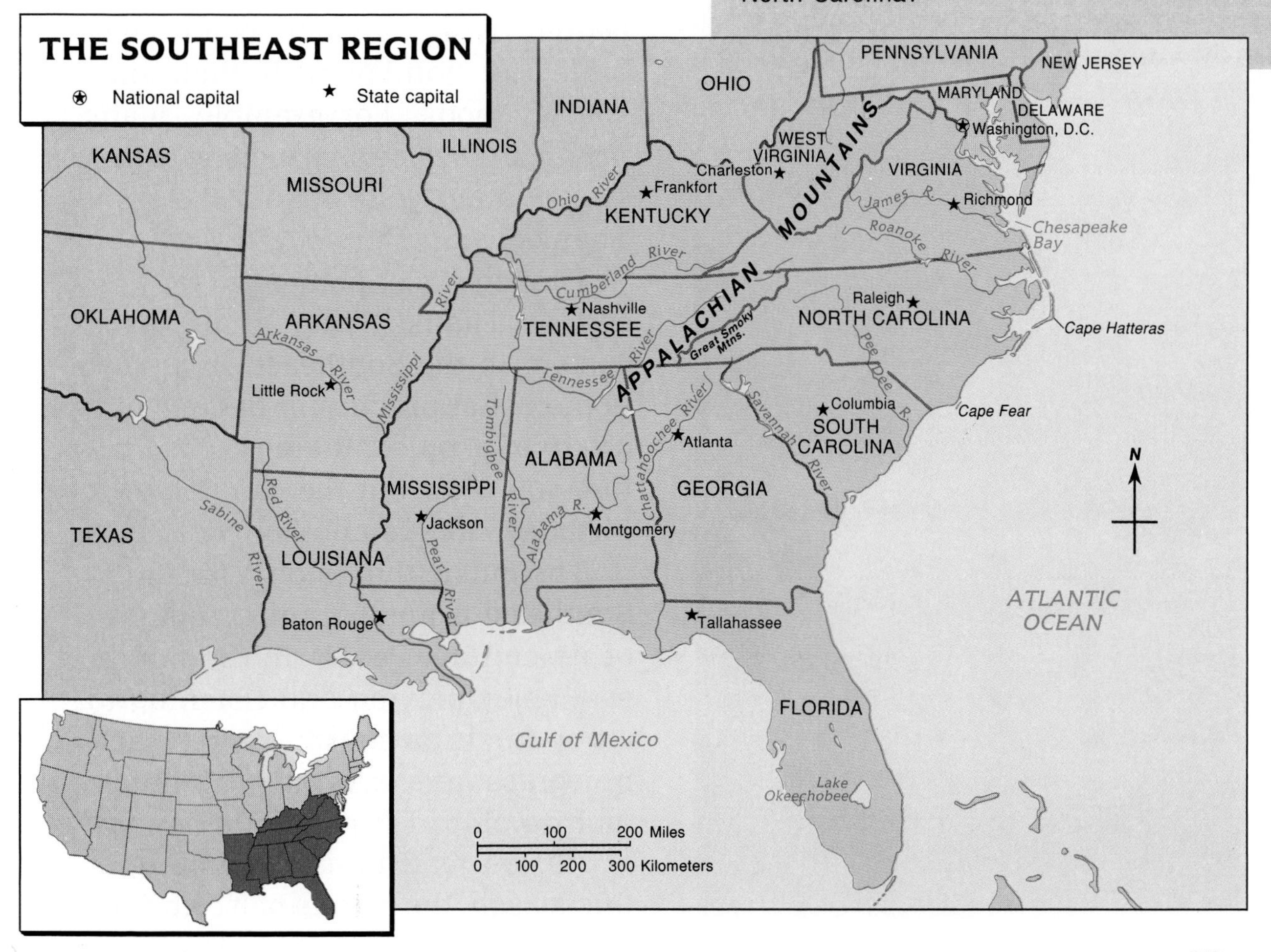

land. For example, 8 of the 12 states of the Southeast are located along the seacoast. The beach near Susan's home is just one of many long, sandy beaches that are found in the Southeast. Find the seacoast on the map on page 27. Notice that the Southeast's seacoast stretches along both the **Atlantic Ocean** and the **Gulf of Mexico**.

Mountains and hills are also found in most of the states in the Southeast. The rolling **Appalachian Mountains** stretch from the state of Alabama north to West Virginia. The **Great Smoky Mountains** are part of the Appalachian Mountains. In Lesson 1 you read about the town of Cherokee. It is located in the Great Smoky Mountains. Find the Appalachian Mountains and the Great Smoky Mountains on the map on page 27.

Thanksgiving dinner is an important **custom** in the United States.

A SHARED CULTURE

We have discussed the land of the Southeast. Did you know that people in the Southeast also share a **culture**, or way of life? The culture of a group includes its language, holidays, art, and music. Let's look at some of the ways in which people in the Southeast share a culture.

As you know, Thanksgiving Day is a holiday that is celebrated in all the regions of the United States. But people living in each region celebrate the holiday with their own special foods. For example, many people in the Southeast enjoy eating sweet-potato pie for dessert on Thanksgiving Day.

Having sweet-potato pie for dessert at Thanksgiving dinner is a **custom** in the Southeast. A custom is the usual practice or actions of a group of people. Making a wish before you blow out the candles on a birthday cake is another custom.

The music that is popular in the Southeast is another important part of its culture. People in the Southeast enjoy playing and listening to many kinds of music. Gospel and bluegrass are examples of music that developed in the Southeast.

As you read in the beginning of this lesson, the people of North Car-

Bluegrass music and gospel have long been part of our state's culture.

olina enjoy telling stories to one another. North Carolinians share this storytelling custom with people living in the other states in the Southeast. In fact, the Southeast is known as a region of storytellers.

A GROWING REGION

The Southeast is also known for being part of the Sunbelt. The Sunbelt is the nickname that has been given to the part of the United States that has mild weather year-round.

In your school, you may have met people who moved to North Carolina from another state. Each year thousands of people come to the Southeast. Why do these people choose to move here? One of the reasons is that many are attracted by the year-round warm weather that the Southeast has.

Another reason that people move here is to find jobs. Many businesses have moved to the Sunbelt from other parts of the country. These new businesses have created many new jobs in the region.

THE SOUTHEAST

As you have read, our state is part of a larger region called the Southeast. The 12 states in this region share many features of geography. The people of the Southeast also share holidays, arts, and other parts of culture.

Check Your Reading

1. What is a region? To what region does North Carolina belong?
2. Why are people moving to the Southeast from other areas?
3. In what ways does North Carolina share its culture and geography with the other states in the Southeast?
4. **THINKING SKILL:** List three questions that you could ask to learn more about the Southeast.

Understanding Latitude and Longitude

Key Vocabulary

latitude	meridian
parallel	prime meridian
longitude	global grid

How would you explain where North Carolina is located to someone who is planning to come here? You could say that it is bordered on one side by the Atlantic Ocean. You could also name the states that are next to it. Suppose that you wanted to explain our state's location more exactly. You could use the imaginary lines that are drawn on maps and globes for just that purpose. These lines help you to pinpoint the exact location of any place on earth. Let's see how they work.

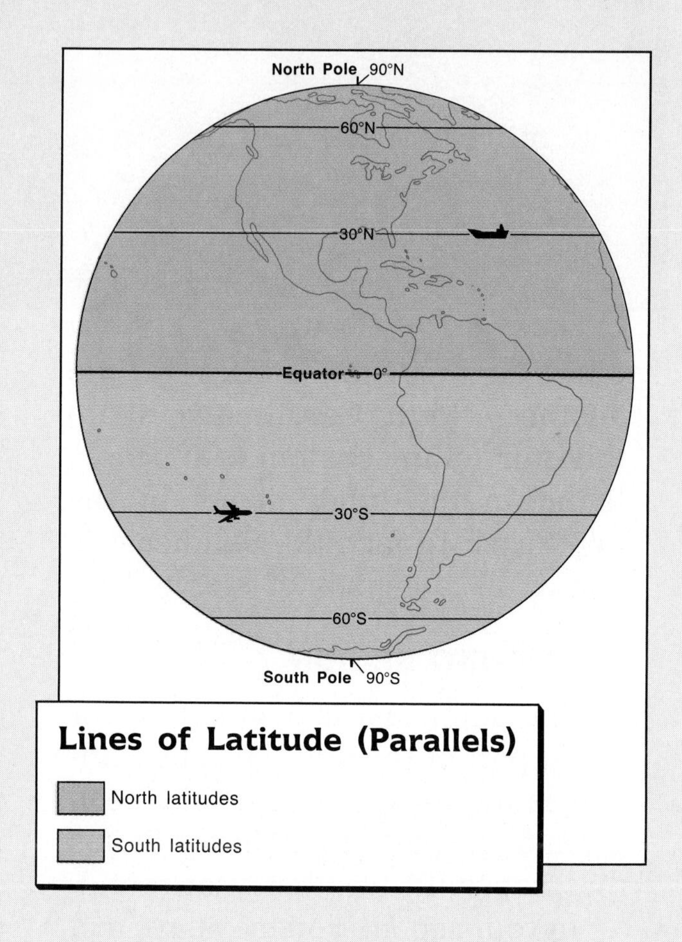

Lines of Latitude

You already know about one of the lines on some maps and globes—the equator. It is the imaginary line that circles the middle of the globe halfway between the North Pole and the South Pole. Locate the equator on the map on this page.

Notice the other lines on the map. They are called lines of **latitude**. Lines of latitude measure distances north and south of the equator. They are also called **parallels** because they are parallel to the equator and to each other. This means that they are always the same distance from the equator and from each other. Lines of latitude never meet.

The distance between lines of latitude is measured in degrees. The symbol ° stands for degrees. Notice on the map that the equator is marked 0°. The first line to the north of the equator is marked 30°N. This means that the line is 30 degrees north of the equator. The latitude of the North Pole is 90°N. The first line to the south of the equator is marked 30°S, which means that it is 30 degrees south of the equator. At which latitude is the South Pole located?

Although lines of latitude measure distance north or south of the equator, they run east and west. The airplane on the map is heading east along the parallel marked 30°S. In which direction is the ship traveling? On which parallel is it traveling?

Lines of Longitude

Maps and globes also show imaginary lines that run north and south. They are called lines of **longitude**. They are also called **meridians**. On the map on this page, find the meridian marked 0°. This is called the **prime meridian** because *prime* means "first." The prime meridian is the starting line from which all of the other meridians are measured.

Lines of longitude are measured in degrees east or west of the prime meridian. Look on the map at the meridians to the west of the prime meridian. They are labeled *W* for "west." The lines to the east are labeled *E* for "east."

Longitude is measured up to 180° east of the prime meridian and 180° west of the prime meridian. Since 180°E and 180°W fall on the same line, this line is marked 180° without an *E* or a *W*.

Meridians are not parallel to each other. They are not always the same distance apart. They are farthest apart at the equator, and meridians come together at the North Pole and the South Pole.

Lines of longitude measure distances east and west, but the lines themselves run north and south. Look at the ship on the map below. The ship is moving south. Along which meridian is it traveling? In which direction is the airplane on the map traveling?

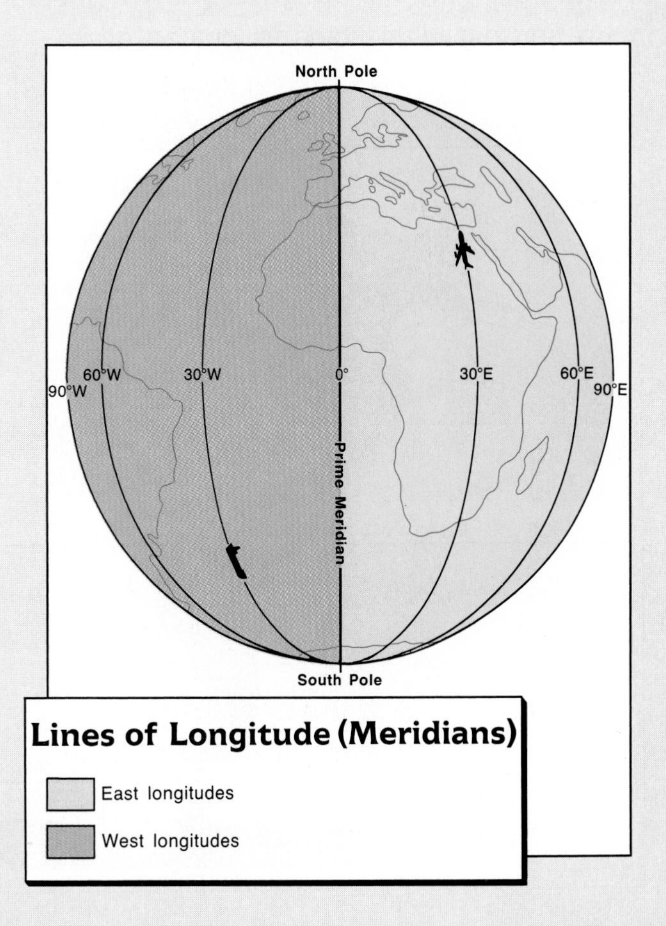

Lines of Longitude (Meridians)

The Global Grid

Together, lines of latitude and lines of longitude form a grid, or a set of crisscrossing lines. The grid on the map below is called a **global grid** because it covers the whole earth. You can use this grid to locate any place in the world if you know its latitude and longitude.

Find the airplane on the map below. Between which lines of latitude is it located? Between which lines of longitude is it located?

Look at the map of the United States on the next page. If you wanted to find out what place is located at 30°N, 90°W, this is what you would do. Put your finger on the bottom of the map on the meridian labeled 90°W. Now move your finger north to the parallel labeled 30°N. Which city is located at that point?

Sometimes a place is not exactly at the point at which two lines cross. Then you have to use the closest lines. Find the city of Charlotte, North Carolina. It is not found at the exact point where two lines cross. You must find the lines the city of Charlotte is closest to on the map. It is closest to 35°N, 80°W. So we can say that Charlotte is located at about 35°N, 80°W.

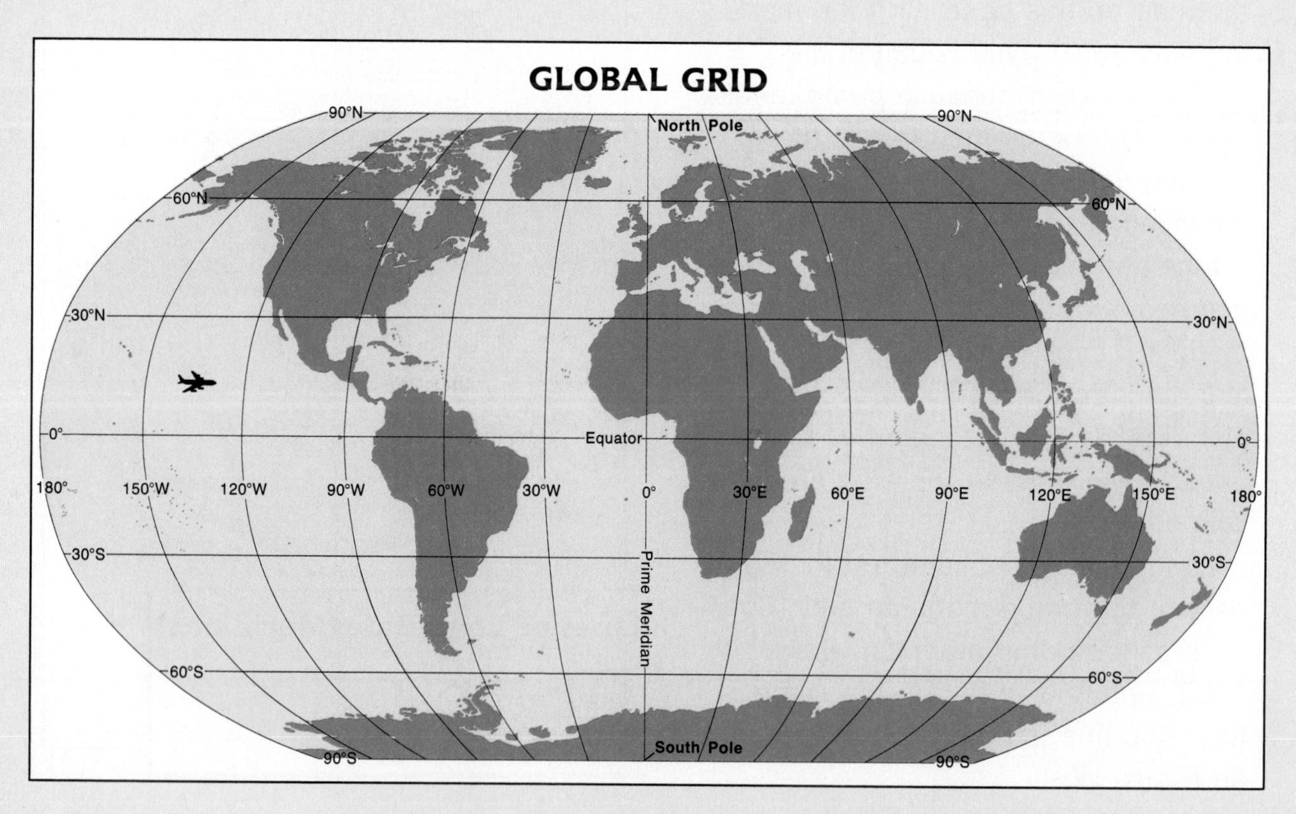

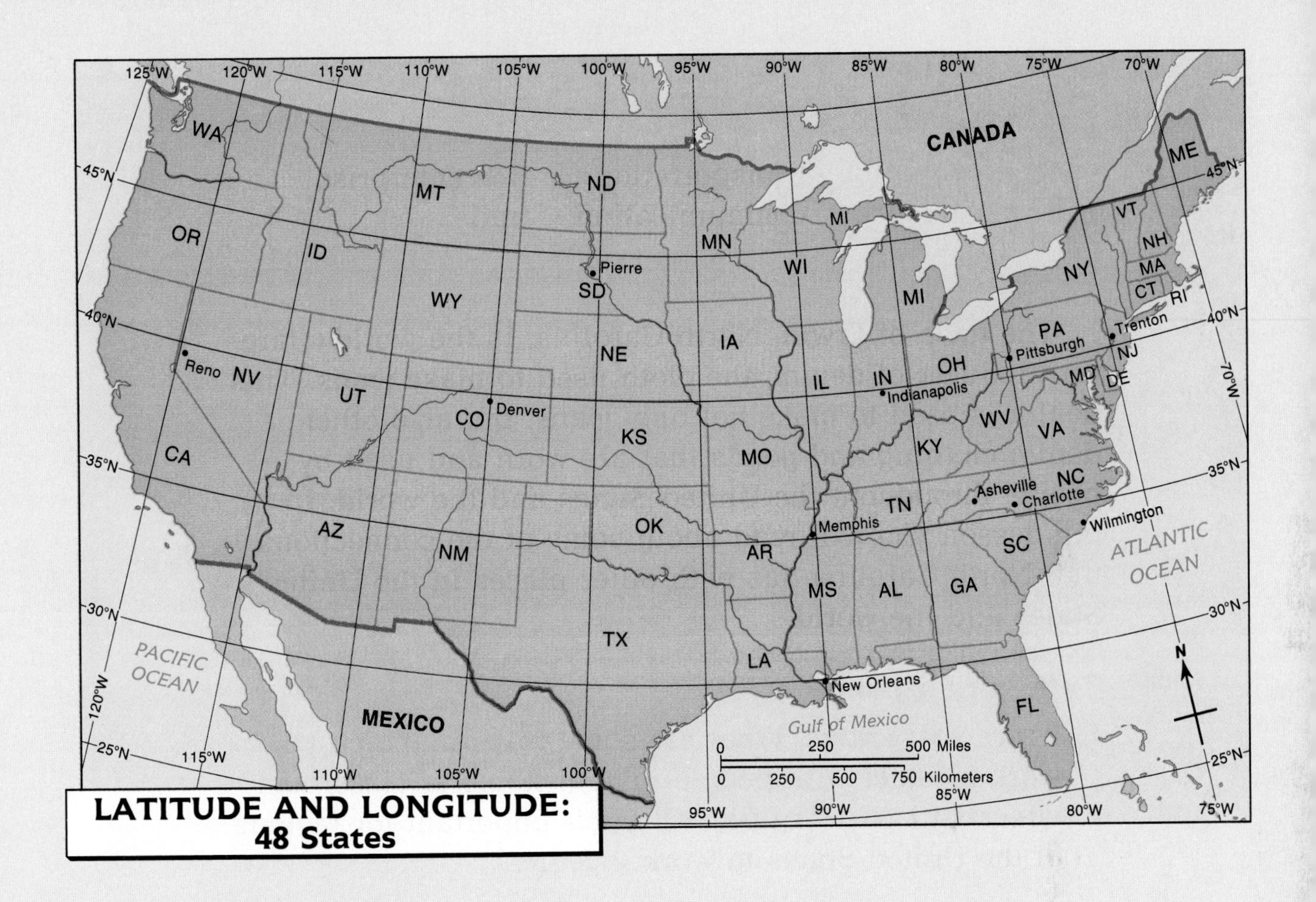

LATITUDE AND LONGITUDE: 48 States

Reviewing the Skill

Use the maps and the information in this lesson to answer these questions.

1. What are lines of latitude and longitude? What do they help you to do?
2. Study the map above. Which line of latitude forms part of the southern border of North Carolina? Which line of longitude forms the western border of Nevada?
3. Which city shown on the map is located at 35°N, 90°W?
4. What is the approximate latitude and longitude of Denver, Colorado?
5. At about which latitude and longitude is Wilmington, North Carolina located?
6. Why is it important to understand how to use latitude and longitude on maps and globes?

LESSON

3 North Carolina Connections

READ TO LEARN

Key Vocabulary

economy
interdependence
transportation
communication
free enterprise
trade

Read Aloud

The town of Erwin, North Carolina, is the world's largest producer of denim, the cloth used to make jeans. This denim is used to make not only jeans, but also other denim clothing and goods that are worn and used by people throughout the United States and the world. In this lesson you will read about some of the connections that North Carolina has with other places in the United States and the world.

Read for Purpose

1. **WHAT YOU KNOW:** What are some ways in which you work together with people in your home or classroom?
2. **WHAT YOU WILL LEARN:** Why is it important for regions of the United States to work together?

THE REGIONS OF THE UNITED STATES

In Lesson 2 you read about the Southeast region of the United States. Did you know that the Southeast is one of five regions in the United States? The other four regions are the Northeast, the Middle West, the Southwest, and the West. Look at the five regions on the map on page 35. Each region has its own special features that are different from those of other regions in the United States.

The people living in the five regions work together to make our country strong. They also work together to make the **economy** of our country strong. An economy is the way in which a state or a country uses its resources to meet its people's needs and wants. Let's find out what part North Carolina plays in the United States economy.

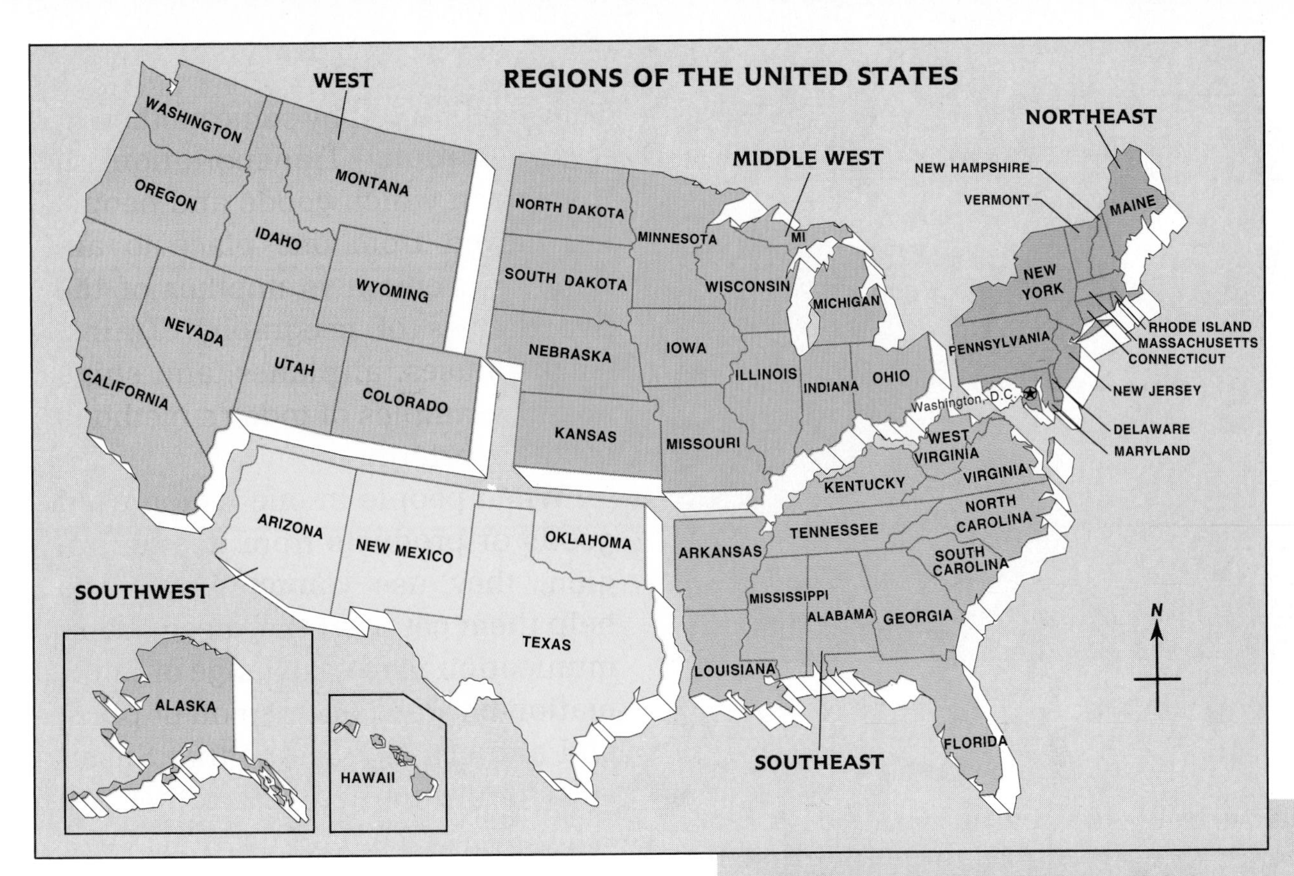

MAP SKILL: From which region of the United States does Julie's computer come? From where do the wheat crackers come?

REGIONS ARE INTERDEPENDENT

The picture on this page shows Julie Williams, who lives in North Carolina. Right now she is using her computer to do her homework. Although Julie's parents bought the computer in a local store, the computer was made in California. The wheat crackers that Julie is eating were made in Illinois. Cloth that was made in North Carolina was used to make the blouse that Julie is wearing.

No region or state can meet all of the needs and wants of its people. For example, few computers are made in North Carolina. Therefore, North Carolina buys computers

Trucks carry goods such as peanuts from North Carolina to other regions of the United States.

from California. On the other hand, California buys much of its cloth from North Carolina.

The buying and selling that the regions of our country do is an example of **interdependence**. This means that people in one region depend on people in other regions of the United States to help them meet their needs and wants.

For example, because the state of Maine has a cold climate, peanuts do not grow there. How do you think that people in Maine get peanuts? They buy them from peanut-growing states like North Carolina.

TRANSPORTATION AND COMMUNICATION

Look at the Atlas map of the United States on pages 354 and 355. You can see that there is a great distance between California and North Carolina. How are goods shipped between the two states? They are brought by some method of **transportation**. Transportation is the way in which goods and people are moved from one place to another. Movement is another of the five themes of geography. Trains, trucks, buses, airplanes, and ships are all examples of today's methods of transportation.

When people in one region need goods or products from another region, they use **communication** to help them get what they need. Communication is the exchange of information between one person or place and another. The letters that Susan and John wrote to each other are examples of communication. Telephones and televisions are other kinds of communication. Together, communication and transportation systems help the economy of our country to work.

BUYING AND SELLING

Do you buy your clothes in a store in your community? Where does your family shop for food? The stores in which you buy food or clothing are probably owned by other North Carolinians. These businesses are examples of the **free enterprise** economy that exists in the United States. In a free enterprise economy, people are free to own and run businesses.

The picture on page 37 shows Ted Johnson working at his furniture store. Mr. Johnson's business is an example of free enterprise. Mr. Johnson sells and fixes wooden furniture. When a customer's chair or table breaks, Mr. Johnson fixes it. Mr. Johnson likes his work and it allows him to pay for the needs and wants of his family.

In our free enterprise economy, people have the right to choose the kinds of work that they want to do.

Free enterprise makes it possible for North Carolinians to run their own businesses.

WORLD CONNECTIONS

North Carolina is also interdependent with other countries. For example, North Carolina sells farm products, furniture, and clothing to countries around the world. North Carolina is connected to these countries by **trade**. Trade is the business of buying, selling, and exchanging goods.

North Carolina also buys goods from other countries. For example, you may know someone who has a camera that was made in Japan. Salt, iron, and oil are among the many goods that North Carolina buys from countries outside the United States.

CONNECTIONS

As you have read, the five regions of the United States work together to keep our country's free-enterprise economy strong. With the help of transportation and communication, North Carolina has connections to other states and to countries around the world.

Check Your Reading

1. Identify two ways in which North Carolina is interdependent with other regions in the United States.
2. Give three examples of the free enterprise system in your area.
3. Why is it important for the regions of the United States to work together?
4. **GEOGRAPHY SKILL:** Look at the map on page 35. Which kind of transportation would be the best for moving peanuts from North Carolina to Maine?
5. **THINKING SKILL:** How do you think that life in our state would be different if we did not trade with other countries?

WOMEN AT WORK

Today women around the world work in all different kinds of businesses. However, often the only jobs that many women can get are low paying. For this reason, many women around the world are poor. Sarah Fields-Davis has worked hard to help many of our state's poor working women, especially African American women. In 1991 she was voted Woman of the Year for North Carolina.

Today Fields-Davis is the director of the Center for Women's Economic Alternatives in Ahoskie. *Alternatives* means "choices." In 1987 members of the Center asked her to come to North Carolina to help them. They had heard about how she had helped women in West Virginia.

After Fields-Davis came to our state, she began trying to improve the factories in which chickens are packaged for food stores. These companies often hire women and pay them very little. Working conditions in some of the factories are poor. There are often no windows, and floors are covered with water. Because of the unsafe conditions, many women are hurt on the job.

Fields-Davis tried to get the factories to pay women better wages. She also asked the women to help themselves by talking with factory owners. Their efforts have begun to make the factories healthier workplaces.

Fields-Davis also helps women to see that they have leadership skills that can be used to gain better jobs. For example, she asks them, "Who is the head of your household? Who takes care of your money? Who teaches your children right from wrong?" Questions such as these show that these women have many responsibilities and make important decisions every day.

Fields-Davis has used her experiences in West Virginia and North Carolina to help women everywhere. She has attended women's meetings around the world and has received many awards for her courageous and caring spirit.

"I want to make a difference while I am here," says Fields-Davis. "I want to make the world a better place." For the many people she has helped, Sarah Fields-Davis is doing just that.

REVIEWING VOCABULARY

county — economy — region
culture — free enterprise

Number a sheet of paper from 1 to 5. Beside each number write the word or the term from the list above that best matches the definition.

1. A large area with common features that set it apart from other areas
2. The way a state or country uses its resources to meet its people's needs and wants
3. One of the divisions of a state
4. An economic system in which people can own businesses
5. The way of life of a group of people

REVIEWING FACTS

1. What is geography?
2. Name one way in which Cherokee and Ocracoke are alike.
3. Which states and bodies of water border North Carolina?
4. In what way are the states of the Southeast like a family?
5. Name two groups of mountains that are located in North Carolina.
6. Give two examples of customs in North Carolina.
7. What is the Sunbelt?
8. Identify two items in your classroom or home that show how North Carolina is interdependent with other states or countries.
9. How does communication help the economy of a state or county?
10. What kinds of transportation are available in your community?

WRITING ABOUT MAIN IDEAS

1. **Writing a Description:** Choose a southeastern custom or an example of our culture with which you are familiar. Describe it so that someone from another region could understand it.
2. **Writing About Perspectives:** Write a letter to John Cornsilk or Susan Carter, telling about your community. Mention ways in which it is the same or different from theirs. You might also ask some questions about Cherokee or Ocracoke.

BUILDING SKILLS: UNDERSTANDING LATITUDE AND LONGITUDE

Use the maps on pages 32 and 33 to answer these questions.

1. What is a global grid?
2. On which parallel is Pittsburgh located?
3. Which city is located at about 40°N, 120°W?
4. At about which latitude and which longitude is Asheville located?
5. Why is it helpful to understand how to use latitude and longitude?

CHAPTER 2

NORTH CAROLINA'S ENVIRONMENT

FOCUS

My dad starts cutting down trees two weeks before Thanksgiving. By the middle of December most of these trees have been sold. You could say that our biggest harvest is Christmas trees.

In Avery County, where Loren Aldridge lives, fall is the busiest time of year for farmers. In this chapter you will read about the weather and land that make it possible to grow a variety of crops in our state.

LESSON

1 Climate

READ TO LEARN

Key Vocabulary

climate
temperature
precipitation
elevation
environment
growing season
rain shadow

Key Places

Gulf of Mexico
Atlantic Ocean

Read Aloud

The wider the stripes on a caterpillar's back, the colder the winter.

This is a saying that some North Carolinians use when they talk about the weather. There are many other sayings that people in our state use when they talk about how hot or cold and how wet or dry it will be. In this lesson you will read about the weather in our state and how it affects the way we live.

Read for Purpose

1. **WHAT YOU KNOW:** What time of year is it hottest where you live? What time of year is it coldest?
2. **WHAT YOU WILL LEARN:** How does North Carolina's climate affect the lives of its people?

WEATHER AND CLIMATE

Look out your window. What is it like outside today? Is it hot or cold? Is it sunny or rainy? These are all questions about the weather. The weather is how hot or cold and wet or dry the air is. As you know, the weather can change at any moment.

The type of weather an area usually has over a long period of time is called **climate** (klī′ mit). As you probably know, a cold winter day high up in the Great Smoky Mountains can be quite cold. However, the weather in our state is usually comfortable during all the months of the year. That is why we North Carolinians say that the Tar Heel state has a mild climate.

TEMPERATURE AND PRECIPITATION

When we talk about how hot or cold something is, we are talking about **temperature** (tem′ pər ə chər). Look at the temperature maps below. They show the average, or usual, temperatures in our state. Notice that the average temperatures in July are about 30°F. (17°C) higher than the average temperatures in January.

Have you ever heard anyone say that "it is raining cats and dogs"? People sometimes use this saying when they talk about **precipitation** (pri sip i tā′ shən). Precipitation is any form of water that falls to the earth. Precipitation may be rain, sleet, hail, or snow.

Our state gets an average of about 50 inches (127 cm) of precipitation each year. However, the amount of precipitation that the coast and the mountains get is not the same. Look at the precipitation map on page 43. How much precipitation falls each year in the place where you live?

CHANGES IN CLIMATE

Three important factors affect climate—latitude, distance from the ocean, and **elevation**. Elevation is the height of a place above sea level. The higher the elevation, the colder the temperature becomes.

As you have read, our state's land includes mountains in the west and plains in the east. Some of these mountains are nearly 7,000 feet (1,800 m) high, and some parts of the coast are at sea level. The land between the mountains and

MAP SKILL: Which part of North Carolina has the highest **temperatures** in both January and July? Describe Asheville's temperatures in January and July.

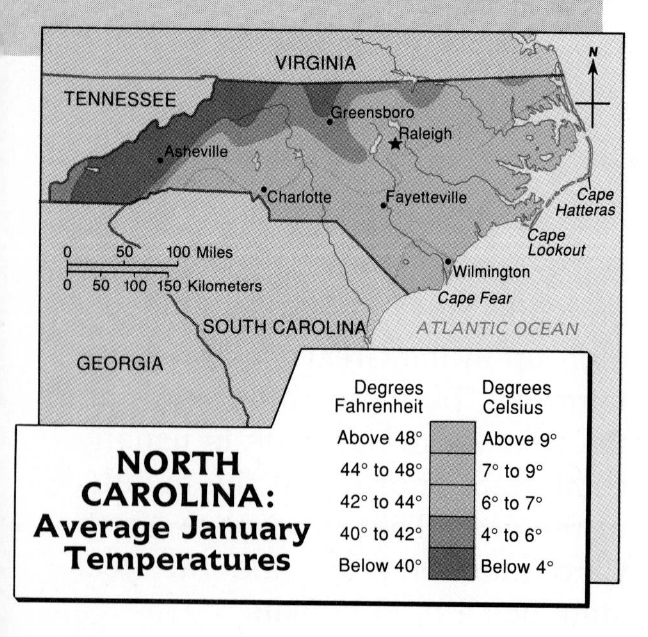

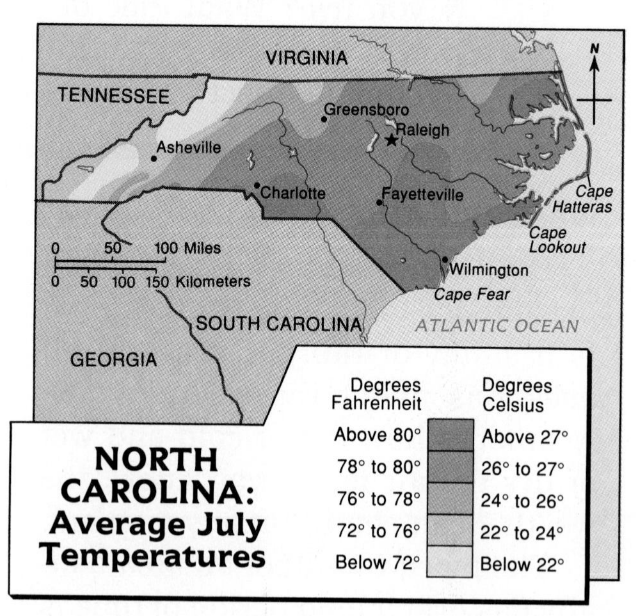

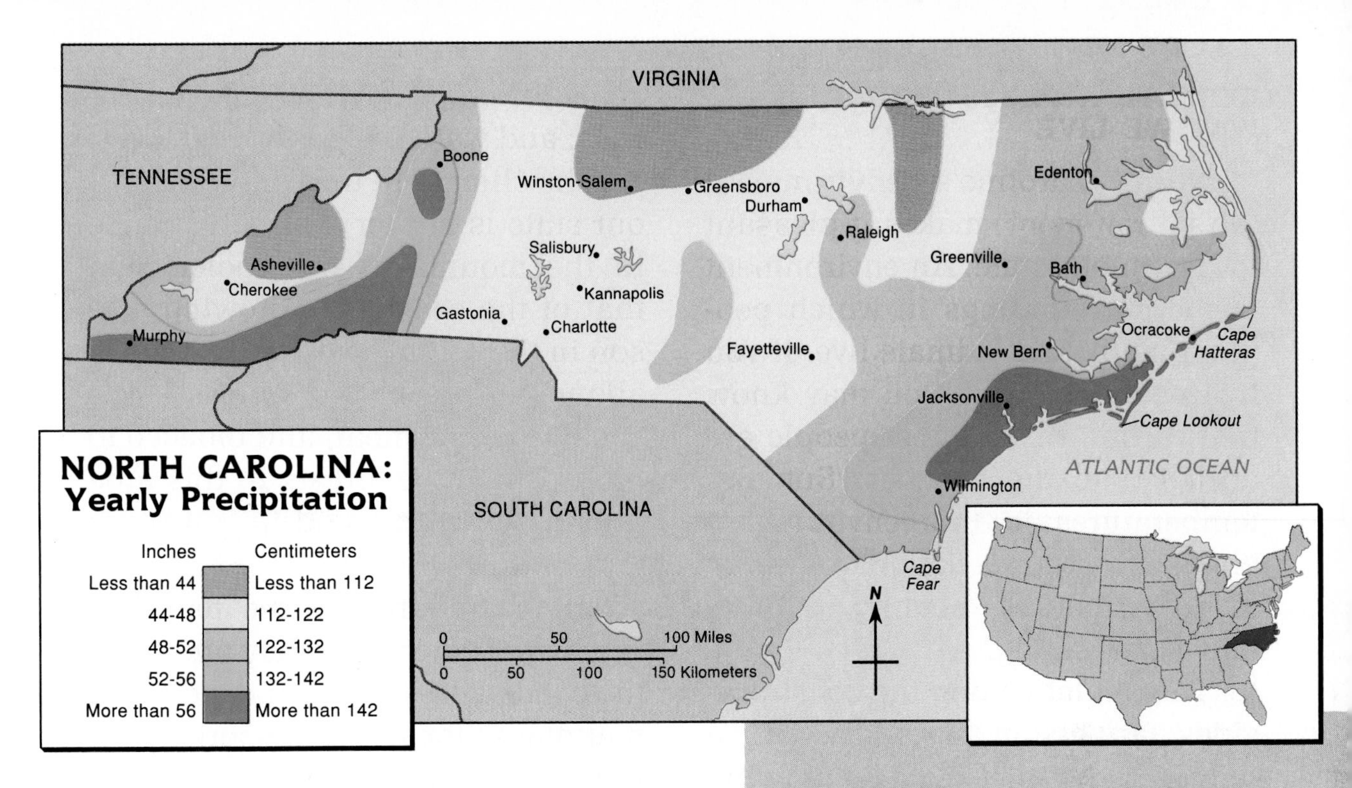

MAP SKILL: How much **precipitation** falls each year in Asheville? How much falls in Wilmington?

the coast is mostly hilly. These differences in elevation are the most important reasons for differences in climate in North Carolina. For example, when it is 90°F. (32°C) along our state's coast, it is about 66°F. (20°C) in the mountains.

The second factor affecting climate is latitude. As you read in the Skills Lesson on pages 30 to 33, latitude measures how close to the equator a place is. Places near the equator have lower latitudes than places farther away from the equator. Because of the angle of the earth as it revolves around the sun, areas closer to the equator receive more direct sunlight than places farther away from the equator. As a result, temperatures are higher in the lower latitudes. Since North Carolina is located in lower latitudes than Maine, our state has a warmer climate than that state.

Distance from the ocean is the third factor that affects climate. You may have noticed that on a hot summer day, it is cooler near the ocean than it is farther inland at the same elevation. The reason is that the ocean warms up more slowly than the land does. Also, breezes from the ocean cool the coastal lands.

In the winter the ocean stays warm longer than the land does. Breezes blowing inland warm the lands along the coast. As a result, the summers near the coast are usually cooler and the winters are usually warmer than they are inland.

CLIMATE AFFECTS THE WAY WE LIVE

North Carolina's **environment** (en vī′ rən mənt) makes it pleasant to live in our state. An environment is the surroundings in which people, plants, and animals live. If you live near the coast, you may know that during the summer people are attracted to the beaches. Summer temperatures in this environment are usually warm enough for people to go swimming, boating, fishing, and water-skiing.

The climate along the coast provides farmers in that area with a long **growing season**. The growing season is the time of the year when the weather is warm enough for crops to grow. The coastal plain has a growing season of more than 270 days. Enough rain falls along the coast for crops such as cotton, peanuts, and watermelon to grow there.

The climate in the central part of our state is milder than the climate in the mountains but cooler than that of the coast. The growing season in the central part of the state is about 210 days. This allows crops such as corn, wheat, and tobacco to grow. The huge forests in this area provide us with wood for furniture and building houses.

In the mountains the temperatures are cooler than they are along the coast. People are attracted to the mountains for fun and sports. During the warmer months people hike on trails through the woods. During the winter many people go to the mountains to ski.

The growing season in the mountains is less than 150 days.

Peanuts *(center)* need a long **growing season** to ripen. Corn *(left)* and apples are grown in areas with shorter growing seasons.

Apples grow very well in the cool climate. The mountains get more precipitation than any other area in North Carolina. Because of colder temperatures, that precipitation is often in the form of snow.

THE RAIN SHADOW

You have read that the mountains affect the kind of precipitation that falls on them. But did you know that the mountains also affect where the precipitation falls? The diagram on this page shows the effect of a rain shadow on parts of our state. A rain shadow is the side of a mountain on which little rain falls.

Look at the diagram above. Air from over the Gulf of Mexico moves toward the mountains. When the air rises up the side of a mountain, the air cools. Cool air cannot hold as much moisture as warm air can. This means that clouds then form and drop most of their moisture on the west side of the mountain as either rain or snow. When the clouds move over to the other side of the mountain, little moisture remains in the clouds. This drier side of the mountain lies in the rain shadow.

Sometimes, however, winds from the Atlantic Ocean blow from the coast toward the mountains. This causes rain to fall on the east side of the mountains. Then the land east of the mountains receives more precipitation than the western slopes.

DIAGRAM SKILL: Which side of the mountain lies in the rain shadow?

A VARIED CLIMATE

The people of North Carolina enjoy a generally mild climate. However, our state's climate can vary, depending upon the elevation, latitude, and distance from the ocean. North Carolinians enjoy changes in climate because of these and other differences in the geography of our state.

Check Your Reading

1. What is the difference between weather and climate?
2. How does North Carolina's climate affect the lives of the people who live here?
3. **THINKING SKILL:** What are three questions that you might ask in order to learn more about the climate of North Carolina?

BUILDING SKILLS
THINKING SKILLS

Decision Making

Key Vocabulary

decision

Imagine that you are having a test tomorrow on the environment of North Carolina. You want to get a high score to improve your grade. You can study in the afternoon when you come home from school. Or you can play with your friends and then study after dinner.

You need to make a **decision** about what to do. Making a decision is the same thing as making a choice.

Trying the Skill

Imagine that you are an adult and that you live in a state other than North Carolina. You have a job that you like, but you get an offer for a job in North Carolina that you really want. Your goal is to find work that both uses your skills and gives you a chance to learn something new. You need to decide whether to move to North Carolina. Consider the following items and then make a decision.

- You can have a job in North Carolina that will teach you new skills.
- Although the job you have now does not use many of your skills, it is enjoyable.
- You have many friends in the state where you live now.
- North Carolina might be a more interesting place in which to live.

1. What is your decision?
2. How did you arrive at this decision?

HELPING YOURSELF

The steps on the left will help you to make good decisions. The example on the right shows one way you might make a decision about moving to North Carolina.

One Way to Make a Decision	Example
1. State your goal, or what it is you want to do.	Your goal is to use all your skills and to learn new ones.
2. Identify some things you could do to reach your goal.	You could move to North Carolina or stay where you live now.
3. Identify what might happen as a result of each choice.	In North Carolina you would be able to learn new skills, but you would have left friends and a pleasant workplace behind.
4. Choose the action that is most likely to help you reach your goal.	You decide it would be best to move to North Carolina.

Applying the Skill

Now apply what you have learned. Imagine that you received some money for your birthday. Your goal is to spend the money in a way that would make you feel good. One thing you could do with the money is donate it to save the Cape Hatteras Lighthouse. On the other hand, there is a good book that you would like to buy. If you donate the money to save the lighthouse, you will feel good about what you have done to help. If you buy the book, you will be doing something that is good for you—reading—but you will be helping only yourself.

Which of the following choices will help you reach your goal?

1. To make your decision, you should first
   - **a.** talk to your best friend.
   - **b.** think about your choices and the possible results of each.
   - **c.** decide what is the best decision.

2. Your decision should help you to
   - **a.** reach your goal.
   - **b.** make up your mind.
   - **c.** get along with your friends.

3. One reason to donate the money to the lighthouse could be that
   - **a.** you don't like to read very much anyway.
   - **b.** it is your birthday.
   - **c.** it will make you feel good about how you spent the money.

Reviewing the Skill

1. What is decision making?

2. What steps could you follow to make a good decision?

3. Why is it important to know how to make good decisions?

LESSON

2 Natural Resources

READ TO LEARN

Key Vocabulary

natural resource
fertile
mineral
dam
renewable resource
nonrenewable resource
conservation
pollution

Key Places

Tusquittee Valley
Cape Fear River
Lake Norman
Lake Mattamuskeet

Read Aloud

He had with his monstrous blow struck the lick of fortune.

These words appeared in a North Carolina newspaper written more than 150 years ago. They tell how John Moore became rich. One day, while he was cutting wood for a fence, John Moore's ax hit a rock. He looked at the rock and saw that his lucky lick, or strike, had uncovered "plenty of shining gold." As you will read, gold is only one of North Carolina's many riches.

Read for Purpose

1. **WHAT YOU KNOW:** What are some of the ways in which you can enjoy nature in our state?
2. **WHAT YOU WILL LEARN:** What are some of North Carolina's most important natural resources?

A LAND OF FORESTS

At the time that John Moore struck gold in the 1800s, North Carolina was covered with forests. He had bought land in the **Tusquittee** (təs kē′ tē) **Valley** in southwestern North Carolina and had begun to cut down its trees. With wood from the trees, Moore built a cabin for his family. What else do you think he could have done with the wood?

The forests have always been an important **natural resource** of our state. A natural resource is something found in nature that is useful to people. Forests cover about half of our state. People have found many uses for the softwood and hardwood trees in our forests.

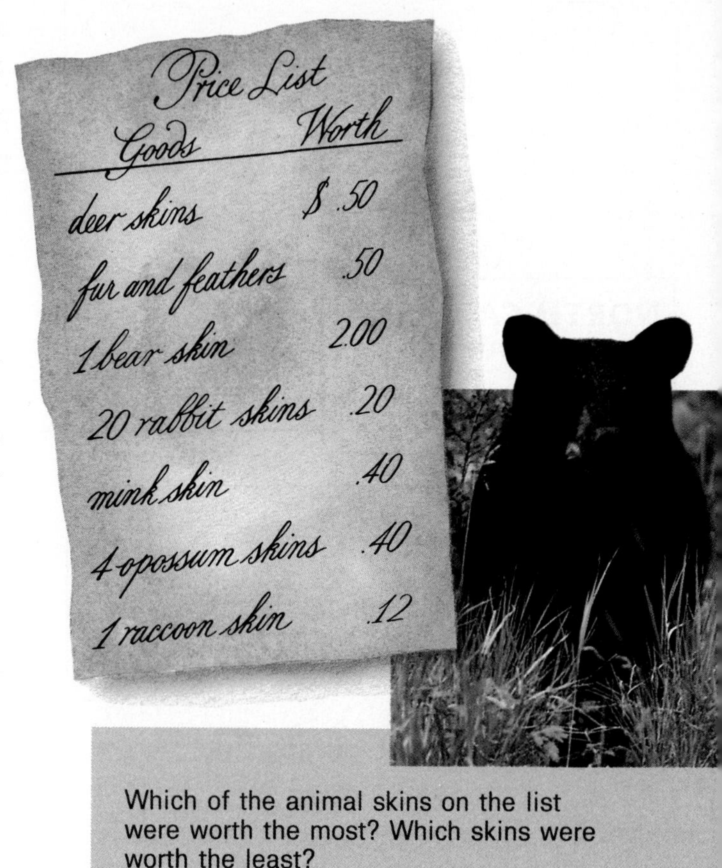

Price List

Goods	Worth
deer skins	$ .50
fur and feathers	.50
1 bear skin	2.00
20 rabbit skins	.20
mink skin	.40
4 opossum skins	.40
1 raccoon skin	.12

Which of the animal skins on the list were worth the most? Which skins were worth the least?

FOREST RESOURCES

After building his home, John Moore built a store in Hayesville. Many of the people who came to the store had so little money that they paid their bills with goods. The price list on this page shows some of the goods that John Moore's customers gave him to pay their bills. What do these goods show about the area's natural resources?

Animals are an important natural resource in North Carolina's forests. In John Moore's time, forest animals were used as a source of food and clothing. Today our forests still are filled with wild animals, such as wild pigs, deer, and many smaller animals and birds. There also are a few black bears. However, most of the meat people eat comes from farm animals, such as hogs.

Trees and animals are not the only living things found in North Carolina's forests. Many unusual plants are also found there. The Venus's-flytrap grows in the swampy forests around Wilmington. This plant's bulblike flower opens wide when an insect comes near it. When the insect is inside the flower, it snaps shut quickly to trap the insect and eat it.

RICH SOIL

Rich soil is another important natural resource in North Carolina. Many parts of the state have **fertile** (fûr′ təl) soil, or soil that is good for growing crops. Some crops, such as corn, are eaten by people or fed to animals. Other crops, such as cotton, are made into cloth.

The eastern part of our state has the most fertile soil because this is where rivers dump fresh mud every year. The mud has minerals that help plants to grow. Look at the farmland map on page 50 to see where this fertile soil has been used for farming.

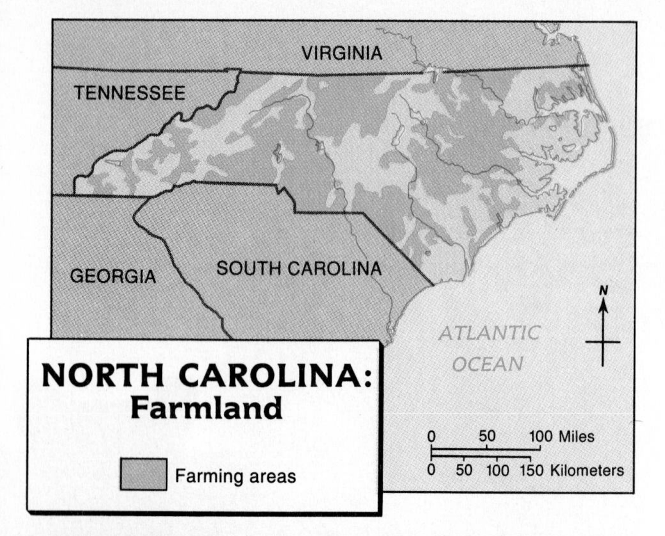

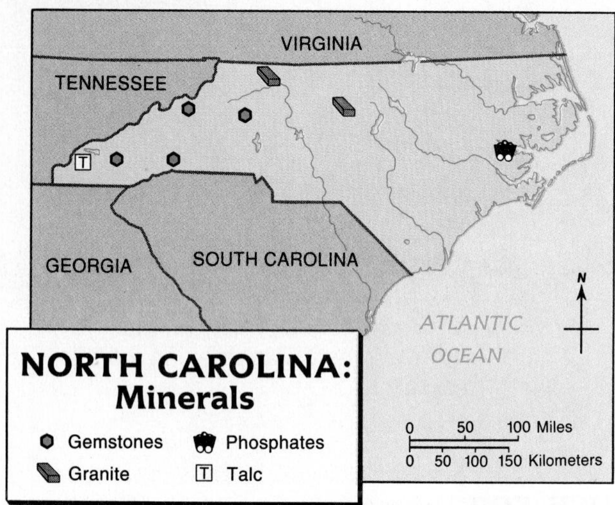

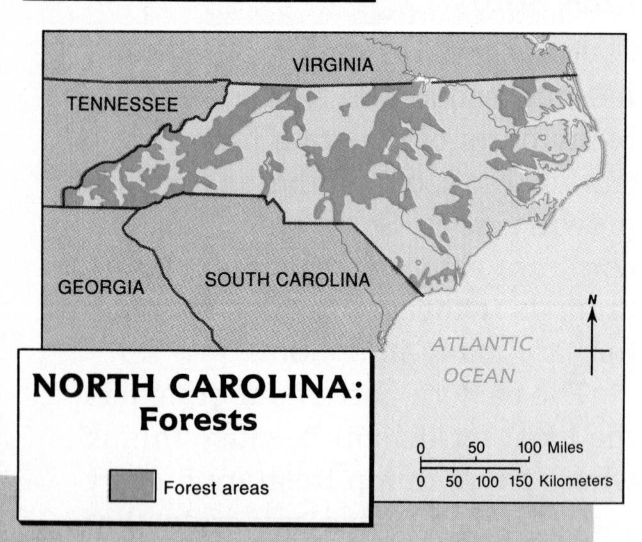

MAP SKILL: Which part of North Carolina has the most minerals? Which part of our state has the largest areas of land covered by forests?

MINERAL RESOURCES

Like John Moore, many other North Carolinians found gold. Although most of our state's gold has been dug out of the earth, small amounts are still being found.

Gold is one of North Carolina's many **minerals**. A mineral is something in nature that is neither an animal nor a plant. Because most minerals are found under the earth's surface, people must mine them, or dig them up, in order to use them. Find phosphate and talc on the minerals map on this page. They are among our state's important minerals. Phosphate is used to make food for plants. Body powder and some building materials are made from talc. Of our state's over 300 minerals, about 70 are mined. Among them are many gemstones.

RIVERS AND LAKES

North Carolina is also rich in water resources. Our many rivers and lakes are used for fishing, travel, and recreation. The **Cape Fear River** is our only river deep enough to be used by large ships.

Lake Norman is the largest lake in North Carolina. But 100 years ago it did not exist. That's because Lake Norman was formed by a **dam**. A dam is a wall built across a river to hold back the flowing water. Many of North Carolina's lakes were made by dams. Our state has few natural lakes, and they are located in the east. Lake Mattamuskeet (mat′ ə mə skēt) is the largest natural lake in our state.

GUARDING OUR RICHES

North Carolina has many natural resources. Some of them, such as water, can be used more freely than others because nature replaces what we use. Such resources are called renewable resources. However, resources like phosphate cannot be replaced. Once taken from the earth, minerals are gone forever. That is why minerals are called nonrenewable resources.

North Carolinians have done much to protect both our state's renewable and nonrenewable resources. The protection of natural resources is called conservation (kon′ sər vā′ shən). For example, to help our people conserve forests, the first forestry school in our country was started near Asheville in 1895. The school taught its students how to use forests wisely.

North Carolinians also try to stop pollution (pə lü′ shən). Pollution is the dirtying of our air and water. You will read more about pollution in the Point/Counterpoint on pages 52 and 53.

RESOURCES FOR THE FUTURE

North Carolina is rich in natural resources. Its people, forests, fertile soil, minerals, and bodies of water

Rafting is a popular sport on many of the swiftly flowing rivers in the western part of our state.

are among our state's important resources. Our state is trying to conserve our resources so that they will be available for the future.

Check Your Reading

1. What is a natural resource?
2. List some of our state's most important natural resources.
3. **GEOGRAPHY SKILL:** Look at the minerals map on page 50. In which part of North Carolina is most of its phosphate found?
4. **THINKING SKILL:** List the natural resources of North Carolina that are renewable. Then list those that are nonrenewable.

BUILDING CITIZENSHIP

POINT/COUNTERPOINT

Should Incinerators Be Used to Burn Chemical Wastes?

You have just read that our state is rich in water resources. Some of our rivers and streams also flow under the surface of the earth. This water is often used as drinking water. It is important to keep both this water and our air clean. If our environment becomes polluted, it may make us sick.

Some products that we use, such as many household cleaners, contain chemicals. Companies that make these products must get rid of the chemicals that are left over after the products are made. These chemical wastes are often called hazardous wastes because they can be hazardous, or dangerous, to our health. Some companies get rid of chemical wastes by burning them in huge furnaces, called incinerators. However, nearby communities sometimes complain that the fumes, or smoke and gases, released into the air from the incinerators are dangerous and pollute our air and water. Other people argue that incinerators can be safe and are necessary because there are not enough places to bury all of our wastes. Should incinerators be used to burn chemical wastes?

POINT

Incinerators Should Not Be Used to Burn Chemical Wastes

Mary Lee Kerr works for the Institute for Southern Studies. This group works to protect our environment. Kerr says that our state should not build incinerators to burn hazardous wastes. Instead, companies should use safer chemicals to make their products.

> Incinerators are dangerous. When hazardous wastes are burned, poisonous fumes go up in their smokestacks. People who work and live near incinerators often get sick from breathing fumes. . . .
>
> We can stop building incinerators because . . . the government has said that companies can change the chemicals they use. . . . If they did that, . . . less waste could get in our water and air to make us sick.

- According to Mary Lee Kerr, why should incinerators not be used to burn chemical wastes?

COUNTERPOINT

Incinerators Should Be Used to Burn Chemical Wastes

George White works for ThermalKEM, a company that builds incinerators that burn chemical wastes. White says that government rules keep incinerators safe. He says that people are afraid of chemical wastes because they are called "hazardous."

> Everything that we use [creates] hazardous waste. Unless our lifestyles are changed, there are always going to be materials to be incinerated. . . . We'll never finish [incinerating the waste].
>
> Our [rules] are . . . stricter than [almost] any other company. . . . The biggest fear that people have . . . is that they call this stuff hazardous waste. If they called [it] chemical waste, we probably wouldn't have as hard a time [building incinerators].

- According to George White, why should incinerators be used to burn chemical wastes?

UNDERSTANDING THE POINT/COUNTERPOINT

1. In your opinion, which side has the stronger argument? Explain your answer.
2. Which other groups of people might have opinions about this issue?
3. Is there anything that the two sides might be able to agree upon? If so, give an example.

LESSON
3 The Outer Banks

READ TO LEARN

Key Vocabulary

barrier island
sound
inlet
dune
erosion
hurricane
current
cape

Key Places

Cape Hatteras

Read Aloud

But the sand! The sand is the greatest thing in Kitty Hawk, and soon will be the only thing.

Orville Wright wrote these words to his sister in 1903. He and his brother Wilbur were near Kitty Hawk on the Outer Banks to test their airplane to see if it would fly. The airplane did fly. Today North Carolina honors this event with the words *First in Flight* on its license plates. In this lesson you will read why Orville Wright and many others have been drawn to the special environment of the Outer Banks.

Read for Purpose

1. **WHAT YOU KNOW:** What are some ways in which people can enjoy the beach?
2. **WHAT YOU WILL LEARN:** What is special about the environment of the Outer Banks?

A STRING OF ISLANDS

Imagine that you, like the Wright Brothers, could glide in an airplane over the Outer Banks. As you look down, you will see that the Outer Banks are a very long string of **barrier** (bar′ ē ər) **islands** made up mostly of sand. A barrier separates things, and a barrier island separates the mainland from the ocean. The barrier islands that make up the Outer Banks separate almost all of North Carolina's coast from the Atlantic Ocean.

Find the Outer Banks on the map on this page. These narrow islands stretch for about 175 miles (280 km) along North Carolina's coast. The longest of these islands are Bodie Island and Hatteras Island.

As you look down from your airplane, you see that some barrier islands are near the mainland. Others are far away. In between the islands and the mainland you will see large bodies of water called **sounds**. A sound is a body of water between the mainland and an island. Pamlico (pam′ li kō) Sound and Albemarle (al′ bə märl) Sound are the largest of the five sounds in this area. Find the others on the map.

The barrier islands are close to one another. Flowing between the islands are narrow openings called **inlets**. Many kinds of fish are found in these inlets and sounds. Some visitors to the Outer Banks have said that the question they hear most often is "Coming to fish?"

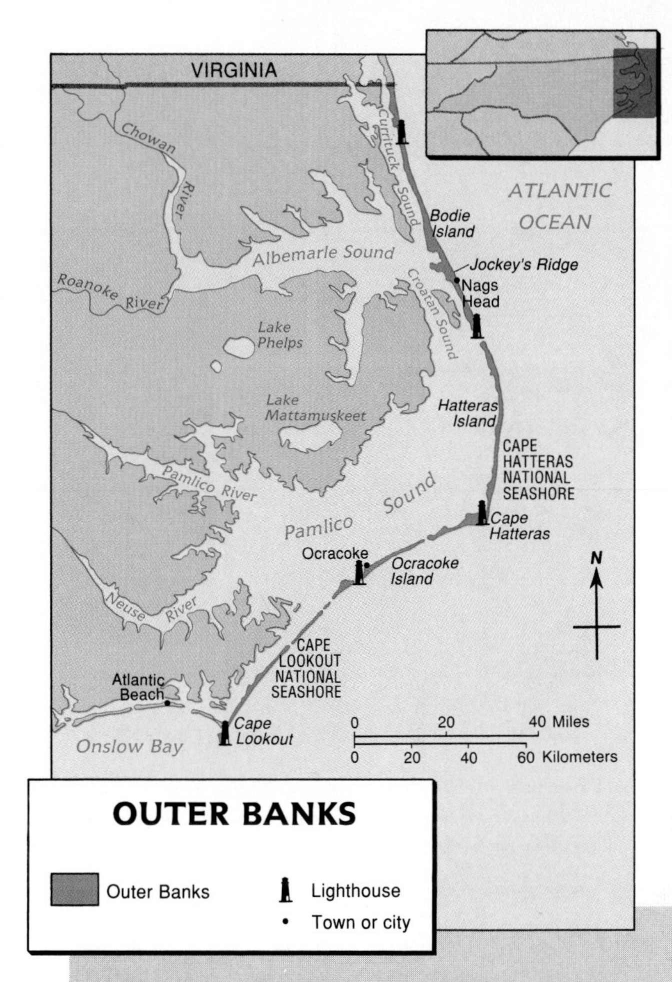

MAP SKILL: On which of the Outer Banks is Cape Hatteras located? Which Outer Banks island has two lighthouses?

LOW LANDS

As you look down from your airplane, you begin to take a good look at the land on the islands. You notice that no place on the Outer Banks is very high. Find Nags Head on Bodie Island on the map on this page. Near Nags Head is a sand **dune** named Jockey's Ridge. A dune is a large pile of sand heaped up by the movement of the wind or the ocean. Jockey's Ridge dune, at 138 feet (42 m), is the highest point on the Outer Banks.

Kitty Hawk, which you read about in the Read Aloud, is near Jockey's Ridge. You will read more about Kitty Hawk and the famous flight of the Wright Brothers in the Traditions lesson on pages 59 to 62.

A SPECIAL ENVIRONMENT

Many people like to spend their summer vacations on the Outer Banks. In summer the weather is

People on the Outer Banks enjoy the sand, sea oats, loggerhead turtles (*above, left*), and killdeer (*below*).

warm. The scenery is beautiful. Seabirds and many kinds of sea plants can be found everywhere on the Outer Banks. As one young woman who works on Ocracoke Island told writer Anthony Bailey:

> *There's nothing like this anywhere on earth. . . . Some of our trees are between 300 and 500 years old. We've got rare aquatic* [sea] *plants—the water violet, for instance—and several endangered birds, like the red-shouldered hawk, and a rare reptile, the yellow-lipped snake.*

Once thousands of sea turtles came ashore here to lay their eggs in the sand. However, few of these turtles can be found today. Almost all of the wild ponies that lived on Ocracoke Island have also gone. New buildings and roads have destroyed many of the natural conditions that these and other special animals need in order to live on the Outer Banks.

THE MOVING SAND

One thing you could not see from your airplane is that the islands of the Outer Banks are slowly moving westward. The ocean both pushes the islands to the west and wears away their Atlantic coastline. The people of the Outer Banks worry about losing their homes. One Outer Banker says, "The ocean keeps on coming. Sooner or later our cottage will go, too."

The reason for this problem is that the Outer Banks are made of sand. Sometimes the waves wash away the sand. At other times the wind blows it away. This washing or blowing away of land is called **erosion** (i rō′ zhən). The wind and the waves also leave behind new piles of sand. During powerful storms so much sand might be moved that small islands disappear and new islands appear. Some islands may be narrower or wider than they were before.

Storms also can cause a lot of damage to property on the islands. **Hurricanes** (hûr′ i kānz), or powerful storms with violent winds, sometimes hit the Outer Banks during the summer and early fall. Hurricane winds blow over 75 miles (120 km) an hour. The heavy rains that come with a hurricane can wash away much of a beach and many homes. Liz Winslow, who has spent summers on the Outer Banks since she was a child, wrote that during one storm "the cottage lost its front porch and kitchen." Many people and animals have died during hurricanes on the Outer Banks.

WHERE CURRENTS MEET

Looking down from your airplane, you will see another interesting sight—several lighthouses. Each lighthouse on the Outer Banks has a different design so that it is easy to recognize. These lighthouses were built to warn ships that they are nearing the shore.

Many ships have run aground and been destroyed near the Outer Banks because of the area's violent storms and strong ocean **currents**. A current is the part of a body of water that keeps flowing in the same path. It is like a river flowing in the ocean. Strong ocean currents have forced many ships into the shallow waters to the east of **Cape Hatteras**. A **cape** is a point of land that stretches into a large body of water. Writer David Stick describes

Starting from the upper right and going clockwise are the Cape Lookout, Ocracoke, Cape Hatteras, and Currituck Beach lighthouses, which have different designs.

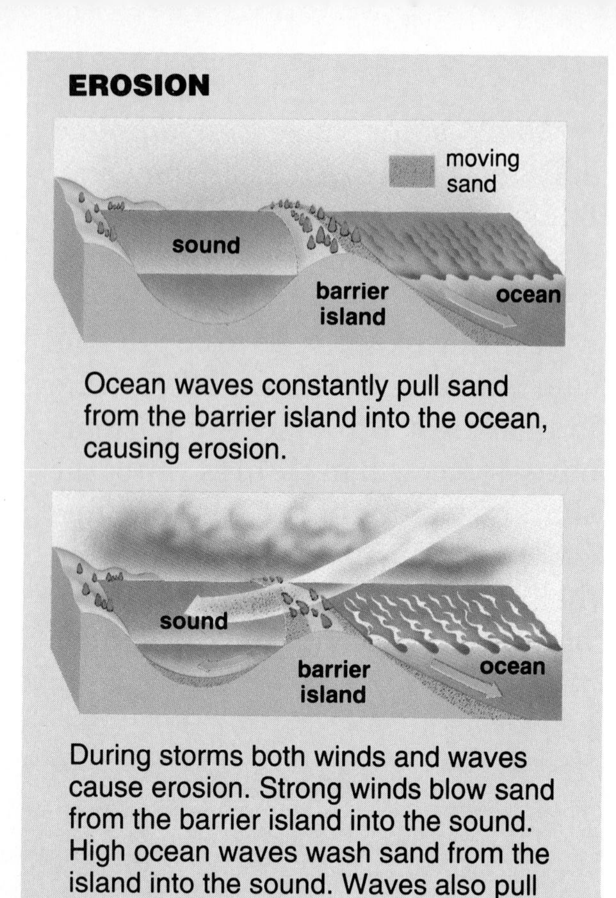

Ocean waves constantly pull sand from the barrier island into the ocean, causing erosion.

During storms both winds and waves cause erosion. Strong winds blow sand from the barrier island into the sound. High ocean waves wash sand from the island into the sound. Waves also pull sand into the ocean.

DIAGRAM SKILL: How do the ocean waves cause **erosion** of the Outer Banks?

what happens when two great currents run into each other.

> *You can stand on Cape Hatteras on a stormy day and watch two [currents] come together in . . . savage fury; for there at the Point [they] . . . run head-on into each other, tossing their . . . spray 100 feet [30 m] . . . into the air.*

So many ships have been wrecked in this area that it is called the "Graveyard of the Atlantic."

One of North Carolina's most famous lighthouses is at Cape Hatteras. It is the tallest lighthouse in the United States. Find Cape Hatteras on the map on page 55. Unfortunately, the Cape Hatteras lighthouse is in danger of falling into the ocean. Erosion has washed away much of the land on which it rests. To save the lighthouse, the United States government has replaced some of the sand around it. A drive to raise money to protect the lighthouse was started in the 1980s.

In 1953 the United States government named Hatteras Island the Cape Hatteras National Seashore. The purpose was to save the unusual environment of the island.

A BARRIER OF SAND

As you have read, the Outer Banks are a long string of barrier islands off the coast of North Carolina. The rough ocean waters that formed the Outer Banks continue to cause erosion and shipwrecks in this area. They give the islands a special environment.

Check Your Reading

1. What is a barrier island?
2. List two reasons why the shape of the Outer Banks changes.
3. What is special about the environment of the Outer Banks?
4. **THINKING SKILL:** Reread David Stick's quote on this page. Do you think that the events he observed happen in all storms?

The Dream of Flying

By Carole Marsh

For thousands of years, people had dreamed of flying. That dream finally came true at Kitty Hawk in 1903 when Wilbur and Orville Wright flew an airplane that they had built. North Carolinians are proud that the Wright brothers chose the Outer Banks to make this dream come true. Continuing to try to make one's dreams come true has long been a tradition in North Carolina. A tradition is a custom or belief that has been handed down from the past. As you read, think about how hard the Wright brothers worked to achieve their dream.

Orville

Wilbur

YOUNG INVENTORS

Wilbur and Orville Wright grew up in the state of Ohio. Wilbur, born in 1867, was four years older than his brother Orville. They were both inventors. An inventor is a person who makes something that no one else has ever made before. Even as young children, the brothers liked to take toys apart and then repair them. Once, their father gave them a flying toy that was powered by rubber bands. The brothers later said that this toy, which they called "the Bat," sparked their interest in flying.

"We built a number of copies of this toy, which flew successfully." —Orville

"... to get at something that interested us. That's happiness." —Orville

In their teens Wilbur and Orville ran a bicycle shop. During their free time they studied flying. They hoped to build a flying machine—one that a pilot could sit in and control. The Wright brothers studied gliders that other inventors had made. A glider is a flying machine that does not have an engine. By 1899 the brothers had built a glider that looked like a big, two-layered kite.

THE FIRST ATTEMPTS TO FLY

Orville and Wilbur needed a place to fly their glider. They wanted a test site, or place, that was far from crowds and had hills and strong winds for gliding. They needed to land the machine on soft sand so that they wouldn't get hurt. In 1900 the brothers picked a place called Kitty Hawk, located on the Outer Banks of our state.

The brothers grew to love Kitty Hawk. Orville wrote home to his sister, "The sunsets here are the prettiest I have ever seen."

During the first test flight Wilbur was the pilot. Orville and a friend held the glider's wings and ran forward. As the glider began to fly Wilbur shouted, "Let go!" The glider lifted, then fell. Wilbur and Orville had not yet found a way to control their machine. They went back to Ohio to work on this problem.

The brothers returned to Kitty Hawk the next fall with a new design, but this plane also failed to fly. Wilbur and

Orville finally decided that the research of other inventors that they were using was wrong. So they began to try out their own ideas. By 1902 they had figured out how to control their machine.

SUCCESS AT LAST

Now Orville and Wilbur were ready to add an engine to power their plane. At home in Ohio, they built a gasoline engine, designed propellers, and sewed cloth wings. In September 1903 they returned to Kitty Hawk.

Wilbur and Orville lay a wooden track down the slope of a large hill for the plane to use during takeoff. Then they dragged their machine to the top. Wilbur won the coin toss to fly first. He lay facedown in the pilot's cradle, between the wings. Whizzing down the track, the world's first airplane rose and then fell to the ground. It had failed to fly.

The brothers repaired the plane and laid the track on flat ground this time. On December 17, 1903, they were ready to fly again. With Orville as the pilot, the plane soared for

"In my experiments I do not expect to rise many feet from the ground, and in case I am upset there is nothing but soft sand to strike on." —Wilbur

12 seconds and landed safely. Wilbur cried, "*Eureka*!"—an old Greek word meaning "I have found it" or "I have succeeded."

For the first time in history, a heavier-than-air machine had been flown and controlled by a pilot. The Wright brothers' dream had finally come true. After this success, Wilbur and Orville decided to spend the rest of their lives making planes. Because of the hard work of the Wright brothers and others, airplanes became a common sight in the world's skies.

KITTY HAWK TODAY

Today, you can visit the Wright Brothers Memorial in Kitty Hawk. There you can see life-size models of their flying machines and the cabin in which they lived and worked. Kitty Hawk is the birthplace of flying. It also is a reminder that invention is a mixture of good ideas, hard work, and the willingness to keep working to make dreams come true.

What did the Wright brothers do to make their dream of flying come true?

REVIEWING VOCABULARY

barrier island
current
erosion
mineral
precipitation

Number a sheet of paper from 1 to 5. Beside each number write the word or term from the list above that best completes the sentence.

1. During the winter ____ sometimes falls in the form of snow.
2. A ____ is a natural substance found in the earth.
3. The ____ is like a river flowing in the ocean.
4. A ____ separates the mainland from the ocean.
5. The ocean can cause ____ , or a wearing away of the land.

REVIEWING FACTS

1. How does elevation affect climate?
2. Name two factors besides elevation that affect climate.
3. What is the main difference between renewable and nonrenewable resources? Give an example of each.
4. What are three ways in which hurricanes can affect the environment of the Outer Banks?
5. Which North Carolina lighthouse is the tallest lighthouse in the United States?

WRITING ABOUT MAIN IDEAS

1. **Writing a Paragraph:** Choose the one natural resource of North Carolina that you think most affects your everyday life. Write a paragraph explaining the ways in which that natural resource affects your life.
2. **Writing About Perspectives:** Write a conversation between two people about our state's climate. The first person can tell what the climate is like in the Piedmont Region. The other person can tell what it is like in the Mountain Region.

BUILDING SKILLS: DECISION MAKING

Suppose that you knew of a plan to clean up a local park. The plan would call for volunteers to spend every Saturday afternoon on the project. Should you join them?

1. To make the decision, you should first
   - **a.** talk with your teacher.
   - **b.** think about your choices and the possible results of each.
   - **c.** visit the park.
2. Your decision should help you to
   - **a.** make money.
   - **b.** reach your goal.
   - **c.** do well in school.
3. Identify some occasions on which you might have to make decisions.

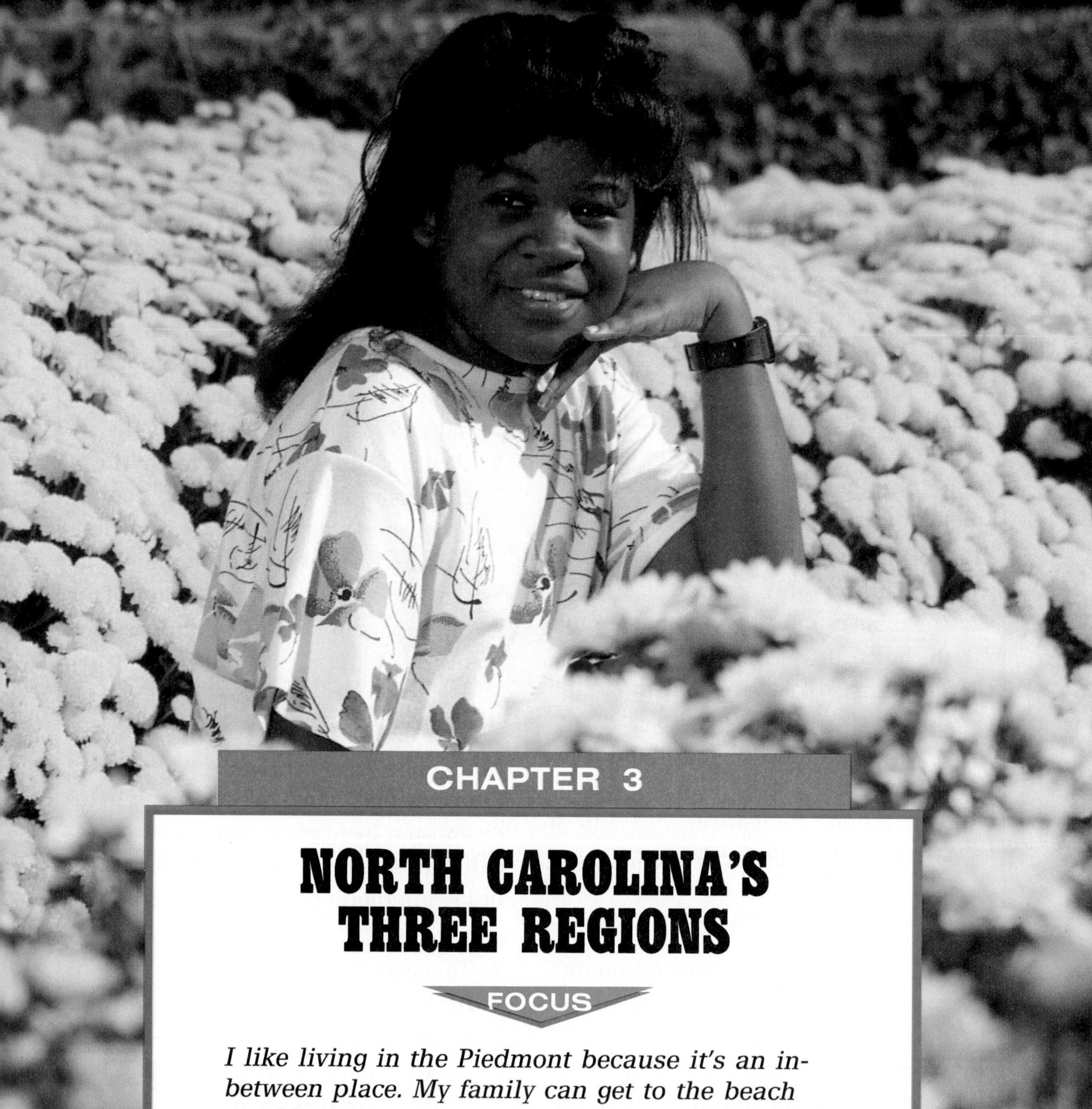

CHAPTER 3

NORTH CAROLINA'S THREE REGIONS

FOCUS

I like living in the Piedmont because it's an in-between place. My family can get to the beach quickly. We can get to the mountains fast, too. Our city has interesting places like Duke Gardens and the Museum of Life and Science.

Madinah Hamidullah lives in Durham, which is a large city in the Piedmont. In this chapter you will read about many special places in our state's regions.

LESSON

1 Three Regions

READ TO LEARN

Key Vocabulary

landform
plain
plateau

Key Places

Coastal Plain Region
Piedmont Region
Mountain Region

Read Aloud

Then let all those who love the land that we live in,
As happy a region as on this side of heaven.
Where plenty and peace, love and joy smile before us,
Raise aloud, raise together the heart-thrilling chorus.

These words are from our state song, "The Old North State." They describe the feelings that North Carolinians have about our state's land. In this lesson you will read about the different kinds of land in North Carolina.

Read for Purpose

1. **WHAT YOU KNOW:** What are the five regions of the United States?
2. **WHAT YOU WILL LEARN:** What are the three regions of North Carolina?

NORTH CAROLINA'S LAND

Jennie Cotten, Willie Green, and Simon Taylor are friends who live in different parts of North Carolina. Jennie lives in Wilmington. Willie lives in Raleigh and Simon lives in Asheville. Recently a newcomer to North Carolina asked each of them to describe our state's land.

"That's very easy," said Jennie. "North Carolina is flat and has beautiful beaches."

Willie shook his head. "That's not true. Our state has soft, green, rolling hills and many wide rivers."

"You're both wrong," said Simon. "North Carolina is covered with steep mountains and deep valleys."

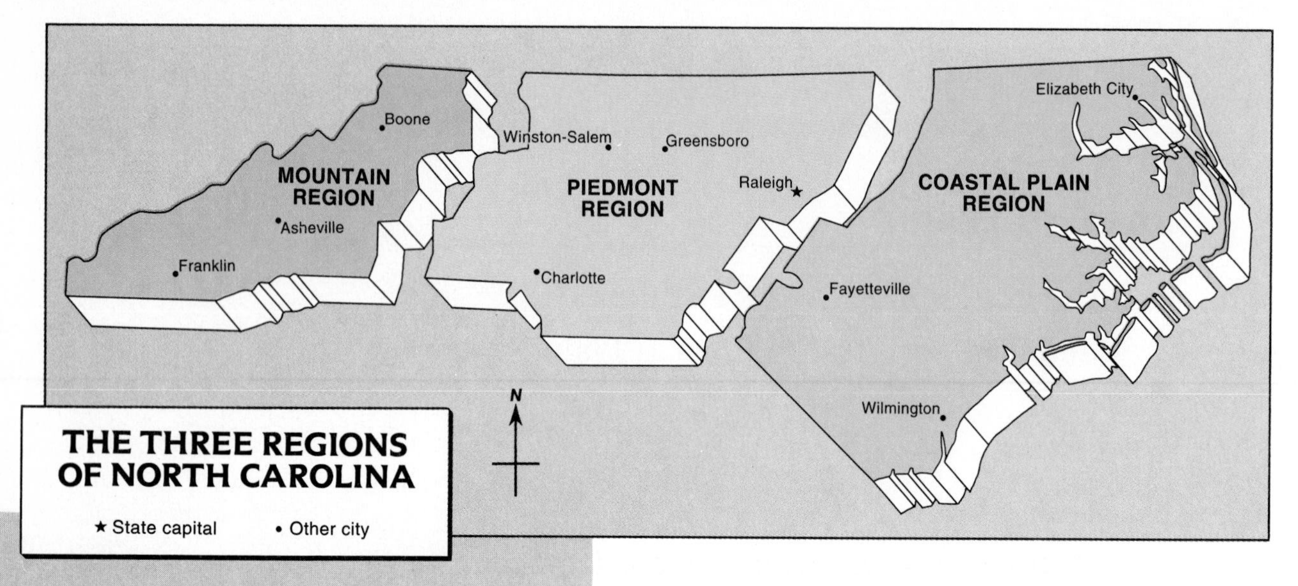

MAP SKILL: In which of North Carolina's regions is the state capital located? Which city is the state capital?

Which one was right? Actually, they all were. They all described North Carolina, but they described the different parts of the state in which they live.

In order to understand a large state like North Carolina, it is helpful to divide the land into regions. You read in Chapter 1 that a region is an area with common features that set it apart from other areas. North Carolina is divided into three regions: the **Coastal Plain Region**, the **Piedmont Region**, and the **Mountain Region**. Find each region on the map above. In which regions do you think Jennie, Willie, and Simon live?

SHAPES OF THE LAND

Each of North Carolina's three regions has different **landforms**. Landforms are shapes that make up the earth's surface. **Plains**, hills, mountains, and **plateaus** (pla tōz′) are some common landforms. A plain is a large area of flat, or nearly flat, land. A plateau is a large area of high, mostly flat land. You can find North Carolina's different landforms on the map on page 67.

The Coastal Plain Region, which is in the eastern part of the state, is made up of plains. The Piedmont Region, in the center of the state, is a plateau with gently rolling hills. The Mountain Region, in the western part of the state, is made up of many high mountains. These landforms are the features that set each area apart and make it a region.

FROM EAST TO WEST

Imagine that you are going to travel across North Carolina from east to west. By the end of your trip, you will have crossed all three of our state's regions. You would begin in the Coastal Plain Region at the Outer Banks. The land along the Outer Banks and along the coast of the mainland is just above sea level. This region of North Carolina has 300 miles (480 km) of coastline. Here you might see swamps and people swimming, fishing, or collecting shells on the beach.

As you cross the Coastal Plain Region to the west, the land begins to rise. When you reach the western edge of the Coastal Plain, you will be about 400 feet (122 m) higher in elevation than you were at the coastline of our state.

Next, you move up onto the plateau of the Piedmont Region. The Piedmont is a much hillier region than is the Coastal Plain. As you move west, you see the land rising.

MAP SKILL: North Carolina's coast includes many wetlands and sandy beaches. Which of the **landforms** on the map do you think the photographs on this page show?

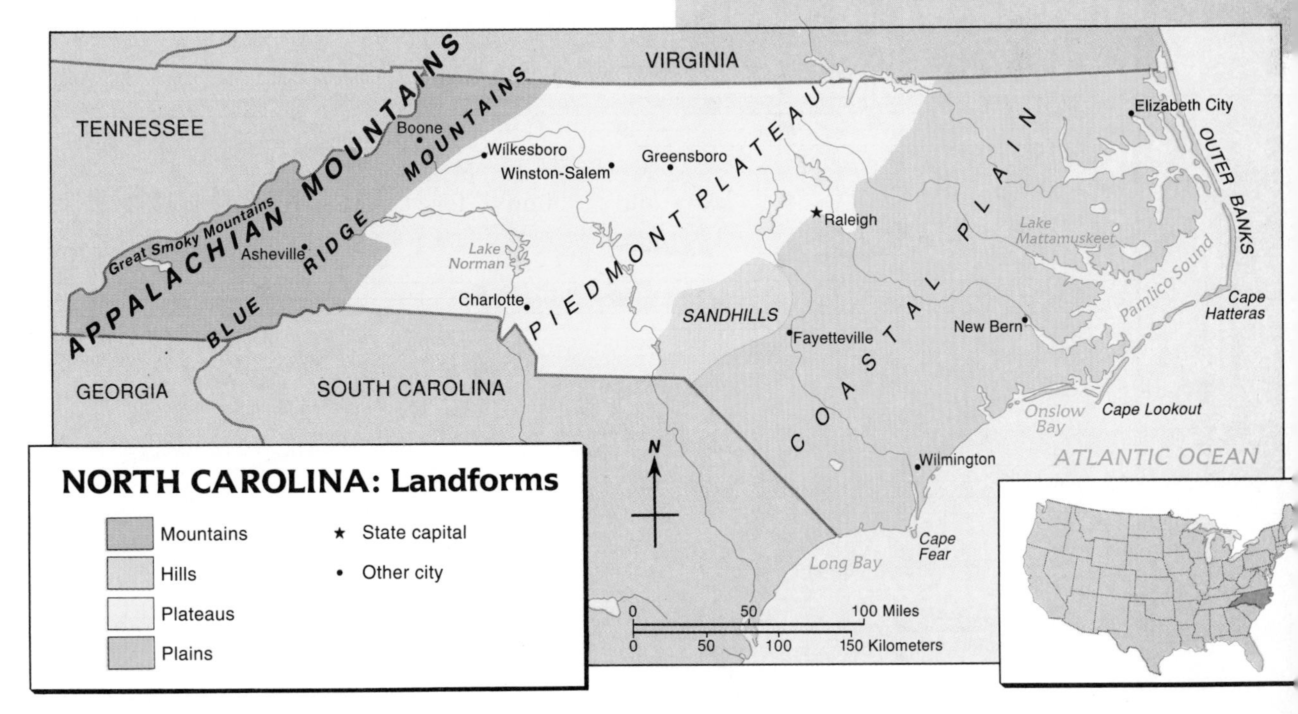

Carolina in the Morning
Words by Gus Kahn
Music by Walter Donaldson
Liltingly
Noth - ing could be fin - er than to be in Car - o -
li - na in the morn - ing,
No - one could be sweet - er than my sweet - ie when I
meet her in the morn - ing.
If I had A - lad - din's lamp for on - ly a day,
I'd make a wish and here's what I'd say:
"No - thing could be fin - er than to be in Car - o -
li - na in the morn - ing."

People use and enjoy their land in different ways in the three regions of our state.

The land rises gradually to about 1,500 feet (457 m) in elevation. You also notice that there are more people, homes, towns, and cities here than in the Coastal Plain.

When you reach the Mountain Region, the land begins to rise steeply. Here mountain peaks are almost as high as 7,000 feet (2,121 m). In this region you find steep mountain trails lined with wildflowers. A blue mist often covers the valleys below. If you were to walk through the mountains in the morning, you might feel as cheerful as the song on the opposite page.

A LAND OF VARIETY

As you have read, our state is made up of three regions with different landforms—plains, plateaus, hills, and mountains. From east to west they are the Coastal Plain Region, the Piedmont Region, and the Mountain Region.

Check Your Reading

1. Name four kinds of landforms found in North Carolina.
2. What are the three regions of North Carolina?
3. In which region do you live? How would you describe the landforms of this region to a person from a different region?
4. **GEOGRAPHY SKILL:** Describe the change in North Carolina's elevation from east to west.
5. **THINKING SKILL:** What are three questions you could ask to learn more about our state's regions?

Reading Elevation Maps

Key Vocabulary

profile

In Lesson 1 you read about the many kinds of land in North Carolina. You learned that our state has a region called the Coastal Plain, which is mostly low, flat land with a long stretch of seacoast. Our state also has hills in the Piedmont Region and mountains in the western part of the state. The map on page 67 shows the landforms of North Carolina.

Landforms and Elevations

The landform map helps you to see how our state's land is different from one region to another. It also shows the location of the Coastal Plain, the Piedmont Plateau, and the Great Smoky Mountains. However, it does not show how high the mountains are or how low the plains are.

That is because landform maps do not show elevation. As you read in Chapter 2, elevation is the height of land above sea level. It is usually measured in feet or meters. Elevation at sea level is 0 feet (0 m). A place

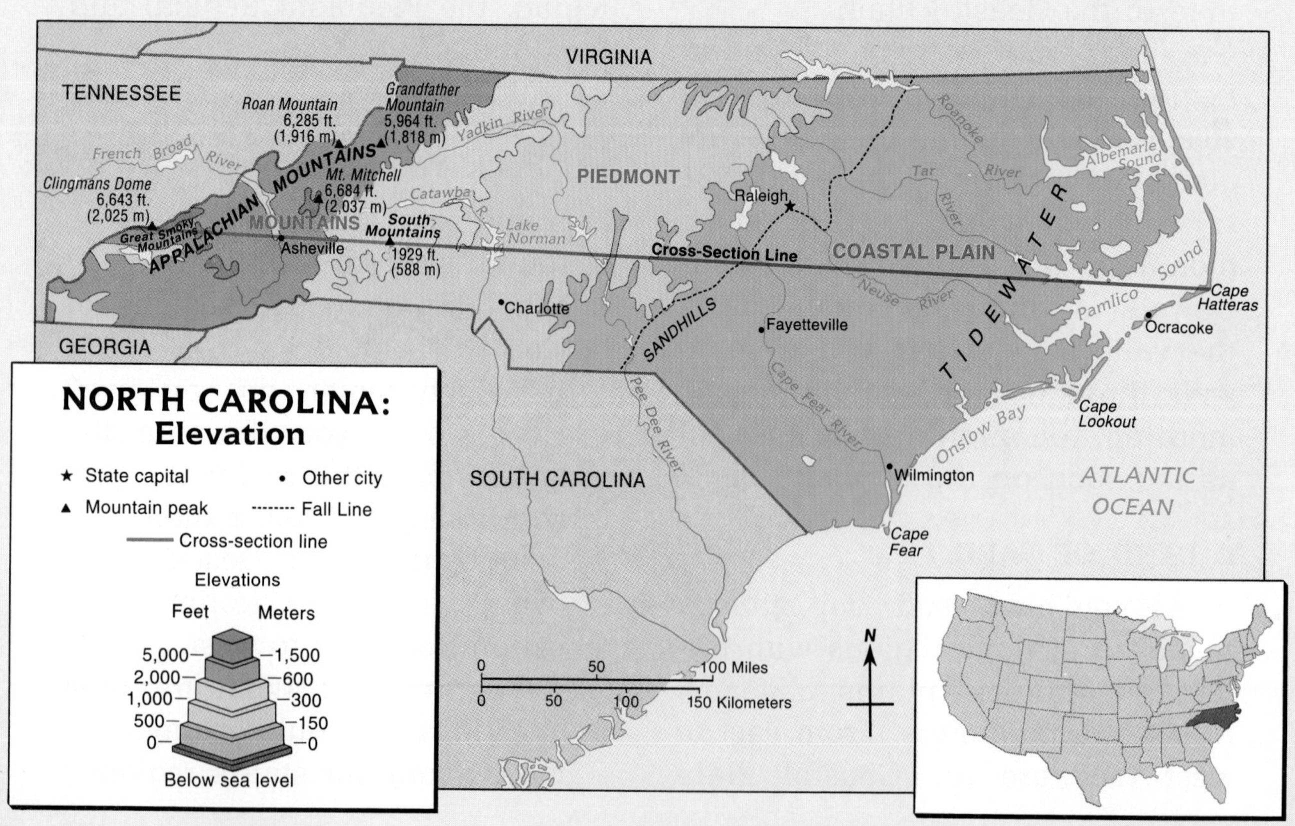

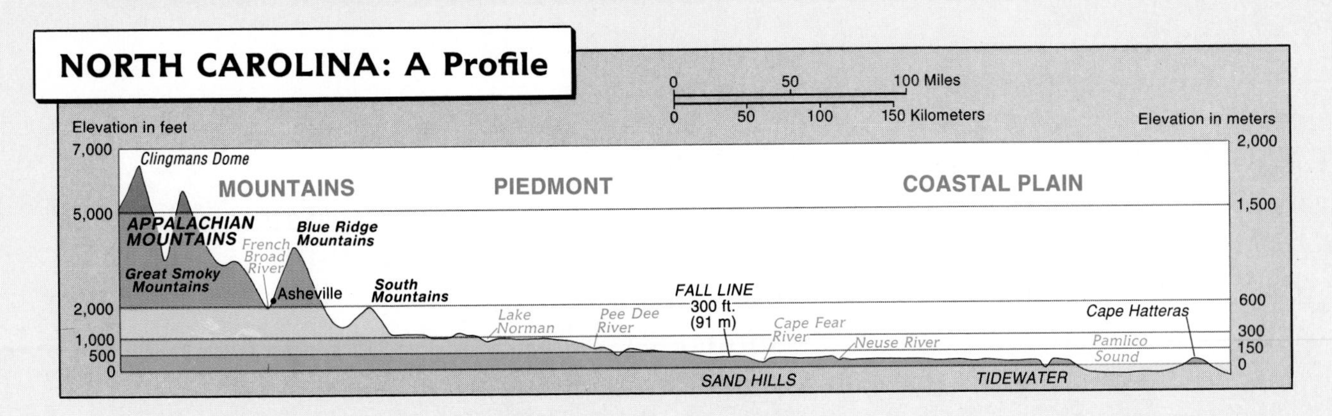

that is close to sea level has a low elevation. A place that rises far above sea level has a high elevation.

Elevation maps show the variations in elevation of a place. Look at the elevation map on page 70. It uses colors to show different elevations. An area that is all one color is almost all the same elevation, whether it is a highland or a lowland area. The elevation that each of the colors stands for is explained on the map key. Which color is used to show elevations of 2,000 feet (600 m)? Which range of elevation is shown by yellow?

A North Carolina Profile

Suppose that you wanted to hike across North Carolina. You might use a diagram called a **profile**. A profile is a side view of a part of the earth. It lets you read the elevation of the land. A profile of the state would be helpful in showing you where you would have to climb up or down.

To understand what a profile is, imagine making a cut straight through North Carolina from east to west and revealing the mountains, lowlands, and the areas in between. The profile shown above was done in this way. It shows a profile of our state from the Atlantic Ocean in the east to the mountains in the west.

Look closely at the profile. Compare it with the cross-section line on the elevation map. What is the elevation of Asheville? Does the map or the profile help you to find the elevation more accurately?

Reviewing the Skill

1. What is an elevation map? What is a profile?
2. Look at the map and profile. What is the elevation of the South Mountains in each? Explain.
3. If you traveled from west to east in North Carolina, would you be going mostly uphill or mostly downhill? How does the profile above help you to answer this question?
4. Why is it helpful to be able to read an elevation map and a profile?

LESSON

2 The Coastal Plain Region

READ TO LEARN

Key Vocabulary

lowlands
tide
peninsula
marsh
swamp

Key Places

Tidewater
Inner Coastal Plain
Neuse River
Pamlico River
Great Dismal Swamp
Lake Mattamuskeet
Sandhills

Read Aloud

A glorious paradise.

These words were spoken by George Washington, our country's first President. President Washington was describing the Great Dismal Swamp, which is part of the Coastal Plain Region. In this lesson you will read more about the various landforms that are in this region of our state.

Read for Purpose

1. **WHAT YOU KNOW:** What are the three regions of North Carolina?
2. **WHAT YOU WILL LEARN:** What is special about the geography of the Coastal Plain Region?

THE LAND ALONG THE COAST

In Chapter 2 you read about the Outer Banks. These barrier islands are part of North Carolina's Coastal Plain Region. The Coastal Plain is a huge area that covers nearly half of North Carolina's land. It stretches 140 miles (225 km) inland from the barrier islands. As you know, a coastal plain is the flat area of land near a coast. North Carolina's Coastal Plain Region has three different areas of **lowlands**. Lowlands are lands that have an elevation just slightly above sea level. One lowland is the Outer Banks. The other two lowlands are the **Tidewater** and

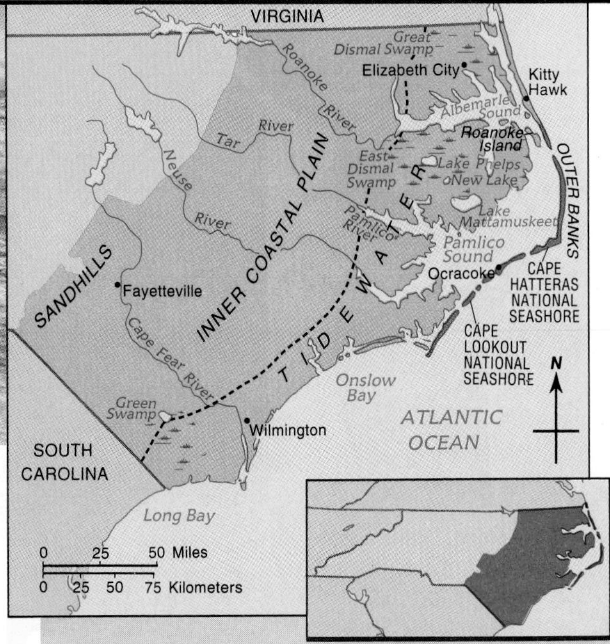

MAP SKILL: Where in the Coastal Plain Region would people go to fish in rough ocean water?

the **Inner Coastal Plain**. Find these lowland areas on the map of the region on this page.

THE TIDEWATER

In Lesson 1 you read about Jennie Cotten, who lives in Wilmington. Living near the ocean, Jennie knows about the effects of **tides**. Tides are the regular rise and fall of the ocean and the bodies of water connected to it. Ocean tides rise two times each day. The Tidewater's name tells us that this area's low-lying coastal land is affected by tides. When the tide is high, some of the low-lying land along the coast is covered with water.

Look at the map of the Coastal Plain Region on this page. Find the **Neuse** (Nüs) **River** and the **Pamlico River**. Notice that as these rivers flow into Pamlico Sound, they nearly surround a body of land. This land is called a **peninsula** (pə nin′ sə lə). A peninsula is a body of land that is almost entirely surrounded by water.

WATER, WATER EVERYWHERE

If you were to visit certain parts of the Tidewater, you might need to wear boots. Some of the lands in the Tidewater are so close to sea level that much of them are wet. In fact, these lands are called wetlands. Wetlands are a very good environment for certain kinds of plants and animals.

One kind of wetland is a **marsh**. A marsh is an area of low, wet land that is covered mostly with tall

The Great Dismal Swamp is home to many plants and animals.
In the photograph above a frog rests on a pitcher plant.

grasses. Near the ocean the Tidewater's marshes are filled with salty seawater. Saltwater marshes are home to many fish and shellfish that find food and safety in these wetlands. Farther inland these marshes become filled with fresh water. The freshwater marshes are home to many kinds of animals, including frogs, turtles, raccoons, ducks, and geese.

THE GREAT DISMAL SWAMP

Inland, the wetlands are covered not only with grasses, but also with trees and shrubs. These wetlands are called **swamps**. In the northeast corner of our state is a large area called the **Great Dismal Swamp**. Even though the word *dismal* means "gloomy," people enjoy visiting the Great Dismal Swamp. The area has miles and miles of wild and beautiful scenery.

Today you can take a boat ride to see the unusual trees and some of the 100 different kinds of birds that live in the Great Dismal Swamp. Part of the swamp is a national wildlife refuge, or a safe home for animals. If you visit the swamp, you might see black bears, otters, and bobcats. Your trip through the swamp will help you to see why President George Washington called the area "a glorious paradise."

NATURAL LAKES

North Carolina has 15 natural lakes. Most of them are small and they are all located in the Tidewater. In Chapter 2 you read about

Lake Mattamuskeet, which is the largest of these natural lakes. Lake Mattamuskeet is very shallow. The deepest spot in the lake is only 5 feet (1.5 m) deep. Lake Mattamuskeet gets its name from the Native American word that means "It is a moving swamp."

If you visit Lake Mattamuskeet, you might see huge birds called ospreys (os′ prēz) and beautiful white egrets (ē′ grits). They are just two of the hundreds of different birds that live in the Lake Mattamuskeet Wildlife Refuge.

Egrets *(top, left)* and ospreys are water birds. Regional crops include peaches and cotton. *(below)*

THE INNER COASTAL PLAIN

As you move westward from the Tidewater, the land rises and becomes drier. You are now in the Inner Coastal Plain, where our state's richest farmland is located. For thousands of years, the rivers of North Carolina have carried rich soil as they flowed to the Atlantic Ocean. Much of this soil was deposited along the Inner Coastal Plain. Today peaches and cotton are just two of the many crops that grow well in this area.

Several of North Carolina's rivers flow through the Inner Coastal Plain on their way to the Atlantic Ocean. The Roanoke River, Tar River, and Cape Fear River are three of the many rivers that flow across the Inner Coastal Plain. You can find these rivers on the map of the Coastal Plain Region on page 73.

THE SANDHILLS

In the southwest corner of the Inner Coastal Plain you will find the Sandhills. This area's name also tells you something about it. The Sandhills are rolling hills of rough, sandy soil. You can find the Sandhills on the map on page 73.

Many visitors to the Coastal Plain Region play golf or relax on the sandy beaches.

The Sandhills are not good for growing most crops. However, people have found that the rolling sandy hills are perfect for building golf courses. People from all over the world come to the Sandhills to play golf on the beautiful courses that are lined with tall pine trees.

A LOW, FLAT REGION

Marshes, swamps, lakes, and sandhills are all part of the huge Coastal Plain Region. In later chapters you will read about why the Coastal Plain Region is a good place for people to live and work.

Check Your Reading

1. How do tides affect the area called the Tidewater?
2. What is special about the geography of the Coastal Plain Region?
3. Why might people want to create more wildlife refuges in the Great Dismal Swamp and around Lake Mattamuskeet?
4. **GEOGRAPHY SKILL:** Describe the changes in the land of the Coastal Plain Region from east to west.
5. **THINKING SKILL:** In what ways are the Tidewater and the Inner Coastal Plain similar? In what ways are they different?

Pirates

By Carole Marsh

About 300 years ago pirates sailed along the coast of North Carolina. A pirate was a sailor who attacked and robbed ships at sea. Today pirates no longer sail the seas, but North Carolinians enjoy the tradition of telling and listening to pirate stories. This tradition helps us to remember stories of the past that are part of our state's history. They keep alive the memories of those days long ago. As you read, think about the reasons that people enjoy the tradition of telling pirate stories.

NORTH CAROLINA'S SHIFTING SANDS

Long ago, English sailors told stories about chasing disappearing pirate ships along North Carolina's coast. These ships seemed to disappear because of the inlets of our coast. As you have read, our sounds and inlets are filled with sand that shifts and creates new inlets. Pirates used these inlets to escape.

However, not all pirates escaped easily. Many ships crashed near the Outer Banks. As you read in Chapter 2, this area is called the "Graveyard of the Atlantic."

BECOMING A PIRATE

A pirate's life was dangerous. Yet many boys became pirates because they were poor and wanted to make money any way they could. Pirates came from many different countries, such as those along the coasts of Africa and Europe. Although most pirates were men, some were women. Around 1720 Anne Bonney, a 16-year-old South Carolinian, ran away from home and became a pirate.

Anne Bonney

Many pirates came to North Carolina to sell their stolen goods. By the early 1700s the town of Bath was the base for most of these pirates. In fact, Bath was the headquarters of the world-famous pirate, "Blackbeard."

BLACKBEARD

Blackbeard, whose real name was Edward Teach, grew up in England. Blackbeard became one of the world's most feared pirates. He was a large man with bushy black hair and eyebrows. He had a long black beard that he braided with colorful ribbons. Just before a battle, Blackbeard would set pieces of cord on fire and stuff them under the brim of his hat. The smoke circling his head made him a frightening sight. Upon seeing his ship, the *Queen Anne's Revenge*, many ships surrendered without a fight.

Blackbeard's house in Bath was at Plum Point, near the home of an important North Carolina leader, Charles Eden. Many people thought that Blackbeard shared his stolen coins and treasure with Eden. Blackbeard wanted to marry Eden's daughter. However, she was engaged to marry another man. Blackbeard became so angry that he killed her future husband.

THE END OF PIRATES

Pirates continued to exist because they made money. North Carolinians and other colonists bought pirates' goods because they were cheaper than goods bought from the English. In the early 1700s the English decided to end piracy. They sent warships to North Carolina and nearby areas to capture the pirates. Those who were brought to trial and found guilty were hanged.

The English wanted to capture Blackbeard. They attacked his ship near Ocracoke in 1718. Although Blackbeard was wounded many times, he fought until he was killed. People felt safer after his death. Other pirates were afraid of being caught and left the area. The inlet of Pamlico Sound where Blackbeard was killed was later named Teach's Hole after him.

Blackbeard

TRACES OF PIRATES TODAY

Some people believe that Blackbeard buried his treasure. It has never been found and people continue to look for it. Today people tell stories about a ship's bell in Bath that is said to have come from Blackbeard's ship. Others tell of Blackbeard's house in Ocracoke. On the Pasquotank (pas′ kwō tank) River there is another house where Blackbeard may have stayed. These places are all traces of the days of pirates, long ago.

Why do people enjoy the tradition of telling pirate stories?

LESSON

3 The Piedmont Region

READ TO LEARN

Key Vocabulary

peak
Fall Line
rapids
population

Key Places

Pilot Mountain
Sauratown Mountains
Brushy Mountains
South Mountains

Read Aloud

The country spreads out below like the ocean [and] an abundance of springs of the purest and finest water—burst out from the side of the [hill].

About 200 years ago a small group of North Carolinians was looking for a place to build the state's first university. The words above tell why the group chose the hill that was later named Chapel Hill, after the chapel that stood there. As you will read, these words about the land and its water can be used to describe many parts of the Piedmont Region.

Read for Purpose

1. **WHAT YOU KNOW:** What kinds of activities might you enjoy doing in a hilly area?
2. **WHAT YOU WILL LEARN:** What is special about the geography of the Piedmont Region?

NORTH CAROLINA'S FOOTHILLS

The name *Piedmont* comes from French and means "foot of the mountain." It's easy to see how the Piedmont got this name. Imagine that you are hiking down the mountains in western North Carolina. Near the bottom, or "foot," of the mountains you see that the land to the east is different from the area you have just passed through. Stretching out before you is a land of gentle, rolling hills.

MAP SKILL: Pilot Mountain, shown in the photograph, is one of the few mountain **peaks** of the Piedmont. Near which other mountains is it located?

The rolling hills of the Piedmont make up the central part of our state. This region is well known for its pleasant climate and beautiful scenery. About 200 years ago a visitor to the Piedmont Region wrote that "no spot on earth can be more beautiful."

WORN DOWN BY WIND AND WATER

Most of the Piedmont Region is a plateau made up of a hard rock called granite. Millions of years ago, the plateau was an area of tall mountains. Although these mountains were hard, they were eroded, or worn down, by one of nature's great forces—water. Many streams rushed down out of the high mountains to the west. As these streams flowed, they slowly eroded the mountains, creating the area that we call the Piedmont.

A few lonely **peaks** stand out above the Piedmont's hills. A peak is the pointed top of a mountain. **Pilot Mountain** to the north of Winston-Salem is one of the most famous of these peaks. Find Pilot Mountain on the map on this page. The Sioux (sü) name for the mountain is *Jo-Mee-O-Kee* (jō mē ō′ kē), a term that means "the Great Guide"

Among the riches of the Piedmont are its beautiful rolling hills and its special gemstones like Hiddenite. *(above)*

in English. Travelers in the area have long used the peak as a guide to their location because it can be seen from a distance.

THE HIGH PIEDMONT

As you read in Lesson 1, the western part of the Piedmont is fairly high in elevation—about 1,500 feet (457 m). There are three groups of low mountains in this area. Use the map on page 81 to find the **Sauratown Mountains**, the **Brushy Mountains**, and the **South Mountains**. Although the Brushy and South mountains are located in the Piedmont, mapmakers often put them in the Mountain Region because they are in counties that are thought of as mountain counties.

These mountains have many caves, springs, and old trails and the people who live in the area tell many stories about them. The Sauratown Mountains are named after the Saura Indians who once lived there. According to one of the Indian stories, a spring that could cure sick people once flowed in these mountains.

The Brushy Mountains are famous for their gemstones, including emeralds and the rare gemstone hiddenite. One of the trails in this area was used by people coming here from other states.

Many kinds of waterfalls are along the **Fall Line**. They may be wide or narrow, or they may fall like steps.

THE FALL LINE

If you were walking east from these three groups of mountains, you would see that the elevation of the Piedmont gets lower. At about 300 to 400 feet (91 to 122 m) above sea level, the Piedmont ends suddenly. On maps this edge of the Piedmont is not shown as the end of the Piedmont Region. Maps divide the regions by counties.

This eastern edge of the Piedmont is called the **Fall Line**. It is where the streams flowing east across the Piedmont fall onto the Coastal Plain. Find the Fall Line on the map on page 81. There, streams tumble for 70 feet (21 m) over waterfalls and **rapids** (rap′ idz). Rapids are places at which the water flows quickly and roughly. Waterfalls and rapids prevent boats from sailing upstream from the coast.

The force of the water rushing over the Fall Line was once used to turn waterwheels. These waterwheels provided energy for small mills near the Fall Line. A mill was used to grind or cut a natural resource such as grain or lumber.

A BUSY REGION

Another important resource of the Piedmont Region besides its water is its soil. If you live in this region, you know that the soil is reddish in color. This color comes from the red iron in the soil. The soil of the Piedmont is not as fertile as that of the Coastal Plain. However, the use of fertilizers has helped to make the Piedmont an important farming area. Fertilizer is something that is added to the soil to make it grow more crops. This region has many beef and dairy farms. It also has farms that grow corn, hay, and other feed for farm animals.

The Piedmont's gentle environment, many sources of water, fertile soil, and other natural resources have attracted many people and businesses to the region. In fact, the Piedmont has more cities and a larger **population** (pop yə lā′ shən) than any other part of our state. Population is the total number of people living in a place. As you can see on the chart, the cities that have the largest populations—Charlotte, Winston-Salem, Greensboro, Durham, and Raleigh (rô′ lē)—are in the Piedmont.

People who fly over the central Piedmont at night get a dazzling view. They can see bluish and orange streetlights that cast light in all directions. Streams of light from automobile headlights flow along

CHART SKILL: Discovery Place *(right)* is an attraction in Charlotte. How many cities have a larger **population** than Raleigh? *(below)*

THE TEN LARGEST CITIES IN NORTH CAROLINA

City	Population 1990 U.S. Census	Region
Charlotte	395,934	Piedmont
Raleigh	207,951	Piedmont
Greensboro	183,521	Piedmont
Winston-Salem	143,485	Piedmont
Durham	136,611	Piedmont
Fayetteville	75,695	Coastal Plain
High Point	69,496	Piedmont
Asheville	61,607	Mountain
Wilmington	55,530	Coastal Plain
Gastonia	54,732	Piedmont

the highways. It seems that every bit of the Piedmont has someone living or traveling on it!

RICH RESOURCES, MANY PEOPLE

As you have read, the Piedmont is a gently rolling region that is located in the central part of our state. Higher in the west than in the east, the Piedmont plateau drops suddenly at the Fall Line. It is there that many of the Piedmont's streams and rivers tumble down waterfalls and rapids onto the Coastal Plain.

Water power and fertile soil have made the Piedmont an important business and farming area. It has more people and cities than any other region in North Carolina.

Check Your Reading

1. How does the Piedmont's name describe the region?
2. What is special about the geography of the Piedmont Region?
3. Many cities in the Piedmont Region are growing rapidly. How might farmers who live on the edge of the cities feel about this?
4. **GEOGRAPHY SKILL:** Look at the map on page 81. Name one large city that is on the Piedmont's eastern edge.
5. **THINKING SKILL:** Compare the Piedmont to the Coastal Plain. List three ways in which the two regions are different.

Writing an Outline

Key Vocabulary
outline

Suppose that you have to write a report about one region of North Carolina. First you need to decide which region to study. For instance, you might choose to do your report on the Piedmont Region.

Then make a list of at least three things that you want to find out about your topic—the Piedmont Region. You might ask these questions: Which landforms are found in the region? Which resources are found there? How do people live and what kinds of work do they do in the Piedmont?

Next read about the Piedmont and take notes to answer your questions. You can see one way to take notes from the example below.

Finally, you need to write your **outline**. An outline is a plan that lets you organize what you want to say about a subject. It presents your thoughts and ideas in a way that is organized.

Plateau of granite (I)
Many businesses (III)
Rushing water (II)
Fall Line (I)
Fertile soil (II)
Many beef and dairy farms (III)
Long growing season (II)
Many cities and highest population in the state (III)
Gentle, rolling hills (I)

Choosing Your Main Ideas

An outline is made up of main ideas and supporting details. You can use the three questions that are given on page 86 as the main ideas in your outline. Label each main idea with a Roman numeral. Your outline should look like this:

I. Which landforms are found in the Piedmont Region?
II. Which resources are found there?
III. How do people live and work in the Piedmont?

Adding Supporting Details

Look at your notes. Your notes are the supporting details for your outline. You need at least two supporting details for each main idea. As you read through your notes, decide which question each note answers.

For example, suppose that you have written down several facts about the Piedmont. Next to each fact, you should write the Roman numeral of the question that it answers.

Putting the Outline Together

Now put each fact, or supporting detail, under the correct main idea in the outline. Label each supporting detail with a capital letter and a period. Write a title at the top. Your outline should look like the one that appears in the next column.

The Piedmont Region

I. Which landforms are found in the Piedmont Region?
 A. Gentle, rolling hills
 B. Plateau of granite
 C. Fall Line
II. Which resources are found there?
 A. Rushing water
 B. Fertile soil
 C. Long growing season
III. How do people live and work in the Piedmont Region?
 A. Many beef and dairy farms
 B. Many cities and highest population in state
 C. Many businesses

Reviewing the Skill

1. What is an outline?
2. Reread the part of Lesson 2 that tells about the wetlands in the Coastal Plain Region. Take notes to answer the question, "What types of plants grow in the wetlands?"
3. Write down two more questions about the Coastal Plain Region. Then find supporting details for each question.
4. Then write an outline from the information you have collected.
5. Why is it helpful to make an outline before writing a report?

LESSON

4 The Mountain Region

READ TO LEARN

Key Vocabulary

gorge
range

Key Places

Blue Ridge Mountains
Great Smoky Mountains
Blue Ridge Escarpment
Grandfather Mountain
Lost Cove
Black Mountains
Asheville
Mount Mitchell

Read Aloud

Never had I seen a town like this before. It was the only town in the entire Graham County, and it was surrounded with . . . steep mountains.

Peter Jenkins wrote the above words about the town of Robbinsville. He visited several towns in western North Carolina during a walk across the United States in 1974. As you will read, the Mountain Region of North Carolina has many high peaks and steep slopes. It also has valleys that are covered with wildflowers in spring and summer.

Read for Purpose

1. **WHAT YOU KNOW:** What kinds of activities might people enjoy in the mountains?
2. **WHAT YOU WILL LEARN:** What is special about the geography of the Mountain Region?

SPECTACULAR SCENERY

The Cherokee writer Traveller Bird lives in the Snowbird Mountains near Robbinsville in the western part of our state. Every day he looks at scenery that he thinks is among the most beautiful on earth.

To me, this region is the top of the whole world . . . . Great billowing clouds sail upon the mountains and in early morning a blue-gray mist hangs just above the treetops.

MAP SKILL: This rock wall *(above)* is southeast of Franklin. Which peaks on the map are closest to Franklin?

North Carolina's Mountain Region is famous for its many high peaks, waterfalls, and spectacular **gorges**. A gorge is a deep passage cut into the rock, usually by a river. These features, along with heavy rainfall, make the western mountains a region that is very different from the rest of our state.

GROUPS OF MOUNTAINS

The Mountain Region has several mountain **ranges**, or rows of mountains. The largest ranges are the **Blue Ridge Mountains** and the **Great Smoky Mountains**. All of the mountains in the region are part of the Appalachian Mountains. As you read in Chapter 1, the Appalachians stretch from southeastern Canada south to the state of Alabama.

The Blue Ridge Mountains are the range that is the farthest east in the Mountain Region. If you were driving west along North Carolina's Highway 421 from Wilkesboro, you would suddenly come to a high wall of stone stretching across the land. This wall is called the **Blue Ridge Escarpment** (e skärp′ mənt) and is the beginning of the Blue Ridge Mountains. An escarpment is a steep rock wall or mountain slope.

The Blue Ridge Escarpment rises about 2,000 feet (606 m) above the Piedmont. It separates the Piedmont from the Mountain Region. In the past the escarpment made it hard for people to travel into the Mountain Region. They found it almost impossible to climb the steep slope with ox-drawn wagons. Today highways and railroads cross the escarpment. They make it easy to travel to the mountain valleys.

THE BLUE RIDGE MOUNTAINS

The Blue Ridge Mountains were named for the blue haze, or smoke-like mist, that hugs the slopes. This haze is caused by the moisture that is given off by the trees in the forests that cover these mountains.

A favorite tourist attraction in the area is Grandfather Mountain. This mountain got its name because of the way it looks when viewed from the side. It looks like an elderly person, perhaps a bearded grandfather, lying back taking a nap.

The Blue Ridge Mountains have a number of unusual places. One of them is Lost Cove. There, on certain nights you might meet people looking at the "Brown Mountain Lights." These lights move through Lost Cove in a ghostly way. Some people think these lights look like the headlights of old railroad engines. Others say they look like the lanterns that the Indians used to carry at night. No one has been able to discover the source of these lights.

SMALL MOUNTAIN RANGES

The region has several small mountain ranges, such as the Black Mountains and the Pisgah Mountains. Find these mountains on the map on page 89. Both of these mountain ranges are well known. The Black Mountains are near Asheville, which is the largest city in the region. Find Asheville on the map on page 89. Many gardens and the Biltmore Estate, which is one of the largest private homes in the world, are near Asheville.

Mount Mitchell, the tallest mountain in the eastern United States, is 6,684 feet (2,037 m) above sea level. The mountain was named for Elisha Mitchell, who was a professor at the

Grandfather Mountain is made up of rock that is believed to be more than 1 billion years old.

University of North Carolina. He explored mountains and measured their heights. Mitchell died in 1857 as a result of a fall in the mountains that now bear his name. He is buried there. Mitchell County is also named for him.

LOW VALLEYS, HIGH PEAKS

The mountains in western North Carolina are the highest in the eastern United States. North Carolina has 174 mountain peaks that are over 5,000 feet (1,524 m) in elevation. Some of these mountains are listed on the table below.

Our mountains are unusual in that they are made up of many separate peaks. Most mountainous areas have long ranges of mountains that are like high walls. In North Carolina several mountains rise and drop sharply. They begin in valley floors at about 2,000 feet (610 m) in elevation. From there they rise steeply, sometimes to almost 7,000 feet (2,134 m).

GREAT SMOKY MOUNTAINS NATIONAL PARK

The southern end of the Appalachian Mountains has been set aside as the Great Smoky Mountains National Park. The mountains here are called "smoky" because of the mist that hangs over them. This mist is similar to the mist in the Blue Ridge Mountains.

This park is more popular than any other national park in the United States. People come to camp, hike, picnic, ski, or just to look at the scenery. Among the

CHART SKILL: Which of these peaks in our state are close to 7,000 feet in elevation?

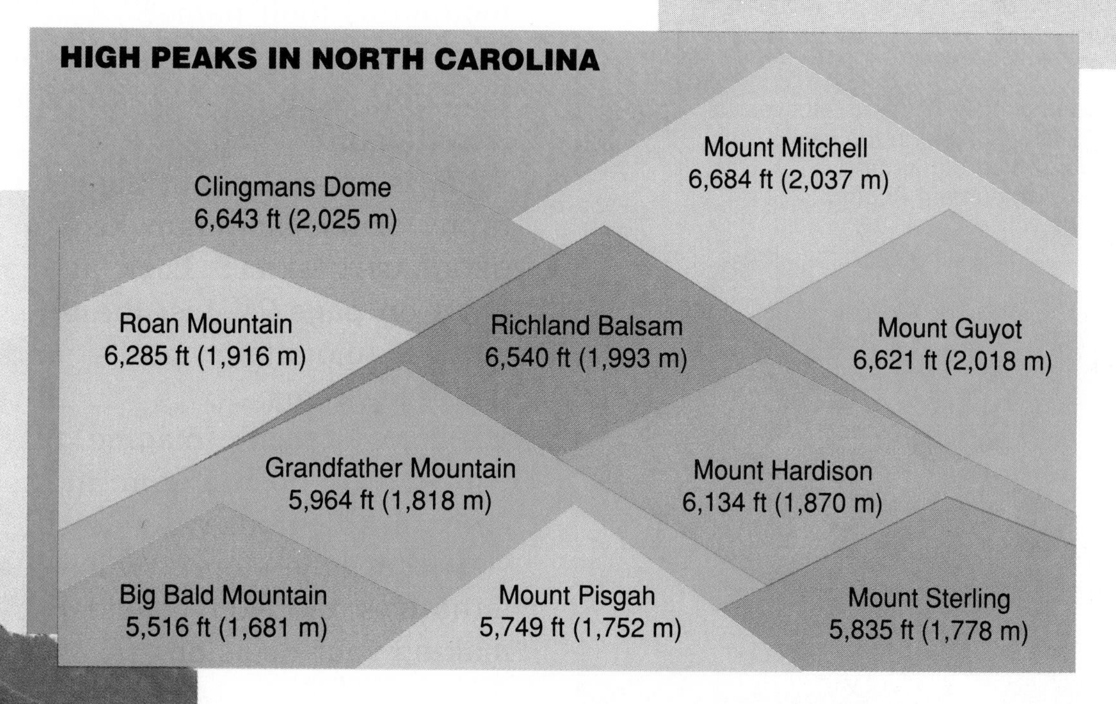

attractions are the gorges and huge old trees. Some of these trees are so big that it takes three or four people with their arms outstretched to reach around them! In spring, flowers cover the mountain slopes. When Peter Jenkins, about whom you read in the Read Aloud, saw the wildflowers, he said, "I couldn't keep myself from them."

LIVING IN THE MOUNTAINS

Although North Carolina has a mild climate and a long growing season, the mountain temperatures are colder in winter than anywhere else in our state. As a result, only small groups of people farm in the high valleys. There people sometimes follow traditions that have changed very little over time. For example, in Robbinsville Peter Jenkins saw people playing handmade musical instruments.

Every summer musicians from all over the United States take part in the music festivals held in our Mountain Region.

In the valleys that are easier to reach, many people have built vacation homes. They go to them every summer to escape the heat of the lowlands. In the valleys are also located most of the cities, such as Boone, Murphy, and Asheville.

A HIGHLAND AREA

As you have read, the Mountain Region of our state has many high mountains and beautiful scenery. The Blue Ridge, Great Smoky, and other mountains in the region are part of the Appalachian Mountains. Among the favorite forms of recreation in the mountains are camping, hiking, and skiing.

Check Your Reading

1. What causes the mist that gives the Blue Ridge and the Smoky mountains their name?
2. Which landform separates the Piedmont Region from the Mountain Region?
3. What is special about the geography of the Mountain Region?
4. **GEOGRAPHY SKILL:** Look at the chart on page 91. List the three highest mountain peaks and their elevations.
5. **THINKING SKILL:** Imagine that you want to open a store in the Mountain Region. Where would you locate the store? Which alternatives did you consider in making your decision?

REVIEWING VOCABULARY

Number a sheet of paper from 1 to 5. Beside each number write **T** if the statement is true. If the statement is false, rewrite it to make it true.

1. A *plateau* is a body of land that is almost completely surrounded by water.
2. The *Fall Line* marks the eastern edge of the Piedmont.
3. A *range* is a deep passage cut into the rock.
4. The total number of people living in a place is called its *population*.
5. A *swamp* is a grassy plain on which many crops can grow.

REVIEWING FACTS

Number a sheet of paper from 1 to 10. Beside each number write the name of the region of North Carolina that you are reminded of by each item below.

1. Outer Banks
2. Great Dismal Swamp
3. granite
4. Great Smoky Mountains
5. Fall Line
6. Tidewater
7. Blue Ridge Mountains
8. highest population
9. Mount Mitchell
10. rich soil

WRITING ABOUT MAIN IDEAS

1. **Writing a Puzzle:** Make up a crossword puzzle using important places and terms mentioned in this chapter. Based on definitions used in the text, write a clue for each word Across and each word Down.
2. **Writing About Perspectives:** Write a poem (or the words to a song) about a special feature of one of our state's regions. The poem should describe what the special feature looks like. It should capture some of your feelings about the place and explore the possibility that not everyone might feel the same way about it.

BUILDING SKILLS: READING ELEVATION MAPS

Use the maps on pages 67 and 70 and the profile on page 71 to answer these questions.

1. What is the difference between a landform map and an elevation map?
2. At about what elevation is the city of Wilmington?
3. Does Lake Norman have a higher or lower elevation than Asheville?
4. What does the profile show at the elevation of 300 ft. (91m)?
5. What could an elevation map of North Carolina show someone who is not familiar with our state?

UNIT 1 • REVIEW

REVIEWING VOCABULARY

climate
culture
economy
environment
Fall Line
landform
natural resource
pollution
region
tide

Number a sheet of paper from 1 to 10. Beside each number write the word or term from the list above that best completes the sentence.

1. A plateau is an example of a ____.
2. The ____ is the boundary between the Piedmont and the Coastal Plain.
3. The ____ of North Carolina, or its weather over a long period of time, is generally mild.
4. The ____ is the regular rise and fall of the ocean.
5. A ____ is a large area with common features.
6. The ____ of a people includes their language and art.
7. Wood, a valuable ____ of North Carolina, is used to build houses and furniture.
8. Dirty air is a type of ____.
9. North Carolina's ____ is the way our state uses its resources to meet our needs.
10. The ____ of the Outer Banks includes sandy beaches and occasional hurricanes.

WRITING ABOUT THE UNIT

1. **Writing an Advertisement for a Newspaper:** Choose one region of North Carolina. Write a newspaper ad that would make people want to visit that region. Think of a catchy saying to use and describe any pictures or illustrations that you might want to include.
2. **Writing About Perspectives:** Write a description of the region of North Carolina in which you live. Include descriptions of both geographical and cultural features. Explain why someone else might choose to live in a different part of the state.

ACTIVITIES

1. **Making a Scrapbook:** Collect newspaper and magazine articles about North Carolina's natural resources. Classify the articles into themes and organize the scrapbook according to those themes. Write a short introduction for each section.
2. **Working Together to Prepare a Weather Chart:** With a classmate, keep a record of the weather in your community. At the end of two weeks, prepare a chart of the weather patterns that you observed. How did your observations compare with the description of our climate presented in Chapter 2?

BUILDING SKILLS: DECISION MAKING

Suppose you want to open a clothing store of your own one day. Your goal is to sell quality clothing and to make money. In which community or part of the state should you locate the store?

1. What steps would you follow to reach your decision?
2. What would be the best decision about where to locate your store?
3. What are some other words that mean *decision making*?
4. When you are making a decision, why is it important to think of several different actions you could take to reach your goal?

LINKING PAST, PRESENT, AND FUTURE

The people of North Carolina have long understood the importance of conservation. As you have read, in 1895 a forestry school was set up in Asheville to protect our state's forests. What steps have the people of our state taken to conserve our natural resources? Do you think we will need to continue these measures in the future?

PLACES TO VISIT

1. Performance of *Unto These Hills* in Cherokee
2. Old Salem
3. Town Creek Indian Mound
4. Moores Creek National Battlefield
5. Bentonville Battleground
6. Somerset Homecoming
7. Walter Raleigh's ship, *Elizabeth II,* at Roanoke Island

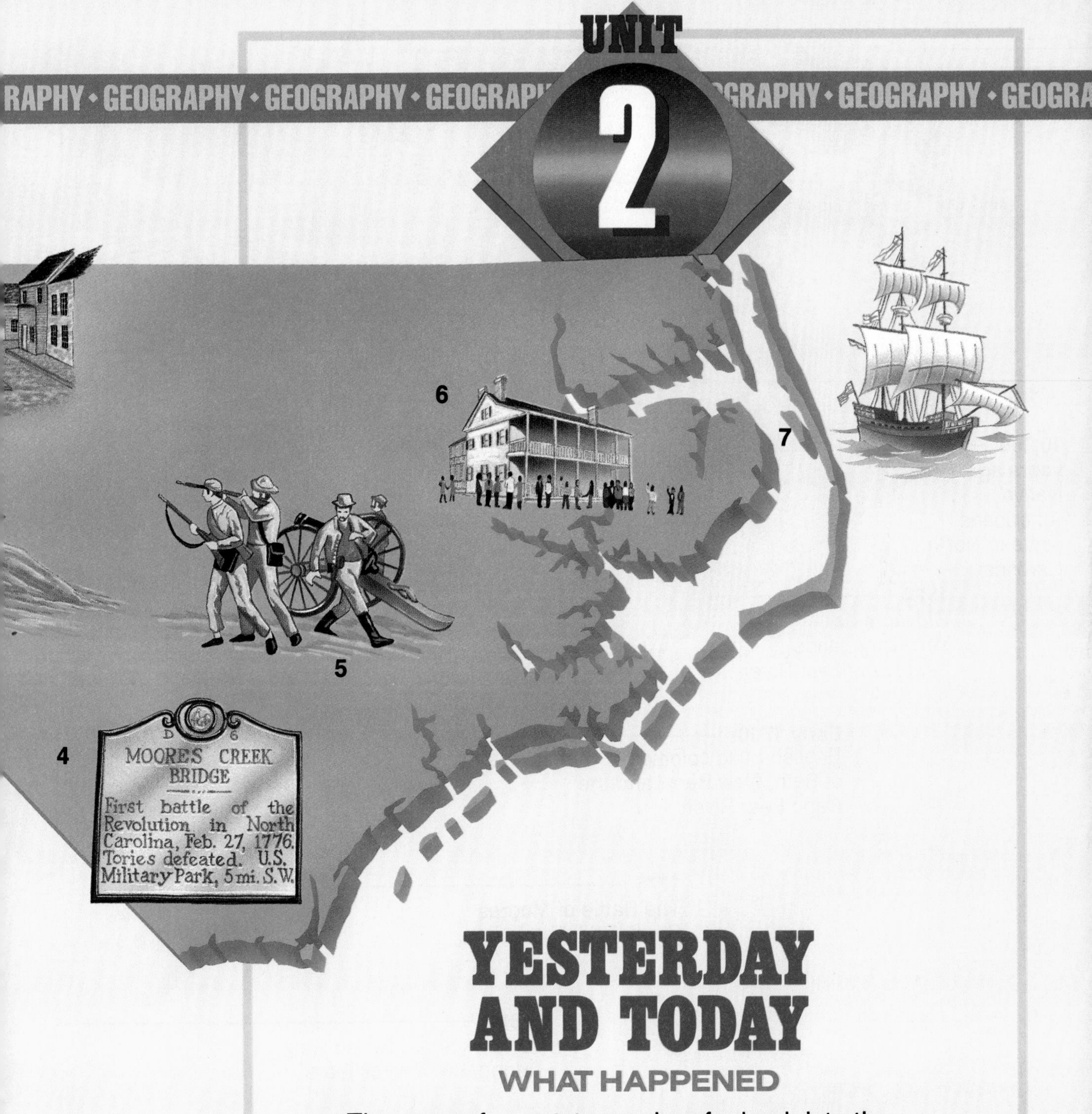

YESTERDAY AND TODAY

WHAT HAPPENED

The story of our state reaches far back into the past and stretches far into the future. The early part of North Carolina's history begins with the Indians, Europeans, and Africans. In this unit you will read about the many groups of people who built their ways of life in the land that became North Carolina.

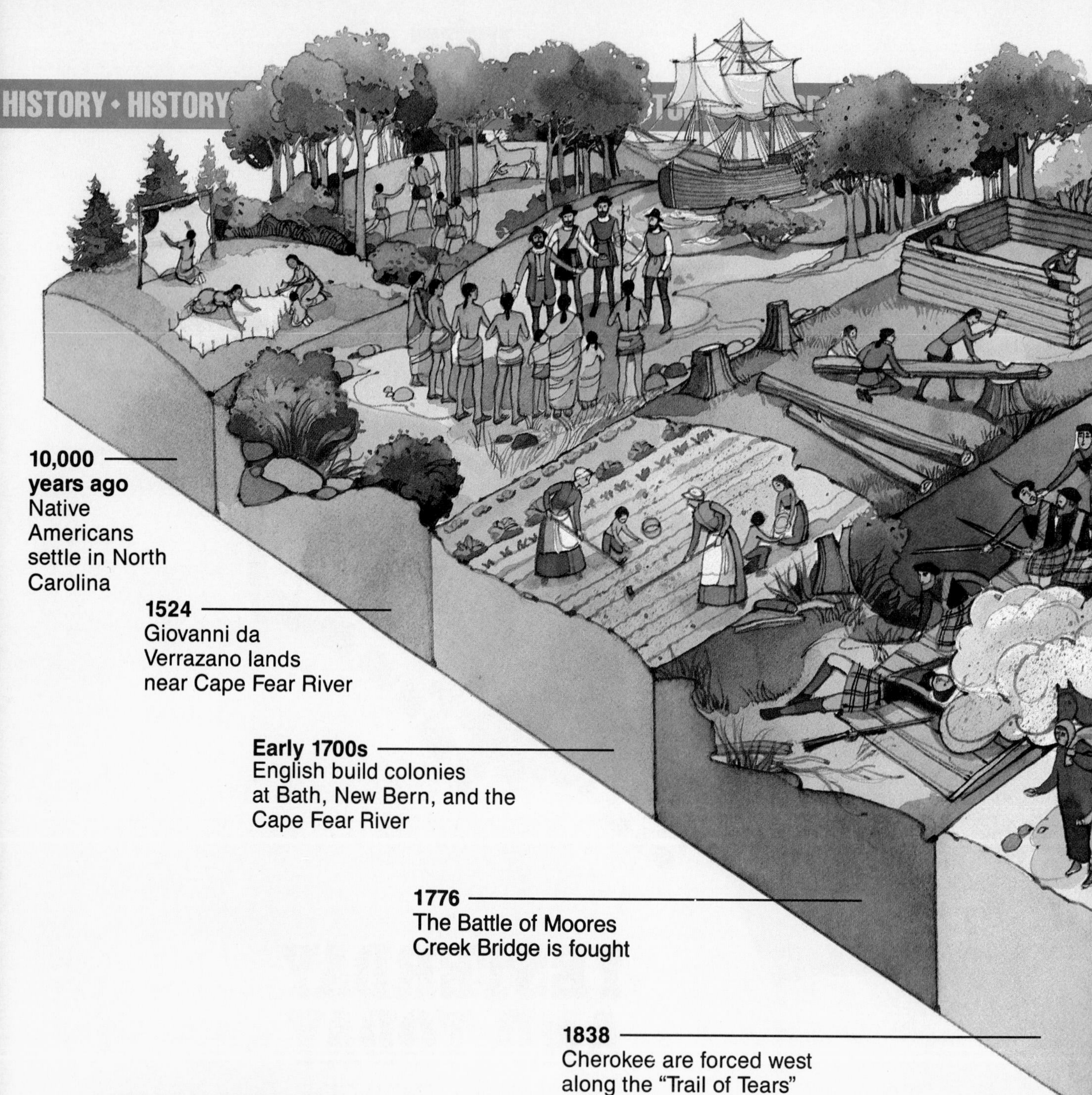

WHAT HAPPENED

Long before North Carolina became a state, Native Americans built communities across the land. In this unit you will read about what happened when Europeans came. You will also read about the challenges that the people in our state faced during the years that followed.

1863
Slavery is ended in the U.S. during the Civil War

CHAPTER 4

TWO CULTURES MEET

FOCUS

I started learning Cherokee dances when I was three years old. My grandfather taught them to me. He said that if the older people didn't teach our dances to us, they might be forgotten.

Andrea Walkingstick lives on the Qualla Boundary Reservation in Cherokee, North Carolina. She is proud of her Native American traditions. In this chapter you will read about the first settlers of North Carolina.

LESSON

1 North Carolina's First Settlers

READ TO LEARN

Key Vocabulary

artifact
archaeologist
migrate
temple
religion

Key Places

Occaneechi Village
Town Creek Indian Mound

Read Aloud

We expect to live on those lands we now possess during our time here.

Chief Hagler of the Catawba (kə tô′ bə) said these words in 1754. At that time the Catawba had been living in the Piedmont Region for hundreds of years. As you will read, the Indians were North Carolina's first settlers.

Read for Purpose

1. **WHAT YOU KNOW:** Why is it important to remember people and events from the past?
2. **WHAT YOU WILL LEARN:** Who were the first people to live in our state? How did they live?

CLUES FROM THE PAST

What was life like in the Piedmont long ago, even before Chief Hagler lived there? Many of the clues to the past have come from **artifacts** (är′ tə fakts) that people have left behind. Artifacts are objects, such as tools, that were made by people long ago.

Scientists called **archaeologists** (är kē ol′ ə jists) use these artifacts to help them piece together a picture of the past. Archaeologists usually dig up the remains of places in which people lived long ago, hoping to find artifacts.

In 1985 archaeologists discovered a 1,000-year-old village near Hillsborough on the Eno River. It gave new clues about the earliest settlers of the Piedmont. This village, called **Occaneechi** (ä kə nē′ chē) **Village**, proved to be one of the earliest settlements of the Piedmont.

These archaeologists are working near the Eno River. The artifacts they have dug up include many spear points.

Stone spear tips and pieces of pottery were found at Occaneechi Village. These artifacts proved to archaeologists that the villagers had both hunted and farmed. Today these early North Carolinians are called Indians or Native Americans. The name *Indians* was first used by the Italian explorer Christopher Columbus when he arrived in the Americas in 1492. Columbus thought he was in India and called the people he saw "Indians." The word *native* means "one of the first people to live in a land."

TRAVELERS ACROSS AMERICA

Archaeologists believe that the first Native Americans began to arrive in North America from Asia thousands of years ago. Many scientists also believe that the early Americans traveled from place to place in search of food. Around 10,000 years ago some of them arrived in North Carolina's Piedmont.

Around 3,000 years ago the early Americans learned to grow their own food. They first grew gourds, beans, squashes, and maize, which is a kind of corn. Slowly the Native Americans cleared more and more land for farming. They also began to settle in one place.

THREE LANGUAGE FAMILIES

By the 1500s, 30 different groups of Native Americans were living in the land that is now North Carolina. All of these groups were alike in one way. They used wood from their forests to make their homes, tools, and weapons.

North Carolina's Native Americans spoke languages that belong to three language families. They were Algonquian (al gong′ kē ən), Iroquoian (ir ə kwoi′ ən), and Siouan (sü′ ən). The chart on page 103 shows some words in one of these languages, Cherokee.

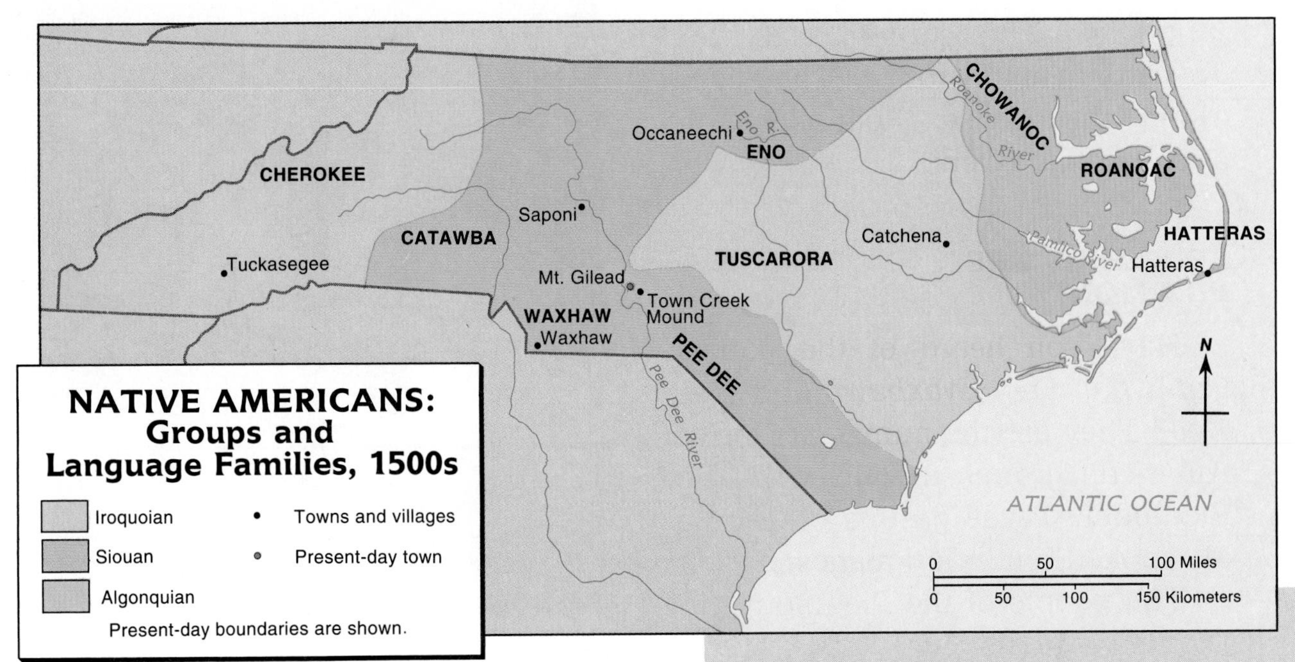

MAP/CHART SKILL: To which language group did Cherokee belong? What is the Cherokee word for *four?*

PEOPLE OF THE COAST

Most of the Native Americans of the Coastal Plain spoke Algonquian languages. If you had visited the Algonquian-speaking people of the coast long ago, you would have heard some words that you know. You might have heard words such as *moccasin* and *woodchuck.* Today, places on the coast such as Hatteras, Pamlico, and Roanoke have Algonquian names. Find these names on the map above.

Most of the Algonquian villages of the Coastal Plain were built along the banks of streams and rivers or where two rivers met. In swampy places, villages often were built high enough to keep them from being flooded.

Algonquian villages each had about 30 houses grouped around a square. To protect themselves from enemies, the Indians built a palisade, which is a fence of tall poles, around each village. Farmers planted beans, squashes, and maize.

Only one group of people of the Coastal Plain spoke an Iroquoian

ONE TO FIVE IN CHEROKEE

1	ᏌᏊ	(sokwoohee)
2	ᏔᎵ	(tha´lee)
3	ᏦᎢ	(tso´ee)
4	ᏅᎩ	(noohkee)
5	ᎯᏍᎩ	(heehskee)

(the ´ sound is like the break in "uh oh")

language. This group was the Tuscarora (tus kə rôr′ ə). They lived along the Neuse, Roanoke, Tar, and Pamlico rivers.

PEOPLE OF THE PIEDMONT

Have you heard of the names *Catawba*, *Eno*, *Waxhaw*, and *Pee Dee*? They are the names of Native American groups that lived in the Piedmont. These groups of people all spoke Siouan languages.

The people of the Piedmont did not live in the same place all year. During the fall and winter they often stayed in hunting camps that they had set up near the forests. The men hunted. The women and children stayed in camp to prepare the meat and hides that the hunters brought back. In spring and summer these people moved nearer to the rivers. The soil there was fertile.

Around the year 1200 a group of Native Americans from the Mississippi River Valley **migrated** to the southern part of the Piedmont. To *migrate* means to "move from one place to another." These Indians are called the Pee Dee because they migrated to the Pee Dee River Valley. They spoke a language like the ones spoken by people on the coast of the Gulf of Mexico.

The Pee Dee farmed along the Pee Dee River Valley for about 300 years. Then the Siouans defeated them, and the Pee Dee moved south.

While in the Piedmont, the Pee Dee built the **Town Creek Indian Mound**, which is near Mount Gilead (gil′ ē əd). A mound is a pile of earth. Indian mounds were large, and many people were needed to pile up the dirt that formed them.

The Pee Dee built their mound as a place to worship their gods and to bury their leaders. Men also came to the mound to discuss problems and to make decisions. A **temple**, or place of worship, was built on the flattened top of the mound. A fire was kept burning in the temple.

GREEN CORN CEREMONY

Every year this temple fire was lit during the Green Corn Ceremony. The ceremony was an important part of the Pee Dee **religion**. Religion is the way in which people worship the God or gods they believe in.

After the corn harvest, the Pee Dee gathered at the Town Creek Mound to celebrate the Green Corn Ceremony.

The Pee Dee believed that the world was filled with spirits that had great power. Ceremonies such as the Green Corn Ceremony helped the Pee Dee to strengthen their ties to these spirits and to each other. The ceremony was held in the late summer after the first corn crop of the year was harvested.

After the priests relit the temple fire, the Indians ate the young corn. They then went home, taking embers, or hot coals, from the temple fire. They used the embers to relight their cooking fires at home.

PEOPLE OF THE MOUNTAINS

The Cherokee, who lived in the mountains, also held a Green Corn Ceremony. They are one of North Carolina's few remaining Indian groups. You will read about the Cherokee in the next lesson.

SETTLING OUR REGIONS

As you have read, Native Americans have lived for thousands of years in the land that is now North Carolina. As they moved into different regions, our state's first settlers built ways of life based on what they knew about their environment.

Check Your Reading

1. Who were the first people to live in our state? How did they live?
2. Name the language families belonging to our state's Indians.
3. **GEOGRAPHY SKILL:** Look at the map on page 103. Which Piedmont rivers are named for an Indian group?
4. **THINKING SKILL:** What three questions would you ask to learn more about the Indians of the Coastal Plain?

LESSON

2 People of the Mountains

READ TO LEARN

Key Vocabulary

council

Read Aloud

When the earth was first made, it was flat, soft, and wet. When at last it dried, the Eagle was sent to earth ahead of all the other animals. He flew all over. When the Eagle reached Cherokee country, he was very tired. His wings began to flap and strike the ground. Wherever they struck, a valley formed. Where they turned up, a mountain appeared.

The Cherokee people tell this story to explain how the tall mountains in their land were formed. In this lesson you will read about the way of life of the Cherokee who live in the Mountain Region.

Read for Purpose

1. **WHAT YOU KNOW:** Who were the first people to settle in North Carolina?
2. **WHAT YOU WILL LEARN:** What was life like for the Cherokee people?

THE CHEROKEE

More than 1,000 years ago the Cherokee settled in the mountains of the land that became North Carolina. At that time they called themselves the *Ani yun wiya* (an ē yun′ wē yə), the "first people." The Ani yun wiya loved their mountain homeland, which they believed was in the center of the world. Later, other Indian groups gave these people the name *Cherokee*, which means "mountain or cave people."

The Cherokee had to overcome many difficulties in order to live in the mountains. The steep sides and deep gorges of the mountains made travel over this land hard. Fast-moving rivers with rapids and waterfalls sometimes made it dangerous to go by canoe. Also, the short growing season in the mountains limited the kinds of crops the Cherokee could grow.

On the other hand, the mountain environment offered certain advantages. The natural resources in the mountains were used for many of the Cherokee's needs. The thick forests had plenty of wood for building homes. The clear mountain streams supplied water for drinking and cooking. The many plants that grew in the woods, along with animals such as bears and deer, were used for food. The Cherokee loved the peaceful mist-covered mountains, which they called "the land of a thousand smokes."

How did the Cherokee of long ago meet their needs? If you could visit the Cherokee of the early 1600s, what would you find? Imagine that you could observe a day in the life of a Cherokee family.

Shooting a bow and arrow was important to Cherokee survival. Cherokee boys began learning this skill at a young age.

STANDING BEAR

Standing Bear is a nine-year-old Cherokee boy. He sits on the grassy riverbank practicing animal calls. He makes these whistling sounds by holding a folded leaf between his lips and blowing. Some day he might whistle to call a fox or a wildcat. Standing Bear knows that such skills will help him to become a good hunter when he is older.

Going Bird, Standing Bear's 16-year-old brother, went on his first hunting trip last winter. He told Standing Bear how the hunters had walked in the woods for many days looking mostly for deer and bears. Going Bird had killed a deer. Then he told its spirit that he was sorry, but his family needed food. You will read more about the customs of the Cherokee in the Traditions lesson on pages 112–115.

QUAIL DANCE
Lightly
Walker Calhoun
Qualla Boundary, NC
Wo yay he yay, Wo he yay,
yay, Wo yay he yay.
1-4
Wo he yay he yay, Wo he yay, Wo he
yay. Wo he yay he yay, Wo he yay,
to 𝄋 on 5
Wo he yay, Wo he yay he yay
Wo he yay, Wo he yay, Wo he yay
he yay, Wo he yay he yay.
5
Wo he yay he yay Oo.

Standing Bear wants to be ready when he goes on his first hunting trip. He sings the hunting song that appears on the opposite page as he picks up his bow and arrow to practice his aim. Soon he hears someone calling his name. It is Going Bird who is calling him. He and his friends want Standing Bear to take part in a ballgame called *anetsa* (ə ne′ tsə). Standing Bear likes playing the ballgame, but he wants to practice using his bow and arrow a little longer.

He watches the other boys pushing each other and running across the field. They hold hickory sticks with deerskin cups at the end. The idea of the game is to bat or throw a deerskin ball from the cup through the goalpost standing at the end of the field. Standing Bear may play with them later. He knows that games help him keep strong.

LITTLE STAR

Standing Bear's sister, Little Star, is returning home from the fields with her mother. They have been planting corn and beans. Now she follows her mother into the house. There she will help with the work. Little Star does not have much time to play today. When she finishes her chores, she will take care of her baby sister.

Little Star is proud that she can do these jobs. She is eight years old now, and the women often let her help. Not long ago her grandmother began teaching her how to weave

Cherokee women had many skills. They made food, clothing, and baskets, and many other things from the natural resources of the mountains.

baskets from the grasses and reeds that grow along the riverbank. Little Star is looking forward to this evening. Then her grandmother will help her finish the basket.

THE COUNCIL

Standing Bear is pulling an arrow from a tree when he notices a group of people gathering nearby. It looks as if there will be a **council** (koun′ səl) meeting. A council is a group of people called together to give advice. The village council will talk about important issues.

Standing Bear's grandmother is arriving for the council meeting. She is one of the most valued members of the council. She and the other members of the council will sit in the council house for many hours. Each member will have a chance to speak. Standing Bear wonders how they can sit for hours.

The council meets in the largest building in the village. Its walls are made of branches and twigs woven together. The walls are covered with clay that is mixed with grass to make them strong. The council house has no windows and only one small door. In the center of the council house, a fire burns in the fire pit.

THE CHEROKEE VILLAGE

In front of the council house is the square. It is a large field used for celebrations and dancing. All around the square are benches on which villagers sit to watch the events that take place there.

Standing Bear and Little Star lived in a village like this one. What kinds of buildings did the village have in it?

Beyond the council house and the square are the homes of the Cherokee. During the summer the Cherokee live in large, open, wooden houses. When winter comes, they move into small, round houses with a fire pit in the middle. The walls of these houses have no windows and they are made of clay, grass, twigs, and branches.

YESTERDAY AND TODAY

The Cherokee have lived in the mountains of North Carolina for over 1,000 years. Their use of natural resources made it possible for them to live in the Mountain Region. As you will read later on, the Cherokee have kept their customs and their traditions through both good times and bad.

Check Your Reading

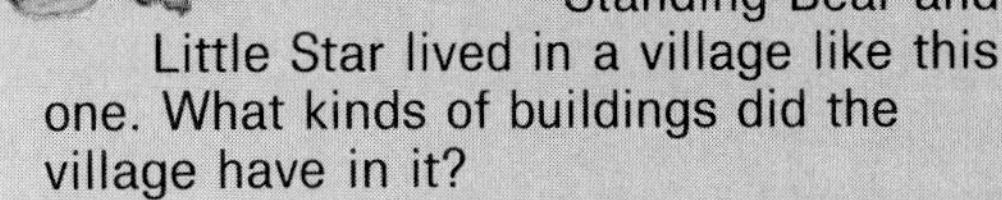

1. What is the meaning of the name *Cherokee*?
2. Name two roles that Standing Bear's grandmother plays in village life.
3. Describe three ways in which Cherokee children help in daily village life.
4. **GEOGRAPHY SKILL:** Name two of the advantages of living in the Mountain Region. Name two of the disadvantages.
5. **THINKING SKILL:** What choices could Standing Bear have considered when he decided not to play anetsa? Explain.

NORTH CAROLINA TRADITIONS

THE STORY OF LITTLE DEER

Retold by Clifford E. Trafzer

In the last lesson you read about the Cherokee way of life many years ago. A special kind of story called a myth (mith) *has long been a part of that way of life. These stories are passed down over the years and they often explain important beliefs. The tradition of telling myths is still important because these stories explain the reasons for many Cherokee customs. In this lesson a woman carries on the tradition by telling her grandson a myth to teach him why the Cherokee have great respect for animals. As you read think about why people should show respect for animal life.*

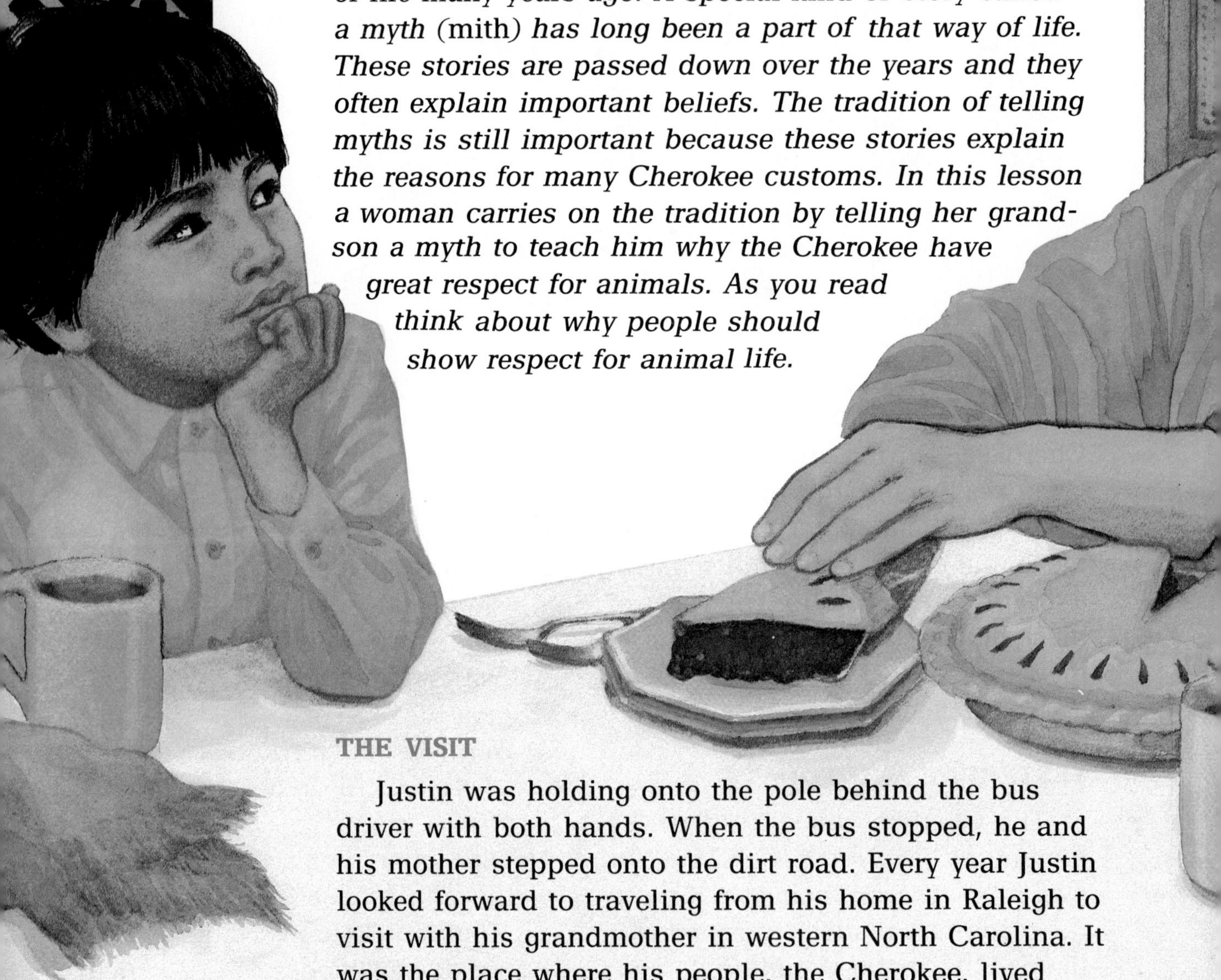

THE VISIT

Justin was holding onto the pole behind the bus driver with both hands. When the bus stopped, he and his mother stepped onto the dirt road. Every year Justin looked forward to traveling from his home in Raleigh to visit with his grandmother in western North Carolina. It was the place where his people, the Cherokee, lived and where he spent his summers.

As Justin and his mother approached his grandmother's house, the scent of freshly baked corn bread and blueberry pie greeted them. Justin happily

stepped onto the wooden porch and ran to his grandmother.

"Justin!" Grandmother said with a start. She bent over and hugged him. "Just look how you've grown!"

Just before supper, Justin's mother kissed him goodbye and left to catch the bus back to Raleigh. The food Grandmother served was Justin's favorite—venison (deer meat) steak, green beans, boiled potatoes, and corn bread. As they ate blueberry pie and drank hot chocolate, he noticed that his grandmother seemed to be deep in thought.

"Is something wrong?" Justin asked, concerned.

Grandmother smiled and said, "You are learning many things at school, but I want you to know more about our people. The Cherokee stories that I tell you about our past are special to us. I want you to know these stories so that you can tell them to your children, just as my parents told them to me."

Justin had learned from his parents that telling stories was an important Cherokee tradition and that he should always listen carefully.

"Which story will you tell me now?" Justin asked his grandmother eagerly.

THE HUNTERS AND THE ANIMAL PEOPLE

"This meal we just had reminds me of one story," Grandmother said. "Justin, you know that venison is deer meat and that we have eaten this meat for years. But a long time ago our hunters became greedy. They killed far more deer and other animals than necessary.

"So the Bear People got together in council," she continued. "They decided to go to war with the Cherokee. The Bear People made bows and arrows, but when they tried to shoot the arrows, their big claws got in the way. They realized that they could not fight as well as the Cherokee hunters could."

Grandmother paused to sip her hot chocolate. Justin sat patiently but, eager to hear more, he pleaded, "Tell me what happened to the Bear People."

Grandmother continued, "The Quail, Rabbit, Squirrel, and many other Animal People met in council. They talked about ways other than fighting to stop the hunters from being so greedy. All of the Animal People—except one—thought that they could do nothing to change the hunters' ways. That animal was Little Deer, chief of the Deer People. Little Deer had great power. He believed that he could convince our people to change their ways."

LITTLE DEER SPEAKS TO THE CHEROKEE

"What did Little Deer do?" asked Justin.

"One night Little Deer visited a Cherokee village," Grandmother answered. "As the people slept, he whispered to them that they had forgotten the old ways. He said, 'Remember that we are all children of the Great

One who made the world, and the Animal People deserve your respect. Give thanks for your meat, and remember that you are relatives of the Animal People. Take no more meat than you need to feed your family and friends.'

"You see, Justin," Grandmother explained, "Little Deer needed to teach us not to be greedy, since we all share one world. Most of the Cherokee awoke from their dreams with a better understanding of why they should hunt for only the meat they needed. However, there were some hunters who were still greedy.

"Little Deer knew how to deal with these hunters. He used his power to weaken the arms and legs of the greedy hunters. Soon they understood that they should hunt only for the meat that they needed. We Cherokee continue to follow Little Deer's teaching today."

Justin sat quietly for a few minutes, thinking about the story. Then he looked at his grandmother and asked, "Will you tell me another story?"

Grandmother laughed. "Tomorrow I'll tell you about how a grandmother like me brought corn to our people. But now it's getting late. You should go to sleep."

The sun had dropped slowly behind the mountains to the west. Justin looked forward to sleeping in a soft bed covered with one of his grandmother's quilts. As he drifted off to sleep, his thoughts were about Little Deer, who had taught the Cherokee an important lesson long ago.

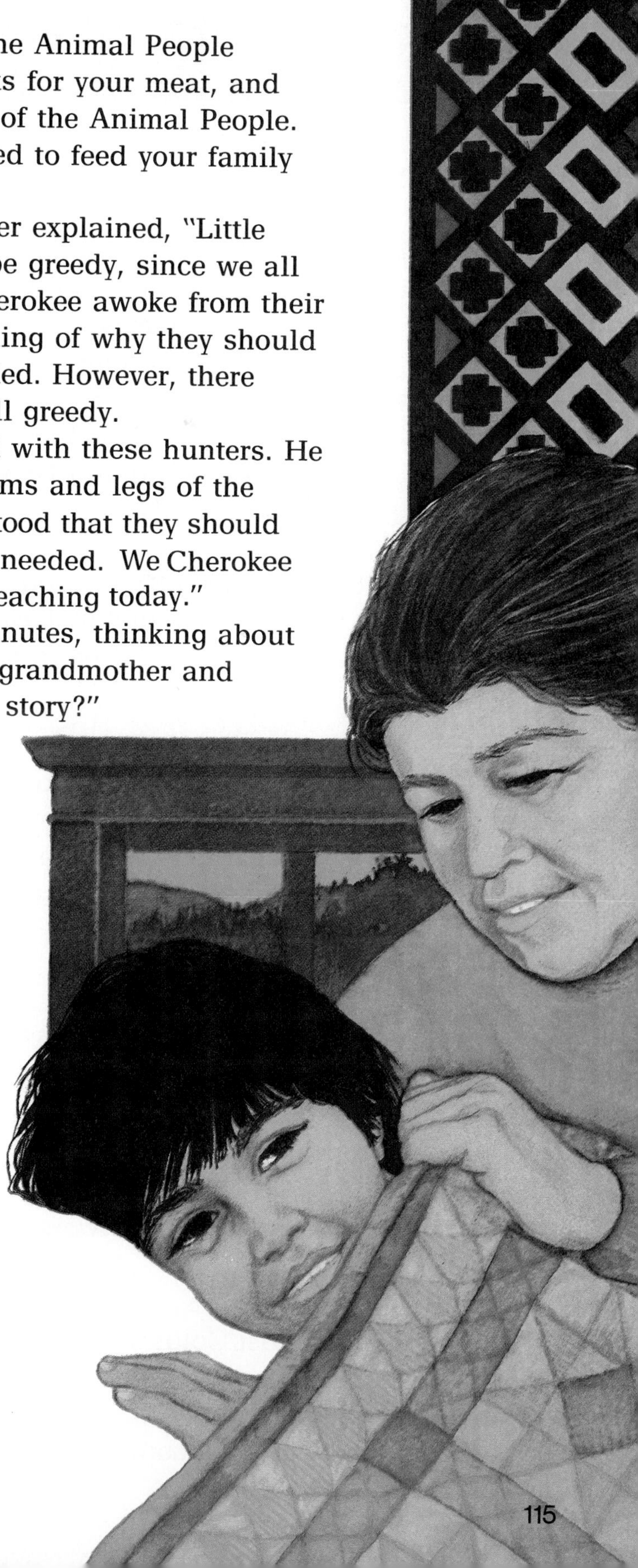

According to the myth, how should people show respect for animal life, and why?

LESSON

3 European Explorers and Settlers

READ TO LEARN

Key Vocabulary

colony

Key People

Giovanni da Verrazano
Lucas Vásquez de Ayllón
Hernando De Soto
Walter Raleigh
John White
Virginia Dare

Key Places

Roanoke Island
Chesapeake Bay

Read Aloud

One of my favorite things about being in the play is getting to wear neat costumes. Last year I played an English settler. . . . This year I'll be in seven scenes. . . . It's hard at first. Then it's fun.

In the summer of 1991, Paul Zuttel from Kitty Hawk acted in a famous North Carolina play called *The Lost Colony.* Every year visitors come to Roanoke Island to see this play, which tells why the island's first English settlement became known as the Lost Colony.

Read for Purpose

1. **WHAT YOU KNOW:** Why do you like to visit places that you have never seen before?
2. **WHAT YOU WILL LEARN:** Why did European explorers come to North Carolina? What happened to the first European settlers in North Carolina?

A WATER ROUTE TO ASIA

The story of the Lost Colony has interested people for a long time. A **colony** is a settlement in one country that is ruled by another country. The colonists whose story is told in the play were not the first Europeans to reach North Carolina.

When the explorer Christopher Columbus sailed west from Spain

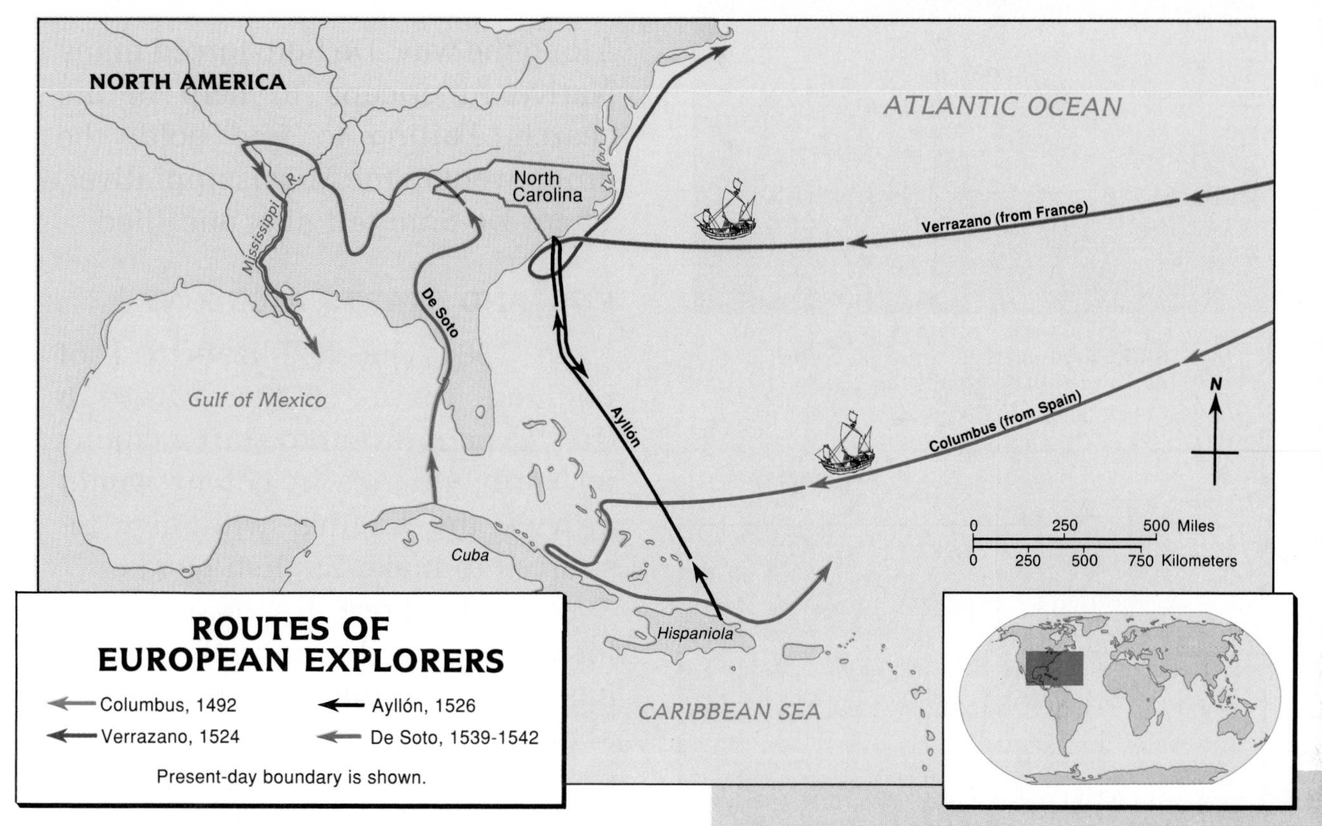

MAP SKILL: Which explorers sailed along the coastline of North Carolina?

in 1492, he was trying to reach Asia. Europeans wanted to trade with the Asians because Asia was a land of great wealth. After Columbus reached the Americas, later explorers hoped to find a waterway through North America to Asia. One of the voyages by these explorers led the Europeans to our state.

EUROPEAN EXPLORERS

In 1524, an Italian explorer named **Giovanni da Verrazano** (jō vän′ nē dā ver ə zän′ ō), sailed to North America for the king of France. He landed on the Atlantic coast near the Cape Fear River. Verrazano and his crew were welcomed by the Native Americans who lived in the area.

Verrazano kept searching for a sea route to Asia by sailing north. When he reached the Outer Banks, Verrazano thought that the body of water he saw to the west was the Pacific Ocean. As the map of the European explorers above shows, what Verrazano had seen was Pamlico Sound.

In 1526 **Lucas Vásquez de Ayllón** (lü′ kas väs′ kās də īl yôn′), a Spanish explorer, reached North Carolina. He was the first European to try to start a colony here. The ship's crew included the first Africans to come to our shore. The colony lasted less than a year. Many of

MAP SKILL: A model of the *Elizabeth II* on which the first English colonists sailed is docked off Roanoke. In what direction is Croatoan Island?

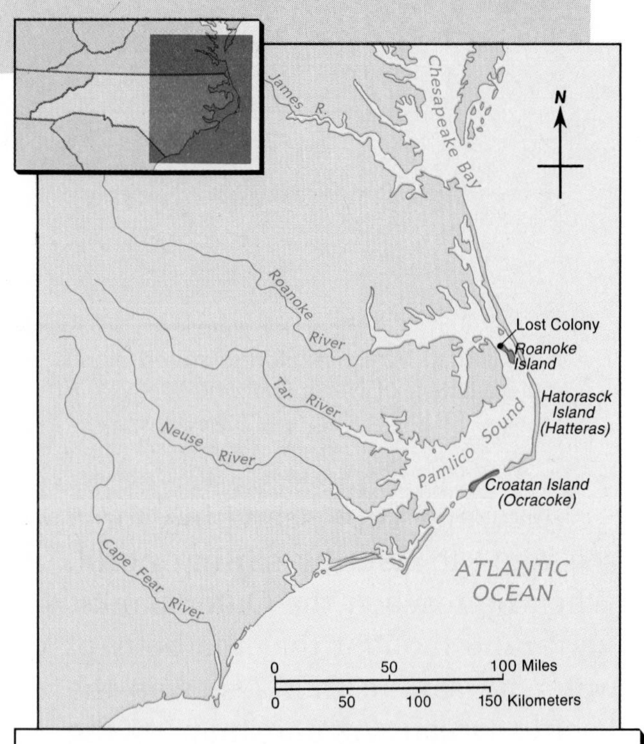

ROANOKE AND CROATAN ISLANDS, 1585

Present-day shoreline is shown.
Modern island names are in parentheses.

its people died from disease and starvation.

In 1539 a group led by the Spanish explorer **Hernando De Soto** (er nän′ dō də sō′ tō) marched from Florida to southwestern North Carolina. It was looking for gold. Along the way, De Soto forced many Native Americans to help in his search. Failing to find gold, the group went to the Mississippi River. There De Soto fell sick and died.

ENGLAND STARTS A COLONY

In 1584 Queen Elizabeth I of England gave **Walter Raleigh** (rô′ lē) permission to start a colony in North America. A colony would provide the English with new resources to make English goods.

Raleigh chose **Roanoke Island** for his colony because the island has a mild climate. In June 1585, about 100 Englishmen reached Roanoke and began to build there.

The colonists had, however, arrived too late in the year to plant crops. At first the Roanoac Indians gave the colonists food. But then the leader of the colonists killed Wingina, the Roanoac's leader. The Indians stopped giving the colonists food. Faced with hunger, the colonists decided to return home.

THE LOST COLONY

Raleigh then planned another colony along **Chesapeake Bay**. Find the bay on the map on this page. This location had a larger and deeper harbor than Roanoke did.

In the spring of 1587, over 100 people set out for the Chesapeake Bay. However, when their ships reached Roanoke, the captain refused to go any farther.

The colonists, led by **John White**, settled on Roanoke Island. But lack of food was a problem. The colonists then sent White to England for supplies. At first, White had refused to leave because he feared for the safety of his family. His new granddaughter, **Virginia Dare**, was the first child born in North America to English parents.

The colonists promised White that they would carve a message on a tree if they had to leave the island. The message would include the name of the place to which they moved and a cross above the name if they were in danger.

White was not able to return to Roanoke for three years. When he did, he found the settlement empty. But he discovered the letters CRO carved on a tree and the word CROATOAN on a doorpost. There was no cross above the writing.

Ever since 1590 people have wondered about the fate of the colonists. Some historians think that they moved north to the Chesapeake Bay area. Others think they went south to Croatoan Island and lived among the Croatoan people.

EXPLORERS AND SETTLERS

The first tries by Europeans to find a water route to Asia and to start colonies in North Carolina failed. At first, the Native Americans welcomed the Europeans. But quarrels soon broke out.

These scenes from *The Lost Colony* include *(above)* John White meeting the Roanoac. *(below)* England's queen receives an Indian pipe.

Check Your Reading

1. What led Europeans to explore the area that is now our state?
2. What happened to the first European colonies in our state?
3. **GEOGRAPHY SKILL:** What geographical features made the Outer Banks a worse location for a colony than Chesapeake Bay was?
4. **THINKING SKILL:** Give three causes for the failure of the early English colonies.

Reading Time Lines

Key Vocabulary

history time line

As you were reading about the early explorers and settlers of our state, you came across a number of phrases that told you when important events took place. These phrases may have had actual dates, such as "in 1524." Or they may have given you other time clues, such as "one year later." To understand the **history**, or story of the past, of our state, you need to know when certain events took place.

A good way to keep track of the order in which events happened is by using a **time line**. A time line is a diagram that shows when events took place. It also shows the amount of time that passed between events.

Reading a Time Line

The time line below shows some of the important events in the early history of our state. The description of each event is written beneath the date on which it happened. The earliest event is located at the left end.

A time line is usually divided into equal parts. Each part of the time line stands for a period of time. This time period can be short, such as one month. It can also be long, such as 100 years. Sometimes a time line covers a long period of time by leaving out some years. Notice the jagged line on the time line below. It shows that some years have been left out. How many years does this time line cover from beginning to end?

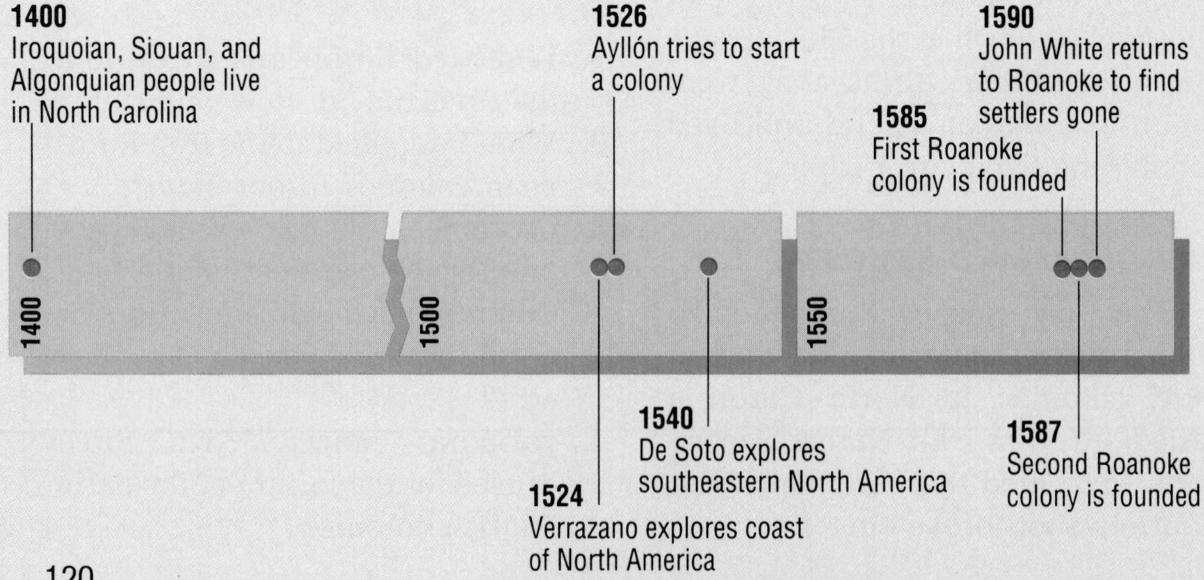

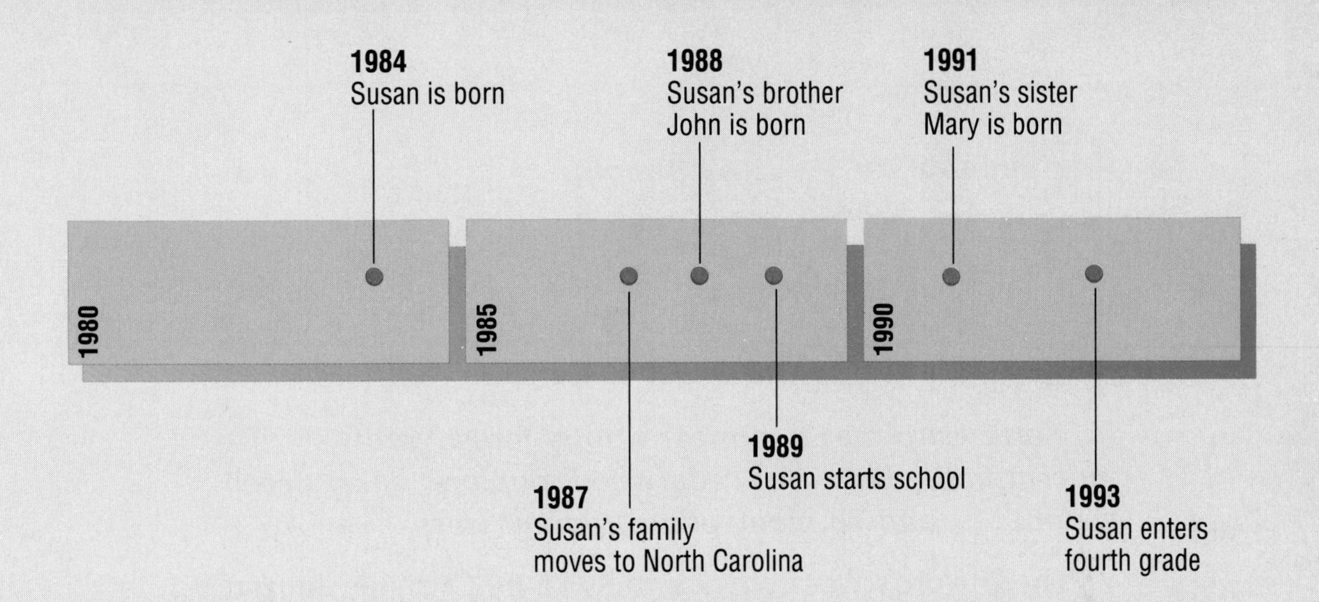

To read a time line, begin by looking for the earliest and latest events. Which is the first event and which is the last event shown on the time line on page 120? Which event is shown between the years 1524 and 1540?

Look again at the time line on page 120 to see the order in which the events took place. Did Ayllón try to start a colony before or after the first Roanoke colony was founded?

Making a Time Line

Time lines can be used for different purposes. The time line above shows the life of Susan, a young girl growing up in North Carolina today. How many years of Susan's life are shown on the time line?

Make a time line of your life using the time line above as a guide. Divide the line into two-year periods. Make the year you were born the first date. Then include the year that you started kindergarten or first grade and the year that you entered the fourth grade. Also include at least three other important events in your life.

Reviewing the Skill

Use the information in this lesson to answer the following questions.

1. What is a time line?
2. How many years before De Soto arrived in North America did Verrazano explore the coast of North America?
3. During which year was the first colony at Roanoke founded?
4. In which year did John White return to the second colony?
5. Why is it important to know how to use a time line?

LESSON

4 English Colonists Arrive in North Carolina

READ TO LEARN

Key Vocabulary

surplus
export
import

Key People

Nathaniel Batts

Key Places

Jamestown
Bath
New Bern

Read Aloud

It [North Carolina] is almost wholly forest, with indescribably beautiful cedarwood, poplars, oaks, beech, walnut . . . and so many other fragrant trees.

These words were written in 1711 by Christen Janzen to describe the land in North Carolina. Janzen was one of the colonists who helped to build the town of New Bern. In this lesson you will read more about New Bern and the other early towns in North Carolina that were settled by Europeans.

Read for Purpose

1. **WHAT YOU KNOW:** Who were the first Europeans to explore the Atlantic coast of North America?
2. **WHAT YOU WILL LEARN:** Why did the first European colonists come to North Carolina? From where did they come?

SETTLERS FROM VIRGINIA

As you have read in Lesson 3, England's first try in starting a colony in North Carolina had failed. In 1607 the English were finally able to build a permanent colony called **Jamestown**. Jamestown was located on Chesapeake Bay in what is now the state of Virginia. Find Jamestown colony on the map on the opposite page.

The Native Americans taught the Jamestown colonists to make use of their environment. One American plant, tobacco, became a source of great wealth for the colonists. They began to grow so much tobacco that they had more than they needed. They decided to sell their **surplus** tobacco to England. Surplus is an amount that is greater than what is used or needed.

Tobacco became an important **export** for Jamestown. An export is something that is sold or traded to another country. It was easy for the colonists to export surplus tobacco from Jamestown. Its harbor on the James River was deep enough to be used by large ships.

The English colonists took more and more Indian land to use for growing tobacco. In time most of the richest farmland in Virginia was used for tobacco. Some colonists decided to move south to what today is North Carolina in order to get land. At that time North Carolina and parts of South Carolina, Georgia, and Florida made up a large area called Carolina. It was named after the king of England, King Charles II. *Carolina* comes from the Latin name for Charles.

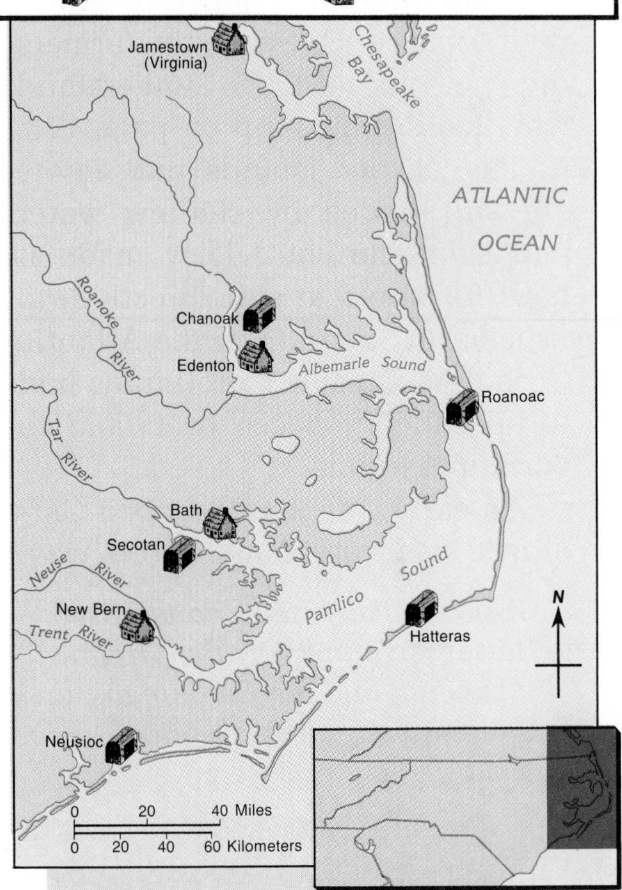

MAP SKILL: Which sound was located near Edenton? What was one way the colonists reached it?

SETTLING THE ALBEMARLE

The first English colonists to settle in Carolina migrated to the area around Albemarle Sound. Find Albemarle Sound on the map on this page. As far as we know, the first Virginian to reach the area was a fur trader named **Nathaniel Batts**. Batts arrived there in 1660 and bought land from the Native Americans.

The colonists who followed cleared the land around Albemarle Sound and planted crops. The crops that grew best there were corn, tobacco, and wheat. Farmers traded surplus corn and wheat for **import** goods such as sugar, tea, and coffee. An import is a good that is brought in from another country for sale or trade.

TRADE PROBLEMS

Like the Jamestown colonists, Carolinian farmers hoped to export their tobacco. However, the farmers did not succeed. To understand why, look at the map on page 123.

The barrier islands and inlets are surrounded by shallow water and swift currents. They made it hard for ships to sail directly into Albemarle Sound from the Atlantic Ocean. As a result, Carolinians had to take their tobacco over land to ports in Virginia.

An early colonist described Carolina's trade problems in this way.

> *A good deal of tobacco is raised, but it is shipped by the Virginia merchant and the Carolinians must accept whatever prices he chooses to pay.*

Taking their tobacco to market in Virginia was not easy for the Carolinian colonists. You have read about the wetlands along the Coastal Plain. In 1672 an English traveler rode along the coast by horseback. He described his route through the Great Dismal Swamp as "full of great bogs and swamps so that we were . . . wet to the knees." A bog is wet ground that is like a swamp. Thick forests and wide, shallow rivers added to travelers' problems. The geography of coastal settlements kept them small.

North Carolinians had to take their tobacco to Jamestown, where ships **exported** it to England.

RIVER TOWNS

Meanwhile people who lived farther inland continued to migrate from Virginia in search of land. In time the northern part of Carolina became known as North Carolina. One settlement there grew into the first town in North Carolina. This town was called **Bath**. Find Bath on the map on page 123.

The second town to be settled by colonists was **New Bern**. Unlike the earlier colonists, the New Bern settlers arrived by ship from Europe in 1710. They found a way through the barrier islands to the coast. These people had left Switzerland and Germany in search of a better life. The name New Bern was taken from the Swiss city of Berne.

Although Bath and New Bern were located on rivers, they did not become successful ports. Both towns were many miles inland. They did not have deep harbors in which oceangoing ships could dock.

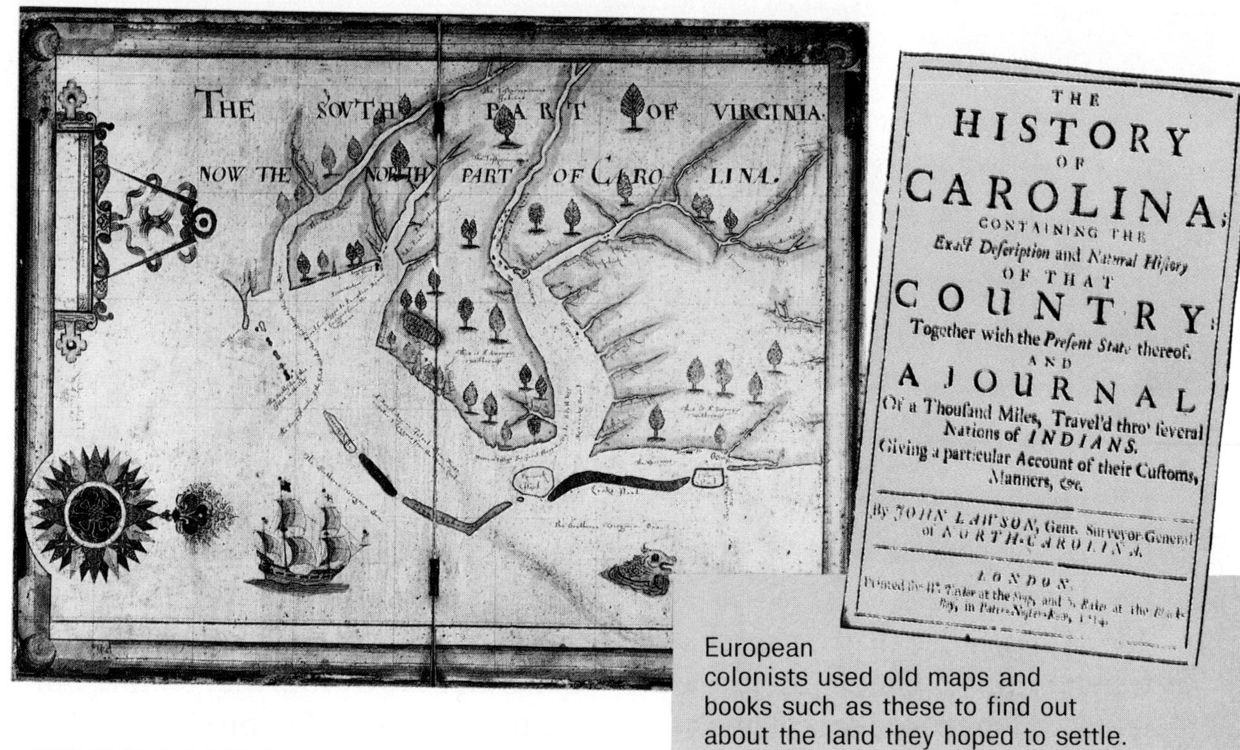

THE
HISTORY
OF
CAROLINA;
CONTAINING THE
Exact Description and Natural History
OF THAT
COUNTRY:
Together with the Present State thereof.
AND
A JOURNAL
Of a Thousand Miles, Travel'd thro' several
Nations of INDIANS.
Giving a particular Account of their Customs,
Manners, &c.

By JOHN LAWSON, Gent. Surveyor-General
of NORTH-CAROLINA.

LONDON:
Printed for W. Taylor at the Ship, and J. Baker at the Black-Boy, in Pater-Noster-Row, 1714.

European colonists used old maps and books such as these to find out about the land they hoped to settle.

INDIAN LOSSES

Around this time, quarrels broke out between the colonists and the Native Americans. At first most of the Indians had welcomed the colonists. However, the colonists began taking Native American land. Several European settlements were built where Indian villages had been located. New Bern was built where the Tuscarora village of Chatooka had stood.

John Lawson, an early English explorer, was saddened by this unfairness. He wrote the following.

> *[The Indians] are really better to us than we are to them; they always give us food . . . we let them walk by our doors hungry.*

Even more harmful to the Native Americans than the loss of land was the loss of life. Diseases brought by the Europeans caused the deaths of many Indians. Smallpox and measles had been unknown to Native Americans. Because they had never had these diseases, thousands of Indians died. In 1695 most of the Pamlico died from smallpox. Other Coastal Plain Indians, hoping to escape sickness, moved west to the Piedmont.

THE TUSCARORA WAR

By the early 1700s the Tuscarora were the largest Indian group still living on the Coastal Plain. As more Europeans arrived, the Tuscarora grew angry. They were tired of being treated unfairly. They also feared the loss of more land.

To start farms such as this recreated one in Old Salem, the colonists cut down forests that the Indians needed in order to survive.

In 1711 the Tuscarora attacked European settlements along the Neuse and Pamlico rivers. The colonists fought back with the help of soldiers from South Carolina. The war lasted three years and ended with the Tuscarora's defeat. The Tuscarora were forced to leave North Carolina. They moved north to New York, where they lived among the Iroquois, to whom they were related.

The defeat of the Tuscarora opened new areas of land for Europeans. Many South Carolinian soldiers who had fought in the war decided to return to North Carolina with their families. Soon new towns were begun along our coast.

THE STRUGGLE TO SURVIVE

As you have read, the English succeeded in starting a permanent colony in North America in 1607. Colonists moved south from the Virginia colony to North Carolina, where they settled. Later, colonists also came from Europe and South Carolina. However, they could not easily export their products. The arrival of the colonists changed the way of life of the Indians. Many lost their land and their lives as a result of war and disease.

Check Your Reading

1. Why was Jamestown a successful colony?
2. Why did many Virginia colonists move to North Carolina?
3. Name three problems that faced the colonists in North Carolina.
4. **GEOGRAPHY SKILL:** Which geographical features of North Carolina affected the colonists' trade with England?
5. **THINKING SKILL:** Compare and contrast the growth of Jamestown in Virginia with the growth of towns in the land that is now North Carolina.

REVIEWING VOCABULARY

archaeologist
colony
export
migrate
surplus

Number a sheet of paper from 1 to 5. Beside each number write the word from the list above that best matches the definition.

1. To move from one place to another
2. A settlement in one country that is ruled by another country
3. An amount that is greater than what is used or needed
4. A person who digs in places hoping to learn more about how people once lived there
5. Something that is sold or traded to another country

REVIEWING FACTS

Number a sheet of paper from 1 to 5. Beside each number write **T** if the statement is true. If the statement is false, rewrite it to make it true.

1. An artifact is a statement that can be proved true.
2. The first Native Americans of both the Coastal Plain and the Piedmont lived in villages.
3. In a Cherokee village council, members discussed important issues and reached decisions.
4. Native Americans were helped by their contact with Europeans.
5. Today we know that the people of the "Lost Colony" of Roanoke resettled on Croatoan Island.

WRITING ABOUT MAIN IDEAS

1. **Writing a Story:** Imagine that you are a Pee Dee leader explaining the Green Corn Ceremony. Tell why the Pee Dee might do these things, why it was important, and what might be learned from the ceremony.
2. **Writing About Perspectives:** Imagine that you are a Virginia tobacco trader and that you buy Carolina tobacco to sell to England. How might your feelings about this trade differ from a Carolinian's? Write a journal entry about your feelings.

BUILDING SKILLS: READING TIME LINES

Read the time line on page 120. Then answer these questions.

1. What does the time line show?
2. When did Verrazano explore the coast of North Carolina?
3. By which date were Native Americans already living in the area?
4. Which is the last event shown on the time line?
5. How does a time line help you to understand the order of events?

CHAPTER 5

NEW WAYS OF LIFE

FOCUS

It was different from any other party that I've ever been to. People at the party told about the Africans who had been forced to work on this big farm called Somerset Place. I found out something else. Way back, my family lived and worked there.

Julius Phelps Santiago and his family had gone to a reunion of people whose ancestors had been enslaved at Somerset Plantation. In this chapter you will read about slavery and about other important parts of North Carolina's past.

LESSON

1 Settling the New Colony

READ TO LEARN

Key Vocabulary

immigrant
backcountry
ancestor

Key Places

Cape Fear River
Wilmington
Fayetteville
Great Wagon Road
Bethabara
Salem
Winston-Salem

Read Aloud

The bad road began. It was uphill and down and we had constantly to push the wagon or hold it back by ropes. . . . [At places] it was so slippery the horses could not keep their footing but fell . . . to their knees.

During the late 1700s a colonist wrote these words to describe the route he followed to get to North Carolina from Pennsylvania. He was one of the thousands of colonists who traveled such roads to North Carolina.

Read for Purpose

1. **WHAT YOU KNOW:** Which region of North Carolina was the first to be colonized by Europeans?
2. **WHAT YOU WILL LEARN:** Which groups of Europeans came to North Carolina after the English?

THE CAPE FEAR RIVER

You have read that the land around Albemarle Sound was the first place in North Carolina to be colonized by Europeans. You may remember that these English colonists had come to North Carolina from Virginia. They were searching for land on which to start farms.

Later, during the 1720s, colonists from South Carolina began moving north to find land with good soil and plenty of trees. They settled along the **Cape Fear River**, where Native Americans had lived for hundreds of years. The colonists soon took the land from the Native Americans who lived there.

The colonists who built homes along the Cape Fear River chose a location that helped their colony to grow. You can see from the map below that this river empties into the Atlantic Ocean. The river is deep enough to be used by large ships. The colonists who lived nearby could trade directly with England.

Because of its location, the Cape Fear River settlement grew quickly. More Europeans arrived there. Soon the town, which was called **Wilmington**, became a busy port. Today Wilmington is our state's most important port.

MAP SKILL: Wilmington *(right)* was the colony's most important port. Which **immigrant** groups lived near the town?

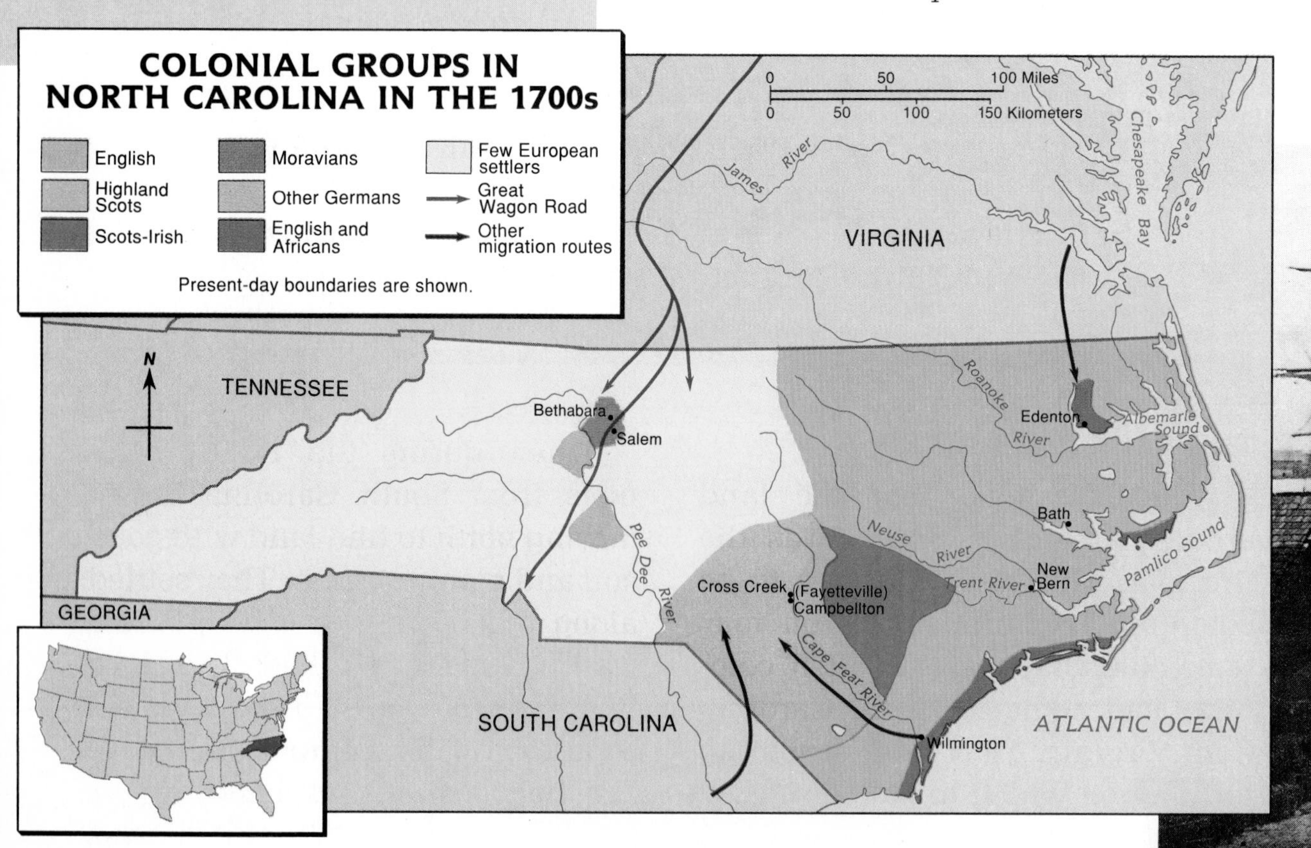

THE HIGHLAND SCOTS

One of the other groups of European **immigrants** that arrived in Wilmington came from Scotland. An immigrant is a person who moves to a new country to live. Because these immigrants came from the mountains of Scotland, they were called the Highland Scots.

After the immigrants arrived at Wilmington, they went by canoes or small boats up the Cape Fear River to settlements called Campbellton and Cross Creek. Later, in 1778, Campbellton and Cross Creek joined to become **Fayetteville**.

As North Carolina grew, Fayetteville's location on the Cape Fear River helped it to become a center of trade. So many Scottish families settled there that the area was called "Little Scotland." Today Fayetteville is the sixth-largest city in North Carolina.

THE BACKCOUNTRY

Few Europeans moved to the Piedmont Region in the 1700s. In fact, colonists called this region the backcountry. The backcountry was "in back of" the Coastal Plain.

The colonists could not travel easily to the backcountry because of the Fall Line. River rapids and waterfalls at the Fall Line made travel across it hard.

THE GREAT WAGON ROAD

As you have read, many Native American groups lived in the Piedmont. You may remember that the Catawba, the Waxhaw, and the Eno made their homes there.

By the 1750s the colonists used Native-American trails through the Piedmont. One Indian trail stretched all the way from Pennsylvania, through the Piedmont, to South Carolina. When many settlers from Pennsylvania began to use this long trail, fighting broke out between them and the Native Americans. The Indians were trying to protect their land, but they soon lost it.

Before long hundreds of other immigrants were using the trail from Pennsylvania to North Carolina. The trail became known as the Great Wagon Road because the travelers carried what they owned on wagons. You read a description of this road in the Read Aloud of this lesson. Find the Great Wagon Road on the map on page 130.

BACKCOUNTRY IMMIGRANTS

The first immigrants to go to the backcountry on the Great Wagon Road were the Scots-Irish. They were called the Scots-Irish because their ancestors were Scots who had lived in Ireland before sailing to North America. An ancestor is a member of your family who lived long before you were born.

The backcountry was also settled by German immigrants from Pennsylvania. Most of these Germans settled on farms. One North Carolinian wrote the following about the German colonists.

> *They raise horses, cows, and hogs with a few sheep; they raise Indian Corn, wheat, barley, rye, and oats, make good butter and tolerable* [fair] *cheese. . . .*

MORAVIANS

In 1753 a small group of German immigrants called Moravians came from Pennsylvania to the Piedmont. The Moravians shared certain religious beliefs and customs that set them apart from other colonists. In the Moravian culture each person worked for the good of the entire community. One Moravian colonist described how their first town, **Bethabara**, was built.

> *Nathanael and Jacob Loesch measured off 8 acres (3.2 ha) of land which is to be cleared at once, so that wheat can be sown* [planted]. *Others began to gather the dead wood and build bonfires. . . . Gottlob, Nathanael, and Grube laid a [floor] of clapboards for our cabin.*

Bethabara grew quickly. In 1766 the Moravians started building a larger town called **Salem**. The Moravian leaders carefully planned the building of the town.

LIFE IN SALEM

Life in Salem was very different from the life in other towns in the backcountry. For example, boys and girls left their parents' homes when they were 14 years old. All the girls then lived in a house called the Single Sisters House. They stayed there until they were married. Fourteen-year-old boys moved into the Single Brothers House, where they lived until they were married. The girls learned how to weave and sew and to make needed goods such as candles and soap. Later this training would help the girls to care for their homes. Boys learned how to build furniture, to bake, and to make bricks. The boys used their training when they went to work.

Farmers in the backcountry traveled to Salem for many of their needs. In Salem they could find goods that were carefully made.

MAP SKILL: These people dressed in colonial clothing are demonstrating colonial skills. On which street on the map do you think they worked?

They also could find a tailor, a blacksmith, or a baker. In time Salem became the center for trade in the Piedmont. Later Salem became part of the city of **Winston-Salem**. Today Old Salem has been rebuilt. You can visit this town to see what Moravian life was like in colonial times.

THE COLONY GROWS

During the 1700s European settlement of the Piedmont Region was slower than that of the Coastal Plain Region. Immigrants came from Scotland and Germany. They also came from colonies to the north and to the south. During this time most Native Americans were driven off their land in the Piedmont Region.

Check Your Reading

1. How did the location of Wilmington help it to grow?
2. Which groups of colonists came to the Cape Fear River valley? Which groups came to the backcountry?
3. **GEOGRAPHY SKILL:** How did the Great Wagon Road affect the population of the backcountry?
4. **THINKING SKILL:** List three questions that you could ask to learn more about population growth in the Piedmont Region during the 1700s.

LESSON

2 Slavery and the Plantation System

READ TO LEARN

Key Vocabulary

slavery
indentured servant
plantation
cash crop
craftsworker
naval stores

Key Places

Somerset Place

Read Aloud

We raise the wheat, They give us the corn;
We bake the bread, They give us the crust;
We peel the meat, They give us the skin.

These lines from an old song express the feelings that many enslaved Africans had about their life in the land that today is the United States. Although most Africans in colonial North Carolina did not come here freely and were forced to work, their work helped the colony to survive and grow.

Read for Purpose

1. **WHAT YOU KNOW:** Which groups of people lived in the Coastal Plain and the Piedmont in the early 1700s?
2. **WHAT YOU WILL LEARN:** What was life like for enslaved Africans on North Carolina's early plantations?

AFRICANS ARE BROUGHT TO NORTH CAROLINA

Today one of every six people in our state is African American. Some of these North Carolinians can trace their roots back to those Africans who were brought here by force in the late 1600s. After they were captured in Africa, these people were separated from their families, put in chains, and sent across the Atlantic Ocean to the colonies. There they began a life under **slavery**. Slavery is the practice of owning people and forcing them to work without pay.

Almost all of the enslaved people were brought to North Carolina from other colonies. Many farmers migrating from Virginia brought them to work on tobacco farms.

FARM WORKERS

The farmers needed workers to make their farms do well. The earliest colonial farmers enslaved some of the Native Americans. But many of these people soon died from European diseases or ran to other areas. Farmers found it hard to hire other European colonists because most of them owned their own land. In addition, few colonists chose to do the backbreaking work needed to keep a large farm going.

North Carolina did have some **indentured servants**, who were mostly English, but there were not enough of them to fill the farmers' needs. An indentured servant agreed to work without pay for someone for several years—usually four to seven. In return the farmer agreed to pay for his or her journey to the colony. The farmer also took care of the servant's needs. At the end of the agreed-upon years, the servant was free at last.

PLANTATIONS

Some farmers believed that the use of enslaved Africans would make their **plantations** do well. A plantation is a huge farm on which large amounts of certain crops were

DIAGRAM SKILL: Plantations were like small towns. Why did some have their own docks?

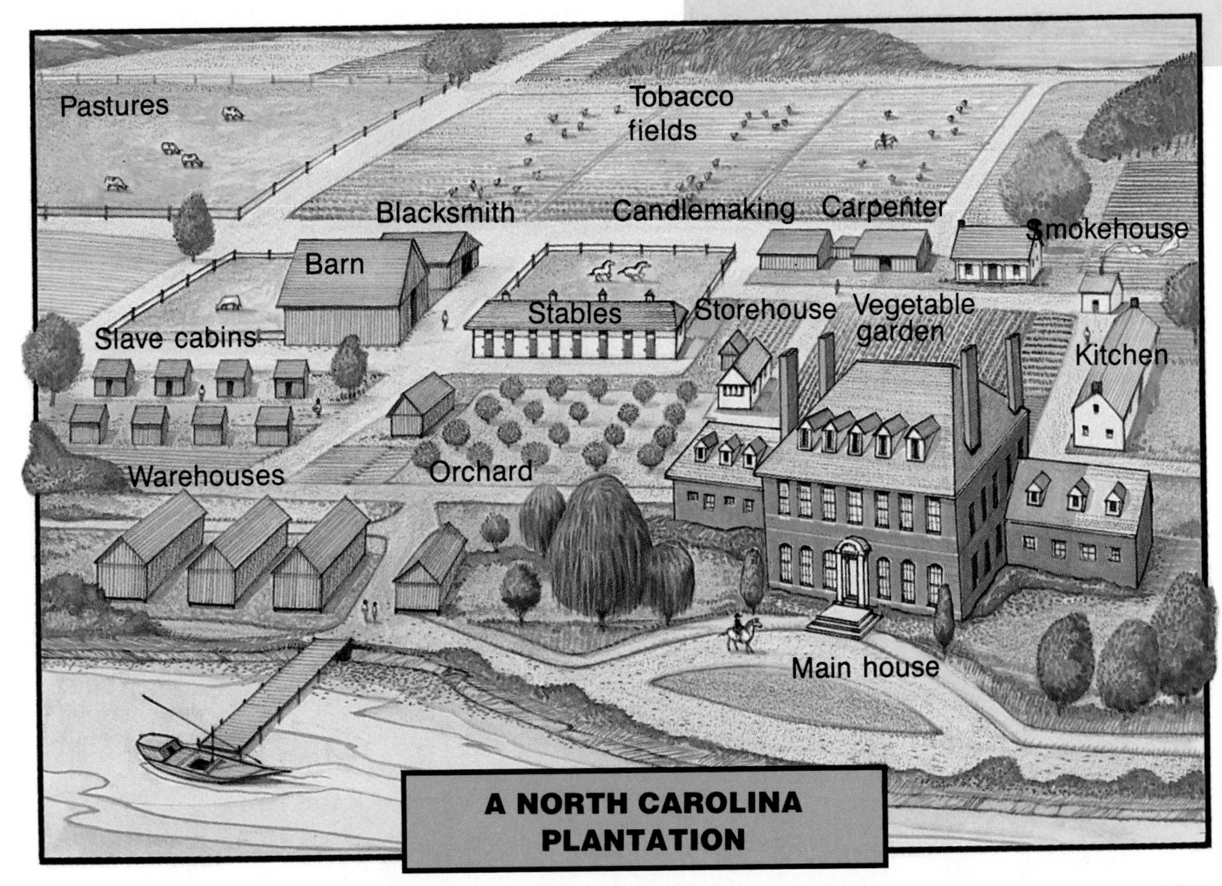

A NORTH CAROLINA PLANTATION

grown. The plantation owners were called planters. They used enslaved Africans to grow tobacco, rice, or cotton. These crops were known as **cash crops** because they were raised for sale rather than for the planter's own use.

A plantation differed from a small farm in that a plantation was like a small town. Its enslaved workers included blacksmiths, carpenters, shoemakers, and weavers. Almost everything a plantation needed was made or grown there. Many plantations had docks where ships came to be loaded. Unlike a plantation, a small farm did not grow cash crops. It grew just enough food for a family's needs.

NAVAL STORES

Some plantation workers made **naval stores**. Naval stores are products that come from pine trees. Naval stores include tar, turpentine, and pitch. Pitch is a dark, sticky material used to pave roads and keep boats from leaking. Do you remember why North Carolinians are called Tar Heels? Many people think that this name goes back to colonial days.

The best customer for the colony's naval stores was the British navy. Its sailors covered the wooden bottoms and the ropes of their ships with tar and pitch to keep the water out.

SLOW GROWTH OF SLAVERY

By 1790 North Carolina had fewer enslaved people than Virginia, South Carolina, and Maryland. Not all African Americans were enslaved. A few came to the colonies as indentured servants. Others earned their freedom or were freed. However, even free African Americans had few rights. They could not travel freely nor meet with enslaved Africans.

These workers are gathering the sap, or sticky liquid, from pine trees in order to make **naval stores**

Enslaved Africans were bought and sold. Their owners could separate children from their mothers.

SLAVE LIFE

By law those Africans who were enslaved in the colonies were the property of other people. Harriet Jacobs, who ran away from North Carolina, wrote the following.

> *[A free person cannot know] what it is to be a slave; to be entirely unprotected by law or custom; to have the laws reduce you to the condition of a [piece of property owned by someone else], entirely subject to . . . another.*

People in slavery could not meet in groups. They had to carry a pass when they traveled. Their families were often broken up, and the parents and children were sold to different people.

SOMERSET PLACE

One of North Carolina's largest plantations was **Somerset Place**. By 1850 over 300 people lived and worked there. Julius Santiago, whom you read about on page 128, traces his roots to one of the enslaved families that lived and worked there in the 1800s.

At Somerset Place, as on many other plantations, enslaved Africans performed all kinds of dangerous and hard work. They drained swamps near Lake Phelps, where many of them died from fevers caused by mosquito bites. Enslaved people cleared thousands of acres of cypress trees and planted crops. Slave labor also built Somerset Place's main house.

Not all enslaved people worked in the fields. Some worked indoors in the main house. Others were **craftsworkers**, or people who make products that need a special skill. Among the craftsworkers were carpenters, blacksmiths, and weavers.

FOLLOW THE DRINKIN' GOURD

Lento, but rhythmic
African-American Folksong
Adapted by Paul Campbell
mp
1. When the sun comes back and the first quail calls,
Fol - low the Drink - in' Gourd. Then the Old Man is a - wait - in' for to
car - ry you to free - dom, Fol - low the Drink - in' Gourd.
Chorus
Fol - low the Drink - in' Gourd, Fol - low the
Drink - in' Gourd, For the Old Man is a - wait - in' for to
car - ry you to free - dom, Fol - low the Drink - in' Gourd.

Visitors to Somerset Place today can see the main house and the places that were known as the outbuildings. Among the outbuildings are the kitchen, laundry, icehouse, and storehouse. What visitors cannot see are the 23 one-room cabins in which the enslaved Africans lived. These cabins no longer exist. You will read more about Somerset Place in the Traditions lesson on pages 157–160.

RESHAPING AFRICAN TRADITIONS

Enslaved Africans contributed in many ways to the culture and economy of the North Carolina colony. For example, the enslaved people brought new ways of growing rice and weaving baskets. One practice that North Carolinians are very fond of, especially on hot summer nights, is sitting on the front porch. Porches were a part of many African houses.

Have you ever heard the blues or listened to gospel music? These well-known music styles can be traced back to enslaved Africans. These Africans brought their music with them. Later they mixed these styles with European music to create exciting new kinds of music. One of the songs of the enslaved Africans was "Follow the Drinkin' Gourd," which appears on page 138. The gourd was another name for the group of stars called the Big Dipper. The two stars in the front of the Big Dipper pointed the way north to freedom.

This grandmother and granddaughter are using their porch to work on a family quilt. The quilt has both European and African designs.

THE PLANTATION SYSTEM

As you have read, Europeans brought Africans to North Carolina and other colonies by force and enslaved them. Slave labor made it possible for plantations to succeed.

Check Your Reading

1. What were some of the crops that enslaved Africans raised on North Carolina's plantations?
2. What are naval stores?
3. Describe the life of the enslaved people on the plantations.
4. **THINKING SKILL:** In what ways do you think the lives of enslaved people were like those of indentured servants? In what ways do you think that they were different?

LESSON

3 Forming a Government

READ TO LEARN

Key Vocabulary

tax
American Revolution
Declaration of Independence
Constitution

Key People

Penelope Barker
Nathanael Greene

Key Places

Moore's Creek Bridge
Kings Mountain
Guilford Courthouse

Read Aloud

We have an invitation to a ball in Wilmington. . . .This is the last that is to be given, as the [colony] has forbidden every kind of [entertainment], even card-playing.

Janet Schaw visited North Carolina from Scotland in 1775. Schaw later wrote a book in which she described what it was like to be in the colonies just before war broke out with Britain. In this lesson you will read about the events that led to this war.

Read for Purpose

1. **WHAT YOU KNOW:** Which country ruled the colony of North Carolina?
2. **WHAT YOU WILL LEARN:** What changes did the American Revolution bring to North Carolina?

UNREST IN THE COLONIES

In 1765 crowds of angry colonists marched along Wilmington's Market Street. Why did the colonists take to the streets? During the 1750s the British had fought the French and Indian War against the French in North America. In this war many Native Americans had sided with the French. The Indians believed that the French were less likely than the British to take their land from them.

After the British won the war in 1763, they wanted the colonists to help them pay for it. The British passed a law in 1763 making the colonists pay a **tax** on paper goods. A tax is money paid by people to support their government. The tax came from the stamps the colonists had to buy from the British. Stamps were put on paper goods such as playing cards and newspapers.

Many colonists thought that they were paying too many taxes already. They were also angry because they had no voice in the British government that was demanding the taxes. In North Carolina colonists in Wilmington, Edenton, New Bern, and Cross Creek held marches.

Penelope Barker gathered together some of Edenton's leading women. She wanted them to do everything they could to end unfair British **taxes**.

During the next ten years the British made more tax laws. The colonists found many ways to show the British that they were against these laws. In 1774 the British placed a tax on tea. A colonist named **Penelope Barker** gathered 51 women who lived near Edenton. They held a meeting called a "tea party." At the meeting, the women signed an agreement to support the 13 colonies. In a letter they said that they would not drink tea or wear clothes made in Great Britain until the British put an end to these laws.

THE AMERICAN REVOLUTION

By 1775 it was clear that the colonists and their British rulers could not agree. This problem led to the war that is called the **American Revolution**. A revolution is a sudden and complete change in government. The colonists fought the American Revolution against the British to gain their freedom.

The first battles of the revolution took place in Massachusetts, in the towns of Lexington and Concord in April 1775. A few weeks later, on May 20, some North Carolinians met in Mecklenburg County. They called for a new government completely under the colonists' control. This date in May marks the beginning of North Carolina's independence from Great Britain.

North Carolina played an important part in the war. On April 12, 1776, the colonial leaders of North

Carolina met in Halifax County. In an agreement called the Halifax Resolves, they suggested that the colonies get together to discuss the actions of the British. They said that the colonies should explain that they wanted to be free.

Partly because of the Halifax Resolves, colonial leaders met in Philadelphia, Pennsylvania. There on July 4, 1776, they signed the **Declaration of Independence**. This statement explained why the colonists wanted to be independent, or free, from Great Britain.

THE WAR IN NORTH CAROLINA

The fighting that followed the signing of the Declaration of Independence lasted until 1781. The first battle in North Carolina took place at **Moore's Creek Bridge** near Wilmington in February 1776. The colonial forces won quickly.

Later, the commander of the British soldiers in the colonies was Charles Cornwallis (kôrn wäl′ is). He believed that North Carolina could be taken easily. Cornwallis was proven wrong at the Battle of **Kings Mountain** on the North Carolina-South Carolina border. In October 1780, small bands of fighters from the Mountain Region defeated the British in a one-hour battle.

In March 1781 the British met North Carolina's army again, at **Guilford Courthouse**, in what is now Greensboro. Cornwallis commanded the British army. General **Nathanael Greene** led the American soldiers. The Americans lost the battle, but Cornwallis was weakened by the great loss of men and supplies. Seven months later Cornwallis surrendered to the leader of the American forces, General George Washington.

A NEW GOVERNMENT

With the war ended, the 13 colonies, now called states, had the hard job of forming a government for their new country. In 1787 leaders from all of the states met in Philadelphia to write a plan for a new government. This plan, called the **Constitution**, set up a strong government for the United States.

This part of the Halifax Resolves says that North Carolina's leaders have the right to meet with other colonists and declare their independence.

HALIFAX RESOLVES

Resolved that the delegates for this colony in the Continental Congress be impowered to concur [act with] the other delegates of the other colonies in declaring independency,...resolving to this colony the sole...right of forming a Constitution and laws for this colony, and of appointing delegates from time to time to meet the delegates of the other colonies....

At the Battle of Kings Mountain, North Carolinians attacked the British from hiding places in the hills.

North Carolina did not vote on the Constitution right away. The main reason for this delay was the fact that the Constitution did not clearly list the rights of the people. North Carolinians wanted to make sure that they would have certain rights. Among these rights were the freedom to speak out and the right to practice their religion freely.

In 1789 the country's lawmakers added a part to the Constitution called the Bill of Rights. This part describes the basic rights of all the citizens of the United States. North Carolina then approved the Constitution and became the twelfth state to join the United States.

The Constitution still did not give everyone equal rights. For one thing, it did not end slavery. It also did not give women or Native Americans the right to vote. Many years would pass before all people in our country gained equal rights.

BECOMING THE UNITED STATES

In this lesson you have read about the events that caused the colonists to demand their independence from the British in 1776. North Carolina played an important part in the American Revolution. After winning the war, the new states set about forming a country.

Check Your Reading

1. Why were the colonists angry about the new British taxes?
2. What changes did the American Revolution bring to North Carolina and the rest of the colonies?
3. **THINKING SKILL:** List three dates in sequence that will help you to remember North Carolina's role in the American Revolution.

Identifying Fact and Opinion

Key Vocabulary

fact opinion

Imagine you were going to visit the national military park at Guilford Courthouse. Your father tells you that the museum is located in Guilford County. This is a statement of a **fact**. You can look in an encyclopedia or on a map to see if it is true. A fact is a statement that can be proved true.

Your father also tells you that this military park is one of the finest historical sites in North Carolina. This statement cannot be proved. It is your father's **opinion**. An opinion is a belief or feeling that a person has about something. One person may believe that a different historical site is more realistic or more interesting. Another person may agree with your father that the military park at Guilford Courthouse is the best.

It is important to be able to tell the difference between fact and opinion. Otherwise you may accept someone's opinion as fact.

Trying the Skill

Tell whether each of the following is a statement of fact or an opinion.

1. In 1774 the British government passed a law to tax tea.
2. The women of Edenton were right to stop drinking British tea.
3. Colonial soldiers won the battle at Moore's Creek Bridge.

HELPING YOURSELF

The steps on the left are one way to tell the difference between a statement of fact and an opinion. The example on the right shows how to use these steps to recognize which statements about the American Revolution in North Carolina are statements of fact and which are opinions.

One Way to Recognize Fact and Opinion	Example
1. Ask yourself if the statement can be proved true.	Could you prove that the British passed a law to tax tea in 1774?
2. If the answer is yes, ask yourself how it could be proved true.	How could you check to see if it is true? You could look it up in a history book or in an encyclopedia.
3. If you do not think a statement can be proved, ask yourself if it gives someone's beliefs or feelings. Look for clue words such as *the best*, *should*, or *I think*.	Is the statement about the women of Edenton someone's belief? The words *were right* are a clue that the statement is an opinion.

Applying the Skill

Tell whether each statement below about the American Revolution and the new country's government is a statement that is a fact or an opinion.

1. Penelope Barker held a "tea party" to show she was against the tea tax.
2. Nathanael Greene was one of the best American generals of the American Revolution.
3. After the Revolution, the former colonies set up a new government under the Constitution.
4. The Bill of Rights should have been included in the Constitution in the first place.

Now answer the following questions.

1. How do you know that Statement 1 is a fact?
   a. It is someone's belief or feeling.
   b. It has word clues.
   c. It can be proved.
2. How do you know that Statement 2 is an opinion?
   a. It can be proved.
   b. It uses word clues that tell you that the writer is giving his or her personal beliefs.
   c. Everyone would agree with it.

Reviewing the Skill

1. What is the difference between a statement of fact and an opinion?
2. Write a statement of fact and a statement of opinion about the Declaration of Independence.
3. Give examples of when it would be helpful to be able to tell the difference between facts and opinions.

LESSON

4 Conflict in the West

READ TO LEARN

Key Vocabulary

frontier
pioneer
self-sufficient
bartering
treaty
Trail of Tears

Key Places

Wilderness Road
Qualla Boundary Reservation

Key People

Daniel Boone
Sequoyah

Read Aloud

Daniel Boone could shoot a tick off a bear's nose.

A friend of Daniel Boone's described him with these words. Boone was a skilled hunter and one of the first colonists to explore the mountains in North Carolina. In this lesson you will read more about how such explorations caused changes in the Mountain Region.

Read for Purpose

1. **WHAT YOU KNOW:** What is it like to travel in the Mountain Region?
2. **WHAT YOU WILL LEARN:** How did the arrival of pioneers affect the Native Americans in the Mountain Region?

NEW ARRIVALS

When the American Revolution ended in 1783, colonists began to move westward into the Mountain Region. Throughout most of the 1700s, few colonists had lived there. To them, the mountains were the **frontier** (frun tîr′). *Frontier* was the word used by the colonists to describe the edge of settlement. Although the area beyond the frontier was settled by Indians, colonists thought of it as a wilderness.

The new arrivals in the Mountain Region have been called **pioneers**. Pioneers are people who lead the way into a land unknown to them. The pioneers in our mountains were the first people to live there who were not Indians. As more pioneers came, the frontier moved farther and farther west.

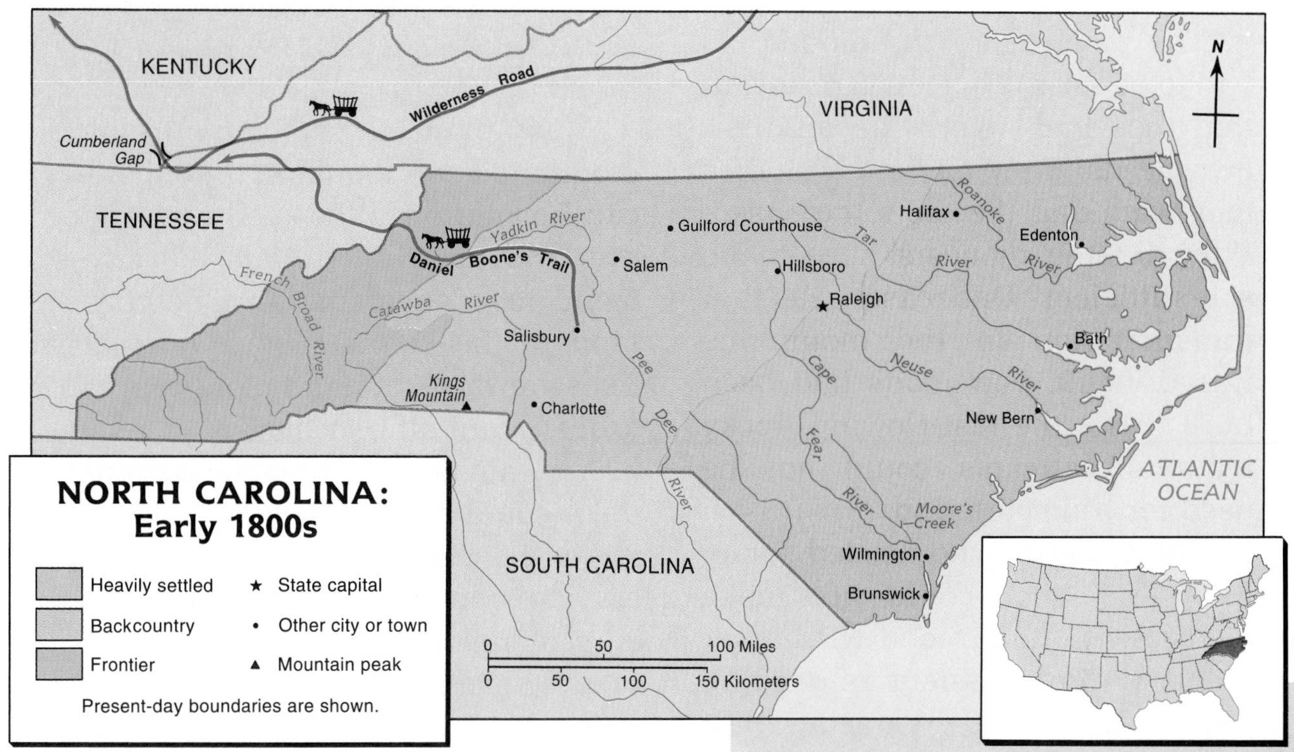

MAP SKILL: Which present-day states could be reached by the pioneers who took the Wilderness Road?

THE WILDERNESS ROAD

The pioneers had a difficult time trying to cross the mountains. Steep slopes and thick forests made the trip dangerous. Most pioneers needed a guide to travel there.

Daniel Boone was one of the first guides to help the pioneers who came to the mountains. Boone had lived in the Piedmont since he was 16 years old. His family had traveled on the Great Wagon Road from Pennsylvania to the Piedmont.

Boone grew up in the woods and enjoyed exploring them. He often followed trails built by Native Americans. One day he found an Indian trail across the mountains that went through a gap, or a natural opening, between mountain peaks. Today that gap is called the Cumberland Gap. In 1769 Boone began to guide pioneers through the gap. This Native American mountain trail soon became known as the **Wilderness Road**. Find the Wilderness Road on the map above.

PIONEER LIFE

Once the pioneers chose a place to stay, they would usually build a cabin made of logs. These log cabins usually had one or two rooms. Most families had only a table and a few chairs. Because they could fit only a few of their belongings with them on a wagon, they had very few pieces of furniture. People slept on mattresses filled with straw.

The pioneers in the mountains had to be **self-sufficient**. This meant that they had to provide for their own needs. They made the clothes they wore and the tools they used. Why did the pioneers have to be self-sufficient? One reason was that transportation in the mountains was difficult. Few roads had been built. Also, the fast-flowing, rocky mountain streams could not be used for transportation.

The pioneers who needed something that they could not make themselves often traded with other pioneers. This system of trading goods was called **bartering**. For example, pioneers bartered corn for jellies or chickens for cloth.

Sequoyah invented the Cherokee alphabet in Georgia in 1821. It helped Cherokee everywhere to learn about the issues that were important to them.

THE CHEROKEE LOSE THEIR LAND

Many pioneers who came to the mountains had fought in the American Revolution. When the war was over, the new United States government gave some of the Cherokee land to the soldiers as a reward. These rewards brought more people to the mountains to live.

You may wonder how the government could give away land belonging to the Cherokee. Cherokee leaders had signed a **treaty**, or a written agreement, with the government. In their treaty, the Cherokee had agreed to sell some of their land to the United States. One reason the Cherokee signed the treaty was that the government promised that no more land would be taken.

Cherokee leaders knew that in the past some Indians had lost land or sold it for too little. To avoid this, leaders such as **Sequoyah** helped the Cherokee read and write. One teacher warned his students to use this knowledge to protect themselves.

> *Unless you can speak their* [the English] *language and read and write as they do, they will be able to cheat you and trample on your rights.*

The Cherokee tried to protect themselves. However, an event occurred that changed their lives. Gold was discovered on Cherokee land in the early 1800s. This led pioneers to come and seek their fortunes. Many of these pioneers attacked Cherokee homes and tried to force the Cherokee off their land. Some Cherokee wanted to fight the pioneers. However, their leaders held them back. The Cherokee leaders felt that being peaceful was the best way for the Cherokee to hold onto their remaining land.

THE TRAIL OF TEARS

In 1830 the United States government passed a law called the Indian Removal Act. The act said that all Native American groups had to be removed from the Southeast to lands west of the Mississippi River. The Cherokee, along with other Indian groups, were very angry. How could they be removed from the land that had been theirs for so long?

The Cherokee refused to move. They tried to persuade United States leaders to change the law. However, in 1838 an army of 7,000 troops entered Cherokee land and forced the people to leave. The route by which they traveled west is shown on the map below.

Nearly 1,000 miles (1,600 km) stretched between Cherokee land and the place set aside for them by the government. They had to travel through swamps, forests, and mountains. Most of the Cherokee traveled this whole distance on foot. Thousands of Cherokee started west on their way to what is now Oklahoma. This terrible journey became known as the **Trail of Tears**. John G. Burnett, a United States

MAP SKILL: In which states did the **Trail of Tears** begin? In which present-day state did it end?

For the Cherokee who were forced to leave their homes, the Trail of Tears was a long, hard journey west to the land that had been set aside for them.

soldier who was there, said, "The trail was a trail of death."

THE OCONALUFTEE

One group of North Carolina's Cherokee, called the Oconaluftee (ō kon ə luf′ tē), lived apart from most other Cherokee. When the Cherokee were forced to leave North Carolina by the Indian Removal Act, the Oconaluftee stayed in the state. Another group of about 1,000 Cherokee hid in the mountains.

Today about 5,500 Oconaluftee and about 3,000 other Cherokee still live in North Carolina. Some live on the **Qualla** (kwä′ lə) **Boundary Reservation**. A reservation is land set aside for Indians to live on. Find the Qualla Boundary Reservation on the map on page 149.

A CHANGED REGION

The arrival of the pioneers in the 1800s caused conflict with the Native Americans who had long lived in the Mountain Region. The Cherokee tried to keep their land peacefully. However, the United States government forced most of the Native Americans to move from North Carolina to land in the west.

Check Your Reading

1. Who were the pioneers?
2. How did the arrival of the pioneers affect the Indians?
3. GEOGRAPHY SKILL: Why did the pioneers find it difficult to travel in the Mountain Region?
4. THINKING SKILL: Arrange the following events in the order in which they occurred: the Trail of Tears; Boone finds the Wilderness Trail; gold is discovered in the mountains.

BUILDING CITIZENSHIP

PEOPLE WHO MAKE A DIFFERENCE

Along the lakes and in the tall mountains of our state, you might hear children singing Cherokee songs. They may say *se-yo,* the Cherokee word for "hello," to greet you. These children can speak and understand Cherokee because of a Cherokee teacher named Edna Chickelela (chik e lā′ la).

When the government set up schools for Cherokees, it did not recommend that the Cherokee language be taught in school. Our government suggested that only English be taught. As a result many Cherokee forgot how to speak their own language.

In 1981 Chickelela began to teach Cherokee at home. She had not learned English until she was 5 years old, and she remembered the 85 sounds of the Cherokee alphabet. In 1982 Chickelela helped to get Cherokee approved as a foreign language in her local school.

She says:

> *Our language comes from the sounds of the brook, the wind, and the running deer. Knowing how to speak our language helps to save our Cherokee way of life.*

Chickelela wanted to keep Cherokee traditions alive. She realized it also was important to teach other parts of Cherokee culture. In 1982 she built a stage at her home in Snow Bird where Cherokee songs and dances could be taught.

Chickelela also teaches people how to make Cherokee white-oak baskets, quilts, and clothes. She designed the first Cherokee flag, and schoolchildren call her "the Betsy Ross of the Cherokee." It is thought that Betsy Ross made the first United States flag.

By keeping alive Cherokee culture, Chickelela is making a difference.

LESSON

5 The Struggle for Equal Rights

READ TO LEARN

Key Vocabulary

Underground Railroad
Confederacy
Union
Civil War
Emancipation Proclamation
segregate
Jim Crow laws
civil rights

Key People

Levi Coffin
Abraham Lincoln

Read Aloud

It was the fourth day of June in 1865 that I began to live.

Katie Rowe used these words to tell how she felt when she learned that she was free. Until then she had been enslaved on a North Carolina plantation. In this lesson you will learn about the struggle for freedom.

Read for Purpose

1. **WHAT YOU KNOW:** What role did slavery play in North Carolina's economy?
2. **WHAT YOU WILL LEARN:** How did African Americans gain freedom and civil rights?

SLAVERY AND STATES' RIGHTS

As you read in Lesson 3, the American Revolution did not end slavery in the United States. By 1850 about one out of every three of all North Carolinians were enslaved African Americans.

By this time several groups had been formed to try to end slavery. However, many southerners believed that their states had the right to decide for themselves about issues such as slavery. This belief became known as "states' rights."

THE UNDERGROUND RAILROAD

Religious groups such as the Quakers were active in the effort to end slavery. They believed that it was their duty to help people who were running away from slavery to escape from the South. Runaways went to northern states or Canada, where slavery was not allowed.

Runaway African Americans often hid in swamps before reaching the **Underground Railroad**. Levi Coffin *(right)* helped to form this network of escape routes.

One of the best-known Quaker leaders was **Levi Coffin**, who came from Guilford County in North Carolina. After moving to Indiana, he put together a network of hiding places for African Americans who were escaping north from slave states. Even though it never had any trains or railroad tracks, this secret network became known as the **Underground Railroad**. Its hiding places were called "stations." Jamestown, Mount Jefferson, and Goldsboro all served as stations.

CAUSES OF THE CIVIL WAR

The slavery question helped to lead to war. **Abraham Lincoln** of Illinois was elected President of the United States in 1860. Lincoln did not support slavery and wanted to keep it from spreading to the new states that were joining the United States. Many southerners were afraid that he might try to end slavery in the South. By doing this, they believed that Lincoln would be taking away their states' rights.

Shortly after Lincoln's election, seven southern states said that they were no longer part of the United States. These states then formed their own country. They called it the Confederate States of America, or the **Confederacy**. Later, four more states joined the Confederacy. The remaining 23 states of the United States were called the **Union**. Look at the map below to see which states finally left the Union and joined the Confederacy.

North Carolina was one of the last states to join the Confederacy. At first North Carolina's leaders voted against leaving the Union. However, in April 1861 President Lincoln called on all states in the Union to send troops to fight the Confederate army. Many North Carolinians did not want to fight against other southerners. Governor Henry Clark of North Carolina told President Lincoln, "You can get no troops from North Carolina."

THE CIVIL WAR

The **Civil War** had begun. A civil war is a war between people in the same country. Even though North Carolina joined the Confederacy, not everyone in the state fought on the Confederate side. Thousands of enslaved people escaped to the North to join the Union army.

In 1862 President Lincoln issued the **Emancipation Proclamation**. To emancipate is to free. The Emancipation Proclamation declared an end to slavery all through the Confederacy. The Emancipation Proclamation took effect on January 1, 1863. However, the President had no way to make the South obey it. What Lincoln's proclamation did

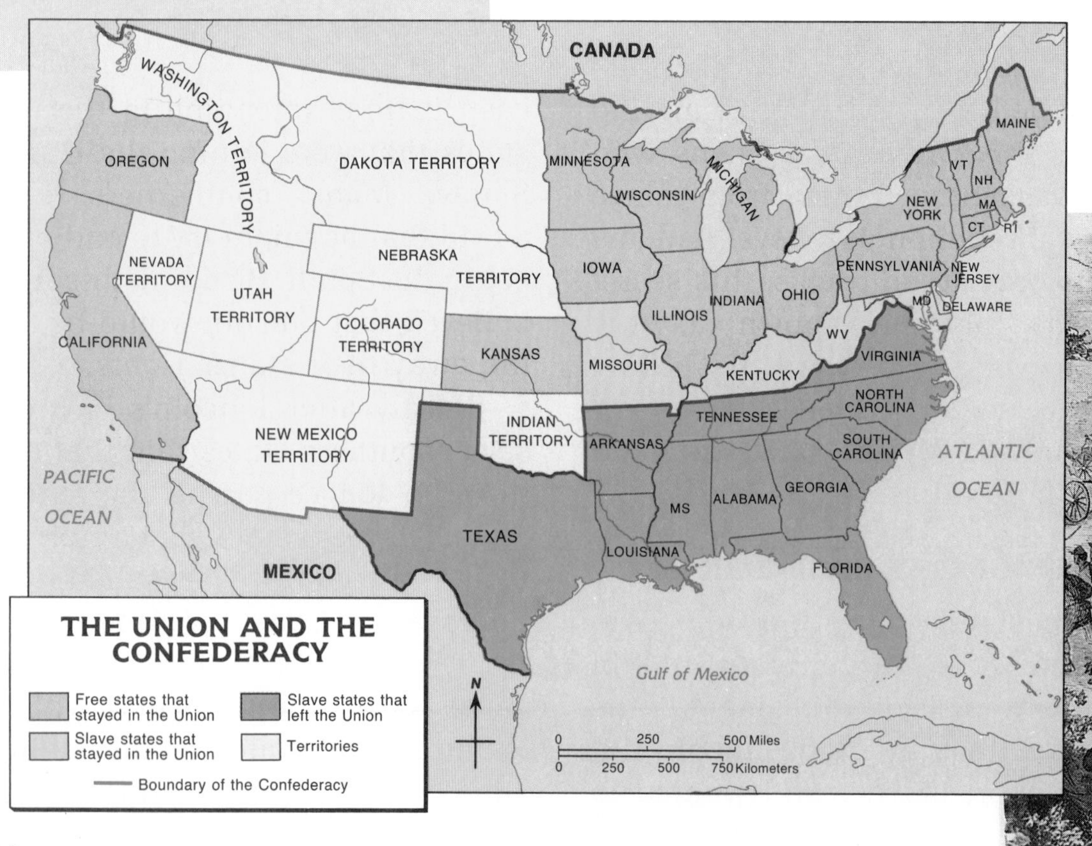

MAP SKILL: Many died in the Battle of Bentonville *(right)*. How many slave states did not join the **Confederacy**?

was to make it clear that the Civil War was being fought both to save the Union and to free people who were in slavery.

During the Civil War the Union navy took much of the eastern part of North Carolina. The last of the 84 battles that were fought in our state took place in Bentonville in March and April of 1865.

This led to the largest surrender of Confederate troops. It took place in North Carolina in April 1865, at the farmhouse of James Bennett. Today Bennett Place is a state historic site in Durham. There you can see the room where generals from both sides met to end the fighting in the Carolinas, Georgia, and Florida.

A NEW TIME OF TROUBLES

In Lesson 3 you read that after the United States Constitution was written, a Bill of Rights was added to protect the rights of American citizens. Four months before the Civil War ended in 1865, Congress passed the Thirteenth Amendment. An amendment is an addition to the Constitution. The Thirteenth Amendment ended slavery everywhere in the United States.

Adding this amendment to the Constitution was an important first step toward fair treatment for African Americans. However, they still did not have equal rights. For one thing, African Americans in North Carolina and many other southern states were not given the right to vote. These African Americans were often frightened into staying away from the voting booths. They were told they would lose their jobs or be beaten if they voted.

JIM CROW LAWS

Southern states also passed a number of laws that **segregated**, or separated, blacks and whites in public places. Such laws were called **Jim Crow laws**, after a song of the time that made fun of African Americans. Under the Jim Crow laws, blacks and whites could not use the same restaurants or hotels. African Americans had to sit in different cars on trains and in the back of buses. Blacks and whites went to separate schools.

Some African Americans challenged these laws in the courts. But they almost never won their cases.

The **Jim Crow laws** of the late 1800s set up separate places, such as this waiting room, for African Americans.

Judges ruled that segregation was legal as long as the two groups were treated equally. However, segregation never meant equality. In North Carolina in the late 1800s, schools for blacks received less money from the state government than schools for whites. Many African-American schools were open only two or three months a year. In 1901 our state had only two public high schools for African Americans, one in Durham and one in Reidsville.

WORKING FOR CHANGE

Segregation lasted a long time in North Carolina. Finally, in the 1950s things began to change. This was the beginning of the struggle known as the **civil rights** movement. Civil rights are the rights of all people to be treated equally under the law. You will read more about civil rights in Chapter 12.

WINNING FREEDOM

As you have read in this lesson, the question of states' rights and slavery in the United States led to the Civil War in 1861. By the end of the war, which the Union won, African Americans were free from slavery. It took over 100 years for segregation to end in our country.

Check Your Reading

1. What is a civil war?
2. What was the Emancipation Proclamation?
3. How have African Americans struggled to gain freedom?
4. GEOGRAPHY SKILL: From what you have just read, why did the Union navy easily gain control of coastal North Carolina?
5. THINKING SKILL: Compare life for African Americans before and after the Civil War.

Tracing Family ROOTS

by Linda Scher

Dorothy Spruill Redford is a North Carolinian who was determined to trace her family's history. This is the story of how nearly ten years of hard work brought her to a former North Carolina plantation called Somerset Place. Today Redford is the director of Somerset Place State Historic Site. North Carolinians take pride in the tradition of finding out about their ancestors and discovering their past. As you read, think about why people value the tradition of tracing their own family histories.

THE SEARCH BEGINS

In 1977 Dorothy Spruill Redford and her 13-year-old daughter, Deborah, were watching the television series, *Roots*. The series was based on a book by Alex Haley, who traced his own roots back to ancestors who had been kidnapped in Africa and forced into slavery in the United States. When Deborah asked her mother, "Who were my great-grandparents? Were they slaves?" Redford had no answer. On that day, Redford's search to discover her family history began. "I felt," Redford said, "this great need to know about my past."

For African Americans like Redford, tracing family roots in the United States can be hard. Enslaved Africans were forced to take their owners' last names. Being sold often meant that their last names were changed to those of their new owners. Tracing a person whose last name was changed several times is not easy.

But Redford was determined. She read family letters, scrapbooks, and old newspapers. She also talked to older family members. From her mother Redford learned the name of her great-grandfather, Alfred Littlejohn.

THE CLUES FALL INTO PLACE

Redford continued her research. In 1981 on a trip to Edenton, North Carolina, near her birthplace, she got lucky. In the Chowan County Courthouse she found a bill of sale from 1826. It listed the names of enslaved Africans, including the name of Elsy Littlejohn, Redford's great-great-great-grandmother! Elsy and her six children had been sold by the Littlejohn family to Josiah Collins. Collins owned a plantation in the next county called Somerset Place, where Elsy's husband, Peter Littlejohn, lived.

Redford found out more about her ancestors by looking through Josiah Collins's letters and records. She also knocked on doors of people who lived in towns near Somerset Place. This step in her search gave her new energy. "After being buried for so long among papers of long-dead people, I was finally back in the land of the living," she said. With this new information, Redford created a family tree of her ancestors. The family tree led back to Somerset Place.

RETURN TO SOMERSET PLACE

Redford remembers the first time she saw Somerset Place. "When I drove past these cypress trees, planted 200 years ago, and looked across the land, I knew I was home. I felt it deep inside." Although Redford was not able to trace her family roots back to Africa as she had hoped, she was able to trace them to Somerset Place. She said, "It's really important for people to be able to identify some place that they can say, 'This is where my ancestors lived.'"

Redford shared her years of hard work by holding a reunion that she called a homecoming. A reunion is a gathering of family members. Redford explains that reunions are a tradition that were popular in the early 1900s. "The tradition was born out of a period when travel was really difficult. People set aside one time each year when they returned home to see family and friends. Everybody came back to their roots."

The first Somerset Place homecoming took place in 1986. Redford's guest list included people whose ancestors had been enslaved on Somerset Place. Redford also invited Josiah Collins, whose great-grandfather had owned Somerset Place. Over 2,000 people came to the homecoming.

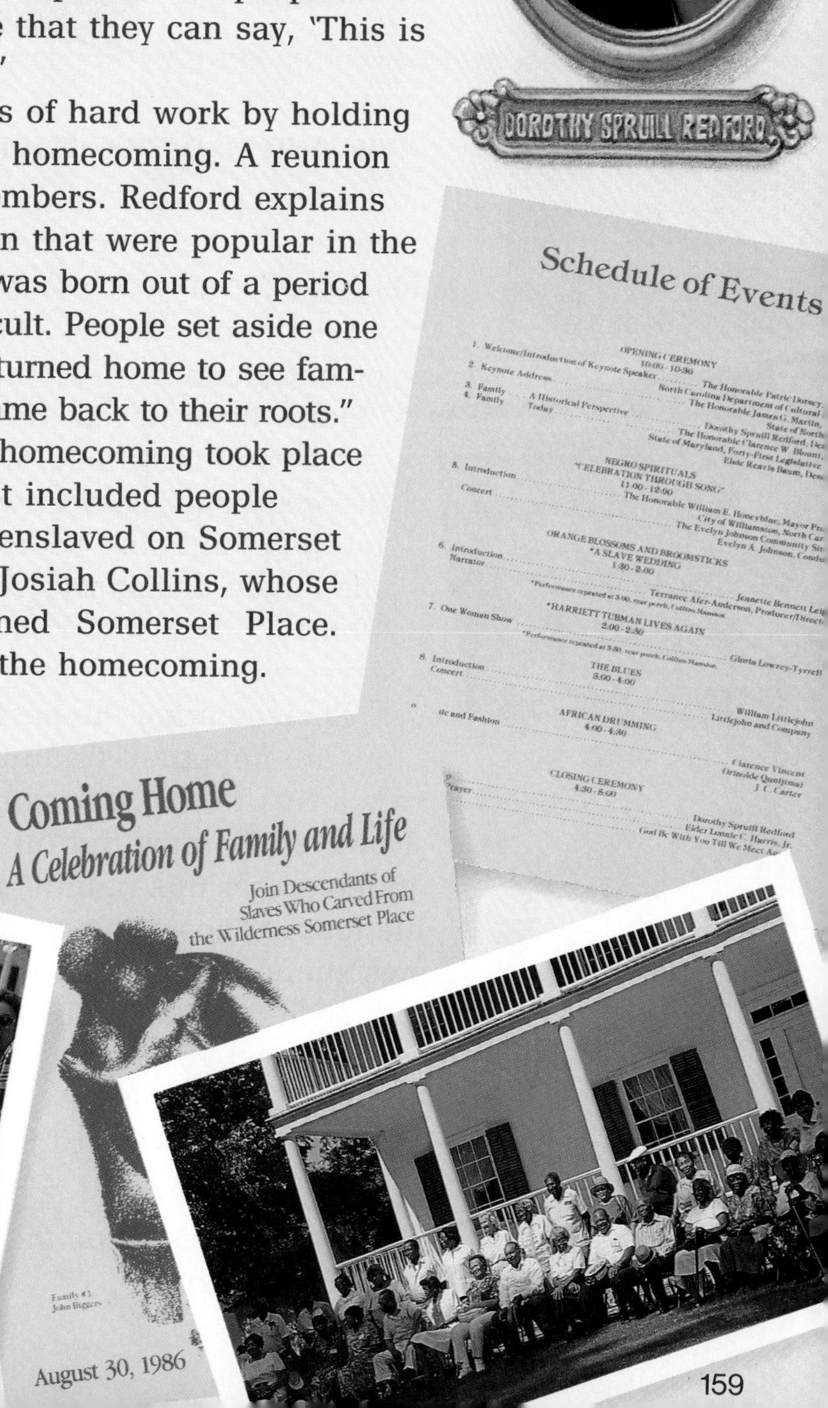

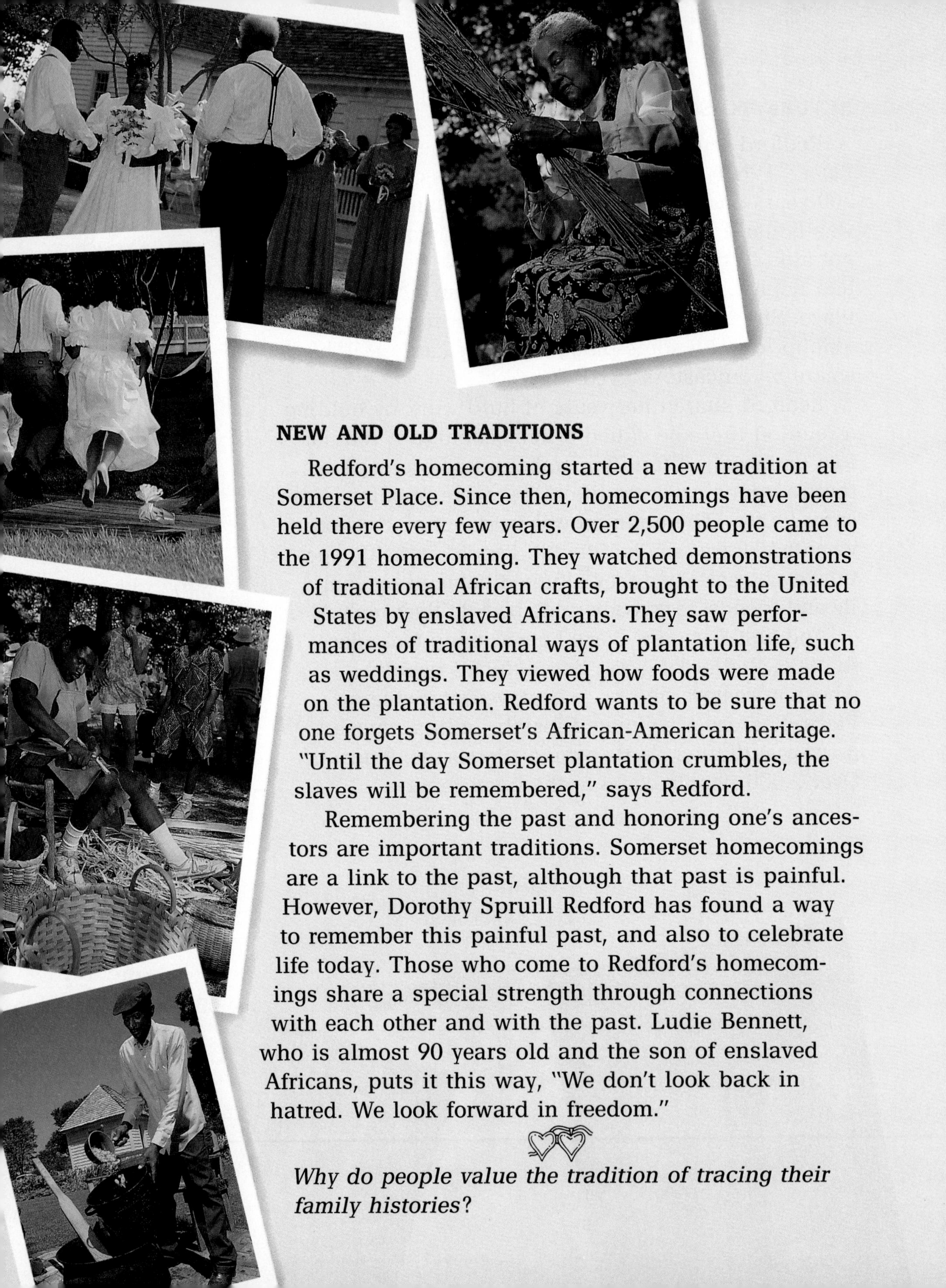

NEW AND OLD TRADITIONS

Redford's homecoming started a new tradition at Somerset Place. Since then, homecomings have been held there every few years. Over 2,500 people came to the 1991 homecoming. They watched demonstrations of traditional African crafts, brought to the United States by enslaved Africans. They saw performances of traditional ways of plantation life, such as weddings. They viewed how foods were made on the plantation. Redford wants to be sure that no one forgets Somerset's African-American heritage. "Until the day Somerset plantation crumbles, the slaves will be remembered," says Redford.

Remembering the past and honoring one's ancestors are important traditions. Somerset homecomings are a link to the past, although that past is painful. However, Dorothy Spruill Redford has found a way to remember this painful past, and also to celebrate life today. Those who come to Redford's homecomings share a special strength through connections with each other and with the past. Ludie Bennett, who is almost 90 years old and the son of enslaved Africans, puts it this way, "We don't look back in hatred. We look forward in freedom."

Why do people value the tradition of tracing their family histories?

REVIEWING VOCABULARY

ancestor
immigrant
pioneer
segregated
treaty

Number a sheet of paper from 1 to 5. Beside each number write the word or term from the list above that best completes each sentence.

1. The Jim Crow laws ____ black people and white people in public places.
2. The ____ from Germany left her homeland and moved to America.
3. The Cherokee agreed to sell some of their land in a ____ they signed with the United States.
4. An ____ of the children lived in this town many years ago.
5. The ____ was one of the first colonists to move into an Indian area.

REVIEWING FACTS

1. From which places did immigrants to colonial North Carolina come?
2. In what ways were the lives of enslaved people controlled?
3. Why did North Carolina not approve the United States Constitution right away?
4. What did the Cherokee do to try to protect their rights? How successful were they?
5. How are the United States Constitution, the 13th Amendment, and Jim Crow laws related to civil rights?

WRITING ABOUT MAIN IDEAS

1. **Writing About History:** North Carolinians fought in the American Revolution in the 1770s and in the Civil War 90 years later. Write about the two wars in terms of: (1) why they were fought, (2) North Carolina's involvement, and (3) results.
2. **Writing About Perspectives:** Not everyone wanted to break away from Britain. Imagine a discussion in a home where the parents want to remain loyal to England. The son and daughter want to be free and to fight on the side of the colonies.

BUILDING SKILLS: IDENTIFYING FACT AND OPINION

Number a sheet of paper from 1 to 5. Beside each number write whether the statement is a fact or an opinion.

1. Today Wilmington is our state's most important port.
2. The Moravians began building Salem in 1766.
3. Indentured servants had a more difficult life than any other group in the colonies.
4. The Constitution should have given equal rights to all Americans.
5. Daniel Boone guided pioneers through the Cumberland Gap.

CHAPTER 6

OUR GROWING ECONOMY

FOCUS

For ten days every April and October my parents are especially busy with their furniture business. Those are the times of the International Furniture Market in the city. I try to help my parents at their showroom by greeting the customers.

Jenny Voysey likes being in her parents' showroom in High Point. Twice a year people from all over the world come to High Point to see the furniture styles. In this chapter you will read about the economic activities that have been important to our state.

LESSON

1 Farms Then and Now

READ TO LEARN

Key Vocabulary

agriculture sharecropping
technology

Read Aloud

When I first began to work on the farm, we used all mule-and-horse power. No tractors anywhere then. Most of the work was done by hand. . . . It was quite a hard job to tend [take care of] *a big crop.*

George Carter, a 77-year-old farmer who lives in Caswell County, tells us that he has seen great changes in farming in our state. In this lesson you will read about how our farms today are different from those of the past.

Read for Purpose

1. **WHAT YOU KNOW:** How do North Carolina's many natural resources help make farming possible?
2. **WHAT YOU WILL LEARN:** In what ways has farming in our state changed since the early 1800s?

A FARMING STATE

Do you enjoy eating peanuts, corn on the cob, and apples? All of these foods are grown by farmers in North Carolina. Tar Heel farmers grow more sweet potatoes and raise more turkeys than farmers do in any other state. Chickens and soybeans are other important products. North Carolina is also our country's top producer of tobacco.

It may surprise you to learn that very few of North Carolina's people earn a living from **agriculture** (ag′ ri kul chər). Agriculture is the business of raising crops and farm animals. Today only 2 out of every 100 North Carolinians are farmers. Yet less than 100 years ago, most workers in our state were farmers.

As you read in Chapter 5, the chance to own land drew farmers to

North Carolina in the past. They were attracted by the mild climate, long growing season, and fertile soil. However, life for these farmers was hard. They began to look for ways to grow more crops and to make their work easier.

CHALLENGES OF EARLY FARMING

Suppose that you are a farmer in the early 1800s. In the spring you rise early to prepare the soil for planting. Your tools are a wooden plow, a pitchfork, a rake, and a horse-drawn wagon. In the summer you weed fields with a hoe. In the fall you harvest the crops with a scythe (sīth). A scythe is a tool with a long, curved blade.

Although you work hard, you do not know if your crops will grow or die. You do not know how to protect crops from insects and disease. You do not know why your fields may grow only small amounts of a crop.

In the early 1800s farmers in North Carolina looked for new land when their fields became less fertile. By about 1820, when all the best land had been taken, many farmers began leaving the state.

BETTER FARMING METHODS

New **technology** (tek nol′ ə jē) brought great changes to agriculture in our state even before the late 1800s. Technology is the use of scientific know-how to find better ways of doing things. New technology produced new farming tools. For example, iron and steel plows and cultivators, or motor-driven machines to break up the soil, made it easier for farmers to prepare the land in the spring. Reapers, which

In the early 1800s farmers used a scythe *(shown below)* to harvest crops by hand. The crops were then taken to mills or to markets by wagon.

are machines for harvesting grain, made it much easier to gather crops in the fall.

Farmers also learned that planting the same crop in the same field year after year would wear out the soil. They learned that they must plant their crops in a different field every few years in order to keep the soil fertile.

New technology and new ways of farming have made farms more productive. To be more productive means that farmers can grow more crops than they did before.

SHARECROPPING

As you read in Chapter 5, slavery and the plantation system ended after the Civil War was over. Since most southern landowners had lost their wealth during the war, they had no money to pay the farm workers that they needed.

For this reason, many owners divided their land and rented it to black workers and white workers. These workers, in turn, paid their rent by giving the owners a large part of their crops. This way of using the land became known as **sharecropping**. These farm workers were called sharecroppers.

At first many sharecroppers were poor. They did not earn enough money from crop sales to pay for seeds and other things that they needed. By 1900 many sharecroppers and people with small family farms had begun to earn a better living. Some had formed groups that helped them work together to get cheaper supplies and higher prices for their crops. New railroads and

After the invention of steel plows *(shown below)*, which were drawn by horses, farmers no longer had to loosen the soil by hand.

roads made it possible for farmers to send their crops to many markets within our state.

A MAJOR CROP

A few farmers became very rich by growing and selling tobacco, which had become our state's leading crop by the early 1920s. Tobacco was first grown and used by Native Americans. They taught the colonists how to grow it.

The steps in growing and curing, or drying, tobacco are shown in the flowchart on page 167. It took farmers about 30 days of work to raise 1 acre (0.4 ha) of tobacco.

As the demand for tobacco grew, better farming machines were invented. Higher demand means that more people want to buy a product. It now takes a farmer about 5 days of work, instead of 30, to raise 1 acre (0.4 ha) of tobacco. A tractor now pulls a machine called a transplanter through the fields. It places young plants in the soil. When the plants are fully grown, farmers gather the crop with a tobacco harvester. Most farmers no longer cure the tobacco leaves over fires in wooden barns. They use natural gas or oil heaters to dry the leaves in large, metal barns.

North Carolina farmers produce two fifths of our country's tobacco. Over 600 million tons (500 metric t) of tobacco are grown here every year. In the past, most people did not know that smoking tobacco was harmful. Scientists have now proved that smoking causes disease, including lung cancer.

FARMING FOR THE FUTURE

Technology has greatly improved Tar Heel agriculture. But it has also caused new problems. For example, did you know that the chemicals used to keep insects away from plants are one cause of water pollution? Rainwater washes the chemicals into lakes and rivers. Scientists are trying to grow plants that do not become diseased.

Another problem for farmers is the high cost of new machines. Many farmers do not have the money to buy them. Also, people who own small farms often have to charge high prices in order to make money. But large farms owned by big companies can produce such large amounts that they can sell

GROWING AND CURING OF TOBACCO

1. In spring workers plant tobacco seeds in beds.

2. Young tobacco plants are planted in fields and cared for during summer.

3. In fall workers tie the leaves into bundles and hang them to dry.

4. Later in fall the tobacco is cured by wood fires in large barns.

DIAGRAM SKILL: During which season did workers often pull weeds and check the plants for disease and insects?

their products for less than small farmers can. George Carter, whom you read about in the Read Aloud, describes the challenges that farmers now face.

> *The farmer has sort of a [hard] time, but it's just like any other business. You've got to . . . plan for whatever you do.*

Many farmers think that growing new crops may help them to stay in business. Fruits and vegetables that were once only grown in other countries are being grown in North Carolina today.

THE IMPORTANCE OF FARMING

You have read that new technology has improved farming in our state. However, some of this technology has added to pollution and made farming more costly. Farmers in North Carolina are working to find answers to these challenges.

Check Your Reading

1. In what ways has farming in North Carolina changed since the early 1800s?
2. What is sharecropping?
3. What are some of the results of the improvements that have been made in agriculture?
4. **THINKING SKILL:** What three questions could you ask a North Carolina farmer in order to learn more about farming today?

Should Chemicals Be Used to Grow Crops?

You have just read how new technology has changed farming methods in our state. This technology helps farmers to produce large amounts of food for North Carolina, and for people in other states and countries. To help them grow so much food, many farmers use chemicals. Farm chemicals include special sprays or powders that prevent crop disease and keep insects away. They also include fertilizers that help plants to grow. Farmers who use chemicals say that they cut down on the number of workers needed to raise crops. They say that using chemicals saves them money.

Some farmers do not think that chemicals should be used to grow food. They argue that our state could produce just as much food without chemicals. For example, insects that eat crops could be kept away by spraying crops with soapy water. Those who are against the use of chemicals also say that chemicals harm our water, soil, and health. They argue that farm soil would last longer if we did not use chemicals. Should chemicals be used to grow crops?

POINT

Farm Chemicals Should Be Used

Many people say that farm chemicals are safe. Without chemicals, they argue, farmers could not grow enough food to feed everyone. They believe it would cost more money to grow food without chemicals because farmers would need to hire more workers to grow and care for crops. This is what Dr. John Anderson, a teacher of agriculture at North Carolina State University, says about farm chemicals.

> Chemicals take the place of more people working on our farms. . . . Without farm chemicals, we would have a lot less food to choose from in our grocery stores.
>
> The new chemicals that farmers use today are safe for our environment. . . . These cause less harm than many people think. If we want a large food supply, we need the help of farm chemicals.

- According to John Anderson, why should chemicals be used to grow our crops?

COUNTERPOINT

Farm Chemicals Should Not Be Used

Some groups of people are against using farm chemicals. They believe that we can grow enough food for everyone without using them. Their concern is that chemicals hurt the health of both people and the soil. Kate Havel, a member of a group called the Carolina Farm Stewardship Association, argues that farming without chemicals is a good idea.

> We can grow as much food [without chemicals] . . . as we do with chemical[s]. . . . We may have to pay more for [workers], but we would not have to pay for chemicals.
>
> Farm chemicals affect our drinking water, . . . stay on our food, and can damage our health. . . .
>
> Chemicals steal [minerals] from the soil. . . . We can use natural ways to build up soil, so that it stays healthy without chemicals.

- According to Kate Havel, why should food be grown without chemicals?

UNDERSTANDING THE POINT/COUNTERPOINT

1. In your opinion, which side has the stronger case? Why?
2. Which other groups of people might have opinions about farming methods?
3. Is there anything the two sides might be able to agree on? If so, give an example.

LESSON

2 Linking the Regions

READ TO LEARN

Key Vocabulary

corduroy road
plank road

Key People

Harriet Morehead Berry

Key Places

Intracoastal Waterway

Read Aloud

Ten o'clock Sunday morning in the hills of North Carolina. Cars, miles of cars, in every direction, millions of cars, pastel cars. . .

Writer Tom Wolfe used these words in 1963 to describe highways crowded with cars going to a car race. However, 40 years earlier many places in our state had had only narrow dirt roads. Read on to find out about the building of our state's transportation system.

Read for Purpose

1. WHAT YOU KNOW: Why was it difficult for North Carolina's farmers to get their goods to market in the past?
2. WHAT YOU WILL LEARN: How has transportation helped to link the three regions of North Carolina with each other and the rest of the world?

A SLOW BEGINNING

You have read about how limited transportation was in North Carolina during the early 1800s. Our state's mountains, swamps, and barrier islands made it hard for farmers to travel to market. The farmers who lived along the Cape Fear River were able to use the river to move their goods. However, other rivers in our state were not wide or deep enough for large ships.

Most farmers had to move their goods over land. At first they followed the trails that the Native Americans had made for trading. However, the Europeans soon made these trails wider to allow wagons to travel over them. They also built many new roads.

During the 1760s farmers who lived in the wetlands began to improve their transportation by building **corduroy roads**. Corduroy roads were made from logs placed side by side. These corduroy roads made it easier for wagons to travel in the wetlands. However, traveling over logs made for a bumpy ride.

BETTER ROADS

Roads in our state improved slowly. In 1753 a wagon could go only 15 miles (24 km) in one day. More than 75 years later, a wagon could travel 30 miles (48 km) a day.

In 1849 the Fayetteville and Western Plank Road Company started building **plank roads**. Planks are long, flat pieces of wood. Workers placed planks over thick, heavy pieces of wood. Then they covered the planks with sand, gravel, or dirt. Plank roads were smoother than corduroy roads.

Plank roads greatly improved transportation. The following news story appeared in the *Fayetteville Observer* on July 15, 1851.

> *One of our most successful farmers, a few days ago, brought to town on the plank road . . . 117 bushels [4,123 L] of meal [and] 200 pounds [91 kgs] of lard. [The] distance traveled to and fro was 26 miles [42 km], which was made with ease in one day.*

RAILROADS

Transportation improved even more after 1840 with the building of the Wilmington and Weldon Railroad. The railroad was named for the two cities it connected. It was 161 miles (259 km) long, which made it the longest railroad in the world. From Wilmington, goods could be shipped to other states.

Both **corduroy roads** *(right)* and **plank roads** *(left)* made it easier for farmers to travel to markets.

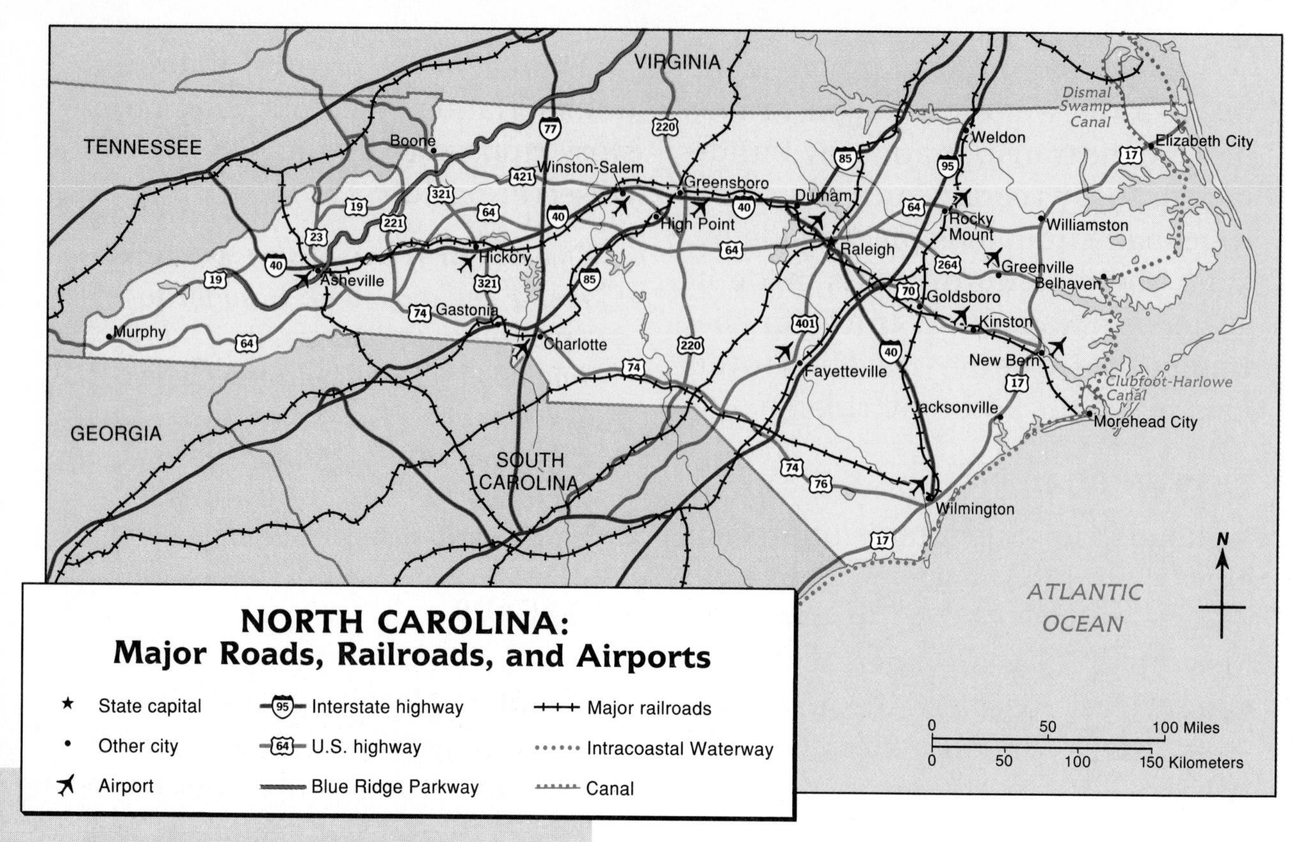

MAP SKILL: Is the shortest route from Wilmington to Fayetteville by railroad or by automobile?

In 1856 another railroad was built. The North Carolina Railroad ran between Goldsboro and Charlotte. It connected the Piedmont with the Coastal Plain.

Once farmers could move their products to market, more of them began to grow cash crops. The railroads especially helped the Piedmont Region. Many towns along the route of the North Carolina Railroad grew into large cities.

WATERWAYS

Find Wilmington on the map. It is located on an important state waterway called the **Intracoastal Waterway**. This water highway is made up of the many inlets, sounds, bays, and rivers that form our coast. As you can see on the map, canals join the different parts of the waterway. They provide a way for ships to travel along the coast.

SUPERHIGHWAYS

In the early 1900s most of the roads in our state were dirt. They turned into mud when it rained. In 1918 **Harriet Morehead Berry** worked for the state government. She suggested that the state build a highway system. Berry went all over the state making speeches about the need for highways.

In 1921 a law was passed that set up our state highway system.

Today North Carolina has more than 76,000 miles (122,000 km) of state highways and roads. We have more roads than any other state has. This is why North Carolina is known as "The Good Roads State."

AIRPORTS

Orville and Wilbur Wright would be surprised if they could see air travel in our state today. Hundreds of airports connect our state with other states and countries. The largest airport is Charlotte–Douglas International in Charlotte.

Every day thousands of people fly into or out of these airports. They come to do business or to visit the many recreation areas that we have in our state.

The Charlotte-Douglas International Airport in Charlotte is one of the busiest airports in the state. It has more than 300 flights a day

COMMUNICATION

Today a letter can be delivered overnight almost anywhere in the world. During the early 1800s, however, North Carolinians had little communication with people outside their own community. This changed in the late 1880s, when electric power began to be used here. Today television, radios, telephones, and fax machines help people to share ideas and information.

A LONG WAY

North Carolina's geography kept the three regions apart for many years. When good roads and railroads were built, they helped to improve the economy of our state. Today railroads, highways, airplanes, and telephones connect us to other places.

Check Your Reading

1. Describe the difference between corduroy roads and plank roads.
2. What is the Intracoastal Waterway? Why is it important?
3. Identify some of the forms of transportation in North Carolina. Explain how they help link our state's regions with each other and the rest of the world.
4. **THINKING SKILL:** Compare and contrast transportation in North Carolina during the 1850s with transportation today.

BUILDING SKILLS
GEOGRAPHY SKILLS

Reading Road Maps and Mileage Charts

Key Vocabulary

road map
mileage chart
interstate highway

You have read that roads in our state have helped to change transportation and to make North Carolina grow. Roads have been built to take you almost anywhere in the state.

Suppose that you wanted to visit Historic Bethabara Park in Winston-Salem. How would you know how to get there?

Road Maps

One way would be to use a **road map**. Road maps show travelers how to get from one place to another by road. A road map of North Carolina shows its cities and towns and the roads that connect them. Look at the road map below. It shows the roads in

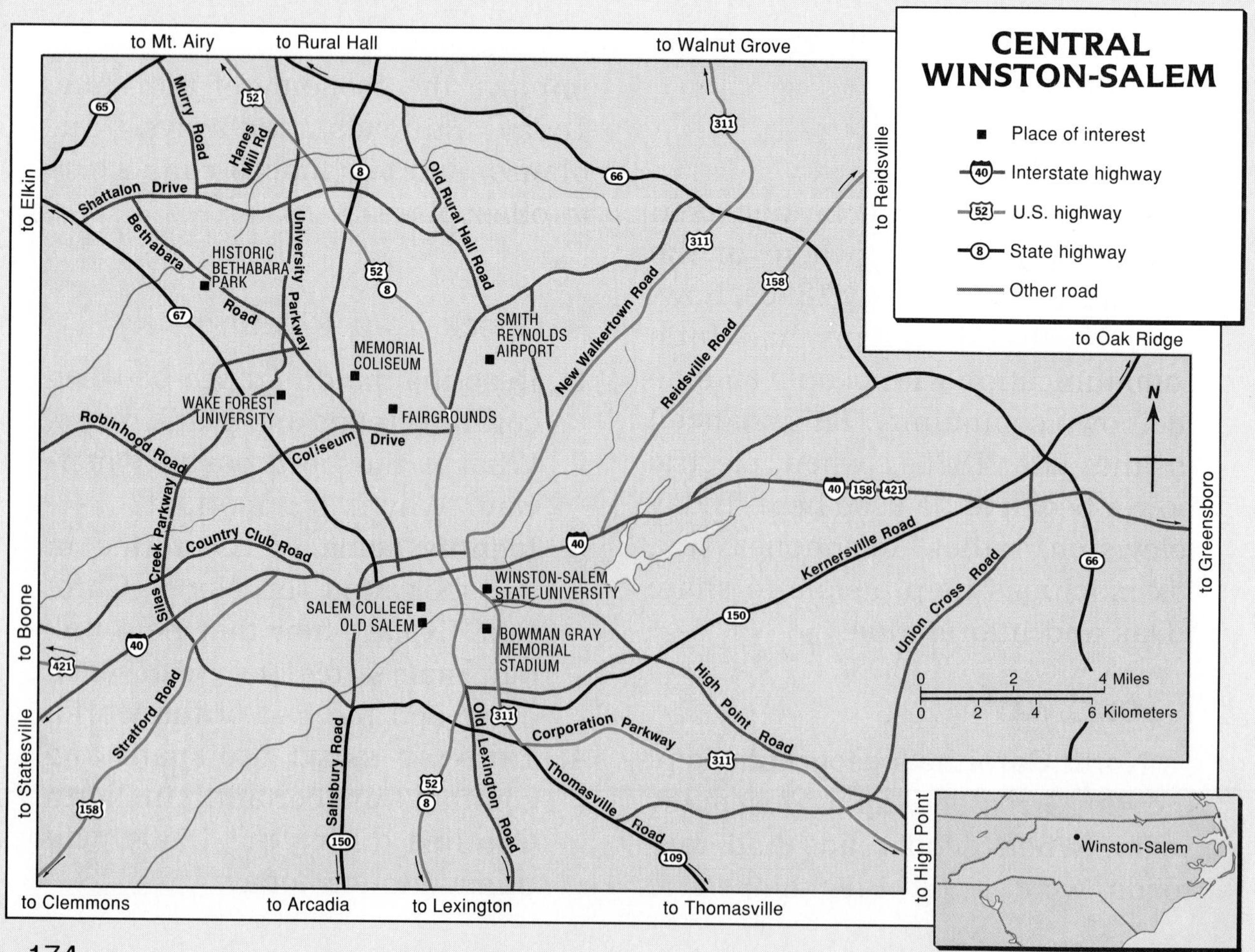

and around the city of Winston-Salem. The **interstate highways** are shown in purple lines. The word *interstate* means "between or among two or more states." Interstate highways are wide, with two or more lanes in each direction. The interstate highway shown on the map is I-40.

The red lines on the map show other United States highways. U.S. highways 311, 158, and 52 run through Winston-Salem.

State highways are built by the state and stop at the state's borders. They are shown in black on the map. Routes 8 and 67 are state highways that run through Winston-Salem.

Road maps that cover a large area, such as a whole state, usually include most of its interstate, U.S., and state roads. The map on page 361 is a good example of this type of map. Maps that cover a smaller area, such as the map of Winston-Salem on page 174, often have only enough space to include some smaller roads and streets. What is another name for State Highway 109? Where is Murry Road?

Numbers and Symbols

Most roads are marked with numbers that are printed inside special symbols. Some roads have more than one number because they are part of more than one highway. For example, U.S. Highway 52 runs together with

State Highway 8 through Winston-Salem. Odd-numbered roads on the road map usually run north and south. Even-numbered roads usually run east and west. 311 is the number of the U.S. highway that runs southeast from Winston-Salem toward High Point. What is the number of the highway that runs north-south through the middle of Winston-Salem? Is it an interstate highway, a U.S. highway, or a North Carolina state highway?

Planning a Route

Suppose that you lived on Hanes Mill Road in the northwestern part of Winston-Salem and you wanted to go to Old Salem. One way to get there would be to go south on U.S. Route 52 and then west on Interstate 40 to the exit for Old Salem. Name one way you could go by car from Old Salem to Historic Bethabara Park.

How Far Is It?

Suppose that you wanted to know how far it is from Winston-Salem to Fayetteville. You might use a map, referring to its scale to measure the distance. Or you might use a **mileage chart** instead. A mileage chart is a table that shows the distances between specific places. Some mileage charts show distances by air, while others show distances by road, railroad, or water. How are distances measured on the mileage chart below?

How to Read a Mileage Chart

Look at the mileage chart. First read the title. It tells you that this is a mileage chart of our state. Next read the labels along the top and the side of the chart. You will notice that the same cities are listed in alphabetical order in both places. The distance between them is in road miles.

Suppose that you want to find the distance between the cities of Charlotte and Raleigh. Find Charlotte listed on the side and place your left index finger there. Now find Raleigh listed on the top and place your right index finger there. Move your fingers, one down and the other across, until they meet. The number *143* means the two cities are 143 miles apart.

Have you noticed that there is a blank space in each row on the chart? The blank space is where each city listed on the side meets the same city listed on the top. There is no distance between a city and itself, so this area of the chart is left blank.

MILEAGE CHART NORTH CAROLINA CITIES

Road Distance in Miles	Charlotte	Fayetteville	New Bern	Raleigh	Winston-Salem
Charlotte		141	246	143	81
Fayetteville	141		110	59	118
New Bern	246	110		112	220
Raleigh	143	59	112		104
Winston-Salem	81	118	220	104	

Reviewing the Skill

1. What is a road map? What is a mileage chart?
2. What kind of road is Route 66?
3. Plan a route from Winston-Salem State University to Wake Forest University.
4. Use the road mileage chart to determine the distance between Winston-Salem and Fayetteville.
5. Why is it important to be able to read a road map? How can reading a mileage chart help you?

LESSON

3 Industry Then and Now

READ TO LEARN

Key Vocabulary	Key Places	Key People
manufacturing	Lincolnton	Michael Schenck
raw material	Gastonia	James W. Cannon
industry		Warren C. Coleman
textile		
labor		
synthetic		
automate		

Read Aloud

We go to the North for everything from a toothpick to a president.

In 1880 the Raleigh newspaper the *News and Observer* worried that the Tar Heel state bought most of its goods from outside the state. In this lesson you will read how North Carolina began to make goods for its own people and for people in other states and countries.

Read for Purpose

1. **WHAT YOU KNOW:** How did most North Carolinians earn their living in the past?
2. **WHAT YOU WILL LEARN:** How has the growth of industry changed North Carolina?

MANUFACTURING

Look around your classroom. Does it have anything in it that was made in North Carolina? Some of the furniture was most likely made in High Point. As you read in Chapter 1, if you're wearing denim, it, too, was probably made here.

Today North Carolina's factories bring more money into the state than any other kind of business does. In fact, North Carolina is one of the country's chief **manufacturing** states. Manufacturing is the making of many goods by machine.

Manufacturing offers jobs for about one fourth of North Carolina's workers. Every day Tar Heel workers turn **raw materials** such as tobacco, cotton, and wood from our forests into finished goods such as tobacco products, clothing, and furniture. A raw material is a natural resource that has not been changed or prepared in any way. Now that so many North Carolinians are working in manufacturing, it may be hard to believe that 150 years ago, our state had few large factories.

EARLY FACTORIES

Our first manufacturing businesses were started about 200 years ago to help farmers. The earliest factories were the mills that people built in the Piedmont along fast-moving rivers or at waterfalls. At sawmills, water-powered saws cut raw materials such as logs into planks and barrel parts. At grist mills, waterwheels moved two large smooth stones against each other to grind corn into cornmeal and wheat into flour.

Another early **industry** in our state was naval stores. An industry is made up of all the businesses that produce the same goods for sale. From the early 1700s until about 1865, North Carolinians produced and sold more turpentine, tar, and other naval stores than any other product. But manufacturing grew slowly in our state.

THE TEXTILE INDUSTRY

An important step in the growth of manufacturing was taken in 1813. At that time **Michael Schenck** began to use water power to make thread. Schenck had come to our state from Pennsylvania in 1790. He built the state's first **textile** mill along a stream near **Lincolnton**. Textiles are cloth and other materials made by knitting or weaving. The word *textile* is also used for the thread and yarn for making cloth.

At Schenck's mill, workers used machines to spin cotton into thread. The thread was sold to northern textile mills, where it was woven into cloth. In 1819 Schenck and other businesspeople opened a larger textile mill, where they made cotton cloth, ropes, and candle wicks.

Poor transportation routes still made it costly to manufacture goods. In the early 1840s a mill owner named Henry Humphreys met this challenge by building a

textile mill near cotton fields. Now he no longer had to transport cotton to his mill from a distance. Humphreys's mill was the first of more than 200 mills in Gaston County. Today the city of **Gastonia** is a textile manufacturing center.

The textile industry grew even larger after **James W. Cannon** decided to manufacture a new textile product. In the 1800s most people used cheap cloth or flour sacks for drying. In 1898 a Cannon mill made the first towel manufactured in the Southeast. By 1914 Cannon mills, such as those at Kannapolis, were making 300,000 towels each day. Find Kannapolis on the map below.

The Cannon Mills Company bought mills from others. One of these mills had been owned by **Warren C. Coleman**. He was the first African American to own a textile mill in our state. His mill in Concord was one of the few that hired African-American workers.

In the 1900s textile mills began to use electricity to power their machines. After more railroads were built in the state, it was easier and cheaper for mill owners to transport raw materials and products. Trains carried almost all of our state's textiles until about 60 years ago, when good roads made shipping textiles by truck possible.

MILL WORKERS

The early textile mills were often built along a stream in the countryside. To attract **labor**, or workers, to these mills, the owners built houses for their workers. Often the owners also built a school, church, and a

MAP SKILL: Early factories such as Michael Schenck's cotton mill *(left)* were run by water power. Which mills were built near rivers?

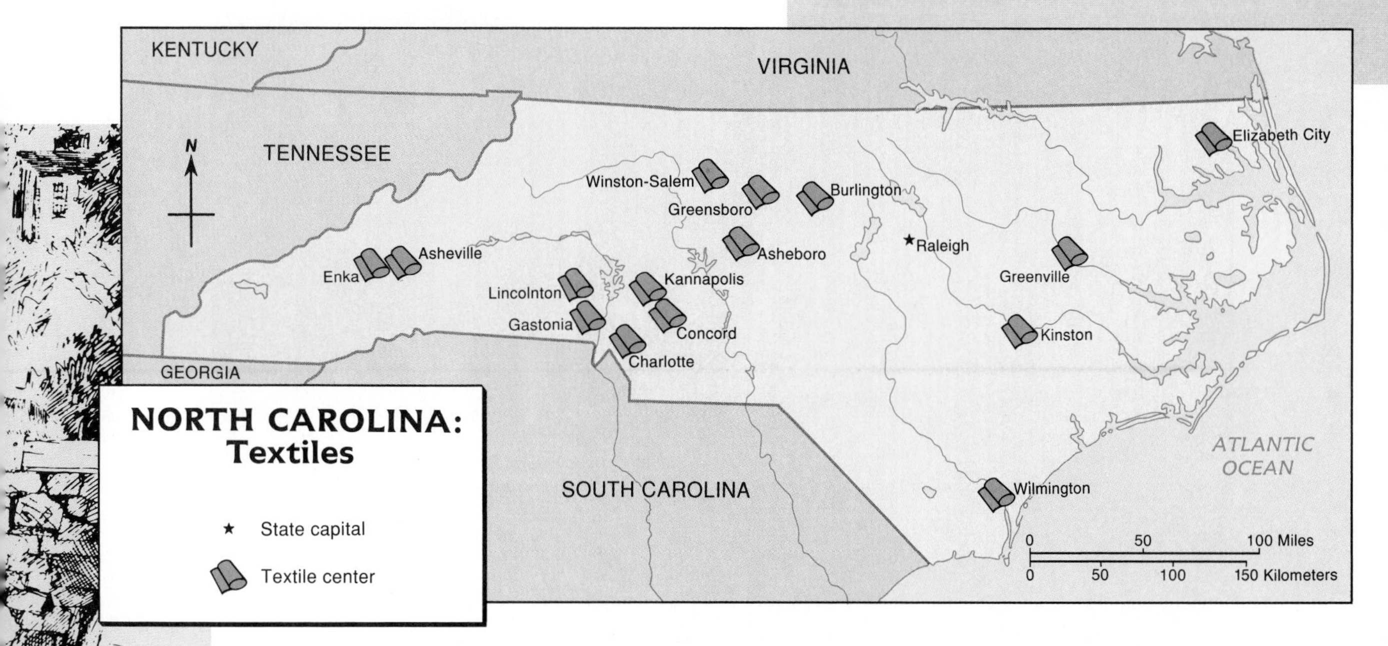

company store where workers could buy the goods they needed. These and other buildings formed a mill village, which was a small town built and owned by a manufacturing company.

Mill jobs were low-paying and dull. Most workers in textile mills were white women. However, mill jobs offered steady work and pay. One textile worker described her job in this way:

> *I like the farm better than the factory any day, but on a farm you just work yourself to a frazzle and don't get a thing for it.*

TEXTILES TODAY

Since 1945 there have been many changes in manufacturing in our state. Some of these changes have been made possible by new technology. For example, for the textile industry technology has created many new kinds of cloth. Have you ever read the labels on your shirts? Each label tells the size of the shirt and the kind of cloth in it.

Many shirts have cotton or wool in them. Cotton is made from a plant, and wool comes from animal hair. However, other shirts are made of materials such as polyester or rayon. These materials do not come from either plants or animals. Instead, they are **synthetic** (sin thət′ ik) materials. Synthetic materials are made in laboratories from chemicals.

Scientists create such synthetic textiles because they have special uses. For example, rayon looks and

Today **synthetic** materials are often used to make products such as elastic *(below)* or are mixed with cotton to make towels.

feels like silk. But it can be washed and cleaned more easily than silk. Nylon makes a good carpet material because it lasts a long time.

AUTOMATION

Another change in textile manufacturing has been in its machinery. Today many factories are **automated**. An automated factory is one in which machines run on their own or are run by other machines. For example, in an automated factory, computers guide machines to make many new designs.

Greater use of machines has meant that less labor is needed in some factory jobs. North Carolina's textile industry has more workers than any other manufacturing industry in our state. However, their number is growing smaller. Our textile industry is also losing business to foreign textile companies. The foreign companies sell products at cheaper prices.

Some of North Carolina's other industries—such as tobacco products and furniture making—have also become automated. You will read more about these industries in Chapters 8, 9, and 10.

INDUSTRY YESTERDAY AND TODAY

As you have read, manufacturing is an important industry in the Tar Heel state. At first, manufacturing grew slowly. However, textile and other industries grew faster after business owners found better ways to run their machines and transport their goods. Today the textile industry remains an important industry in North Carolina.

Many modern textile factories in our state use large, **automated** knitting machines to make cloth.

Check Your Reading

1. What is an industry?
2. Why did early manufacturing grow slowly in our state?
3. How has the growth of industry changed North Carolina?
4. **THINKING SKILL:** How are automated factories different from older factories? Explain how the two might be the same.

Understanding Cause and Effect

Key Vocabulary

cause effect

Lisa studied hard for the social studies test. When she took the test, she got all the answers right. Studying hard was the **cause** of her getting the answers right. A cause is something that makes something else happen. Answering correctly was the **effect** of careful studying. An effect is what happens as a result of something else.

Read the two sentences below.

- Alex has the largest baseball card collection in his class.
- Alex walks his neighbor's dog every afternoon to earn money.

The first sentence states a fact that exists. The second sentence states the cause, or reason that the fact came to be. Alex has a large baseball card collection because he earns the extra money to buy the cards.

Identifying cause and effect will help you to understand how events are related. You will see how one event leads to another.

Trying the Skill

Read each sentence below. Then tell which sentence states a cause and which sentence states an effect.

- The Piedmont Region of North Carolina is famous for the manufacture of fine wood furniture.
- Almost half of North Carolina is covered with trees.

HELPING YOURSELF

The steps on the left can help you to identify causes and effects. The example on the right shows one way to apply these steps to the two sentences on the previous page.

One Way to Find Cause and Effect	Example
1. Look at the events or situations being described.	A great deal of wood furniture is manufactured in the Piedmont.
2. In each sentence look for words that signal causes, such as *because*, *since*, and *as a result of*. If you do not find any word clues, ask yourself if one event is the reason that something else happened.	Does the presence of many trees in the area help to make a furniture industry successful?
3. If the answer is yes, you have found a cause.	The fact that there are many trees could lead to the growth of a furniture industry.
4. Look for words that signal effects, such as *so*, *therefore*, and *as a result*. If you do not find any of these word clues, ask yourself what happened as a result of the cause. What happened is an effect.	Because there are many trees, North Carolina can manufacture large amounts of fine furniture.

Applying the Skill

Now apply what you have learned. Read each pair of sentences below. Which of the sentences states the cause and which states the effect?

- The Durham Bulls practice hard many times a week.
- The Bulls win almost every game.
- Karen received a Good Citizen's Award.
- Karen spent Saturday helping to clean up Eno River Park.

Now check yourself by answering the following questions.

1. What is the first thing you should do to identify cause and effect?
   - **a.** Find the cause.
   - **b.** Look at the events described.
   - **c.** Ask what happened.
2. What is one effect of practicing hard?
3. What is one effect of cleaning up a public park?

Reviewing the Skill

1. What is the difference between a cause and an effect?
2. Why is it important to tell the difference between causes and effects?

LESSON

4 Cities Grow

READ TO LEARN

Key Vocabulary

metropolitan area
population density
hydroelectric

Key Places

High Point
Piedmont Urban Crescent
Charlotte
Durham
Winston-Salem

Read Aloud

Quail hunting was good in fields that now are suburbs. . . . An airplane flying over was a big event.

These words describe how Mary Kratt remembers her hometown of Charlotte in the 1940s. Charlotte has changed in many ways since then. In this lesson you will read about how some of North Carolina's cities have grown and changed.

Read for Purpose

1. **WHAT YOU KNOW:** Do you live in a city, a town, or a village?
2. **WHAT YOU WILL LEARN:** How have cities in North Carolina changed and grown?

RAILROADS AND CITIES

During the years following the Civil War, some of North Carolina's cities began to grow. Gastonia, Raleigh, Greensboro, and Charlotte all started to be lively, busy places.

In the past these cities were mostly centers where farmers went to buy supplies and exchange news with their neighbors. In the late 1860s people went there to start businesses and to open factories. These factories and businesses offered new jobs for people who were leaving the farms in our state.

The railroads played an important part in these changes. Once a place became a railroad center, factories often followed, turning small towns into cities.

For example, because of the North Carolina Railroad, **High Point** became a center for the furniture industry. The railroad made it possible to ship furniture to regions all over the United States. Today thousands of people work in the furniture industry in and near High Point. Our state's Southern Furniture Exposition Building in High Point is an important furniture market for the entire country.

SPREADING CITIES

The people who live and work in High Point are part of what is called a **metropolitan area**. A metropolitan area is a large city or a group of cities together with their nearby suburbs. Find the city of High Point on the map below.

High Point is part of a crowded area called the **Piedmont Urban Crescent** (kres′ ənt). This curved area is formed by several cities. Find the inset, or small map, of the Piedmont Urban Crescent on the **population density** map below. Population density is the number of people living in a square mile or square kilometer of an area.

CITY LIFE

Good transportation connects our state's metropolitan areas. An example is given by Charles Tompkins, who manages a furniture factory in High Point. He describes city life in the following way.

> *I live in Lexington. I'm 20 minutes from my office in High Point and 35 minutes from Greensboro. I can live in one [city] and still be a citizen of the whole Piedmont.*

MAP SKILL: What is the **population density** of Charlotte, Winston-Salem, Raleigh, and Wilmington? Are they all in the **Piedmont Urban Crescent**?

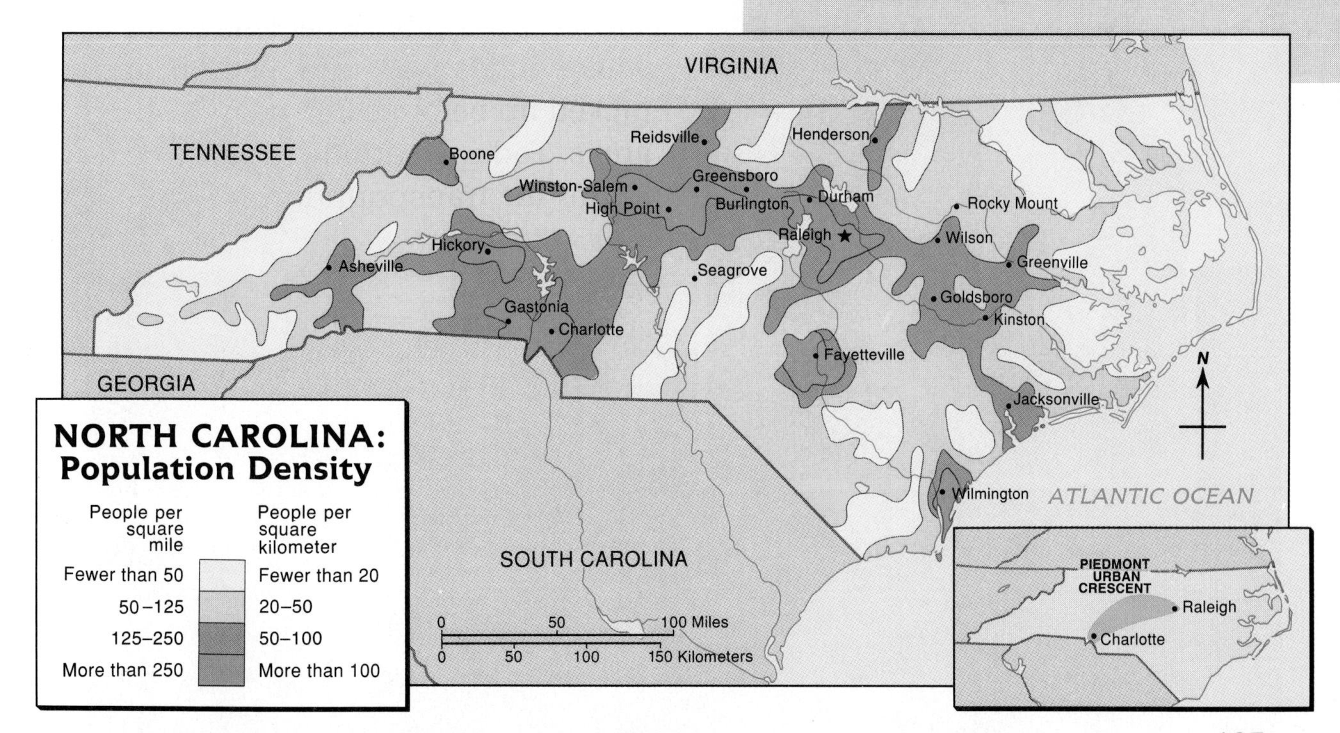

Our state's good roads and superhighways make it possible to live in one place, work in a second place, and find entertainment in a third. Today nearly half of our state's population lives in areas with high population densities.

CHARLOTTE

In 1791 our country's first president, George Washington, visited the small town of Charlotte. He called it a "trifling place," or one that was not important. Washington might be surprised if he visited Charlotte today. He would see that the small town had become a city with nearly 400,000 people.

Charlotte grew mostly because of its location on the North Carolina Railroad. In fact, Charlotte became a railroad hub, or center, for many different railroad lines that connected with other states. By the year 1900 Charlotte had six major railroad lines.

Charlotte grew even more after 1904. At that time a hydroelectric plant was built on the Catawba River. Hydroelectric means the production of electricity by water. As you can see from the map on page 187, many hydroelectric plants have been built on the river. Hydroelectric power drew more factories to Charlotte. By 1920 there were more than 300 textile mills in the area around Charlotte.

Manufacturing firms also were attracted to Charlotte because of its highways and railroads. Its location caused Charlotte to become a place where goods were dropped off and picked up before being sent to other areas. Today Charlotte is also a center for air transportation.

The metropolitan area of Charlotte has many open spaces in which people can meet, relax, and shop.

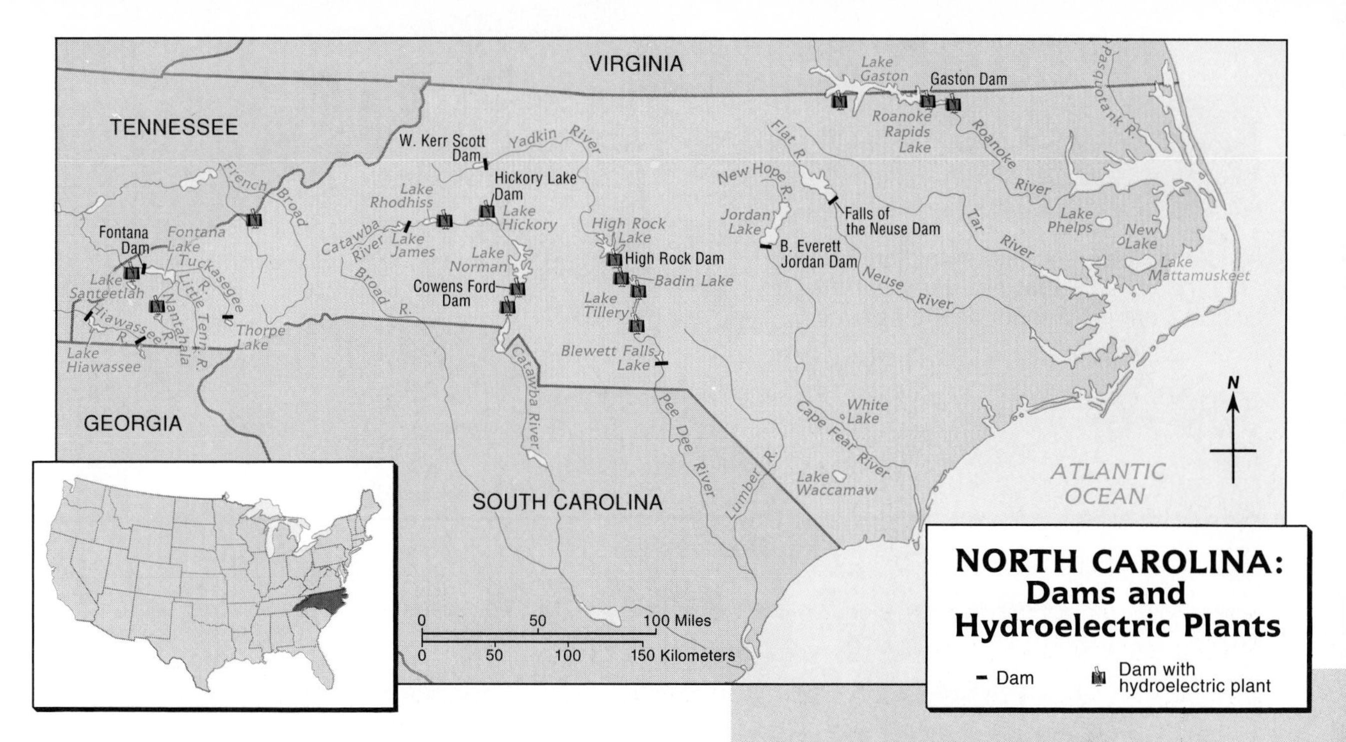

MAP SKILL: Which rivers on the map have more than one dam with a hydroelectric plant on them?

IMPROVING THE FUTURE

Raleigh, Durham, and Chapel Hill are all cities in the Piedmont Urban Crescent. Raleigh is the capital of our state. Durham is the fifth-largest city in North Carolina. Chapel Hill is an education center. These cities all share one thing. They are part of a metropolitan area in which people work to improve life in the future.

As you will read in Chapter 8, Durham is near the Research Triangle Park. The Park was built near three well-known universities. They are the University of North Carolina at Chapel Hill, Duke University in Durham, and North Carolina State University at Raleigh. Students and teachers from all three universities work in the Park.

Many different studies are being done at the Park. For example, some people are trying to improve crops. Others are trying to find ways to get rid of chemical waste safely. Each day new information is being discovered by workers at the Research Triangle Park.

WINSTON-SALEM

In Chapter 4 you read about the town of Salem that was settled by the Moravians. The Moravians planned Salem as a center for trade. As you read, people went to Salem for the fine goods produced by the Moravians. Later, mills such as gristmills and sawmills began to open in Salem.

Nearby, a small town called Winston was growing. The town planners in Salem liked the idea of

Fashion designing and music are two of the many skills that are taught at the North Carolina School of the Arts in Winston-Salem.

having another town nearby. It was good for their trade. In 1913 the two towns became Winston-Salem.

Today Winston-Salem is part of a large metropolitan area. Like many large cities, it has tall buildings filled with offices, shops, and eating places. Some of the city's older buildings have been fixed up and put to new uses. For example, an old movie theater is now the home of the North Carolina School of the Arts. Its students come from all over the country.

CENTERS OF INDUSTRY

After the Civil War, towns in North Carolina began to grow faster and to change. Railroads, highways, and both new and growing industries all helped to bring about these changes. Some small towns became centers of certain industries. Today our metropolitan areas are creating even more jobs for many people in North Carolina.

Check Your Reading

1. Of which industry is High Point the center?
2. What is a metropolitan area?
3. How have cities in North Carolina changed and grown?
4. **GEOGRAPHY SKILL:** Look at the map on page 185. Name five large cities that are part of the Piedmont Urban Crescent.
5. **THINKING SKILL:** How did railroads cause our cities to grow?

LESSON

5 Growth of Services

READ TO LEARN

Key Vocabulary

service industries
retire
tourism
insurance

Key People

John Merrick
Aaron Moore
Charles C. Spaulding

Read Aloud

Although my part in the movie was only two minutes long, we did it over and over until the director got the scene just the way he wanted it. In the scene I was sitting on a bench at the school lunch table, and another boy kept pushing me off. . . . It was harder work than I [had] thought, but it was neat.

Eleven-year-old Evan Dalrymple is describing his role in a "monster movie" made in Wilmington. Many North Carolinians have worked as actors on movies filmed here. Filmmaking is one of our fast-growing industries.

Read for Purpose

1. **WHAT YOU KNOW:** How do farming and manufacturing contribute to our state's economy?
2. **WHAT YOU WILL LEARN:** What kinds of services are part of our state's economy? Why are they important?

A GROWING INDUSTRY

In this chapter you have read about how farmers and manufacturing workers help our state's economy. Another group of people who help our economy are those in the service industries. Service industries are ones in which workers do things that help people. For example, service workers may put out fires or deliver the mail.

There have always been service workers in our state. But today, more North Carolinians work in services than they did in the past. Look at the circle graph on page 371 of the Almanac. How many North Carolinians hold service jobs?

Police officers and the workers who care for our roads are part of the service industries. They make our state a safe place in which to live.

One reason for the rise in services is the gain in the number of people in our state. Every year about 10,000 people retire in North Carolina. To retire means to stop working, usually when a person is older and has worked many years.

People who retire to our state enjoy the mild climate and the many services that North Carolina provides. Among them are our fine medical services. In fact, one city, Durham, is called the "City of Medicine" because of its many hospitals and medical services.

GOVERNMENT SERVICES

Our local, state, and federal governments also provide services. These are paid for by the taxes we pay. Local government workers include firefighters, police officers, and garbage collectors. State workers include those who build roads and help care for the environment.

Many North Carolinians are in the military. They are part of the armed services branch of the federal government. Men and women in the military fight and risk their lives for our country in wartime.

SERVING TOURISTS

Some parts of the service industry are growing faster than others. One of these industries is tourism (tůr′ iz əm). Tourism is the business of offering services to people who are on vacation. Over 200,000 North Carolinians work in tourism. They include tour guides, hotel workers, and ski instructors.

Imagine that you are planning to travel around our state. You would

The Biltmore Estate, the USS *North Carolina*, and the zoo all provide jobs for service workers.

probably first write to the tourism office in Raleigh, the state capital, for information about areas to see.

After you decide where you want to go, you might go to a person called a travel agent. He or she can help you plan your trip, obtain a place to stay, and buy bus, plane, or train tickets.

The travel agent most likely will give you facts about places to see, such as the battleship USS *North Carolina*. It is docked near Wilmington. For the Piedmont Region, the travel agent may say that you might visit the North Carolina Zoological Park near Asheboro. A well-known place in the mountains is the 225-room Biltmore Estate. These places have service workers who give tours, care for the places, and answer questions.

BANKING AND INSURANCE

Many service workers help to take care of money. Several of our country's largest banks are located in North Carolina. They provide many banking services for people, businesses, and governments.

Another widely used service is **insurance**. Insurance is a protection against financial loss. People buy insurance to help them in the event of sickness and emergencies. For example, if a flood causes damage to a home, insurance money will help pay for the repairs.

Durham is home to an important African-American business, the North Carolina Mutual Life Insurance Company. The company was begun in 1899 by **John Merrick**, a barber, and **Aaron Moore**, a doctor. The company sold insurance to African Americans. At that time few southern companies sold insurance to African Americans.

The partners hired Moore's nephew **Charles C. Spaulding** to run their insurance company. By 1950, when Spaulding retired, North Carolina Mutual was making millions of dollars.

THAT'S ENTERTAINMENT

North Carolina has become an important filmmaking center. In the last 20 years more than 150 films have been made here. Many filmmakers come to our state because of its many landforms. As one film director, Dino de Laurentiis, says,

> *You can find any geographical setting for filming you want in North Carolina, except the desert.*

Filmmaking is a service industry that helps our economy to grow. Filmmakers spend a lot of money in hotels and restaurants. They also rent cars and office equipment.

One of the largest film studios in the country is in Wilmington. The "monster movie" you read about in the Read Aloud was filmed here.

Setting up and running the movie cameras is one of the many interesting jobs in filmmaking.

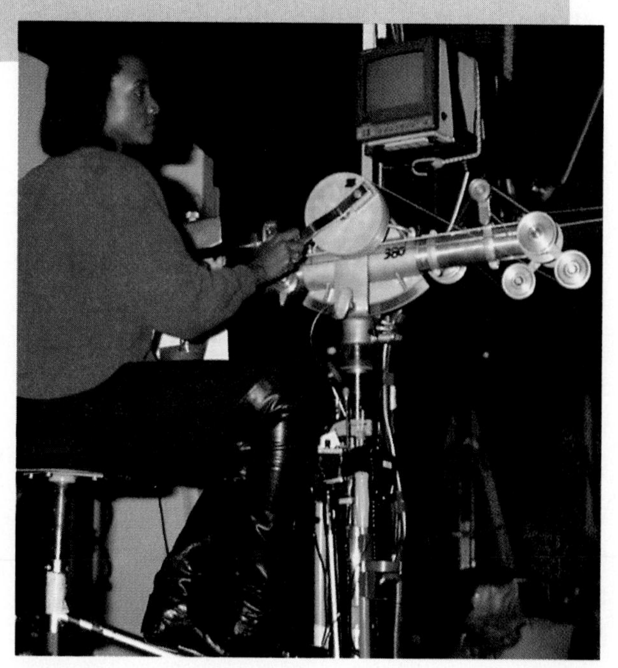

MEETING PEOPLE'S NEEDS

You have read about the kinds of services that have become a big part of North Carolina's economy. These services provide jobs that help our state's economy to grow and meet the varied needs of our people.

Check Your Reading

1. What are the major service industries in North Carolina? Why are they important?
2. Name some service jobs that are not mentioned in this lesson.
3. Why is Charles Spaulding important?
4. **THINKING SKILL:** List three questions that you could ask a service worker to find out more about her or his job.

REVIEWING VOCABULARY

Number a sheet of paper from 1 to 5. Beside each number write **T** if the statement is true. If the statement is false, rewrite it to make it true.

1. *Sharecroppers* paid their rent by giving the owner of their land a large part of their crop.
2. *Industry* is the making of goods by machine.
3. The *textile mill* produced flour.
4. In the *metropolitan area* there are many farms and small towns.
5. The making of blue jeans is an example of a *service industry*.

REVIEWING FACTS

1. Name three challenges faced by farmers in the early 1800s. Name three different challenges faced by farmers today.
2. Why did Charlotte grow from a small community to a large city?
3. How did each of the following means of transportation improve on the type used before: corduroy roads, plank roads, railroads?
4. Name two advances in technology that have helped to speed communication in our state.
5. How did the following people help to make North Carolina into a manufacturing state: Michael Schenck and Warren C. Coleman?

WRITING ABOUT MAIN IDEAS

1. **Writing Then-and-Now Statements:** Write a then-and-now statement about each of these topics: (1) farming, (2) roads, (3) cities.
2. **Writing About Perspectives:** Imagine a young man named John Robertson, who has been freed from slavery after the Civil War. He has rented land from his former owner and has become a sharecropper. How do you think John would have felt about the change in his life since slavery?

BUILDING SKILLS: UNDERSTANDING CAUSE AND EFFECT

1. What is a cause? What is an effect?
2. Write an effect statement for each of the following:
   a. Reaping machines and cultivators were invented.
   b. In 1840 the Wilmington and Weldon Railroad was built.
3. Write a cause statement for each of the following:
   a. Gastonia is a textile manufacturing center.
   b. Charlotte is our largest city today.
4. Why is it useful to be able to understand the difference between causes and effects?

UNIT 2 • REVIEW

REVIEWING VOCABULARY

ancestor
archaeologist
colony
export
immigrant
industry
migrate
segregated
service industry
technology

Number a sheet of paper from 1 to 10. Beside each number write the word or term from the list above that best matches the definition.

1. Separate public areas for blacks and whites
2. All the businesses that produce a certain product or provide a certain service for sale
3. To move from one place to another to live
4. A person who moves to another country to live
5. A person who digs where people lived long ago, hoping to learn more about their way of life
6. A business in which the workers do something of use for other people for a fee
7. A settlement or area in one country that is ruled by another country
8. A person's relative who lived a long time ago
9. Something that is sold or traded to another country
10. The use of tools and scientific knowledge to make things

WRITING ABOUT THE UNIT

1. **Writing About People:** Write one or two sentences about how each of the following people helped North Carolina to develop: Nathaniel Batts, Daniel Boone, and Harriet Moorehead Berry.
2. **Writing About Perspectives:** Imagine that you are the owner of a company that manufactures cotton shirts and dresses. Write a paragraph about the changes you might have made in your factory when synthetic materials were introduced and became popular.

ACTIVITIES

1. **Making a Model:** Make a model that illustrates the work that archaeologists do. Try to show how they dig at a site and the types of artifacts they find.
2. **Researching:** Find out more about one of the following topics: attempts by the Cherokee to remain in their homes; Braxton Bragg, a Confederate general during the Civil War; how methods of manufacturing wooden furniture have changed.
3. **Working Together to Put on a Skit:** With a group of classmates, write and perform a skit about life in Old Salem. If possible, try to use some interesting costumes and props.

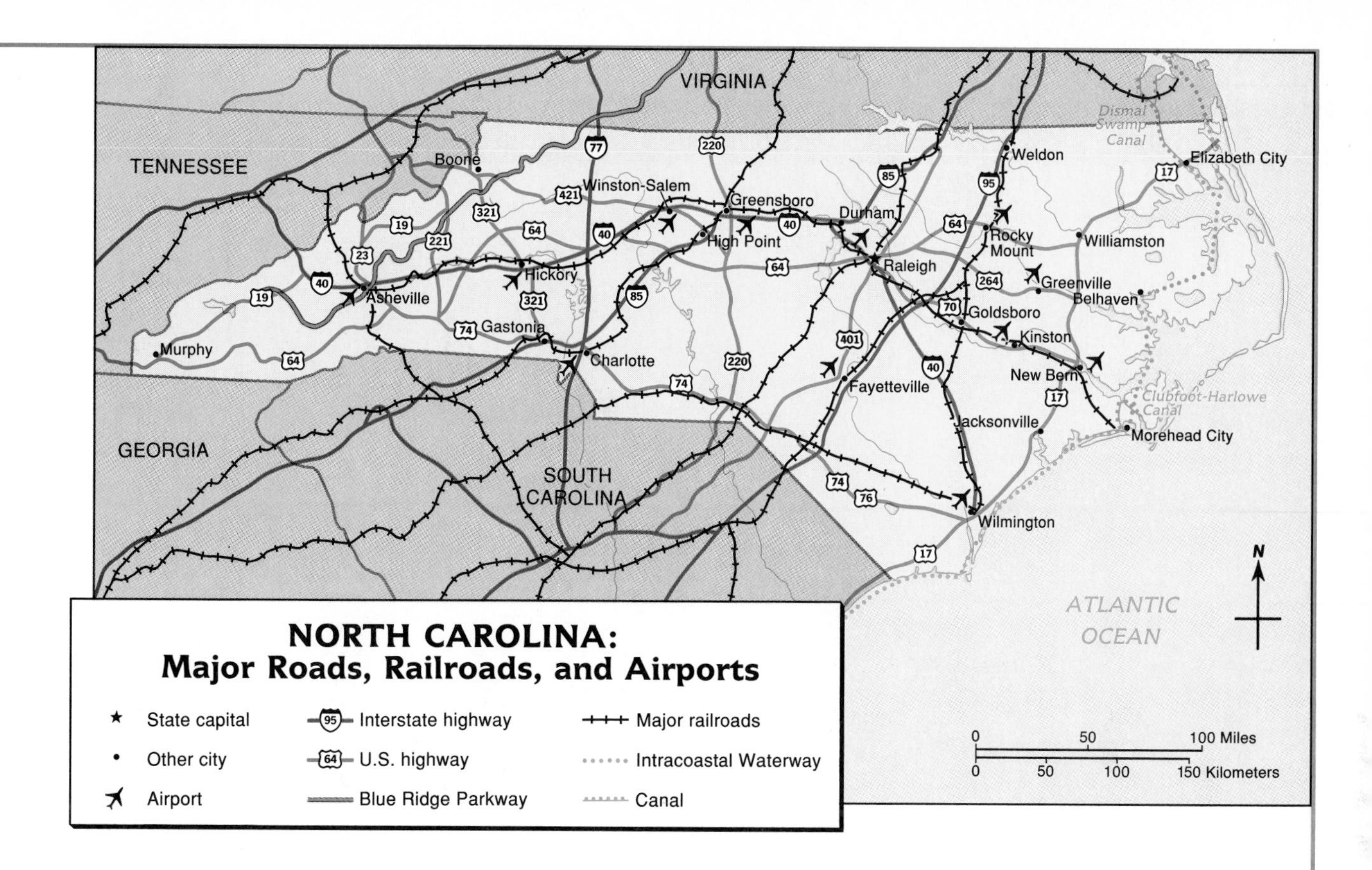

NORTH CAROLINA: Major Roads, Railroads, and Airports

BUILDING SKILLS: USING ROAD MAPS AND MILEAGE CHARTS

Use the map shown above to answer the following questions.

1. What is a road map?
2. Which color and symbol is used to show interstate highways? Which is used for U.S. highways?
3. Which highway would you use to get from Raleigh to Fayetteville? Is it a U.S. or interstate highway?
4. Use the mileage chart on page 176 to find out the total road miles of a trip from Raleigh to Winston-Salem to Charlotte.
5. Give an example of a time when you might need to know how to read a road map.

LINKING PAST, PRESENT, AND FUTURE

You have read about the changes in transportation that have come to North Carolina since the early days. We have gone from muddy trails to superhighways, from wagons to trains and airplanes. What challenges have arisen because of changes in transportation? What types of transportation do you think we will see in the future?

NORTH CAROLINA TODAY

1. Folkmoot USA, international dance festival at Maggie Valley
2. Forestry and woodmaking industries
3. Textile industry
4. Golfing at Pinehurst and Pines
5. Research Triangle Park
6. Completion of Interstate 40
7. Tryon Palace at New Bern
8. The Wright Brothers Memorial

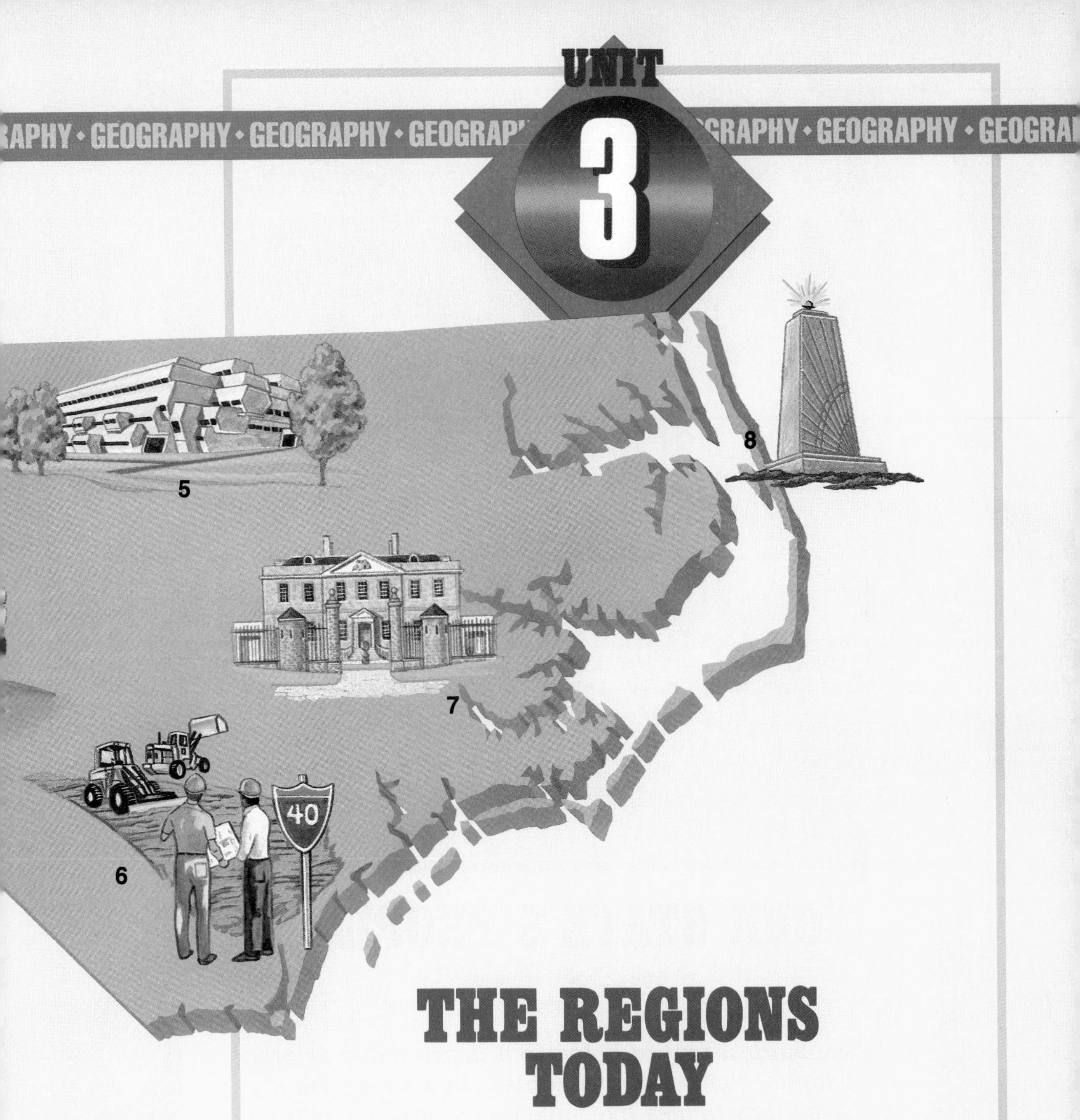

THE REGIONS TODAY

LIFE IN OUR STATE

Today North Carolina is growing and changing faster than ever before. In this unit you will read about the people and ideas that have brought changes to the three regions of our state. You will also read about how the mixture of the old and new are forming new ways of living and working.

CHAPTER 7

OUR STATE'S PEOPLE

FOCUS

The hardest part of being in a dance group is practicing all the twists and turns. The dance steps have funny names like "open and close the garden gate," " wild goose chase," and "four leaf clover."

Janna and Shanna Reno of Waynesville enjoy being in a dance group called the Billy Bob Cloggers. Clogging is a kind of traditional dancing done in our Mountain Region. In this chapter you will read about the traditions that are special to our state.

LESSON

1 Way of Life

READ TO LEARN

Key Vocabulary

rural urban suburban

Read Aloud

We offer mild climate and just plain friendliness.

Former North Carolina governor James Hunt used these words to describe the Tar Heel state. As you have already read, climate is one of our state's most important natural resources. But North Carolina's most important resource is its people.

Read for Purpose

1. **WHAT YOU KNOW:** What are some of the jobs that North Carolinians have?
2. **WHAT YOU WILL LEARN:** How has North Carolina's population been changing?

A GROWING POPULATION

Travel writers Patricia L. Hudson and Sandra L. Ballard believe that "people who are born in North Carolina like to live in North Carolina." Many North Carolinians live near the same places where their parents and ancestors lived.

Nearly 400,000 people lived in North Carolina when it became a state in 1789. As you have read, some were Native Americans. Other people, such as the Scots-Irish, the Highland Scots, the English, and the Germans, came from Europe. Many people also came from Africa.

Today over 6.6 million people live in our state. Only nine states in our country have more people than North Carolina. Look at the bar graph on page 200. It shows the rise in North Carolina's population since 1790. As you can see, North Carolina's population has grown very fast over the last 40 years. In fact, our state is one of the fastest-growing states in the United States.

NORTH CAROLINA POPULATION 1790-1990

Millions of people: 0, 1, 2, 3, 4, 5, 6, 7

Years: 1790 1830 1870 1910 1950 1990

GRAPH SKILL: People of many ethnic groups live in our state. By how many people did our state's population increase between 1950 and 1990?

A CHANGING STATE

In recent years nearly half of the gain in our state's population has been caused by the movement of people from other places. Many people come to find jobs. Some come for the climate. Others come to enjoy North Carolina's great natural beauty.

As you read in Chapter 6, many of the North Carolinians who have come from other states are senior citizens. They are drawn by our state's fine weather and have chosen to move to our state after they have stopped working. Others are immigrants who have moved to our country in search of better lives. Our state's economy offers these people many kinds of jobs.

North Carolina has welcomed immigrants from Asia, Central America, and South America. Many of these immigrants speak Spanish, Vietnamese, or other languages. They bring their own culture to North Carolina. They also make our state a more interesting place.

The move to a new country can be hard. Businesses and church groups in North Carolina are working to help immigrants. One immigrant, Heng Som, is a Cambodian who moved to Greensboro a few years ago. He says that:

> *[W]hen I [came] here, a lot of people [helped] me find a job, a school for my kids, and housing. People have been very good.*

WHERE WE LIVE

How has a growing population changed North Carolina? Until the 1940's most North Carolinians lived in **rural** areas. Rural areas are country areas with few houses or people. Today only about half of our state's people live in rural areas. The other half of the people live in **urban** areas. A city and the communities around it make up an urban area. The urban areas of Charlotte, Raleigh, and Greensboro are the three largest ones in North Carolina.

The communities outside a city are called **suburban** areas. Suburban areas are the fastest-growing communities in our state. Do you live in an urban, a suburban, or a rural area?

RELIGION

The pitch comes in. Jimmy Wilson swings, and the bat cracks against the ball. The crowd roars as Jimmy slides into second base.

It is Saturday afternoon. The youth group from Jimmy's church is winning a game in the Baptist Church Softball League. On Sunday morning Jimmy and the team will sing in the youth choir.

For Jimmy and millions of other North Carolinians, religion is an important part of everyday life. Jimmy attends church services every week and sings in the choir.

The Baptists, Presbyterians, and Methodists are the largest religious groups in our state. There are also Catholics, other Christians, and Jewish groups. The number of religious groups in our state is growing. This growth is caused by the new North Carolinians who have brought their religions with them.

Today churches may hold services in languages such as Korean, Laotian, and Vietnamese. People

This Baptist church and Hindu temple are only two of the many different places of worship in our state today.

who practice religions such as Buddhism, Hinduism, and Islam have their own places of worship in our large cities.

Of course, not all North Carolinians are members of religious groups. Religious traditions in North Carolina are as different as are our state's land and its people.

NEW AND OLD WAYS OF LIFE

As more people move to North Carolina, the way of life in our state keeps changing. The growth of new religions is just one sign of the changes in our ways of life.

Another sign of change can be found in the new festivals that we hold. Several of our state's immigrant groups now have festivals. For example, every spring Winston-Salem holds a festival that honors Greek culture through its food, dance, and crafts.

Performing Greek dances is one way that Greek Americans in North Carolina celebrate their culture.

Many of their old customs and traditions remain important to North Carolinians today. Some of these customs, such as Thanksgiving, are celebrated by people all over our country. Other customs are marked by people just in North Carolina. Among these customs are annual festivals and county fairs.

One fair that you might enjoy is the homecoming gathering that is held by the Lumbee Indians. It takes place in Robeson County.

A GROWING STATE

North Carolina's population has been growing. A mix of people with different cultures from many countries makes North Carolina an exciting, changing state.

Check Your Reading

1. What has been happening to the size of our state's population?
2. From which parts of the world have people moved to our state?
3. In what ways have immigrants and other new citizens to our state changed the way of life of North Carolinians?
4. **THINKING SKILL:** What questions would you ask an immigrant to find out what it is like to live in another country?

A Gift to Others

Many different people live in our state. Some people in our state have come here from other countries and are not citizens of the United States. Many have come from countries where life is different from life in the United States. They have come to work or live in our state. Many of these people have left their countries because of difficult conditions there. For example, many Mexican farm workers in our state could not find jobs in Mexico.

Manlin Chee is a lawyer who helps these people. They arrive in our state hoping to make their lives better. But sometimes they run into trouble. When people do not speak or read English well, they may break our laws because they do not know or understand them.

While growing up in Singapore, a country in southeast Asia, Chee's parents taught her to help the poor. In 1969 Chee left Singapore to attend Guilford College in North Carolina. Her father had said, "America is a great country . . . because it protects its weakest citizens. Go and find out how they do it." Chee's parents and her school gave her courage. She decided to become a lawyer so that she could help people in need.

Today Chee has her own law office. When people do not have money to pay her, she works for free. Recently Chee received a national award for her hard work.

Here is the advice Chee gives to her three children:

> *If you work for money, you will always worry that someone will try to take your money from you. If you work for power, someone may take that. But if you work for the good of the world, you will always be free.*

Chee has helped many people. She is a person who makes a difference.

Reading Line and Circle Graphs

Key Vocabulary

graph   line graph   circle graph

In 1990 the population count, or census, showed North Carolina's population to be 6,628,637 people. This made it the tenth-largest populated state in the United States. Since the first census in 1790, the population has grown steadily. One way to show this growth is by using a **graph**. A graph is a diagram that allows you to compare different facts and figures. Graphs can show a lot of information without using many words.

Reading a Line Graph

One kind of graph is a **line graph**. A line graph shows changes that have taken place over a given period of time. The line graph below shows the population of North Carolina from 1940 to 1990.

To read a line graph, first look at the title. Next read the label on the bottom of the graph. What information

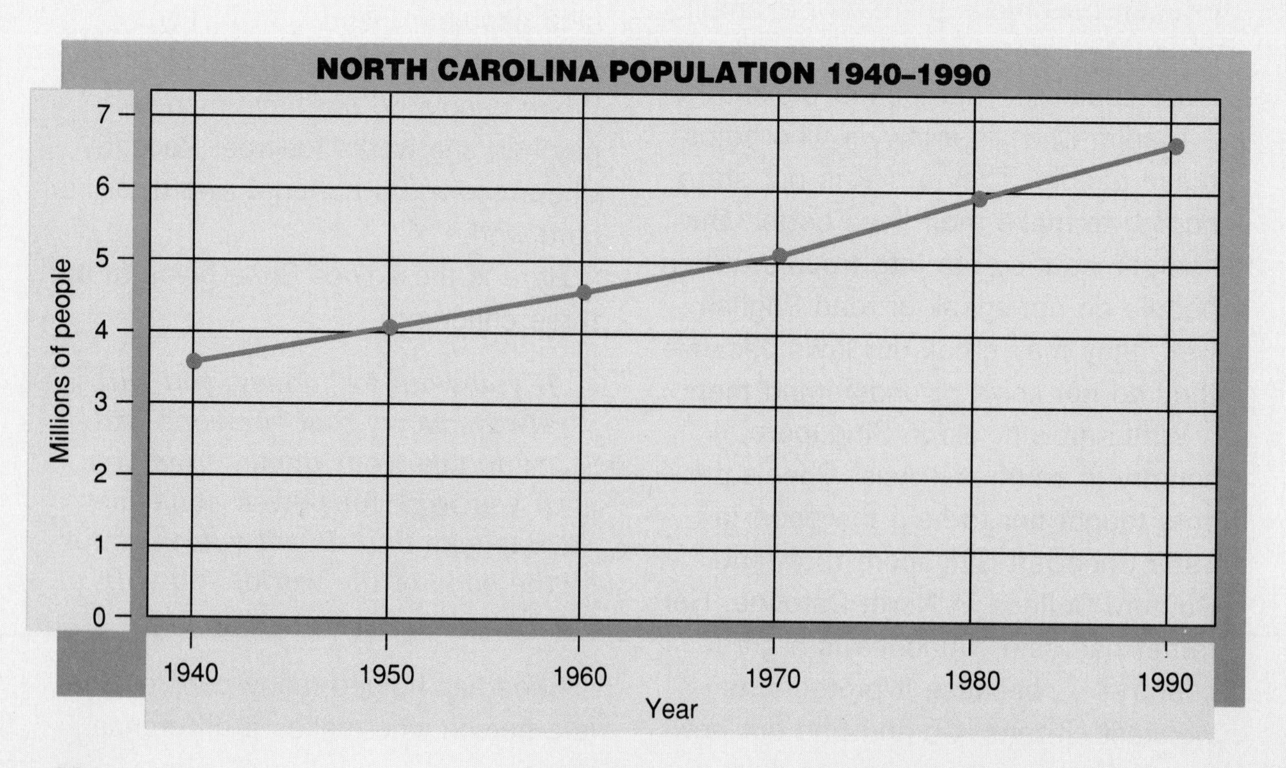

does this label give? Find the label on the left side of the graph. What information does this label give?

Now locate the year 1940 at the bottom of the graph. To find out the population of North Carolina in the year 1940, look at the dot above 1940. The dot is between the numbers 3 and 4 on the left side of the graph. Since the 3 and 4 stand for millions of people, the population of North Carolina in 1940 was between 3 and 4 million people. Notice that the dots are connected to make a line that rises on the graph as the population increases.

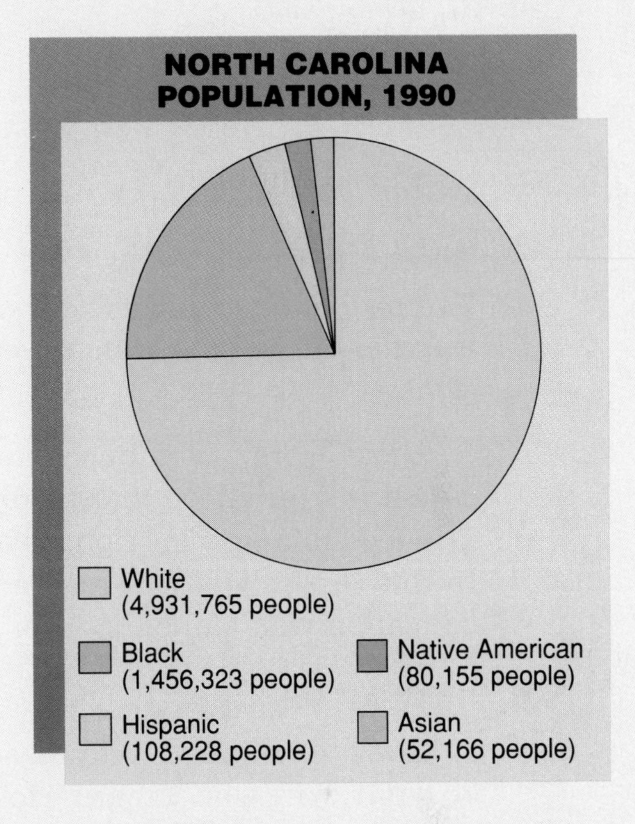

Reading a Circle Graph

Another kind of graph is a **circle graph**. This kind of graph shows how something can be divided into parts. Together, all the parts make up the whole. A circle graph is sometimes called a pie graph because the parts look like slices of a pie.

The circle graph on this page shows that the population of North Carolina is made up of several groups, such as black Americans, white Americans, and Asians. Suppose that you wanted to compare the part of the population that is black to the part that is white. First read the title of the graph. The circle represents the total population of North Carolina in 1990. Each part of the circle represents a different group in the population. Which group of North Carolinians is larger, black or white? By how much?

Reviewing the Skill

1. What is a graph? Name two kinds of graphs.
2. By what year had the population of our state reached 4 million?
3. What was the population in 1980?
4. What part of the population of North Carolina is Asian?
5. Why is it useful to understand how to read graphs?

LESSON

2 Education

READ TO LEARN

Key People

John Chavis
Archibald Murphey
Charles B. Aycock

Read Aloud

The people have a right to the privilege of education, and it is the duty of the state to guard and maintain that right.

These words from our state's constitution say that education is a privilege that belongs to all of our people. A privilege is a special right given to a person or a group. In this lesson you will read about how the right to an education was gained by everyone in our state.

Read for Purpose

1. **WHAT YOU KNOW:** Why is education important to you?
2. **WHAT YOU WILL LEARN:** How do North Carolina's schools provide a good education for our state's people?

EDUCATION IN OUR STATE

Do you sometimes dream about what you want to be when you are older? Perhaps you would like to be a farmer, a teacher, or an animal doctor. Today our state has thousands of schools and colleges. They have helped North Carolinians make their dreams come true. Education offers the skills that are needed for you to do well.

EARLY SCHOOLING

Before 1840 there were very few schools for children in our state. Rich white families sent their sons to schools that had been started by several religious groups. Girls were taught at home.

Many poor white families did not have the money or time to send their children to school. These children learned the skills they needed at home or at work. At this time almost all of the Native American children learned important values, traditions, and skills from the older people in their communities.

In the early 1800s most African-American children were enslaved. They learned customs, beliefs, and skills from their families. In many places it was against the law to teach African Americans to read and write. Some free blacks were able to go to a school started in the early 1800s in Raleigh by an African-American minister named John Chavis. Chavis taught both black children and white children.

EDUCATION IMPROVES

The right to an education was slowly gained by the different groups in our state. In the early 1800s a state lawmaker named Archibald Murphey wanted all of our state's white children to have a free education. He thought that more schools should be built.

Murphey's ideas were put to use in 1840, when the first public school was started in Rockingham County. Public schools are free elementary and high schools that are paid for by tax money. At that time, most public schools were one-room buildings in which children of all ages were taught together.

EDUCATION FOR ALL

In 1901 Charles B. Aycock (ā′ kok) became the governor, or leader, of our state. Aycock helped to improve education in our state. He had thousands of schools built. The school year was changed from

Most of our state's public schools in the 1800s were one-room schoolhouses for children of all ages like the one shown here.

four months to six months, and then to nine months.

As you have read, blacks and whites went to separate schools in the later part of the 1800s. Indians also went to separate schools. Their schools were not as good as those for whites.

It took a long time, however, for all children to go to the same schools. In 1954 the Supreme Court, which is the most important court in the United States, said that segregated schools were against the law.

However, it was difficult to end the practice of separate schools. During the 1950s many African Americans took part in the civil rights movement. Civil rights are the rights of all people to be treated the same under the law. Because of the struggles of many African Americans, more black children and white children began to go to school together. By 1980 most North Carolina public schools were integrated.

Today North Carolina has over 2,000 public elementary and high schools. These schools offer a free education for all. There are many public schools in every county in our state. Some of these schools are for students who have special interests in the arts and sciences.

HIGHER EDUCATION

North Carolina has over 100 colleges and technical schools that prepare students for work when they are older. Some of these schools are community colleges, which are two-year colleges that are paid for by their communities. A few of these community colleges are shown on the map on page 209.

The University of North Carolina (UNC) was started in 1795. It was the first public college in the United

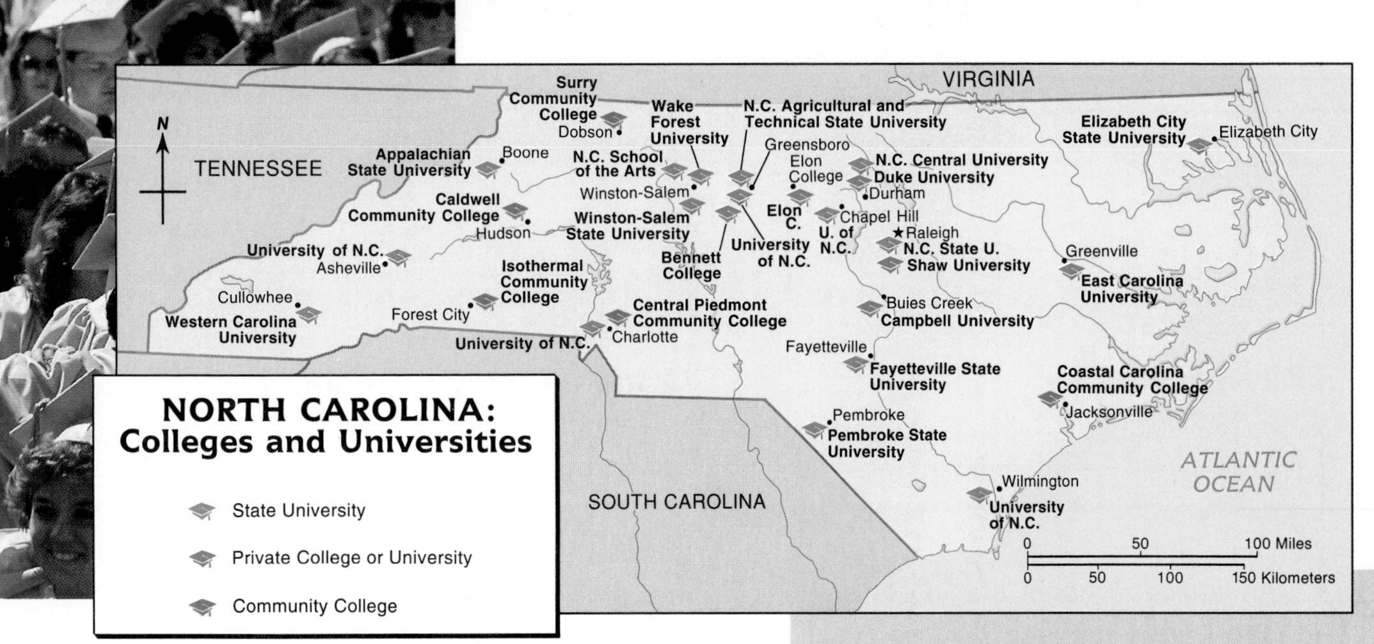

MAP SKILL: All Tar Heels have the right to an education. From the map, which region has the most schools?

States. A public college is one that is set up by the state. Since the state helps to pay for running a public college, the cost of going there is low. UNC has grown from a small university in Chapel Hill to one with schools in 16 different cities. People from around the world come to UNC to study.

Our state also has many private colleges. Private colleges are those that were started by religious groups or wealthy people. Most private colleges cost more to go to than public ones. Trinity College in Durham was started by the Methodists in 1839. Now called Duke University, it is well known for its school of medicine.

North Carolina also has colleges that were started for African Americans. Among these are Shaw University in Raleigh and North Carolina Agricultural and Technical State University in Greensboro.

A RIGHT AND A PRIVILEGE

As you have read, education has a long history in North Carolina. Today everyone has the right to go to school. This right gives each of us a chance to follow our dreams and to make our state a better place in which to live.

Check Your Reading

1. How do North Carolina's schools provide a good education for our people?
2. Why is John Chavis important?
3. **GEOGRAPHY SKILL:** Using the map above, find two colleges or universities that are close to your home.
4. **THINKING SKILL:** Compare education in our state in the past with that of today.

Using the Library

Key Vocabulary

reference book
encyclopedia
atlas
dictionary
almanac
call number

As you read about life in our state today, you might want to find out more about certain subjects. For instance, you might want an answer to the question: What led to the founding of the University of North Carolina?

You can find information about many different subjects in a library. The reference section is a good place to start. Here you will find **reference books**, which are books that are full of facts about different subjects.

Using an Encyclopedia

One kind of reference book is an **encyclopedia**. An encyclopedia is a book or set of books that contains information about famous people and places and about important events and subjects.

Encyclopedia articles are arranged in alphabetical order from *A* to *Z* by title. On the spine of each volume, or book, of an encyclopedia are the letters of the alphabet of the subjects covered in that volume. The last volume usually contains an index. The index is arranged in alphabetical order by subject. If you look up your subject in the index, you will find a list of all

the articles in the encyclopedia that include information about your subject.

Other Reference Books

Another useful reference book is an **atlas**. An atlas is a book of maps. Some atlases have maps that show the specific locations of places in the world. Other atlases have maps that illustrate events from the past. These are called historical atlases.

Other reference books include **dictionaries** and **almanacs**. A dictionary is an alphabetical list of words, along with their meanings and pronunciations. An almanac is published every year and contains up-to-date facts and information on many different subjects.

Finding Books

You may also want to find books that are not in the reference section. You can use the card catalog or computer listings to find where these books are located. Each book is listed there in three different ways: by author, by title, and by subject. The card in the catalog or entry in the computer tells the title of the book and the author's name. It also gives information about where and when the book was

NORTH CAROLINA—HISTORY
975.6 Claiborne, Jack, and William Price
Discovering North Carolina:
A Tar Heel Reader
Chapel Hill: University of
North Carolina Press, 1991
372 pages, collection of articles on
North Carolina history

printed, as well as a brief description of the book. Each card or entry has a **call number** that will help you locate the book you are looking for on the shelves.

Shown on this page is a card from a card catalog. It is a subject card. What is the name of the book? Who are the authors? What number would you look for on the shelf to find the book?

Reviewing the Skill

1. Name four kinds of reference books.
2. How would you find information about Wake Forest University in an encyclopedia?
3. Which reference book would you use to find out how many North Carolinians attended public school last year?
4. How would you go about finding a book about Chapel Hill?
5. Why is it important to know how to use the library?

LESSON

3 The Arts

READ TO LEARN

Key Vocabulary

folk art

Key People

Charles W. Chesnutt
O. Henry
Carl Sandburg
Thomas Wolfe
Doris Betts
James Larkin Pearson
Earl Scruggs
Doc Watson
John Coltrane

Read Aloud

I always carried my notebook and pencil to the field with me, and as I trudged [walked slowly] *between the plow handles . . . my mind was busy working out a poem.*

These words were written by the Tar Heel poet James Larkin Pearson. Pearson wrote poetry while he worked on a farm in Wilkes County in the late 1800s. In this lesson you will read about some of North Carolina's famous writers and musicians.

Read for Purpose

1. **WHAT YOU KNOW:** What kinds of music, theater, dance, writing, or painting do you like?
2. **WHAT YOU WILL LEARN:** Which arts are popular in North Carolina? Why are the arts an important part of our state's culture?

THE ARTS IN OUR STATE

Mr. Lenox asked his students to name which of the following activities they enjoy: quilting, reading, painting, music, or dancing? "My grandmother makes quilts by sewing together different patches of cloth," said Diane Gardner. "I think they're really beautiful."

"I like to read books," said Tom Davidson. "Some of my favorite stories are about the people who settled our state."

This carved wooden horse, decorated plate, and cloth doll are examples of folk art.

"I like country music most of all," said Jackie Stone.

These students are talking about the arts. The arts include creative activities such as writing, painting, or music. When you listen to music, read a book, or see a painting or beautiful building, you may begin to understand things in a new way. The arts are an important part of our culture.

FOLK ART

The quilts sewn by Diane's grandmother are examples of folk art. Folk art is the traditional art of a community.

The crafts of weaving, rug making, quilting, pottery, glassblowing, and cabinetmaking are all kinds of folk art. Even telling stories, which you will read about on pages 218–221, is a kind of folk art.

Some of the skills used in making these crafts were almost forgotten when people began making goods by machine in factories. Many people, though, continued to value goods made by hand in the old ways.

Two important places where such crafts are taught are the John C. Campbell School in Brasstown and the Penland School of Crafts near Spruce Pines. The photographs above show some of the craftspeople who are keeping our folk-art tradition alive.

O. Henry, Charles Chesnutt, Carl Sandburg, and Doris Betts are among our state's many famous writers.

WRITERS

Our state has long been proud of its authors. One of our country's well-known African-American authors is **Charles W. Chesnutt**, who grew up in Fayetteville in the middle 1800s. His short stories and books are about blacks who lived under segregation. One of our most famous authors is **O. Henry**, who was born near Greensboro in 1862. O. Henry's real name was William Sydney Porter. He wrote hundreds of short stories. Some of these stories take place in North Carolina.

Even though the poet and historian **Carl Sandburg** was born in the Midwest, he lived in North Carolina for many years. You will read more about Sandburg in the Traditions lesson on page 218.

The following poem, "Window," shows how, with a few words, Sandburg describes the night from a moving train.

Night from a railroad car
window
Is a great, dark, soft thing
Broken across with slashes
of light.

Another well-known North Carolinian author is **Thomas Wolfe**, who was born in Asheville in 1900. Wolfe later wrote several books based on his early years. One of these books was *Look Homeward, Angel*. Wolfe's writing powerfully describes the beauty of our state's land and mountains.

Among our state's well-known writers today is **Doris Betts**. In her first book Betts wrote about her hometown of Statesville. Another important writer is the poet **James Larkin Pearson**. You read about him in the Read Aloud.

MUSIC

Jazz and folk music have long been loved in our state. Several singers of these kinds of music have become famous. Jackie's favorite bluegrass star, **Earl Scruggs**, was born in Flint Hill. **Doc Watson**, who comes from the Blue Ridge Mountains, is a well-known country music singer. Bluegrass and country music are kinds of folk music. The saxophonist **John Coltrane** was born in Hamlet. He became one of the world's great jazz musicians. Nina Simone, a jazz singer, is also well known.

You can hear country music, folk music, rock, pop, and rap played in concert halls all over our state. Fiddle tunes such as "Old Joe Clark" also can be heard in North Carolina. The words to "Old Joe Clark" appear on page 216.

SUMMER ENTERTAINMENT

Summer is a time for dance, music, and theater festivals in North Carolina. Dance companies from countries around the world come to the American Dance Festival in Durham to perform.

Singer Nina Simone, saxophonist John Coltrane, and singer Doc Watson are all part of North Carolina's rich musical heritage.

Old Joe Clark

You can hear music and operas at the Summer Festival of Music in Brevard. You can also hear music from many countries being performed at the Eastern Music Festival in Greensboro.

In summer North Carolinians can see plays and musicals at our state's oldest theater. This is the Flat Rock Playhouse near Hendersonville. Among the best-known plays, however, are the historical plays that are staged outdoors every summer. Thousands of Tar Heels and tourists flock to plays such as *The Lost Colony,* about which you read in Chapter 4. They also enjoy *Unto These Hills,* which tells the story of the forced migration of the Cherokee along the Trail of Tears.

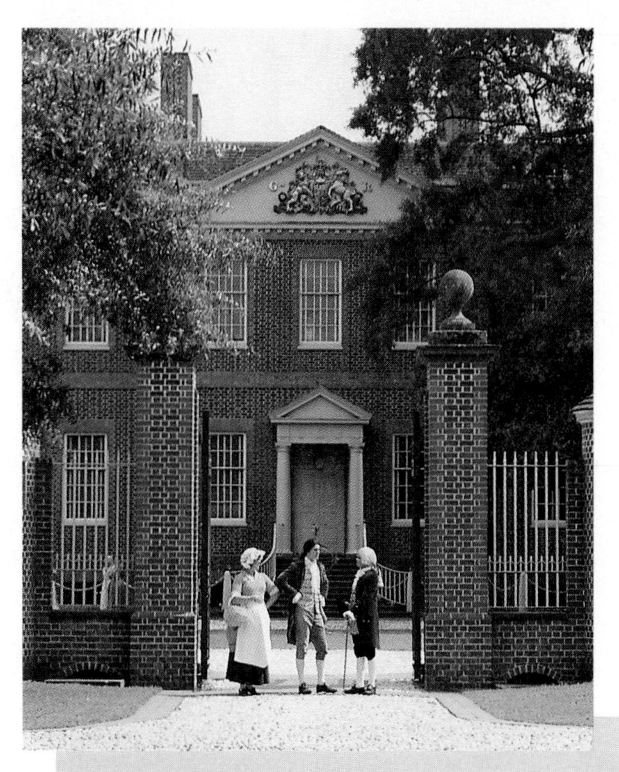

Guides dressed in clothes like those worn in colonial times offer tours of Tryon Palace in New Bern.

MUSEUMS AND HISTORIC BUILDINGS

Year-round you can visit many historic homes and art museums in our state. In New Bern you can tour Tryon Palace. It was the first capitol building of our state. At museums such as the North Carolina Museum of Art in Raleigh, you can see many fine artworks.

ART FOR EVERYONE

As you have read, many North Carolinian authors, musicians, and folk artists have added to the arts in our state. Our concert halls, music festivals, theaters, and museums offer our state's people many chances to enjoy the arts.

Check Your Reading

1. What kinds of art are popular in North Carolina? Why are the arts an important part of our state's culture?
2. What is folk art?
3. Name places in your community or county in which you can enjoy some of the types of art discussed in this lesson.
4. **THINKING SKILL:** List the following artists according to whether they are writers or musicians: Earl Scruggs, Thomas Wolfe, O. Henry, Doris Betts, John Coltrane, Carl Sandburg. Tell why each artist is important.

Storytelling

by Lila Summer

North Carolina's arts include many different kinds of stories. These stories make up our rich storytelling tradition. Some stories are special to certain regions of our state, such as the Piedmont. Others are special to different cultures. Some are told out loud, while others are written down. Stories are ways in which people pass on their history, their beliefs, and their way of looking at the world. As you read, think about how the tradition of storytelling helps us to learn about our state.

OUR ORAL TRADITION

Long ago, few people knew how to read or write. They learned about the past by telling stories out loud to each other. These stories that we tell out loud and pass along from person to person are part of our oral, or spoken, history.

Our state has many storytellers who help to carry on this oral storytelling tradition. One of these storytellers is Jackie Torrence of High Point. Look at the photo of Jackie Torrence on this page. What kind of story do you think that she is telling?

North Carolina storytellers tell many different kinds of stories. Among the kinds of made-up stories that Jackie Torrence tells are ghost stories. Many of these scary stories originally came from the Piedmont. Imagine a Piedmont pine forest late at night. It is

not hard to guess why people in the Piedmont tell ghost stories!

Besides made-up stories, North Carolinians also like to tell tales that begin with something real. For example, there are many stories about the scary pirate Blackbeard. Stories are also told about the lost colonists of Roanoke Island, whom you read about in Chapter 4. The following story, "Betsy Dowdy's Ride," is about a real person. Although all the facts are not known about Dowdy, she was a hero of the American Revolution.

It was a dark, cold December night in the year 1775. Inside her home on the Currituck Banks, just south of the Virginia boundary line, 16-year-old Betsy Dowdy was trying to decide what to do. She had heard her father talking about the danger that the colony of North Carolina faced. He had learned that the British planned to attack the Albemarle Sound area and capture its wild ponies for their troops. There were not enough armed colonists to stop the British.

Betsy decided to warn the American army. After leaving a note for her father, she went outside and saddled her horse. Although it was night, Betsy and her horse slid down the sand banks and swam across Currituck Sound to the mainland. They galloped across the Dismal Swamp and past Camden, Elizabeth City, and Hertford. As the sun rose, Betsy reached the colonial army in Perquimans County.

Because of Betsy's warning, the Americans acted quickly. They defeated the British at the Battle of Great Bridge, and North Carolina was saved.

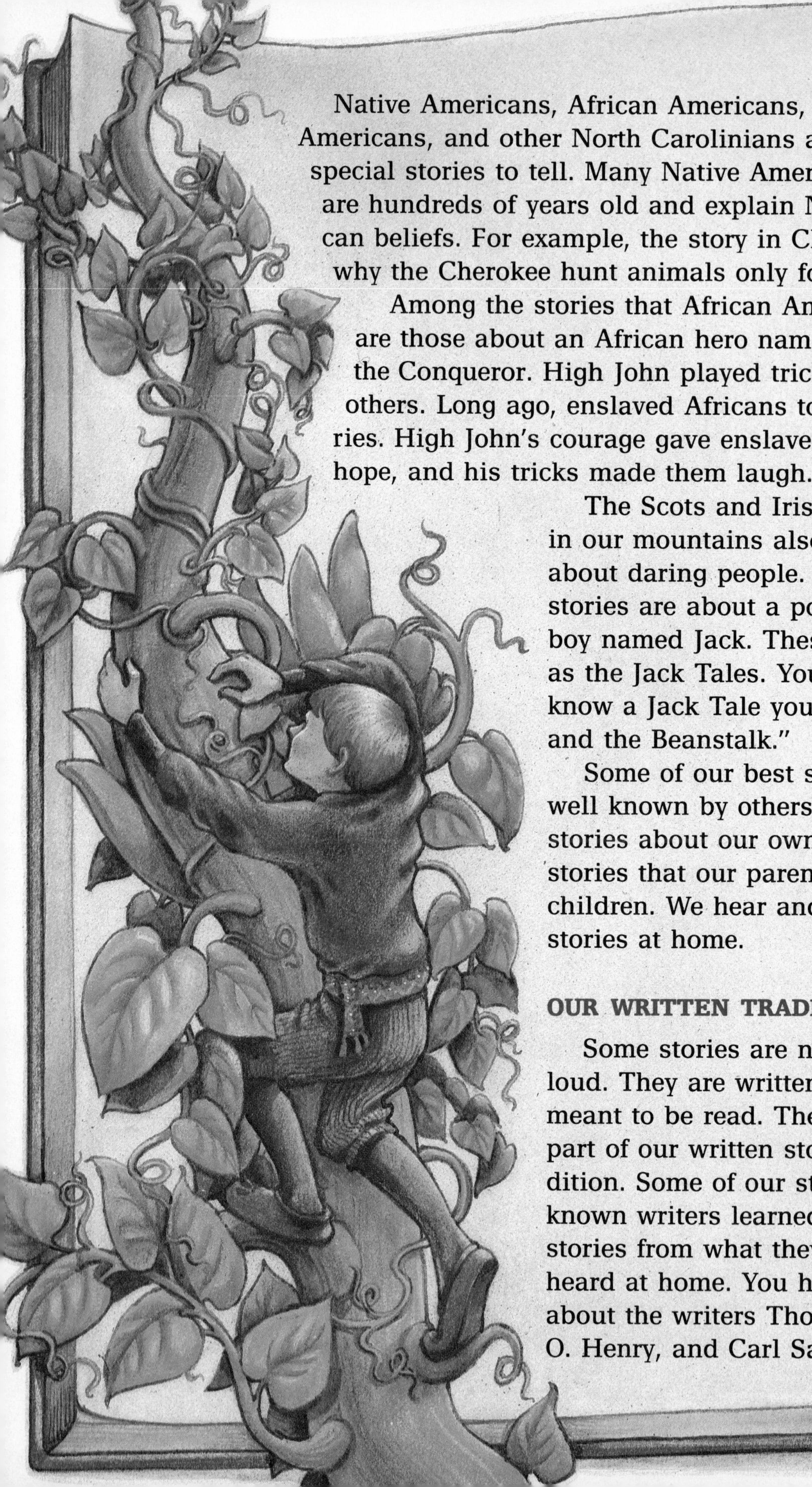

Native Americans, African Americans, European Americans, and other North Carolinians all have special stories to tell. Many Native American stories are hundreds of years old and explain Native American beliefs. For example, the story in Chapter 4 tells why the Cherokee hunt animals only for food.

Among the stories that African Americans tell are those about an African hero named High John the Conqueror. High John played tricks to outsmart others. Long ago, enslaved Africans told these stories. High John's courage gave enslaved Africans hope, and his tricks made them laugh.

The Scots and Irish who settled in our mountains also told stories about daring people. Many of the stories are about a poor but lucky boy named Jack. These are known as the Jack Tales. You probably know a Jack Tale yourself—"Jack and the Beanstalk."

Some of our best stories are not well known by others. They are stories about our own families or stories that our parents heard as children. We hear and tell these stories at home.

OUR WRITTEN TRADITION

Some stories are not told out loud. They are written down and meant to be read. These stories are part of our written storytelling tradition. Some of our state's best-known writers learned about telling stories from what they saw and heard at home. You have read about the writers Thomas Wolfe, O. Henry, and Carl Sandburg.

After he became famous, Thomas Wolfe said, "I wrote about things that I had known, the life of my childhood." Like Wolfe, O. Henry also told stories about his home. When he was a teenager, he worked in his uncle's drugstore, and drew pictures that told funny stories about the store.

Carl Sandburg was already famous when he moved to our state in 1945. Originally from Illinois, Sandburg was a writer and a poet. Some of Sandburg's stories and poems were written for children. While he was living in our state, he published a book of poems for children called *Wind Song*. The following poem from *Wind Song* is called "Bubbles." It tells a very short story.

Bubbles

Two bubbles found they had rainbows on their curves.
They flickered out saying:
"It was worth being a bubble just to have held that rainbow thirty seconds."

CARRYING ON THE TRADITION

Today someone may tell you a story. Or you might tell a story to a friend about something that happened to you. Perhaps you will read or write a story before the day is over. That is how we pass along our rich storytelling tradition.

In what ways does North Carolina's storytelling tradition help us to learn about our state?

LESSON

4 Sports and Recreation

READ TO LEARN

Key Vocabulary

recreation
spectator
professional team
amateur team

Key People

Michael Jordan
Richard Petty

Key Places

Cape Lookout National Seashore
Jockey's Ridge
Lake Norman
Great Smoky Mountains National Park

Read Aloud

I'm a Tar Heel born
And a Tar Heel bred
And when I die,
I'll be a Tar Heel dead

So Rah Rah Carolina-lina
Rah Rah Carolina-lina
Rah Rah Carolina
Rah! Rah! Rah!

Students at the University of North Carolina sing this song at sports events. In this lesson you will read about some of the games and events that North Carolinians enjoy. You will also read about some of the other ways in which people in our state have fun.

Read for Purpose

1. **WHAT YOU KNOW:** What are some of your favorite ways of spending free time?
2. **WHAT YOU WILL LEARN:** What kinds of sports and recreational activities do people in North Carolina enjoy?

RECREATION

Do you play basketball in your free time? Or do you enjoy watching team sports? These activities are kinds of **recreation**. Recreation is the way in which people relax and enjoy themselves.

Different places offer different kinds of recreation. You may remember the pen pals, Susan and John, whom you met in Chapter 1. Susan often goes to the beach to swim. John enjoys hiking in the mountains near his home.

Bicycle riding, jogging, and whitewater canoeing are among the many kinds of **recreation** that are enjoyed in North Carolina.

PARKS, LAKES, AND SEASHORES

Our state's varied geography offers North Carolinians many kinds of recreation. As you have read, people who live in the Coastal Plain Region can visit the beaches to swim or sail. The **Cape Lookout National Seashore** has miles of sandy beaches. Here visitors can gather beautiful shells. At **Jockey's Ridge** it is fun to climb the high sand dunes. You have already read about the Sandhills. There are many golf courses in this part of our state. People from all over the world play golf in the Southern Pines-Pinehurst area. The World Golf Hall of Fame is in Pinehurst. Visitors to the Hall of Fame can see the golf clubs and other items once used by well-known golfers.

In the Piedmont Region people enjoy activities on our state's lakes. **Lake Norman** is the largest human-made lake in North Carolina. The lake draws people who want to go fishing, boating, and swimming.

In the Mountain Region many people visit the **Great Smoky Mountains National Park**. Each year millions of people visit the park to hike its trails and enjoy the outdoors. Did you know that more than one half of our state is covered by forests? People from all over the United States come to these forests for recreation. White-water canoeing is another favorite sport.

SPECTATOR SPORTS

"You know you make me want to shout." Sometimes as many as 23,000 voices join in with this cheer for the Charlotte Hornets, a basketball team. Basketball is one of North Carolina's favorite **spectator** sports. A spectator is a person who watches but does not take part in an event. Football, baseball, soccer, and golf are among the other favorite spectator sports in our state.

The Charlotte Hornets are one of our **professional teams**. Professional teams are made up of players who have special training and earn money for their work.

In 1988 the Charlotte Hornets began playing in the National Basketball Association (NBA). That year the Hornets had so many spectators they broke the NBA's first-year team-attendance record.

College teams, such as the Duke University basketball team, are also popular. In addition, Tar Heels enjoy watching their favorite players.

SUPERSTARS

The pass is very wide. **Michael Jordan** darts to his left and grabs the ball. He moves quickly toward the basket, spins around, bounces the ball twice, and then leaps. The crowd gasps as Jordan seems to float through the air. The basketball rolls slowly from his fingers as

Soccer and golf are **spectator sports** that Tar Heels like to watch. Amateurs young and old also enjoy playing these sports.

he shoots it at the basket. The ball sails cleanly through the net.

Michael Jordan grew up in Wilmington. When he was a young boy, he played many sports. At the age of 14, he decided that he liked basketball the best. Later Jordan attended the University of North Carolina at Chapel Hill. There he played for the Tar Heels, an **amateur team**. Amateur teams are ones that play mostly for fun and that are not paid.

Jordan was given the nickname "Air" because he could jump very high. After graduating, he went to play for the Chicago Bulls. In 1988 Jordan was named the Most Valuable Player of the National Basketball Association.

Another favorite spectator sport in North Carolina is stock-car racing. Thousands of Tar Heels watch these races at the Charlotte Speedway. Many people come just to watch **Richard Petty**. Petty is the most successful stock-car racer in the history of the sport.

Basketball, baseball, and stock-car racing are also popular sports. Basketball star Michael Jordan (left) is shown in action.

Tennis and races are some of the sports events that are held for people with some kind of limited ability.

TIME FOR FUN

Tar Heels enjoy many kinds of recreation. They can swim on the coast, play golf in the Sandhills, or climb in the mountains. They also can enjoy watching sports such as basketball and car racing.

A SPECIAL SPORT

Each year in our state, many of our counties hold a sports event called the Special Olympics. The Special Olympics are held for North Carolinian children and adults who have some kind of limited ability.

At the Special Olympics Tar Heels can take part in many kinds of athletic activities. They include races, tennis, and team sports. A parade, music, and large, cheering crowds make the Special Olympics an important day for both the spectators and the athletes.

Check Your Reading

1. What is recreation?
2. How is a professional team the same as an amateur team? How is it different?
3. What are the Special Olympics?
4. GEOGRAPHY SKILL: For each region of our state, identify two kinds of recreational activities that people can enjoy.
5. THINKING SKILL: Imagine that you could interview Michael Jordan. List three questions you would ask him.

REVIEWING VOCABULARY

folk art
suburban
recreation
spectator
rural

Number a sheet of paper from 1 to 5. Beside each number write the word or term from the list above that best completes the sentence.

1. Quilting is an example of ____.
2. People who live in ____ areas are likely to see many farms.
3. The way people relax and enjoy themselves is called ____.
4. A ____ is a person who looks on, or watches, an event.
5. People who live in ____ areas live on the edge of cities.

REVIEWING FACTS

Number a sheet of paper from 1 to 5. Beside each number write the letter of the phrase that best completes the sentence or answers the question.

1. North Carolina's population
   a. includes people from many different countries.
   b. has fewer people than in 1965.
2. Public schools in North Carolina
   a. were founded in the 1700s.
   b. were aided greatly by the work of Governor Charles B. Aycock.
3. The University of North Carolina
   a. was founded 50 years ago.
   b. has schools in 16 locations.
4. A well-known author of our state is
   a. John Chavis.
   b. Doris Betts.
5. Which of the following is not an example of recreation?
   a. spectator sports
   b. driving to work each day

WRITING ABOUT MAIN IDEAS

1. **Writing a Description:** Look closely at one of the examples of our state's folk art shown in Lesson 3 or that you have seen somewhere else. Write a paragraph describing the example.
2. **Writing About Perspectives:** Imagine that a girl from another country came to live next door. Tell the girl about your favorite North Carolina art form. Assume that she speaks English but has not heard of the art form before.

BUILDING SKILLS: USING THE LIBRARY

1. Name three sources you could use in a library to find information about the Raleigh-Durham Airport.
2. Which reference book would you use to find out how to pronounce the word *amateur*?
3. What steps would you follow to find a book in the library?

CHAPTER 8

LIFE IN THE COASTAL PLAIN

FOCUS

When I first came to school in Mount Olive, I sometimes mixed up Spanish and English words because I learned Spanish first. Now I help the Spanish teacher at school.

Yina Maldonado's family comes to our state every spring to work on a farm in the Coastal Plain Region. When the harvest season ends in October, Yina's family returns home to Texas. In this chapter you will read about ways of life in the Coastal Plain Region.

LESSON

1 Living in the Coastal Plain Region

READ TO LEARN

Key Vocabulary	Key People	Key Places
migrant worker festival auction	Henry Berry Lowry	Cape Lookout National Seashore

Read Aloud

Would you like a bite of fried stingray or shark stew? Or maybe you'd rather try some pickled eel or squid salad.

You might hear someone say these words at the Strange Seafood Exhibition. This event is held in the seaport of Beaufort every August. At this event you can taste over 40 kinds of seafood found in our state's waters. Celebrating the resources of the sea and the land is an important part of the way of life of people in the Coastal Plain Region.

Read for Purpose

1. **WHAT YOU KNOW:** Which customs and traditions do you and your family follow and enjoy?
2. **WHAT YOU WILL LEARN:** How have history and geography affected the way of life of the people of the Coastal Plain Region?

VISITING THE COASTAL PLAIN

In Chapter 1 you read about John Cornsilk and Susan Carter, two pen pals who live in different regions of North Carolina. Imagine that John leaves the Mountain Region to visit Susan and her family in the Coastal Plain Region. He wants to learn more about the culture of the Coastal Plain. Susan will take him on a trip through her region.

ROOTS IN THE PAST

Our history and geography have shaped the way of life of the people who live in the Coastal Plain. Susan tells John that the largest number of people in the region can trace their roots to the English, Germans, Swiss, and Scots. These groups first came here in the early 1700s.

Susan and John begin their trip by visiting Edenton. This town was started by English colonists in the 1700s. Here they see many signs of the past. They walk along tree-shaded streets lined with homes from colonial times. Susan shows her friend St. Paul's Episcopal Church. It was built in the mid-1700s and is still being used today.

Having the sea nearby has also shaped how people live in the Coastal Plain Region. Susan takes John home to the small fishing village of Ocracoke on Ocracoke Island. There he learns that North Carolinians both in the past and the present have earned a living by fishing off the Atlantic Coast.

The Cupola House is one of Edenton's beautiful colonial buildings. It was built around 1725.

In recent years the sea has drawn people who like to spend their vacations by the water. This has led to new jobs, such as tour guides, in the tourism industry. You will read more about tourism and about growing coastal towns, such as Beaufort, in Lesson 3.

Visiting the beach is important to the way of life of people in this region, especially during the summer. Over 100 miles (160 km) of sandy white beaches line the Outer Banks. Susan and John plan to swim and climb some sand dunes at **Cape Lookout National Seashore**.

THE LUMBEE

As you have read in Chapter 3, our state's richest land is in the Coastal Plain. This region's fertile soil has made farming a way of life for many people. For hundreds of years before the Europeans arrived, many Native Americans farmed along the coast. Even though the European colonists took most of their land, some Indians still farm the land that was left to them.

The largest Native American group now living in the Inner Coastal Plain is the Lumbee. Today there are more than 40,000 Lumbee

Many Lumbee women and children wear traditional clothing at their yearly homecoming celebration. It is held in Robeson County.

living in Robeson County. Many are farmers, teachers, lawyers, and local government leaders.

The ancestors of the Lumbee include several groups of Indians on the coast. Over the years, the Lumbee, along with other Indian groups, have had to struggle for their rights. As you read, most of the Cherokee had to leave their land in the 1830s and migrate west. The Lumbee, though, were able to keep their land. However, state laws were soon changed. The Lumbee then lost certain rights, such as the right to vote and go to school.

During the Civil War the Confederate government made the Lumbee build forts for Southern soldiers. Some of the Lumbee refused. Henry Berry Lowry became a leader of this group. Lowry and his followers helped many poor white, black, and Indian people. For many years Lowry fought for the rights of the Lumbee of the coast.

A CHANGING WAY OF LIFE

John learns that almost one half of North Carolina's African Americans live in the Coastal Plain. Their lives also have been shaped by the history and geography of this region. As you know, before the Civil War, many African Americans were enslaved workers. When slavery was ended after the war, many of these African Americans began to farm for themselves.

Farming still is a way of life for some African Americans today. However, because of the changes in farming that you read about in Chapter 6, many young African Americans are leaving the farms. They are finding jobs in other parts of the state and in other parts of the country.

NEW NORTH CAROLINIANS

Susan plans to take John to a restaurant that serves Mexican foods. These restaurants are a sign of the growing number of Hispanic people who now live in eastern North Carolina. Hispanics are people with Spanish or Latin American ancestors. Many Hispanics in North Carolina come from Mexico. Some come from Guatemala and El Salvador. Find these countries on the Atlas map on page 350.

John discovers that most Hispanics first came to our state as **migrant workers**. Migrant workers are farm workers who move from one region to another in search of work. They are often not paid well. Some migrant workers have settled in the Inner Coastal Plain. There they hope to improve their lives. As one migrant farm worker, Margarito Moreno, said:

> *I want a lot of things for my children . . . a room for each of them . . . good food and certain kinds of meat and fish that I cannot now afford.*

Cucumbers are just one of the crops picked by **migrant workers** in the Coastal Plain.

COMMON TRADITIONS

As you have read, the groups of people who call the Coastal Plain Region home come from different cultures. However, these groups share many customs that are important to the region. People here often celebrate their customs at farm **festivals**. A festival is a celebration that takes place every year.

In fact, there are so many farm festivals in this region that John might have to come back to see them all! He also wants to see the Strange Seafood Exhibition, which you read about in the Read Aloud. John thinks that he would enjoy the Peanut Festival in Edenton and the Strawberry Festival in Chadbourn.

Visitors at the Strange Seafood Exhibit (*left*) decide which fish to taste. Buyers (*right*) at a tobacco **auction** look at the tobacco leaves.

Before John leaves, Susan wants to take him to a tobacco **auction**. An auction is a public sale at which goods are sold to the person who makes the highest bid. Tobacco auctions have been a Coastal Plain tradition for over 150 years.

In late July farmers sell their tobacco in Rocky Mount and Goldsboro. Buyers from companies that make tobacco products come to these auctions. An auctioneer stands in front of the tobacco leaves, calling out the prices:

> *Fifty-five cents a pound, five, five, five. Give me 56 cents. I got 57—give me 58!*

The tobacco goes to the person offering the highest price for it.

PEOPLE IN THE COASTAL PLAIN

Soon it is time for John to say good-bye to Susan. He returns home. John's visit has taught him how the history and geography of the Coastal Plain have shaped the lives of the region's people. He has also enjoyed some of the traditions that are shared by the different groups in the region.

Check Your Reading

1. Name the major groups of people who live in the Coastal Plain Region.
2. Name one way that history and geography have shaped the lives of the region's people.
3. Why is Henry Berry Lowry important in our state's history?
4. **THINKING SKILL:** Imagine that a friend is coming to your area for a vacation. List the attractions that best represent your area's culture. Then divide the list into two groups: Places and Events.

Drawing Conclusions

Key Vocabulary

conclusion

Tim likes to visit the zoo. One day he saw the monkeys jump up when a woman went up to their cage. Tim thought about why the monkeys jumped up. He decided that it was because they knew the woman. A few minutes later she went into the cage and gave the monkeys some bananas.

Tim's thinking led him to draw a **conclusion**. Drawing a conclusion means pulling together pieces of information so that they mean something. A conclusion is a final opinion about information that you have been given and thought about without repeating that information.

You can draw conclusions from several facts. For example, if you look outside and see that it is sunny with a stiff breeze, you might conclude that the weather is good for flying a kite. In drawing that conclusion you have used the facts you have learned, and you have given meaning to them.

Trying the Skill

Read each of the following facts. Then draw a conclusion about the population of the Coastal Plain.

- Recently, a few Mexican restaurants have opened in nearby communities.
- Two new Spanish-language radio programs have become popular in the community in the last few years.

1. What conclusion did you draw?
2. What did you do to draw your conclusion?

HELPING YOURSELF

The steps on the left will help you to draw conclusions. The example on the right shows you one way to apply these steps to the statements on page 234.

One Way to Draw Conclusions	Example
1. Identify the subject of all the information that is given.	The subject is population change in your town.
2. Skim, or read through the information quickly.	Quickly read the information to get a general idea of the facts.
3. Look for ideas that are common to all the information that is given.	The information has to do with the new presence of Hispanic people in your community.
4. Write a sentence that tells about the common features and how they are connected to the subject. This is your conclusion.	One conclusion that you might draw is that your town has a growing Hispanic population.

Applying the Skill

Now apply what you have learned by drawing a conclusion from the following statements.

- Many tourists visit the Tryon Palace in New Bern each year.
- The Wright Brothers National Memorial near Kitty Hawk is a popular tourist attraction.
- Fort Raleigh National Historic Site has a busy visitor's center.

1. What is the subject of all the information above?
   - **a.** how many people spend their vacations
   - **b.** interesting sites to visit
   - **c.** the Coastal Plain Tourist Bureau
2. What idea is common to all the statements?
   - **a.** The Coastal Plain Region is attractive to tourists.
   - **b.** The main industry in the Coastal Plain Region is tourism.
   - **c.** The Tryon Palace, the Wright Brothers National Memorial, and Fort Raleigh are the most popular attractions in the region.
3. Write a sentence that draws a conclusion from all the information that you have been given.

Reviewing the Skill

1. What does drawing a conclusion mean?
2. List four steps that you can follow to help you draw conclusions.
3. Name some occasions that might arise in school when you might find it useful to draw conclusions.

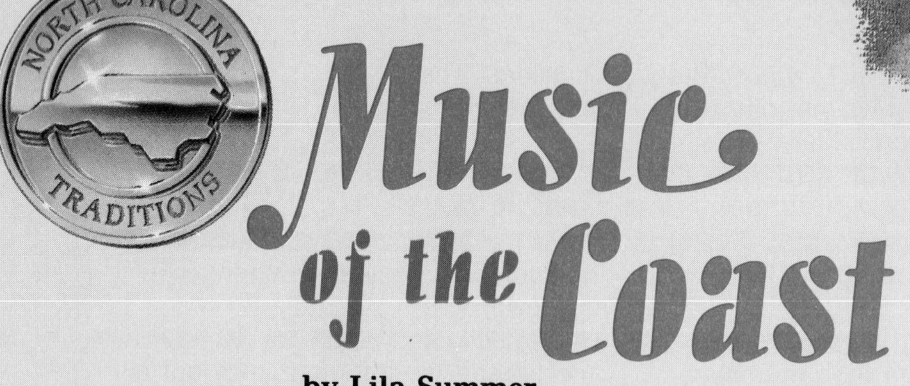

Music of the Coast

by Lila Summer

Our state's Coastal Plain Region has many special features. Several of them, such as the sea and the beach, are sung about in the songs of the region. This tradition of music captures the way of life and spirit of people living in the Coastal Plain. As you read, think about what the tradition of music tells us about the people of the Coastal Plain and our state.

SONGS OF THE SEA

Connie Mason, a singer from Morehead City, learned many songs while she was growing up. Today Mason works at the North Carolina Maritime Museum, collecting songs, including folk songs. *Folk* means "people," and folk songs are written by people in a community about their lives, homes, and ideas. Mason talks about the folk songs that she has collected.

I used to think all our music was in the mountains. Then I discovered I was part of a tradition. The coast is the doorway to the music in our state. In this door blow sea chanteys, or work songs of boatmen and fishermen. You find navy songs and old Irish and English ballads, or story songs. Of course, many of these are about sailing and shipwrecks.

One song is about the shipwreck of the *Florence C. McGee*, which happened during a storm in 1894. This song was written by a young man who lived on Roanoke Island, not far from where the ship went down. Here is the first verse of the song.

Come all ye friends and sailors too
And listen unto me,
While I relate the sad, sad fate
Of the Florence C. McGee.

Mason sings folk songs about life on or near the sea. Some songs are work songs, which many kinds of workers sang as they worked. "Big Boy" Henry, shown in the photograph to the right, is a singer who once worked on a boat in Beaufort. The boat workers sang "Help Me to Raise 'Em" as they worked to let each other know when they should pull on the heavy nets filled with fish. Today machines lift these heavy nets, but "Big Boy" still sings work songs that help us to remember those days.

SONGS OF HOPE

Another kind of folk song is called a spiritual. Spirituals are religious songs that were often written by African Americans in the southern United States. Lloyd Wilson, a Wilmington musician, says that the spirituals that enslaved Africans used to sing "were full of hope and promise of a new world. They were about leaving this world and flying to freedom 'over yonder'."

Many spirituals were sung by enslaved Africans in a special style. While working in the fields, one person would lead the song by singing the first line. Then others would join in together on the second line. Then the leader would call out a third line, and others would respond, or answer, again. This kind of song is known as a call-and-response song. Many of these songs are still sung today by groups of singers in churches.

Here's a verse of a call-and-response song called "Wade in the Water." This song is about a Bible story that told how Moses helped his people to escape from slavery by crossing the sea. Enslaved Africans sang this song, hoping to escape slavery as well.

Who's that yonder all dressed in red?
God's a-goin' to trouble the water.
Looks like the children that Moses led.
God's a-goin' to trouble the water.

MUSIC TO DANCE BY

Another kind of popular coastal music is heard along our beaches, where bands play at dance clubs. These bands play a kind of dance music called beach music. Beach music is a mixture of many different kinds of music. Some people think it sounds like old rock 'n' roll music.

People do the shag dance to beach music. The shag dance, which has many different steps, is a fast dance that is done with a partner. This dance was invented in our state in the 1950s. A well-known shag dancer from Wilmington is Nelson Burton, shown here with his wife and two of his grandchildren. He says:

> *I pick up a step in Morehead City and take it to Wrightsville. Then I learn another step in Atlantic Beach. . . . My granddaughters take shag lessons. They're carrying on the tradition.*

If you go to do the shag dance at a resort or dance club on our beaches, you will hear beach music. Or instead you may hear Connie Mason singing old and new folk songs along the beach. You will find old and young people having fun carrying on the tradition of music in our state.

How does the tradition of music help us to learn about the way of life of the people of the Coastal Plain?

LESSON

2 Working in the Coastal Plain

READ TO LEARN

Key Vocabulary

mixed farming	contract growers	pulpwood
food processing	livestock	commercial fishing

Read Aloud

Cooking is my favorite part of the bed-and-breakfast business.

Ann Erlinghaus enjoys cooking best, but she likes every part of her bed-and-breakfast business. She runs an inn for tourists on Ocracoke Island. In this lesson you will read about other ways that people work on the Coastal Plain.

Read for Purpose

1. **WHAT YOU KNOW:** What are some of the ways people earn their living in your community?
2. **WHAT YOU WILL LEARN:** What are some of the ways people earn their living in the Coastal Plain Region?

FARMING ON THE COAST

When John Cornsilk returned home from the Coastal Plain, he told his friends about his trip. He described the long sandy beaches and the miles of farms. John had expected to see beaches along the coast. However, he was surprised to see so many farms.

Many people earn their living from farming or making products out of the region's crops. The rich sandy soil, regular rainfall, and long growing season give our state miles of fertile land.

Nearly half of our state's tobacco is grown in the Coastal Plain. You read in Chapter 6 that because smoking causes disease, the demand for tobacco has dropped. This drop in demand caused many farmers to grow other cash crops. Some farmers raise soybeans and sweet potatoes with tobacco. This kind of farming is called **mixed farming**. Today most farmers in the Coastal Plain practice mixed farming.

FOOD PRODUCTS

Do you like peanuts or peanut butter? Peanuts grow well in the Coastal Plain. When you eat raw peanuts from the shell, you are eating them in their natural form. When you eat peanut butter, you are eating peanuts that have been changed by a method called **food processing**. Food processing is the method used to turn raw food into different kinds of products.

Peanuts are just one of many crops from which products that are not food are made. For example, did you know that peanuts are used to make glue and paint? Scientists have discovered more than 200 uses for the peanut plant.

Do you like pickles sweet or sour? Like peanut butter, pickles are the end product of food processing. You can see how pickles are processed in the flowchart below.

CHART SKILL: Cucumbers are being **processed** at this pickle plant in Mount Olive. At which step do the cucumbers turn into pickles?

FOOD PROCESSING: FROM CUCUMBERS TO PICKLES

1. Cucumbers are unloaded at the factory.

2. The best cucumbers are chosen for making pickles.

3. Cucumbers soak first in a salty liquid, then in vinegar.

4. Pickles that look bad are removed.

5. The pickles are placed in a jar by hand.

6. Machines add the jar tops and labels.

Perhaps you already know that pickles are made from cucumbers.

Many farmers who grow crops such as cucumbers for food processing are contract growers. A contract grower agrees to raise a certain crop for the food processors. The food processors agree to buy the crop.

LIVESTOCK

On a farm where mixed farming takes place, you might see farmers working in fields of soybean and peanut plants. You might also see fenced-in fields filled with turkeys as far as you can see. Imagine the noise that they make!

In the United States the demand for turkeys is great. Our state is one of the country's leaders in turkey production. As you can imagine, that demand is quite high at Thanksgiving. Each Thanksgiving, North Carolina farmers send a turkey to the President in the White House in Washington, D.C.

Hundreds of turkeys can be raised in huge pens such as this outdoor one shown above.

Turkeys are only one kind of livestock raised on our farms. Livestock are farm animals raised for profit. Hogs are another kind of livestock. Farmers in Sampson County raise more hogs than any other county in the United States. They sell nearly 1 million hogs each year.

FOREST PRODUCTS

Rich soil for farming is not the only natural resource in the Coastal Plain. Miles of woods and forests give us a large supply of trees. Did you know that our state tree is the pine? You read in Chapter 5 about the longleaf pine forests that grow near Cape Fear. You also read about the colonists who made lumber and naval stores from these trees.

Today different kinds of products are made from trees. Pine trees are used to make pulpwood and then paper. Pulpwood is the raw material from which paper is made. This book or the paper on which you write might have been made from North Carolina pine trees.

Imagine the different kinds of work that people do to produce paper products from a pine tree. First the tree is cut down by loggers. Then it is transported by truck to the pulp and paper mills. At the mills the logs are ground into pulp by machine. From the pulp paper products such as bags, wrapping paper, and boxes are made.

COMMERCIAL FISHING

During John's visit to Ocracoke he saw commercial fishing boats off the coast. Commercial fishing is the business of catching fish that are then sold. In North Carolina, commercial fishing is a very important industry.

Many different kinds of fish are in the Atlantic Ocean off the North Carolina coast. One kind of fish, menhaden (men hā′ dən), is caught in huge numbers. They swim close to the surface of the water, which makes them easy to catch. Long ago, Native Americans discovered that menhaden could be used as fertilizer. Today the oil from menhaden is also used to make some soaps and paints.

You have read about farm products that are sold to food processing factories. Fish are also sold to factories. There they are canned or packaged. North Carolina's waters are rich in flounder, mackerel, and striped bass. Commercial fishers also catch shellfish.

FARMS, FISH, AND FORESTS

People who live in the Coastal Plain Region work in many different kinds of jobs. Farming, commercial fishing, and food processing are important businesses. The forests in the region also have many different kinds of resources to process.

The commercial fishing industry provides shellfish for fish markets and food processing factories.

Check Your Reading

1. What is mixed farming?
2. What are some of the ways in which people earn their living in the Coastal Plain Region?
3. GEOGRAPHY SKILL: Name two ways that the geography of the Coastal Plain affects the kinds of work people do.
4. THINKING SKILL: What effect does Thanksgiving Day have on the business of raising turkeys in the Coastal Plain?

BUILDING CITIZENSHIP

POINT/COUNTERPOINT

Should We Build Jetties to Save Our Beaches?

You have just read about different businesses in the Coastal Plain. Many people worry that businesses along the beaches are in danger. Storms and high tides cause our beaches to erode, or wear away. These beaches get smaller every year and water gets closer to our businesses.

Some people think we should build jetties to save our beaches. Jetties are special walls that are built in the water. People in favor of building jetties argue that jetties slow down erosion by stopping sand from washing out to sea. The sand that piles up near the jetties is then pumped back onto the beaches through long pipes. These people believe that building jetties would help protect our beaches and nearby homes and businesses.

Other people believe that we should not build jetties. They say that jetties do more harm than good. They argue that jetties stop sand from washing ashore. They think that jetties only make beaches erode more quickly. If we want wide beaches, they argue, we should move the buildings farther back from the shore. Should jetties be built?

POINT

Jetties Will Save Our Beaches

Kip Oppengaard is the mayor of Topsail Island, which is north of Wilmington. He thinks that building jetties will help our beaches to last longer. Oppengaard would like to bring in pumps to push the sand back up onto his town's beaches. Before that can happen, however, he says that jetties must be built.

> North Carolina's corps of engineers [*a group of builders*] studied our beaches and found that jetties will hold back erosion. The jetties will keep the sand that we pump in from moving out again. This is the way it is being done in Masonboro's inlet [*near Wilmington*], and it works there. This is our beach. If we want to go ahead and take care of it, we have a right to.

- According to Oppengaard, how will jetties help Topsail Island?

COUNTERPOINT

Jetties Will Harm Our Beaches

Orrin Pilkey teaches geology at Duke University. Geology is the study of the earth's surface. Pilkey says that jetties will only make our beaches erode faster. Nothing can stop storms and strong currents from eating away at the beaches, he says. Pilkey argues that the building of jetties is a waste of money.

> Jetties create the problems they are built to prevent. [Almost] all jetties built on the east coast barrier islands have caused more erosion. Masonboro is probably the most rapidly eroding island on the coast. Building jetties is harmful. [Pumping sand] takes almost constant [repairs]. It's like throwing money into the waves. The beach will wear away. Why do a short-term solution?

- According to Pilkey, why is the building of jetties not a good idea?

UNDERSTANDING THE POINT/COUNTERPOINT

1. In your opinion, which side has the stronger argument? Why?
2. What other opinions might people have about jetties?
3. Do you think that an agreement can be reached between those people who are against jetties and those who want to build them? If so, what might it be?

LESSON

3 Population Changes

READ TO LEARN

Key Vocabulary

census

Key Places

Beaufort
Wilmington
Fayetteville
Jacksonville
Pinehurst
Southern Pines

Read Aloud

We expect the next big explosion of growth in North Carolina to come in Wilmington.

Joe Augustine, a business leader in Wilmington, used these words to express his hopes for Wilmington's future. In this lesson you will read about changes that are taking place in the Coastal Plain Region.

Read for Purpose

1. **WHAT YOU KNOW:** Do you live in a large community or a small community?
2. **WHAT YOU WILL LEARN:** How is the growth or loss of population causing life in the Coastal Plain to change?

NEW PATTERNS OF GROWTH

Do you know whether the number of people in your community has stayed the same since you were born? Suppose you live in the Coastal Plain Region. Then the chances are good that the number of people in your area has either grown much larger or much smaller than it was.

We know that the population in this region has changed because every ten years the United States government takes a **census**. A census is an official count of the population in an area. The 1990 census showed that the number of people in most of the region's counties increased between 1980 to 1990. In fact, in some of these counties the population rose sharply. The census also showed that in a few counties the number of people fell. The map on page 247 shows which counties gained and which lost population over the last ten years.

Why are some areas growing faster than others? You have just read about how people live and work in the Coastal Plain. Tourism and commercial fishing have led to growth in certain places. Other places have not grown because they have fewer jobs.

CHANGING RURAL AREAS

The loss of population has been greatest in rural counties. These places already have few people. Many people are leaving rural areas because they cannot find good jobs. Some factories making textiles or tobacco have closed or moved to foreign countries. Many people have moved out of state or to growing Coastal Plain cities.

What happens when people leave an area? For one thing, businesses lose customers. Without customers, some of these businesses fail. When businesses fail and people are out of work, the economy suffers. To stay strong, rural counties must attract businesses that will make new jobs.

GROWTH OF COASTAL AREAS

Some of the counties that have grown rapidly over the last ten years are in the Tidewater area. Find Currituck, Dare, Carteret, and Brunswick counties on the map on this page. The populations of these counties grew because of a rise in the number of tourists and people buying vacation homes. This rise

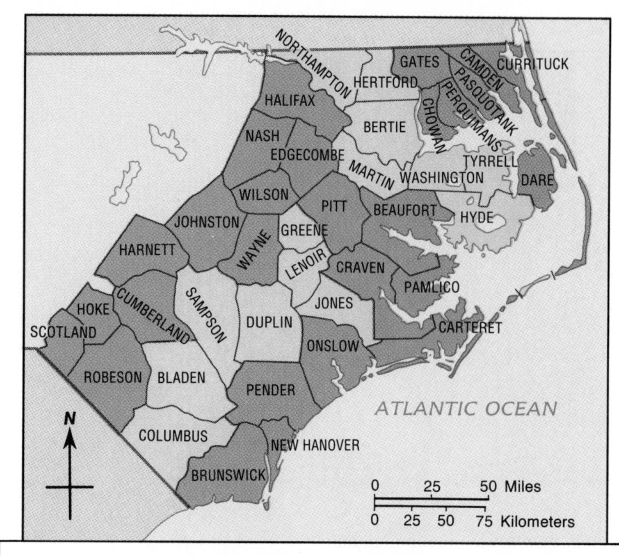

COASTAL PLAIN: County Population Changes, 1980–1990

Gained population

Lost population

MAP SKILL: Study the map key carefully. Did more counties in the Coastal Plain Region gain or lose population between 1980 and 1990?

has meant more jobs in home building and tourism.

Long ago many places along the Outer Banks were connected to the mainland by only one bridge. Travel was hard. Local leaders saw the need to improve transportation. Now bridges, ferryboats, and highways connect the mainland with the Outer Banks.

More people are also visiting the coastal towns in the Tidewater area. For many years **Beaufort** continued to lose population. Then in the 1970s the people in the town decided to repair many houses that had been built more than 200 years ago. Now Beaufort looks much as it

People of all ages enjoy visiting the exhibits at the North Carolina Maritime Museum in Beaufort.

did in the 1700s. The North Carolina Maritime Museum, which has exhibits on coastal sea life, was also rebuilt. Today Beaufort has visitors year-round, and the town's economy has improved.

However, the growth of towns along the coast has also meant challenges. As you have read, the plant and sea life of these areas are part of a special environment. Population growth has harmed this environment in some areas.

To keep themselves from growing too fast, some towns are taxing people who rent hotel rooms or buy and sell land. Others are allowing only a certain number of businesses in their towns.

INTERSTATE 40

People hope that the newest section of Interstate 40 will help the economy of the Inner Coastal Plain. Find I-40 on the Atlas map on page 361. In 1990 the final stretch of this superhighway was finished. I-40 now connects the port of **Wilmington** with Raleigh, the state capital. The highway continues west through North Carolina, six other states, and ends in California.

Johnston County has already changed because of I-40. Now it is just 45 minutes by car from Raleigh. People can afford to buy houses in Johnston County and work in Raleigh where there are more jobs.

Other counties that expect to grow because of the highway are Sampson and Duplin counties. Poultry and hogs are raised and processed there. Using the highway nearby, trucks now can speed these products to markets in states west of North Carolina.

THE LARGEST PORT

Perhaps the place that hopes to gain the most from I-40 is the city of Wilmington. Today Wilmington is the state's ninth-largest city. I-40 has cut the time it takes to get from Wilmington to Raleigh from $3\frac{1}{2}$ hours to 2 hours. As a result, more people are visiting Wilmington and buying land in the nearby area.

Each year millions of dollars in goods pass through Wilmington, our state's largest port. The new part of I-40 will help Wilmington to move more goods. Now businesses in the states west of North Carolina can bring goods by truck to Wilmington. From there the goods will be shipped overseas. Goods arriving at the port can be carried by truck to businesses that are in western states.

OTHER AREAS OF GROWTH

Several cities and towns in the region have grown because of the work that people there do. They have also grown because of the special services that they offer. Many men and women in our country's armed services are stationed at two large army bases near **Fayetteville** and **Jacksonville**. They keep many

Riverboats dock at Wilmington. The *Henrietta II* ferries passengers along the Cape Fear River.

These soldiers are at an army base. Army bases are important to the defense of our country and to the economy of our state.

businesses booming there. Among the businesses that depend upon the bases are food stores, dry cleaners, and barbershops. The size of the army base at Fort Bragg gives Fayetteville the largest population of any city in the Coastal Plain—75,000 people.

RETIREMENT CENTERS

You read in Chapter 3 that people come from all over the world to the Sandhills area. These visitors come to the southwestern part of the Coastal Plain to play golf. The Sandhills offer golfers a choice of 31 courses on which to play. Recently many retired people have settled in the communities of Pinehurst and Southern Pines. They like the pleasant climate, beautiful views, and good services. Meeting the needs of retired people, golfers, and others who enjoy sports gives jobs to people in these towns. It also keeps the area's economy strong.

CHALLENGE FOR THE FUTURE

Today the Coastal Plain Region has better roads, more recreational areas, and new industries. These changes are attracting people to move to new parts of the region. Now the leaders of the region must help all parts of the Coastal Plain to share in this growth. They must also try to guide future growth so that it helps everyone.

Check Your Reading

1. Name two problems that are caused by the loss of population in some rural areas of the Coastal Plain.
2. What are some of the challenges that growing coastal areas and Coastal Plain cities face?
3. Name two kinds of special communities that help to strengthen the economy of the Coastal Plain.
4. GEOGRAPHY SKILL: Use the map showing I-40 on page 361 with the one on page 247 to name the counties that might grow as a result of the highway.
5. THINKING SKILL: Predict what might happen to the growing Coastal Plain communities if they do not find ways to control their growth.

REVIEWING VOCABULARY

auction
census
commercial fishing
food processing
migrant worker

Number a sheet of paper from 1 to 5. Beside each number write the word or term from the list above that best matches the definition.

1. The turning of raw food into finished products
2. The business of catching fish to be sold
3. A farm worker who moves around in search of work
4. An official count of the population
5. A public sale in which goods are sold to the highest bidder

REVIEWING FACTS

Number a sheet of paper from 1 to 5. Beside each number write **T** if the statement is true. If it is false, rewrite the statement to make it true.

1. The Lumbee were forced off their land in the 1830s.
2. One important product made from peanuts is pulpwood.
3. Contract growers agree to sell their produce to a certain supermarket.
4. The livestock raised in our state includes turkeys and hogs.
5. Interstate 40 connects Raleigh with Fayetteville, North Carolina's largest port.

WRITING ABOUT MAIN IDEAS

1. **Writing a Poem:** Choose one feature of the Coastal Plain Region, such as its people, an interesting sight, or ways of earning a living there. Write a poem about that feature, that both tells about it and expresses your feelings about it.
2. **Writing a List:** Make a list of some of the cities that I-40 goes through in our state. You might want to read Lesson 3 again and to study the road map on page 361.
3. **Writing About Perspectives:** Suppose that the United States government wanted to save money by closing certain military bases, including one near your town or city. How do you think a store owner in the area might feel about this decision? Write a letter that the store owner might write to the government about the base closing.

BUILDING SKILLS: DRAWING CONCLUSIONS

1. Tell in your own words what it means to draw a conclusion.
2. Why is it important to draw conclusions about the information that you read or hear?
3. What do you suppose might cause you to change a conclusion once you have drawn it?

CHAPTER 9

LIFE IN THE PIEDMONT

FOCUS

You can really enjoy yourself in Charlotte. You can go downtown to the park. You can also go to Discovery Place and experiment with science the fun way on your own. It's a sports town, too. I have a favorite basketball team, the Charlotte Hornets.

Sharhonda Mayes lives in Charlotte, which is our state's largest city. In this chapter you will read about the special places in the Piedmont Region.

LESSON

1 Living in the Piedmont

READ TO LEARN

Key Vocabulary
scarce

Key People
Conrad Reed
John Baker

Key Places
Metrolina
Charlotte
Raleigh
Greensboro
Triad
Seagrove

Read Aloud

A wide-awake town is a town where folks want new folks and welcome strangers.

These words appeared in the North Carolina magazine *The State* close to 60 years ago. "Wide-awake" still describes many places in the Piedmont Region. Only now these places are big, busy cities. In this lesson you will read about the way of life of people in many parts of the Piedmont Region.

Read for Purpose

1. **WHAT YOU KNOW:** Which large cities are located in the Piedmont Region?
2. **WHAT YOU WILL LEARN:** How has the way of life of people in the Piedmont changed over time?

PIEDMONT URBAN CRESCENT

As you have read, more people live in the Piedmont than in any other region of our state. Nearly all of our largest cities can be found in this region. Together they form the Piedmont Urban Crescent. These cities grew during the mid-1800s, when railroads were first built in North Carolina.

CITY LIFE

Today the Piedmont Urban Crescent has three metropolitan areas within it. As you know, a metropolitan area is a large city or group of cities and the suburbs surrounding them. The Piedmont's largest metropolitan area is called **Metrolina**. **Charlotte** is its largest city. As you can see on the map on page 254, some of the cities that make up Metrolina are in South Carolina.

The region's second-largest metropolitan area is the Piedmont Triangle, which is also known as the Research Triangle. As you have read, it is made up of Raleigh, which is the state capital, Durham, and Chapel Hill. The cities of Greensboro, Winston-Salem, and High Point form another large metropolitan area called the Triad.

The lives of people in the Triangle and the Triad are connected in many ways. For example, people living in Chapel Hill might go to Durham to see the Durham Bulls play baseball and to Raleigh to hear music played by the North Carolina Symphony. Tar Heels living in Greensboro might work in the furniture factories in High Point and shop in nearby Winston-Salem.

MAP SKILL: The Piedmont Urban Crescent is made up of three large metropolitan areas. Which city is the largest in each of these areas?

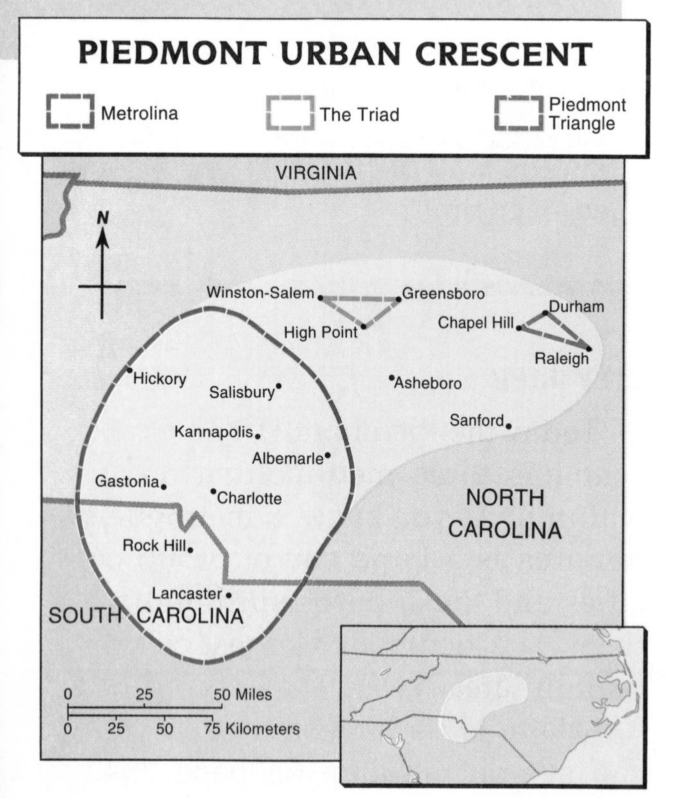

CHARLOTTE

Most North Carolinians work, shop, and have fun in the "wide-awake" centers of the cities. Not long ago, these centers, or the busy parts of cities such as Charlotte, were smaller than they are today.

You have read that Charlotte is part of Metrolina. But do you know how Charlotte grew to become North Carolina's largest city? The following story will help to explain the changes that took place in Charlotte during the early 1800s. It will also tell you what the city's people have done to preserve, or keep, their past.

The story begins in 1799. A young boy named Conrad Reed went fishing in the creek on his father's farm. Conrad was about to toss his fishing line into the water when he saw a large yellow rock near the water's edge. The rock was so unusual that Conrad took it home, where it was used as a doorstop.

Several years later John Reed, Conrad's father, sold the rock to a jeweler in Fayetteville for $3.50. Later, Reed learned that the rock was a 17-pound (7.7-kg) piece of gold. At the time that amount of

Discovery Place in Charlotte has hands-on science exhibits. Paintings can be seen at the city's Mint Museum of Art.

gold was worth thousands of dollars because gold was **scarce**. The word *scarce* means that there is less of something than is needed or wanted.

Conrad Reed's discovery led to a gold boom, or a rapid growth in gold mining. This boom helped Charlotte to grow. In fact, it was the first gold boom in the United States. In 1837 our country's government built the first branch of the United States Mint in Charlotte. A mint is a place where coins are made. The mint in Charlotte made gold coins until the 1860s, when it began to make coins from other metals.

In 1935 the Charlotte mint was about to be torn down and replaced by a post office. The people of Charlotte worked to preserve their mint. The building was moved to its present location, where it was named the Charlotte Mint Museum of Art.

RALEIGH

Raleigh, the capital of our state, is located in the Piedmont Triangle. State government buildings and many universities are located in Raleigh. Today the city is a rapidly growing metropolitan area that has more than 200,000 people. Its largest groups are made up of people whose ancestors came from England, Germany, and Scotland.

In recent years some African Americans have come back to live in Raleigh. Years ago many blacks left North Carolina because they could not find work and were not treated equally. Today there are more jobs in the Piedmont Region. And African Americans now feel surer that their rights will be protected.

John Baker is one African American who has returned to Raleigh. Baker was a professional football player for many years. During that time he lived in different parts of the country. After Baker stopped playing football, he returned to North Carolina, where he had been born. Baker explains why he returned.

> *I've always wanted to come home. Now the jobs are here and [also] laws to uphold our rights.*

Today Baker is the sheriff of Wake County. He is the first African-American sheriff in our state.

Lively cities and traditional crafts, like pottery, are important parts of the Piedmont way of life.

GREENSBORO

During the past 20 years, thousands of Asian families have moved to North Carolina. Church groups, businesses, and local governments have helped many of these families to find homes and jobs.

Hien Dai (hů′ yen dī) was born in Greensboro, our state's third-largest city, in 1982. Her family had moved to Greensboro in 1976. They had come from Vietnam, a country in southeast Asia. Hien Dai's parents work at one of the textile mills in Greensboro. They go to religious services that are held in Vietnamese. They buy Vietnamese foods at local supermarkets.

Hien enjoys visiting Greensboro's natural science center and planetarium. She describes some of the other places she has seen.

> *My class went on a trip to High Point, where we watched people making furniture. Another time we went to see the village at Old Salem. Now I want my parents to go there to see how the Moravians lived.*

SEAGROVE

Seagrove is a town in the Piedmont near Asheboro that draws many tourists. In Seagrove many people preserve their traditions through their work. The Europeans who settled there long ago used the town's red-clay soil and timber from the forests to make clay. After shaping the clay into pots, they used

At the state fair in Raleigh, Tar Heels celebrate their traditions and have fun.

timber to fire the ovens that baked the clay into pottery. You will read more about this pottery in the Traditions lesson on pages 258–261.

THE STATE FAIR

During October of each year, Tar Heels from all of our regions celebrate their farming traditions at the state fair in Raleigh. Visitors can see examples of prize-winning fruits and vegetables such as huge watermelons and cucumbers. The winners of baking and cooking contests proudly show their jellies, cookies, and cakes. Members of 4-H clubs parade their award-winning livestock. The fair is also a time to enjoy thrilling rides on the Ferris wheel and the roller coaster.

A CHANGING WAY OF LIFE

As you have read, the Piedmont is a region with large, busy cities. During recent years, several groups of people have been drawn to the Piedmont's urban areas because of the jobs that can be found in the cities. The Piedmont is a growing region with a changing way of life.

Check Your Reading

1. Name the important cities that make up the Metrolina, the Piedmont Triangle, and the Triad.
2. What features of the Piedmont have brought more people to the region in recent years?
3. GEOGRAPHY SKILL: Which natural resources affected the way that the town of Seagrove grew?
4. THINKING SKILL: What effect did Conrad Reed's discovery of a gold rock on his father's farm have on the city of Charlotte?

by Lila Summer

You have read that Seagrove is a popular location for tourists and a center for pottery. Making pottery is a craft that people in the Piedmont have become especially skilled at doing. A craft is a special skill that people use to make objects. Other Piedmont crafts include quilt making and furniture making. As you read, think about how North Carolinians use the resources of the Piedmont to carry on the tradition of their crafts.

PIEDMONT POTTERY

The best clay for making pottery in our state comes from the Piedmont. This is why Mark Hewitt, a potter, lives in Chatham County. He digs clay close to his home because he does not like store-bought clay. "You can't end up with a pot that is alive without starting with clay that is alive," he says.

Hewitt takes the clay to his workshop, where hundreds of simple pots line the walls. Piedmont potters are famous for jars, pitchers, and jugs, which are used for juice, milk, and molasses.

With a "splat!" Hewitt throws wet clay onto a round spinning wheel, called a potter's wheel. The photos on this page show how he shapes the clay into a pot. Making pottery takes practice.

After Hewitt finishes forming the pot, he places it to dry on a shelf with other pots. Dried pots are coated with a glaze, or a shiny covering, that makes them waterproof. After Hewitt has glazed many pots, they are ready to be fired, or baked in a kiln, which is a huge oven. Firing makes the pots hard so that they won't break easily.

The kiln that Hewitt built is as big as a school bus. He puts small pots on a shelf and stacks big pots on the floor of the kiln. Then he lights a wood fire and heats the pots for two days and nights until they are done. Piedmont potters are lucky that they do not have to travel far for wood. The Piedmont forests have plenty of it.

There was a time when most people did not value pottery making. Farmers made pots because they needed jugs. People called one pottery-making area of the Piedmont "Jugtown" as an insult. Luckily, farmers in the Piedmont carried on this craft tradition. Today people are proud to own handmade pottery from this region. Jugtown is now one of the most famous pottery centers in the world. Its plain glazed jugs are similar to the ones that the early European settlers made.

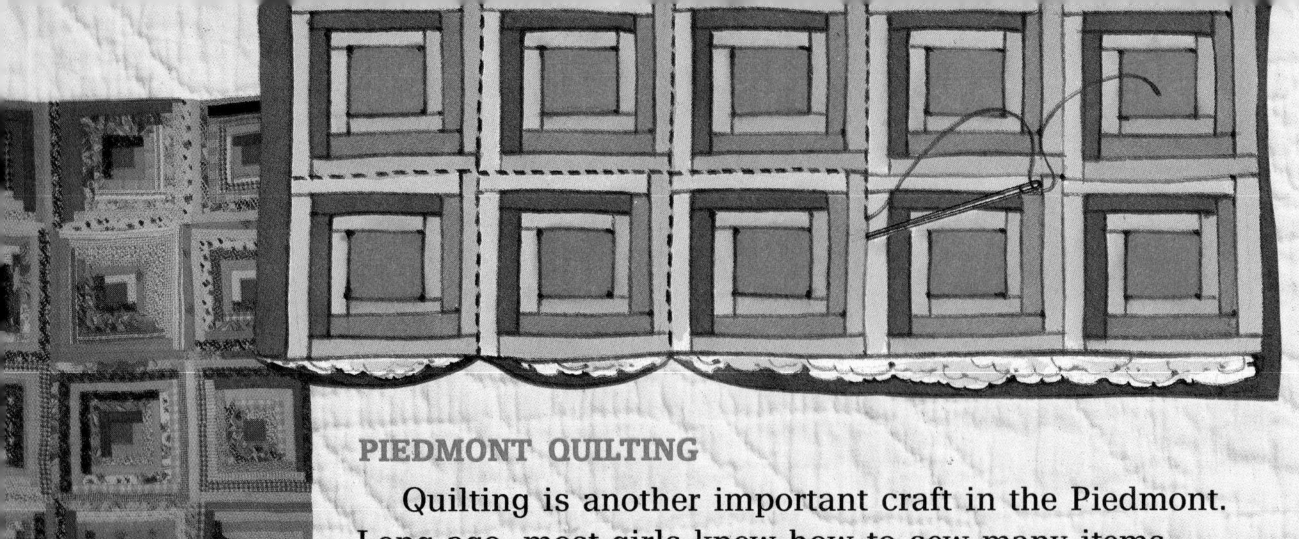

PIEDMONT QUILTING

Quilting is another important craft in the Piedmont. Long ago, most girls knew how to sew many items including clothing, towels, and tablecloths. Sewing skills were also used to make bed covers, or quilts.

A quilt is a kind of cloth sandwich. The bottom is usually a plain cloth. The middle is filled with stuffing such as heavy cotton fluff. The top cloth is often made by sewing together different pieces of cloth so that they form designs. Sewing the three layers together is called quilting. Quilting is a lot of work.

Long ago, many quilters had to make their own cloth before they could begin sewing. Today, many quilters use cloth made by Piedmont textile manufacturers.

There are many different quilt designs. Tulip patterns were often used by German settlers. Quilts that had patterns of large stars or a bright red sun with yellow points were often made by Scots-Irish settlers. Many quilts made of long log-shaped strips were created by African Americans. Strip designs are still used today in Africa.

A few years ago, a group of women was concerned that an important tradition would be lost because many of our state's old quilts were being thrown away. They formed a group called the North Carolina Quilt Project and collected information about these old quilts so that people would always remember them. They hope to keep alive the tradition of quilt making.

CRAFTS TODAY

Long ago, people made many more things by hand than they do today. There were no factories, and people made good dishes and warm blankets by hand. Today, people still carry on the tradition of making these items. They are made with such skill and beauty that people from all around the country come to see them.

Quilting and pottery making are only two Piedmont crafts. The Piedmont Region is also known for other crafts, such as furniture making. Our huge furniture industry grew from the traditions of the Moravians and others who settled in the region. Today you can see quilts, pottery, and furniture at Piedmont agricultural fairs, crafts festivals, and museums such as the Southern Decorative Arts Museum in Winston-Salem. The Ackland Museum in Chapel Hill and the Southern Regional Furniture Market in High Point are also places where you can find handmade items. Maybe you own something made by a person who used a craft to create it. It may be a quilt or a little brown jug. Each one tells a story of a Piedmont tradition.

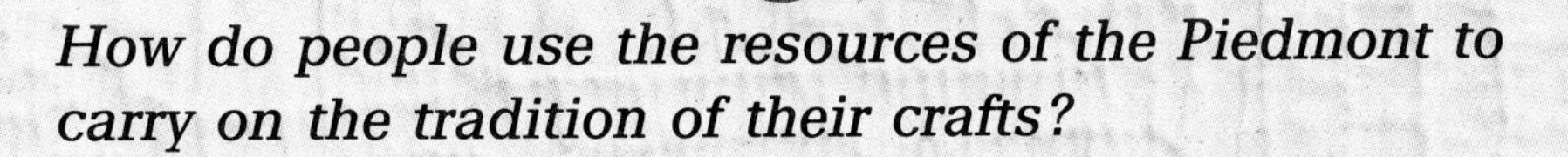

How do people use the resources of the Piedmont to carry on the tradition of their crafts?

LESSON

2 Working in the Piedmont

READ TO LEARN

Key Vocabulary
finished goods
capital resources

Key People
Thomas Day
Washington Duke
James Buchanan Duke
Richard Joshua Reynolds

Key Places
High Point

Read Aloud

I used to work with children. Now my classrooms are filled with adults. With the communications [industry] changing so quickly, there is always new information to teach.

This is how Rachel Strauss describes her job as a teacher at a company in Raleigh that makes telephone equipment. Strauss teaches hundreds of workers how to send calls during emergencies such as hurricanes. In this lesson you will read about some of the thousands of people like Strauss who have helped the Piedmont to become the industrial center of our state.

Read for Purpose

1. WHAT YOU KNOW: What are some of the jobs that the people in your community have?
2. WHAT YOU WILL LEARN: How are many of the Piedmont's industries changing?

PIEDMONT INDUSTRIES

You have just read about the urban way of life of many people in the Piedmont. A large number of them work in several big industries, such as furniture and textiles.

As you have read, many Piedmont industries use the region's natural resources to make products. Wood from the Piedmont's oak, hickory, maple, and pine trees is used in making furniture. You have also read that this region's fast-moving rivers helped run machines in early textile mills. The red-clay soil of the region's northern counties is good for growing tobacco and for making bricks.

Today automation is changing the brickmaking, textile, and furniture industries. As you know, in an automated factory machines run by themselves or are run by other machines. These machines now do much of the work at a much faster pace than workers can. As a result, some companies now need fewer workers than they did before. This means that many workers have had to look for new jobs.

EARLY FURNITURE MAKERS

One of the industries that technology is changing is the furniture industry. More than 300 years ago, skilled craftsworkers realized that the Piedmont's trees could be used to make many kinds of furniture. Moravian craftsworkers, about whom you read in Chapter 5, became known for the beautiful furniture that they made by hand.

One well-known craftsworker was a cabinetmaker named Thomas Day. He made furniture that was popular in many southeastern states. Day was a free African American who started a furniture workshop in Caswell County in the 1850s. Many of his customers were wealthy Tar Heel planters.

AN INDUSTRY STARTS

Several of the earliest furniture factories in the Piedmont were opened in the 1880s. They were started by the owners of lumber companies in High Point. The town is close to forests of hardwood trees. In the past the owners had mostly sold their lumber. By the 1880s these owners saw a way of earning more money. Instead of selling their lumber as a raw material, they began to use it to make wooden products. Furniture and other products that are made from raw materials are called finished goods. Soon factory workers were producing many kinds of furniture, which were bought by people in northern and southeastern states.

This bureau and armchair are among the many kinds of furniture that were made by cabinetmaker Thomas Day.

Workers use machines such as the one shown here to shape some chair parts. The pieces are then glued together.

MAKING FURNITURE TODAY

Today over 86,000 Tar Heels make furniture in Piedmont cities such as Thomasville, High Point, and Hickory.

Thomasville is known as "Chair City." Imagine that you are visiting a factory there to see how the parts of a chair are put together. You see workers cut the chair pieces so that they fit when they are glued together. Workers then attach the chair legs. Other workers sand the wood and use a liquid to preserve and protect it. After the liquid has dried, the chair is sanded again to give it a smoother finish. Then the chair is ready to be sold.

Today more and more workers are using the newest technology to help make chairs and other furniture. Computer programs help to design furniture, and computer-controlled tools cut the wood. Such tools are called **capital resources**. These are the tools and machines used to produce goods and services.

THE FURNITURE SHOW

People who do not actually make furniture also work in this Piedmont industry. In fact, making furniture is only one part of this very large industry. For example, a number of people in the Piedmont have jobs connected with furniture sales.

Each year in April and October, a show in High Point called the International Home Furnishings Market is crowded with home decorators and buyers from over 50 countries. They come to see the new furniture styles.

On page 162 you read about Jenny Voysey, who helps her family in a furniture showroom. Many people like the Voyseys have jobs in the hundreds of furniture showrooms in High Point. The furniture show also creates jobs for the people of High Point and nearby areas. What services do you think are needed by the people who come to the International Home Furnishings Market?

TEXTILES

As you have read, textile production was one of our state's important early industries. Today, though, Piedmont mills are competing with mills in other countries. In some countries, textiles can be made more cheaply because their workers are paid less than workers in our country. This has caused many mills in the Piedmont to close or to make other finished goods.

BRICKMAKING

Brickmaking is another large Piedmont industry. Tar Heels make about 1 billion bricks yearly—more than do people in any other state.

Automation has helped workers to make more bricks in less time. Instead of shaping and cutting clay into bricks by hand, workers now use machines to mix clay and water in molds. These molds form the clay into logs. Other machines then cut these clay logs into bricks.

TOBACCO INDUSTRY LEADERS

As you know, the Piedmont is a major producer of tobacco. Here the leaders of the tobacco industry started their companies in the mid-1800s. Washington Duke started growing tobacco shortly before the Civil War.

In 1884 the Duke family began making cigarettes with a machine that could roll 200 cigarettes a minute. Using this capital resource, Duke's American Tobacco Company became the country's largest cigarette producer by 1894.

James Buchanan Duke was the son of Washington Duke. In the early 1900s, when he headed the company, Duke gave part of his family's wealth to a small Methodist school named Trinity College. In honor of the $40 million gift, the school changed its name to Duke University. Today Duke is one of our country's finest private universities.

A WINSTON-SALEM FORTUNE

Richard Joshua Reynolds was another leader in the tobacco industry. The factories that Reynolds built in Winston-Salem in the 1870s helped the city to become a center for making tobacco.

His company, now called RJR Nabisco, is still a leading tobacco company. However, it now makes many kinds of products, like cookies, crackers, and pet food.

James B. Duke (*left*) and Richard Joshua Reynolds (*right*) were two leaders of North Carolina's tobacco industry.

Tar Heel poultry workers sort and package thousands of chicken parts every day.

POULTRY PROCESSING

Many Piedmont farmers are contract growers who raise chickens and turkeys, or poultry, for food-processing factories. In fact, poultry processing is the largest agricultural business in the Southeast.

Today the owners of poultry factories, or plants, in all parts of the state face a challenge. They need to improve the safety of their plants. The importance of plant safety was seen in 1991 when a poultry-plant fire killed 25 workers in the Piedmont town of Hamlet.

NEW JOBS AND SKILLS

Automation and the demand for better machines are forcing Piedmont workers to learn new skills. Some workers now run the new machines in automated factories. Others are engineers who design these machines. Have you ever thought about who decides whether a tool should be made of plastic or metal, or whether the wires in an electric cord should be thick or thin? Highly skilled workers are trained to deal with questions like these. These workers are important resources of our state.

More businesses are hiring people to study the ways in which products can be improved. Jobs in which people work to improve products are an important part of the region's economy. Many of these jobs are done in Research Triangle Park, which you will read about in Lesson 3.

INDUSTRIES OLD AND NEW

As you have read, people working in industries both old and new have contributed to the growth of the Piedmont. Today automation is changing many industries and the ways in which people work.

Check Your Reading

1. In which industries do many people in the Piedmont work?
2. How are many of the Piedmont's industries changing?
3. How have Thomas Day, Richard Joshua Reynolds, and the Duke family helped Piedmont industries to grow?
4. **THINKING SKILL:** Identify some of the effects of automation on the larger Piedmont industries.

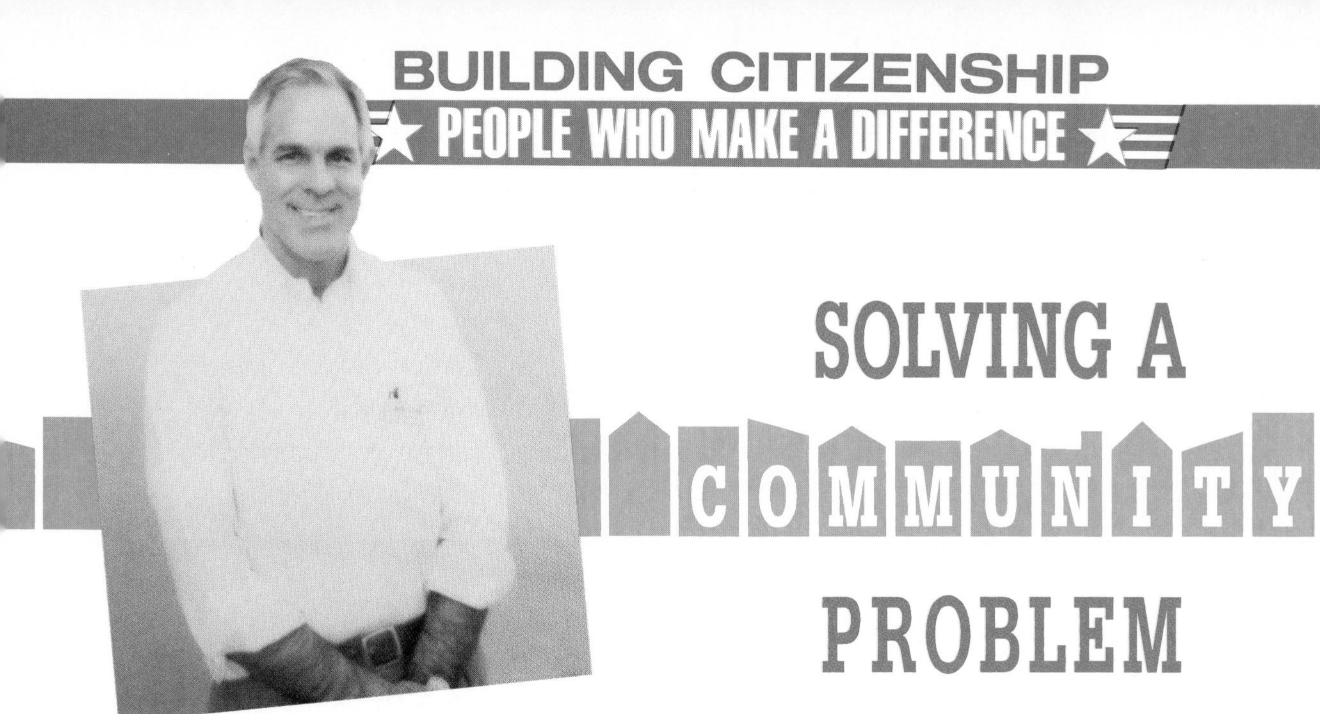

SOLVING A COMMUNITY PROBLEM

Ed Spence lives and works in the Piedmont Region. In 1987 Spence discovered that some of his young employees had been stealing money from his cash register to buy dangerous drugs. "If these kids are stealing money, drugs are a bigger problem than I realized," Spence thought. He decided to do something to make his city a safer and healthier place in which to live.

Within a week Spence had called a town meeting in the library to talk about drugs. To his surprise, hundreds of people showed up—so many that the meeting had to be moved from the library to the high school auditorium.

Spence kept working on the problem. In 1988 he began to form drug education programs in schools and in other places in the city. He set up a 24-hour phoneline staffed with volunteers to answer questions about drugs. He worked to have the courts give tougher punishments to drug dealers. Spence also made himself available to anyone who needed help with a drug problem. He offered jobs to people who had stopped using drugs.

Some people in Siler City did not want to admit that people were using dangerous drugs. They said that Spence was wrong and became less friendly toward him. Drug dealers were angry with him and threatened his life.

However Spence did not give up, and his efforts paid off. The police added two drug agents to the police force. The courts gave drug dealers longer prison terms. Spence continued to give talks about the dangers of using drugs.

Because of Spence, many people in Siler City have turned their lives around. Siler City is trying to end the use of dangerous drugs, and it is now a better place for all to live.

Comparing Maps

Key Vocabulary
population density map
land use map

Throughout this book you have been using maps to learn about the geography, history, and economy of North Carolina. Each of the maps has helped you to understand something different about our state.

As you have seen, maps show information in a special way. Each map, however, usually shows only one kind of information. By comparing maps that show different kinds of information, you can learn even more about North Carolina.

Both maps on page 269 show North Carolina. However, each map presents different information about the state. What kind of information is shown on each of the maps?

Different Kinds of Maps

Map A is a population density map. As you know, it shows the number of people living in a square mile (or a square kilometer) in different areas of the state. You can use this map to discover in which areas many people live and in which areas few people live.

Map A uses different colors to show the number of people that live in a particular area. Which color is used to show areas in which there are fewer than 50 people for each square mile (fewer than 20 people for each square kilometer)?

Map B is a land use map. It shows some of the different ways in which people in the Piedmont use the land to earn a living. You already know that many people in the region work in manufacturing. The land use map shows the areas in the Piedmont in which there are factories. The land use map also shows how much land is used for forests and for farming. Study the key for each map to make sure that you understand what the colors used on the map stand for.

The key on **Map B** uses different colors to show how people use the land. Which color is used to show manufacturing areas? Which color shows forest areas?

You can also use the information on these maps to compare areas. Together, the maps can show you how population and land use affect one another. For example, first find the most heavily populated areas in the Piedmont Region. Then look at the manufacturing areas on the land use map. Are the areas that are used for manufacturing heavily populated? Why do you think this is true?

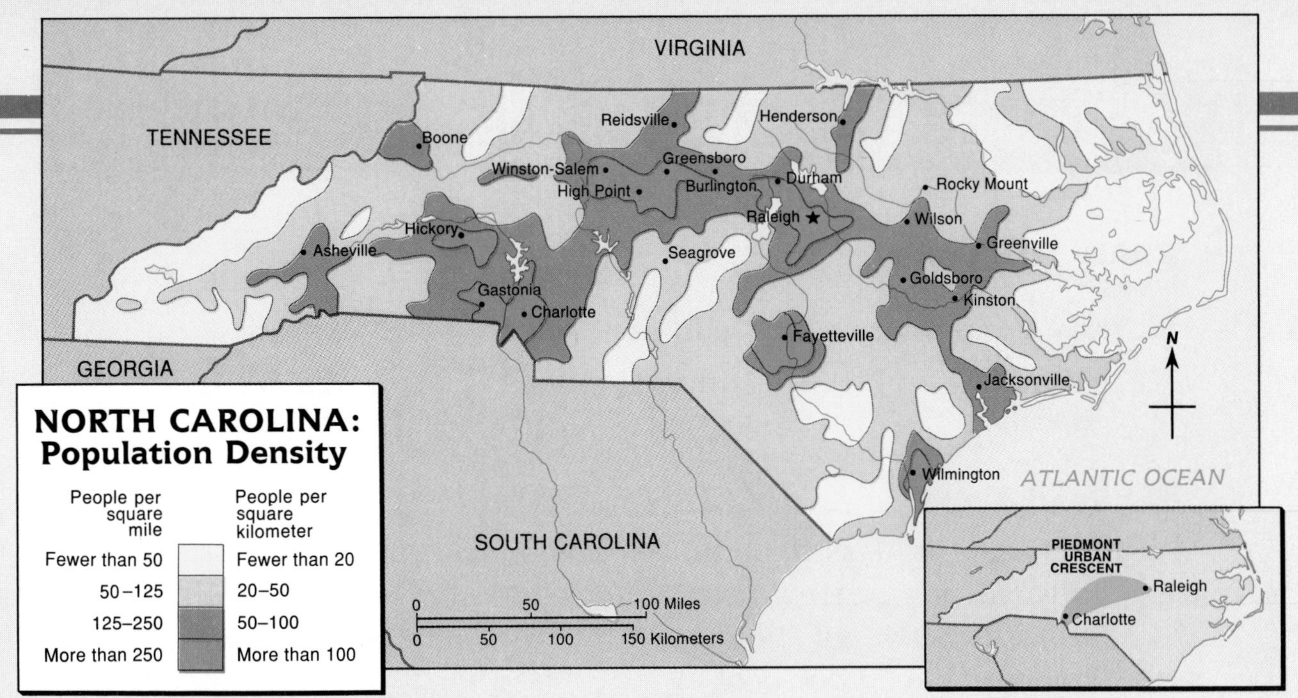

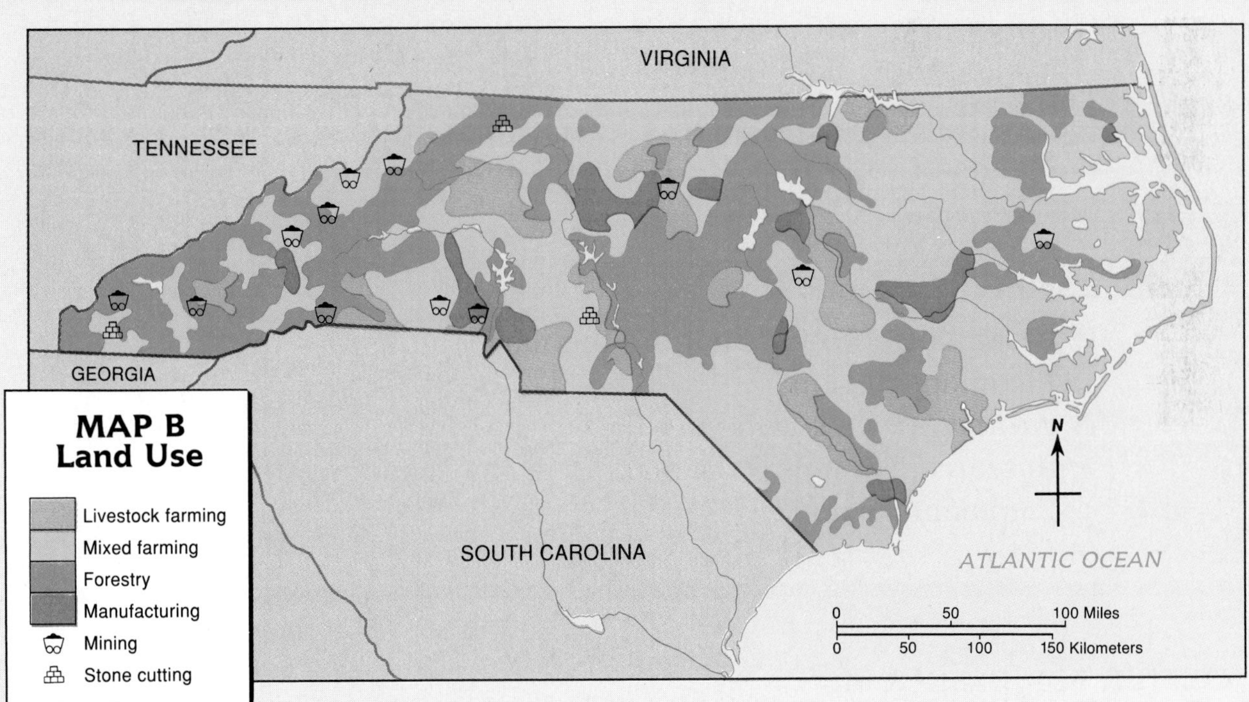

Reviewing the Skill

Compare the maps on this page to answer the following questions.

1. Approximately how many people are there per square mile (or per square kilometer) in Raleigh?
2. Which city is located in a more heavily populated area—Rocky Mount or Winston-Salem?
3. Compare the two maps above. Are the areas in which timber is grown heavily populated?
4. Why is it helpful to compare different maps of the same place?

LESSON

3 Research Triangle Park

READ TO LEARN

Key Vocabulary
research
high tech

Key People
Luther Hodges
Archie Davis

Key Places
Research Triangle Park

Read Aloud

This [area is] less than half an hour's drive from three universities. . . . We'd been agricultural: tobacco, textiles, furniture, brick, all [products] from the land. We had to do more to keep our best.

Ned Huffman, a Tar Heel businessman, used these words to explain the need to create different kinds of jobs for our state's people. In this lesson you will read about the kinds of work that Tar Heels do at a special place in the Piedmont.

Read for Purpose:

1. WHAT YOU KNOW: What are the major industries in the Piedmont Region?
2. WHAT YOU WILL LEARN: What special contribution is Research Triangle Park making to the economy of the Piedmont Region?

CENTER FOR RESEARCH

You have read that the Piedmont is a region of busy cities in which many people work in large industries. The Piedmont Region is also the home of a famous research center. The word *research* means to search for new ideas or for new ways of doing things.

Some day you may need to take a new medicine to cure an illness, or you may use a talking computer. Products such as these are developed by the people who work at **Research Triangle Park**. Research Triangle Park covers 6,700 acres (2,712 ha) near the Piedmont cities of Raleigh, Durham, and Chapel Hill. It is the largest research center in the United States.

The research center has provided jobs for over 30,000 people from North Carolina and around the world. Their work brings in $1 billion every year to our state's economy. It has also created jobs for people in other parts of North Carolina and for people in nearby communities who provide services for the Park's workers.

The name Research Triangle Park tells what its workers do. The people at the Park work on medical and scientific research. They try to find cures for diseases, make better drugs, and find new ones. Other scientists study how pollution changes the environment. They then try to make chemicals that are not harmful. They also look for safe ways to handle the chemical wastes that industries produce.

The word *triangle* in the Park's name comes from an imaginary triangle. This triangle is formed by the three large universities located nearby. They are Duke University, North Carolina State University, and the University of North Carolina. Teachers at these schools work closely with Park researchers. Find the Park on the map on this page. In which cities are the three universities located?

If you were to view Research Triangle Park from an airplane, you would understand why *Park* is part of its name. Most of the Research Triangle is covered with trees. Its founders asked companies that wanted to build in the Park to use only a small part of the land and to keep the rest natural. One worker has described it as "city life in a country setting."

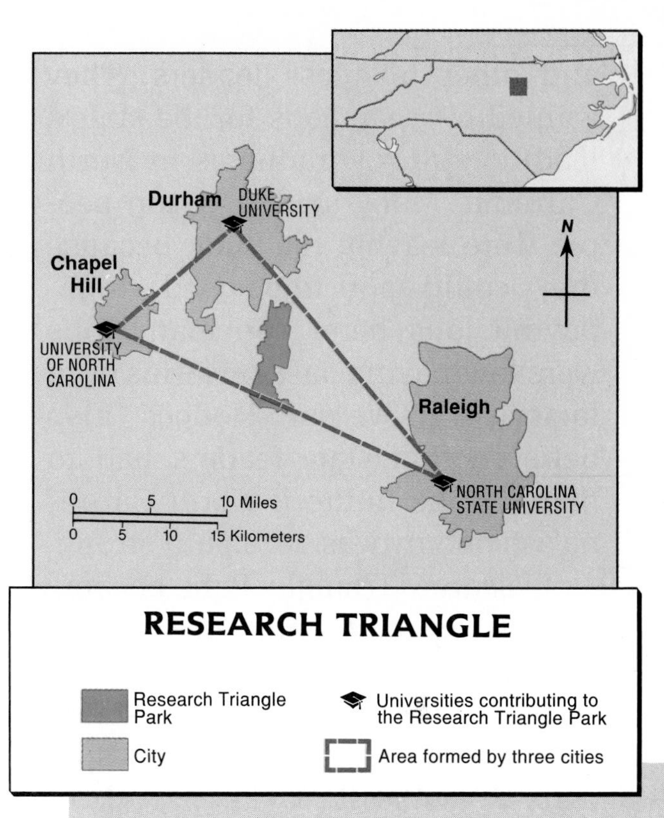

MAP SKILL: Research Triangle Park is located in the center of the Research Triangle. Which university of the Triangle is the farthest south?

HOW RESEARCH TRIANGLE PARK BEGAN

Research Triangle Park was built in 1959, but planning for it began years earlier. **Luther Hodges**, who was North Carolina's governor in the 1950s, met with **Archie Davis** and other business leaders. They wanted to create jobs for the state's leading college graduates in North Carolina. Many skilled young people were leaving the state because they could not find good, high-paying jobs here. Too many jobs were low-paying ones on farms or in factories. Governor Hodges also believed that state leaders had to plan for the future if North Carolina's economy was to remain strong.

Research Triangle Park became the answer to stopping this loss of skilled people. Today many of our state's college graduates are scientists, engineers, and computer specialists at the Park. They work in **high-tech** research jobs. The term *high tech* refers to work that makes use of advanced scientific learning or equipment, such as computers.

A GOOD LOCATION

Many large businesses have offices and laboratories in Research Triangle Park. Several United States government agencies also have offices in the Park.

These companies and government agencies chose the research center for several reasons. One reason is that researchers are able to work with teachers at nearby universities. Another reason is that the Park is close to many highways and airports. They make traveling easy for the many people who work at the Park. Business and government officials also thought that workers would enjoy living in the surrounding Piedmont communities.

Scientists at many large companies in the Research Triangle use **high-tech** equipment in their research.

LINKING BUSINESS AND RESEARCH

Do you think that we live in a high-speed world? Some workers in the Park are trying to make things work even faster. One large Canadian company makes electrical switches that speed up the sending of information over telephone wires.

Have you ever seen a symbol with a series of lines and spaces on the products that you buy? This symbol is called a bar code. One type of bar code is called the Universal Product Code (UPC). It was created by a large computer company in the Park. A bar code has important information about a product. For example, the code on a box of cereal tells the name of the cereal, its price, and how many boxes of that cereal are left in a store. The book you are now reading has a bar code on its back cover. The code is "read" when a scanner is passed across the item.

Some companies in the Research Triangle also have helped the economy of other parts of our state. Today factories in the Coastal Plain make many of the products developed at the Park. A number of these factories make medical supplies. Such factories provide jobs for the people in a region.

The UPC symbol *(below)*, developed at the Park, is shown on many products. Sales workers use machines called scanners to "read" the code.

A PARK RESEARCHER

Maria Elena Lapetina, who is nine years old, lives with her family in Chapel Hill. Every day Maria's father, Eduardo Lapetina, drives the short distance to his office in Research Triangle Park. Eduardo Lapetina is a doctor and a scientist for a large company that does medical research.

Lapetina works as the head of a research group that creates new medicines to help treat people with heart disease. His coworkers are scientists from Sweden, Japan, Germany, and Italy. Quite often, he travels around the United States

Dr. Eduardo Lapetina helps to make new medicines to treat heart disease. Maria Lapetina meets her father at the Park.

and to many foreign countries to speak at meetings and to discuss his research with other scientists.

Lapetina and his family came to North Carolina over 16 years ago from Argentina in South America. He decided to move to Chapel Hill because of the chance to work at the Research Triangle.

> *I can do my medical research with the resources that are needed for it. . . . [Also] the people I work with . . . are very well trained.*

Maria Elena is glad that her family moved to North Carolina. She likes living in Chapel Hill and being close to other lively Piedmont cities. Perhaps one day she, too, will work at Research Triangle Park.

PARTNERS IN RESEARCH

You have read about an important part of the Piedmont's economy—the Research Triangle. The people who work at the Park's businesses and government offices and at nearby universities are partners in research. Together they are finding ways to improve the lives of people in North Carolina and the world.

Check Your Reading

1. What kinds of jobs are done by people who work at Research Triangle Park?
2. How have the Research Triangle companies created jobs for people in other parts of the state?
3. What does the term *high tech* mean?
4. **THINKING SKILL:** Imagine that you are interviewing a scientist who works at Research Triangle Park. List three questions that you would ask to find out more about his or her work.

REVIEWING VOCABULARY

Number a sheet of paper from 1 to 4. Beside each number write the letter of the choice that best completes each sentence.

1. *Scarce* means that
   - **a.** you should go away.
   - **b.** there is less than needed.
   - **c.** something is growing.
2. Examples of *finished goods* are
   - **a.** shoes.
   - **b.** salads.
   - **c.** trees.
3. A person who does *research*
   - **a.** produces goods in a factory.
   - **b.** grows food for sale.
   - **c.** searches for new ways of doing things or for new ideas about something.
4. *High tech* is
   - **a.** work that makes use of advanced scientific learning or equipment.
   - **b.** work that is performed at high altitudes.
   - **c.** another way of saying "fancy, fashionable clothes."

REVIEWING FACTS

1. How did the following affect the growth of cities in the Piedmont: railroads, the discovery of gold, the use of modern machinery?
2. Give two examples of Piedmont industries whose growth has been influenced by local geography.
3. What are two challenges that the textile industry and the poultry-processing industry face today?
4. Why was the Research Triangle Park started?
5. Explain the reason for each part of the name *Research Triangle Park*.

WRITING ABOUT MAIN IDEAS

1. **Writing a Journal Entry:** Imagine you attended the state fair in Raleigh or the International Home Furnishings Market in High Point. Write a journal entry about the things you saw and did there.
2. **Writing About Perspectives:** Write a sentence or two telling how each of these people might feel about the work done at the Research Triangle Park: the president of Duke University, a video-store owner in Chapel Hill, a research scientist in Japan.

BUILDING SKILLS: COMPARING MAPS

Refer to the maps on page 269 to answer these questions.

1. Name four cities that are located in the most densely populated area of the Piedmont.
2. How is most of the land used in the most densely populated areas?
3. When might you want to know how to compare two kinds of maps?

CHAPTER 10

LIFE IN THE MOUNTAINS

FOCUS

I always have a great time at the Highland Games. I get to wear my kilt. Some people call it a skirt but it's not. I also wear my tartan, a special plaid cloth of my family. Wearing this clothing is one way of showing my Scottish heritage.

For Robert Cocke, the Highland Games are special. His great-grandmother Agnes MacRae Morton started them near Grandfather Mountain. The games are a reminder of the many Scots who settled in the Mountain Region.

LESSON

1 Living in the Mountains

READ TO LEARN

Key Places

Asheville
Hendersonville
Blue Ridge Parkway
Linville Caverns

Read Aloud

If you come here you're either coming to see somebody or you're lost.

Bishop Holder, the mayor of Robbinsville, was smiling when he said this about his town. Robbinsville is a small town in the mountains where everybody knows everybody else. In this lesson you will read about the way of life of the people in the Mountain Region.

Read for Purpose:

1. WHAT YOU KNOW: Which group of people was the first to live in the Mountain Region?
2. WHAT YOU WILL LEARN: What is life like for people in the Mountain Region today?

WHERE PEOPLE LIVE

There are only 800 people living in Robbinsville. As you read on page 88, the town is located in Graham County. The land in the county is steep. In some places in the Mountain Region the mountains make it very hard to build roads. Many towns are small because roads leading to them are narrow. The mayor of Robbinsville says that the only way the town will grow is if it gets a four-lane highway.

Asheville is a city that has a four-lane highway connecting it with Winston-Salem. Asheville was a small town until the North Carolina Railroad connected it with other parts of the state. Today Asheville is the eighth-largest city in North Carolina. Many people come to Asheville to vacation in the cool, fresh air of the mountains. So many people spend their holidays here that the city's population more than doubles every summer.

THE PEOPLE

Most of the people living in the Mountain Region are from families that came here from England, Scotland, Ireland, and Germany. As you have read, these groups came to the region during the 1700s.

Other groups of people also live in the Mountain Region. Marshall Logan is an African American who was born and raised in Asheville. Marshall says that he likes living in the place where he was born.

> *I go to the church that I grew up in, and I have restored an old home next door to my 93-year-old uncle. I really feel at home.*

In Chapter 4 you read about the Cherokee, who were the first people to live in the Mountain Region. Today there are many Cherokee in the region. Most of them live on the Qualla Boundary Indian Reservation. About 6,800 members of the Eastern Band of Cherokee live here.

NEWCOMERS

New roads have helped some small mountain towns to grow. Now that transportation is better, many retired people have come to live in the mountains. You may know some retired people in your community. Retired people choose mountain towns like **Hendersonville** because of their mild climate, beautiful views, and many outdoor activities.

Frank Bogardus of Florida lives in Hendersonville from May until October. He explains why by saying that "it cools off here every night. After you live in Florida, you appreciate this."

TRADITIONS

The Tar Heels of the Mountain Region keep their traditions alive. In fact, the region has three schools

Many retired people who live in the Mountain Region work as volunteers to help others.

that teach traditional crafts. The Penland School of Crafts, near Spruce Pine, is well known. The other two schools are the Southern Highland Handicraft Guild in Asheville and the John C. Campbell Folk School in Brasstown.

At these schools people learn how to weave baskets, blankets, and wall hangings. They also learn to sew quilts in traditional patterns, with names like Bear Paw, Log Cabin, and Double Wedding Ring. Cherokee crafts such as jewelry making and basketry are taught at Oconaluftee Indian Village.

Traditional crafts and customs of the Mountain Region include weaving and clogging.

CELEBRATIONS

Do you think of dancing as a tradition? Kyle Edwards of Maggie Valley does. He explains why dancing is important to his family.

> *When I was growing up, this place was so isolated [set apart] that dancing was our only way of relaxing. We danced our way through our problems. My mother, my aunts, uncles and friends—we all danced.*

Today Edwards owns the dance hall where one local clogging contest takes place. Clogging is a lively mountain dance in which dancers wear tap shoes called clogs. Every October, crowds come to Maggie Valley for the Clogging Hall of Fame Dance-Off. Clogging grew out of the folk dances of the English, Irish, and Scottish settlers.

Early European immigrants brought their music and instruments to the region. Scots-Irish musicians played the bagpipe. Germans brought a stringed instrument that they held on their laps. It was like the Appalachian dulcimer (dul′ sə mər) of today.

Bagpipes can be heard at events such as the Highland Games, which you will read about in the Traditions lesson on pages 282–285. Traditional kinds of music also can be enjoyed at the Old Time Fiddlers and Bluegrass Convention held at Grandfather Mountain.

Along the Blue Ridge Parkway you can see the Mile-High Swinging Bridge and beautiful views.

THE BLUE RIDGE PARKWAY

The Tar Heels of the Mountain Region also have tried to keep the beauty of their region. The Blue Ridge Parkway was built so that people can enjoy the views in this part of our state. The Parkway winds along the top of many mountains for 470 miles (756 km).

There are many sights along the Blue Ridge Parkway. On top of Grandfather Mountain visitors can walk across the Mile-High Swinging Bridge connecting two of its peaks. At Linville Caverns, which are large caves, guides lead visitors under Humpback Mountain to see the huge rocks.

LIVING IN THE MOUNTAIN REGION

In this lesson you have read about the different groups of people who live in the Mountain Region. The people of this region are proud of their traditions and share a love for their land.

Check Your Reading

1. Name three groups of people that live in the Mountain Region.
2. What are three traditions that are kept alive by the people of the Mountain Region?
3. **GEOGRAPHY SKILL:** How has the geography of the Mountain Region affected how the region's people live?
4. **THINKING SKILL:** Compare and contrast Robbinsville with Asheville. How are they alike and how are they different?

BUILDING CITIZENSHIP

★ PEOPLE WHO MAKE A DIFFERENCE ★

Working for a Clean ENVIRONMENT

People who live in the three regions of our state work hard to make sure that North Carolina is a clean, safe place in which to live. L. C. Coonse, who lives in the Mountain Region, works hard to keep his community free of pollution.

Coonse lives in Caldwell County and teaches chemistry at Hickory High School in nearby Catawba County. In 1976 Caldwell County began using a new incinerator to burn wastes. Soon after the incinerator was in use, many of Coonse's students and neighbors started getting sick. As a chemistry teacher, Coonse understood that the incinerator could be affecting people's health. He found out that it was burning harmful chemicals. He decided he had to do something to close it down.

Coonse wrote letters to state officials about the problem. He held community meetings to educate people about the dangers of the harmful chemicals that were being burned.

It wasn't easy. Some people didn't want to admit that there was a problem. They didn't want to lose their jobs if the incinerator closed down. They wondered whether Coonse was correct. Some state officials did not want to be bothered with the problem.

In time, Coonse's hard work paid off. People in the community supported his efforts to close down the incinerator, and state officials finally agreed. At last Caldwell County closed down the incinerator.

However, there is still a problem. The chemicals released into the air have polluted the water and the land. Many people in the community still suffer from ill health, possibly caused by the pollution.

Coonse's efforts have helped to put pressure on our government to look at incinerators all over the country. Every day people call Coonse to learn how to close down dangerous incinerators in their communities. As you can see, L. C. Coonse is making a difference.

Highland Games

by Lila Summer

As you have read, many people who settled in our mountains long ago came from Scotland. Many settlers came from the mountainous region of Scotland known as the Scottish Highlands. These settlers brought with them the tradition of the Highland Games, which are still held in Scotland. These games are also a North Carolina tradition. They help North Carolinians remember life long ago. As you read, think about how the Highland Games have changed over time.

THE GAMES BEGIN

It is night on Grandfather Mountain. Fog curls in MacRae Meadows below. From faraway comes the sound of footsteps. Suddenly a torch of fire appears. A man holds the flame high and yells, "The MacRaes are here!" One by one, torches light up by the hundreds. For each torch, a voice yells out. "The Camerons are here!" "The MacBeths are here!" Thousands of people watch, hushed. The Grandfather Mountain Highland Games have begun.

This ceremony is known as "the calling of the clans." The word *clan* comes from the Gaelic (gāl′ ik) word *clann* and means "a group of families that are related." Long ago, Scots spoke the Gaelic language. Back then, over 900 years ago, Scottish leaders held games to test the strength of men for war. Today the Highland Games are held for fun. On Grandfather Mountain, over 40,000 people come to this 4-day event. Many are Scottish Americans. Other people also come to enjoy the games, which have been held every July since 1956, when Agnes MacRae Morton helped to start them. These games are one of the largest Highland Games festivals in our country.

TAKING PART IN THE GAMES

"You have bagpipes ringing in your ears for days," says 12-year-old Megan Monroe. The bagpipe is a musical instrument often played in Scotland.

Megan is a dancer who has won many Scottish dance contests. Bagpipers wearing kilts often play the music for the dances. A kilt is a pleated skirt with a plaid pattern called a tartan. Each clan has its own special tartan.

Megan sits in her clan's tent. It is one of hundreds of tents in the meadow. Megan watches people preparing for the games. The first game is the caber toss. A caber is a tree trunk about as tall as a telephone pole.

Two people help to place the caber on another person's shoulder. To win, the person must toss the caber, making it flip and land flat, pointing straight ahead.

Like the caber toss, most Highland Games take strength and skill because they were originally tests for war. Today people test their own skills. For example, in the stone toss, people try to throw a heavy stone the farthest distance. This game comes from the time when Scottish Highland leaders kept a stone outside their home. Visitors showed off their strength by throwing the stone as far as they could.

Megan leaves her tent to watch the games. As she walks, she hears the music of a Scottish harp, bagpipes, and a strolling fiddler mixing in the air. She visits the booths where jams, tartans, and other items are for sale. She arrives in time for the sheepdog event. A small Border Collie moves among the sheep. The dog does not bark but herds the sheep together by staring into their eyes. One of these Scottish farm dogs can herd 100 sheep.

HIGHLAND DANCING

When it is time for the Scottish dances, Megan, now wearing a kilt, hops on stage and begins the Highland fling. This dance is performed on one small spot because the fling used to be danced on a soldier's shield. Megan's favorite dance is called *seann triubhas* (shawn trews), which means "old trousers" in Gaelic. After the English defeated the Scots, they made it against the law for Scots to wear kilts. The English made the Scots wear trousers, or pants, to try to do away with Scottish traditions. The "old trousers" dance is about kicking off trousers, which Scots found uncomfortable. "You kick and wiggle and twist. It is really a funny dance," Megan says.

Megan also dances the sword dance. This is one of the oldest Scottish dances. Scottish soldiers used to perform this dance to celebrate winning a battle. They placed two swords on the ground and leaped on their toes in and out of the crossed blades. In this dance, Megan would lose the contest if her feet touched the swords.

A HAPPY ENDING

Finally comes the clan tug of war. It is a huge show of strength and great fun. Two teams pull a rope and try to topple the other team. In Scotland, villagers used to compete like this for fun, too. After this game everyone joins hands. They sing "Auld Lang Syne," a Scottish song about keeping old friends. Then anyone who wishes to, goes to a *ceilidh* (kā′ lē). A ceilidh is a Scottish get-together at which people sing, dance, and tell stories.

People have many different ways of celebrating their past. But only at the Highland Games do the bagpipes ring in your ears.

How have the Highland Games changed over time?

LESSON

2 Working in the Mountains

READ TO LEARN

Key Vocabulary

orchard quarry

Key People

George Vanderbilt

Read Aloud

People used to live very simply, but very rich[ly]. . . . I can remember, we got the first TV in the whole area when I was a child. And all the neighbors would come in to watch TV. All the new people, the ski resort, summer people, [and] everything else that came in [have] changed things. It's hard to be a farmer when you can make more money building houses for the tourists.

Mark Phillips was born in Cow Camp near Newland in Avery County over 40 years ago. During the years that he has lived in the mountains, he has seen many changes in the way people live and work in the region.

Read for Purpose

1. **WHAT YOU KNOW:** How has agriculture been important to our state's history?
2. **WHAT YOU WILL LEARN:** How has the economy of the Mountain Region changed?

A CHANGING ECONOMY

Long ago some people called the Mountain Region "the land of do without." Many people who lived there were poor. They had small farms on rough mountain land. Today some of the region's people still farm, but their farms grow more crops than older farms did.

The natural resources of the Mountain Region have long been an important part of its economy. Today service industries such as tourism are using these natural resources in new kinds of jobs. As a result, the Mountain Region can now be described better as "the land of do with."

AGRICULTURE

You have read that tobacco is an important crop in the Coastal Plain and Piedmont regions. Tobacco is also an important crop in the Mountain Region. Farmers there grow burley tobacco, which is darker in color than the bright leaf tobacco grown in the other regions.

Many farmers in the mountains also raise cattle. The fields of the mountain hillsides and river valleys make good grazing land for beef cattle. The grass and hay that feed the cattle grow well in the valley soil.

Sheep's Nose, Golden Delicious, Crow's Egg, and Granny Smith are the names of which fruit? If you said "apple," you would be right. Farmers grow more than 20 kinds of apples in the **orchards** of the region. An orchard is land on which fruit trees are grown.

In earlier times many mountain families ate apples at nearly every meal. They also dried, cooked, and canned them for use in the winter.

Today apples are our state's leading fruit crop. Almost all of the apples grown as cash crops in North Carolina orchards are of three kinds: Red Delicious, Golden Delicious, and Rome Beauty.

People in the Mountain Region are proud of the many food products they make from the apples grown in **orchards**.

FOREST PRODUCTS

Another important cash crop in the Mountain Region is the fir tree, which is used as a Christmas tree. Kathy and Randall Aldridge have a tree farm in Crossnore. You read about the Aldridges in the Chapter Opener on page 40. The Aldridges raise over 65,000 fir and pine trees each year. They send the trees all over the United States.

Other forest products that are important to the region's economy are lumber and paper. Furniture makers in the Piedmont buy lumber cut from forests in the Mountain Region. Hardwoods such as oak, hickory, and beech grow well there. One of the world's largest paper mills is in Canton in Haywood

Natural resources provide jobs for many people in the Mountain Region. This region has many Christmas-tree farms and stone quarries.

County. The Canton mill makes paper for millions of postcards that are produced every year.

MINING

Rocks and minerals are other natural resources of the mountains. Nearly every mountain county has at least one quarry, where crushed stone is mined. A quarry is a place where stone is cut or blasted out of the ground. Stone from the quarries is used to build things such as houses and highways.

The area near Franklin in the Cowee Valley is known for its precious stones. Gems such as rubies and sapphires can be found in the ground. Visitors to the gem mines can sift through buckets of rocks looking for the precious stones.

MANUFACTURING

The factories in the Mountain Region make many different products, from textiles and clothing to electrical and leather goods. The town Enka in Buncombe County is one of the largest producers of a machine-made textile called nylon.

For many years small mountain towns depended on one industry for jobs. If a factory closed or moved, everyone in the town suffered. Today many communities in the Mountain Region are developing service industries so that they will have more kinds of jobs.

TOURISM

Many of the jobs in the Mountain Region are in tourism. During the late 1800s the region began to draw tourists. Many of them came from places in the South to escape the hot, sticky, summer weather.

Some millionaires, such as **George Vanderbilt**, built large, beautiful summer homes in the Mountain Region. The most famous home was Vanderbilt's Biltmore Estate. As you have read, each year thousands of visitors tour its many beautiful rooms and gardens.

During the 1890s businesspeople built several big resorts in the region. Resorts are places to go to have fun and to relax. A number of resorts were near Blowing Rock, Linville, and Asheville. Even more tourists came to the resorts after the North Carolina Railroad was built. The resorts gave people jobs—as managers, gardeners, tour guides, and cooks, for example.

Today Asheville is still a center of tourism. As the region's largest city, Asheville is also a center for shopping, banking, educational, and government services.

RETIREMENT COMMUNITIES

You read in Lesson 1 that many retired people have moved to Hendersonville. When the population of a place increases, the goods and services also increase. Businesses in Henderson County offer many goods and services for retired people. These include houses, clothing, and medical care.

In Henderson County the population nearly doubles during the summer. Tourists there spend $65 million every year.

This huge, sunlit entranceway is one of the many beautiful rooms in the Biltmore Estate.

THE LAND OF DO WITH

Many of the jobs in the Mountain Region come from the region's natural resources. As the economies of the mountain towns grow, the old image of the region is changing to "the land of do with."

Check Your Reading

1. Name three natural resources that are important to the economy of the Mountain Region.
2. How has the economy of the Mountain Region changed?
3. What effects has tourism had on the economy of the Mountain Region?
4. **THINKING SKILL:** What effects have retired people in Hendersonville had on the economy of the town?

Reading Contour Maps

Key Vocabulary

contour map
contour line
contour interval
relief

The geography of North Carolina includes many kinds of landforms, ranging from a flat coastal plain to rugged mountains. As you know, these landforms have different elevations, or heights above sea level. Mapmakers can use elevation maps to show these differences in height. The map on page 70 is an elevation map.

The elevation of a place can also be shown on a **contour map**. Contour means "shape." Contour maps help us to picture the shape of the surface of the earth. Contour maps use lines or colors to show different elevations.

A **contour line** on a map connects areas that have the same elevation. If you were to walk along an area shown on the map by a contour line, you would not go up or down. You would remain at about the same elevation.

Understanding Contour Maps

The diagrams on page 291 will help you to understand contour lines. They explain how a contour map shows both the elevation and the shape of Grandfather Mountain.

Diagram A shows the mountain in a side view. Contour lines are marked in feet and meters. The lines show the elevation in steps that are always the same distance above sea level. If you walked around the mountain at the contour line marked 5,600 feet, you would always be at about 5,600 feet (1,700 m) above sea level.

Diagram B shows the mountain divided up into four sections. The elevation of each contour line is marked in feet and meters. These sections are the same areas as those shown in **Diagram A**. However, they are also shown in slices of different colors. The legend shows the elevation that each color represents.

Each section shows the elevation as a **contour interval**, which is the distance between two contour lines. All of the section shown in one color is the same contour interval. The part shown in yellow is between 4,800 and 5,200 feet (1,460 and 1,580 m). When using contour maps, it is a good idea first to check the contour intervals. These intervals vary from one map to another, and are usually given in the legend. In the diagrams on page 291 the interval is 400 feet (122 m).

Diagram C shows the mountain in a view from the top. It uses the same colors as **Diagram B** to show the elevation and shape of the sections.

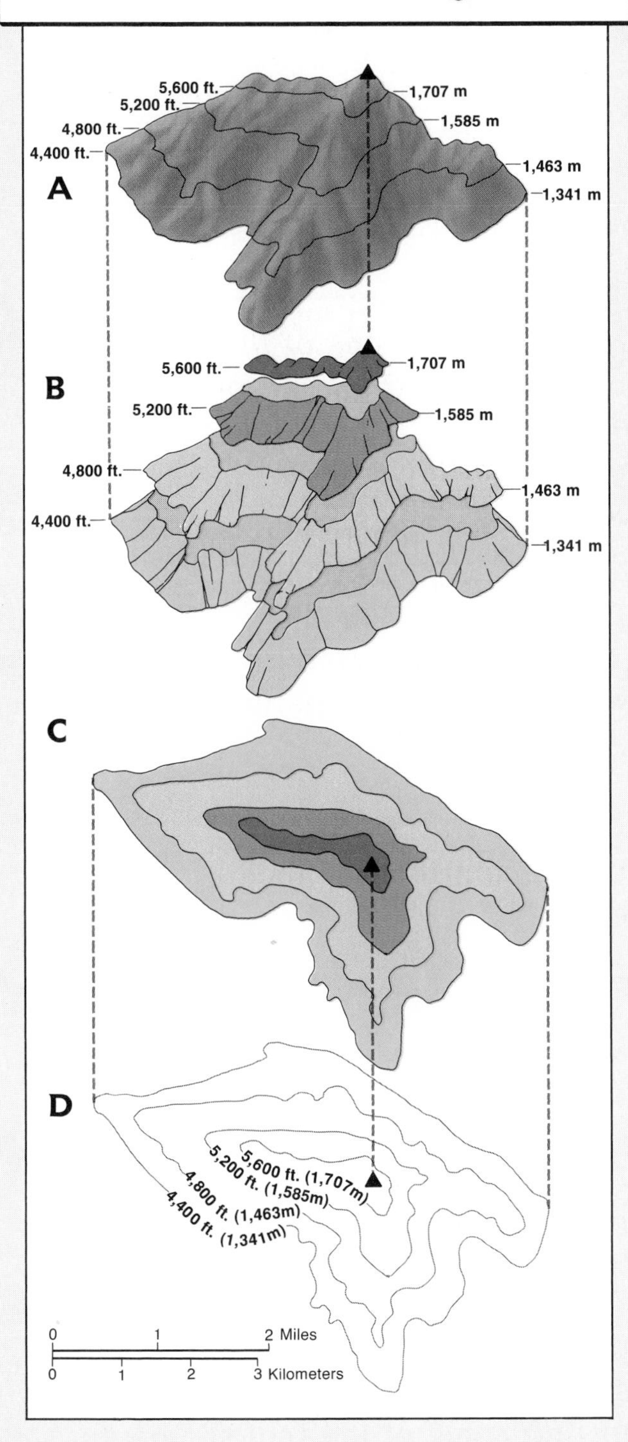

In **Diagram D** the sections are all one color. The contour lines of the sections are marked with feet and meters. The numbers give the elevation and the lines show the contour of the area. This is the type of contour map that you are most likely to see.

Contour Maps Show Relief

When you look at a contour map, you also see the **relief** of an area. Relief is the change in elevation. High mountains are said to have high relief. Flat plains with little differences in elevation are areas of low relief.

Relief on a contour map is shown by the spacing of the lines. Widely spaced contour lines mean that the land is flat or gently sloping. A steep slope, or mountainside, is shown by lines that are drawn close together.

In **Diagrams C** and **D**, which area shows the highest relief? In which area is the relief lower?

Reviewing the Skill

Use the diagrams on this page to answer the following questions.

1. What are contour maps?
2. What do the lines on a contour map show you?
3. What is a contour interval?
4. What does the term *relief* mean?
5. How do contour maps help you picture the shape of the land?

LESSON

3 Parks and Forests of the Mountains

READ TO LEARN

Key Vocabulary	Key People	Key Places
forestry	Gifford Pinchot	Pisgah National Forest
smog	Carl Schenck	Great Smoky Mountains National Park
acid rain		Mount Mitchell State Park

Read Aloud

I think about how peaceful it was and about one of those beautiful mountain streams. You could just drink out of most of the streams without any fear. . . . I really would like to build a fence around western North Carolina.

Former governor of North Carolina Dan Moore was born in Asheville and raised in Webster. Since Moore lived in these mountain towns, he knew the region's parks and forests well. In this lesson you will read about how people are finding ways to protect its natural resources.

Read for Purpose

1. **WHAT YOU KNOW:** How do forests contribute to the economy of the Mountain Region?
2. **WHAT YOU WILL LEARN:** What is being done to preserve the forests? Why is it important to do this?

SAVING AND SHARING THE LAND

Many people share Dan Moore's feelings about the Mountain Region. They also want to preserve its beauty. They know that it is important to protect the land in order to save its resources. Our state's waterways, trees, plants, and animals can continue to live only if the land is protected. However, as more people come to the region to live, protecting the land becomes harder.

The Mountain Region has more parkland than any other part of our state. Look at the map on page 293 to find some of the region's parks.

FORESTS

George Vanderbilt built one of the Mountain Region's best-known tourist spots—the Biltmore Estate. He also gave our state its first national forest. This was the Pisgah National Forest, near Brevard.

Vanderbilt began building the Biltmore Estate in 1892. He hired a forester named Gifford Pinchot (pin′ shō) to manage the forestlands around his new home. The idea of managing forestland was new in the United States. Usually a lumber company would cut down trees whenever it needed wood. Often these trees never grew back.

Pinchot believed that forests could be used in many ways. They could be enjoyed by visitors for hiking and camping. They could also be used as lumber for wood products. The forests could also provide jobs for workers in the region's lumber industry.

In 1895 Carl Schenck came from Germany to manage the forestlands of the Vanderbilt estate. Schenck started the first forestry school in our country near Mount Pisgah. Forestry is the science of managing,

MAP SKILL: Our forests must be used carefully. Which national forests can you reach by using the Blue Ridge Parkway?

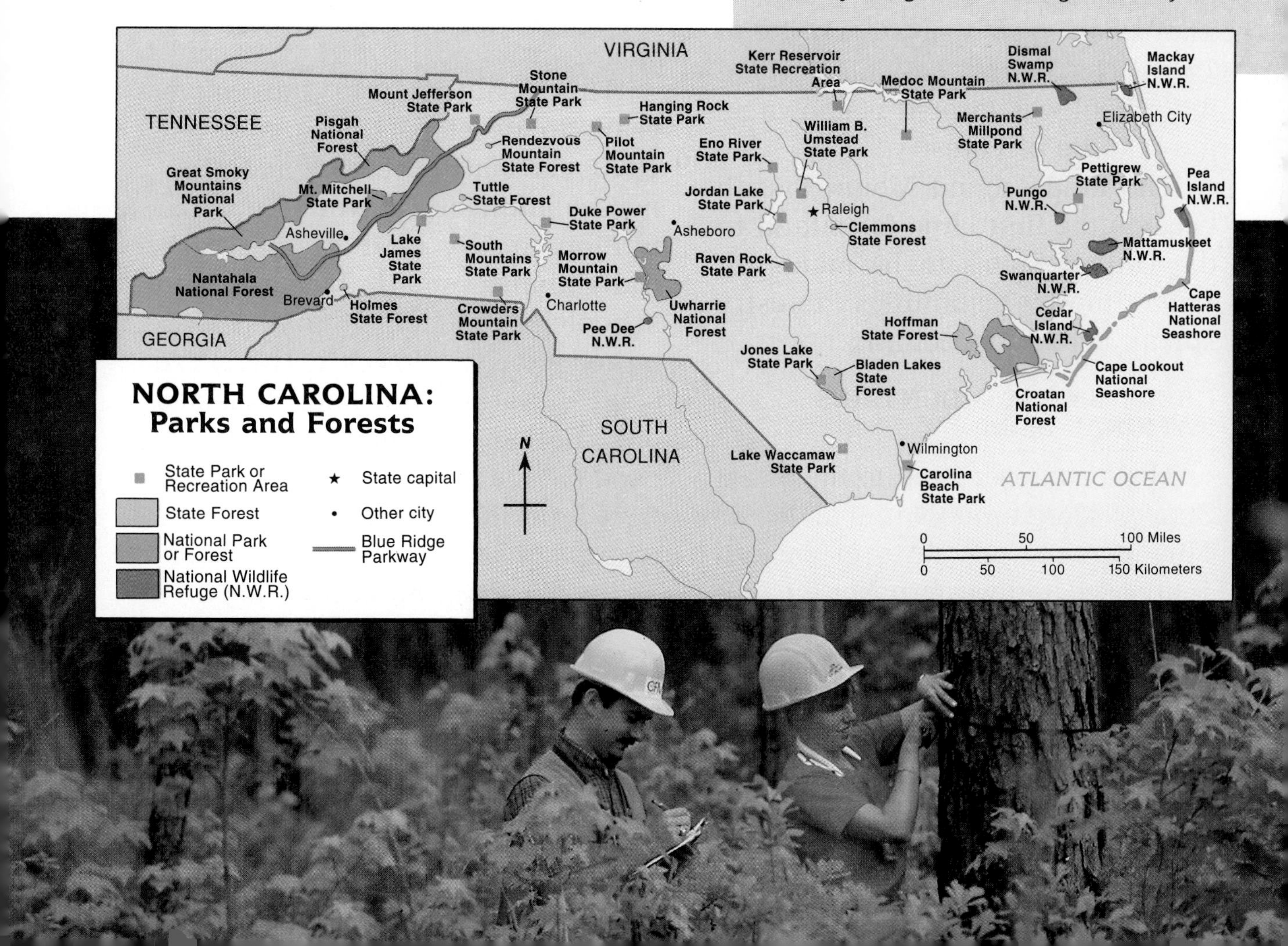

People in the Mountain Region can enjoy its hiking trails and many kinds of rocks, plants, and animals.

developing, and protecting forests. The school was open from 1898 to 1914. The mountain valley where the school was located is known as the "Cradle of Forestry."

The land around Mount Pisgah became the first large forestland in the United States to be managed. From these beginnings forestry spread across the country.

GREAT SMOKY MOUNTAINS NATIONAL PARK

Have you ever been to the Great Smoky Mountains National Park? This park covers parts of eastern Tennessee and western North Carolina. As you read in Chapter 7, more people visit this park than any other national park in our country. Every year more than 8 million visitors come here to camp, fish, and hike along the Appalachian Trail.

This beautiful park took many years to develop. During the late 1920s the state governments of Tennessee and North Carolina gave $2 million to buy land for the park. Individuals, small groups, and schoolchildren helped to raise even more money. However, by 1928 state governments had collected only half of the amount that was needed. Many of the people who were working to get the park were ready to give up. Then John D. Rockefeller, Jr., gave $5 million for it.

The Great Smoky Mountains National Park is a wonderful place to enjoy nature. It is also a home for many plants and animals. Today hundreds of different kinds of plants and animals have a safe

home in the forests of the park. This was not true several years ago.

At one time large animals such as elk and bison lived in the Great Smoky Mountains. By 1800 these animals had disappeared. During the early 1900s there were still beavers, wolves, and mountain lions living there. Today most of these animals also are gone.

Why did these animals disappear? Some were killed by hunters. But the major reason was that their food supply had shrunk. As land was cleared for roads and houses, there was less space for many plants and smaller animals to survive. Since they provided food for the larger animals, many of the larger animals died as well.

Today park rangers make sure that people obey the park's hunting and fishing laws. As a result, black bears, white-tailed deer, foxes, squirrels, bobcats, and jumping mice live in the park. The rangers also make sure that the park is used properly by its visitors.

OUR OLDEST STATE PARK

In 1991 Mount Mitchell State Park in the Black Mountains had its seventy-fifth birthday. The park is the oldest state park in North Carolina. It is also the home of the highest mountain peak east of the Mississippi River.

Imagine that you are making the long drive up to the top of this 6,684-foot (2,037-m) mountain. You would notice a sudden drop in temperature. The air would seem colder. You might also notice how different the plants look. At higher elevations the plants here are like those found in Canada.

The park's seventy-fifth birthday was not a very happy one. Many trees on the mountaintop are dying. Scientists give many reasons for this. Wind and ice have caused older trees to fall. Also, a tiny insect called the woolly aphid is eating away at the fir trees.

Air pollution is also killing the trees. Some of the air pollution comes from smoke and gases from cars and nearby factories. This polluted air rises and mixes with moisture in the air to become smog. Smog is a mixture of smoke and fog.

Plants on Mount Mitchell also suffer from a form of pollution called acid rain. Chemicals are

Many of the trees on Mount Mitchell have died because of the acid rain caused by the burning of chemicals.

given off when coal, gas, and oil are burned at power plants and factories. These chemicals are then carried by winds moving east. This dirty air mixes with drops of water to form clouds that drop poisonous acid rain on the mountain's plants.

Many people hope that Mount Mitchell's one-hundredth birthday will find the trees in better shape. Perhaps by then healthy trees will cover our state's tallest mountain. In order for this to happen, North Carolina will have to find ways to work with other states to keep the air clean of smog and acid rain.

SAVING THE LAND

Lumber companies continue to use wood from the national forests of the Mountain Region. However, today foresters are careful about the number of trees that are cut down. They decide which trees can be cut. In this way they leave enough trees to protect the plants and animals living in the forests.

In places where forests have been cut down or paved over, water flows quickly over the surface of the ground. Then it does not have time to soak in. This water may carry away the soil. Rapidly moving water can cause erosion and flooding along its path. Foresters and lumber companies are working to limit erosion and flooding in the Mountain Region. The success of their work will benefit all the people in our state.

THE FUTURE OF OUR FORESTS

People from all regions of the country depend on the forests of the Mountain Region for recreation and for jobs. The future of the forests depends on people finding solutions to problems such as pollution and erosion.

Check Your Reading

1. How did Gifford Pinchot believe that forests should be used?
2. How is acid rain created?
3. What is being done to preserve the forests? Why is it important to do this?
4. **GEOGRAPHY SKILL:** Look at the map on page 293. Name three national parks that are in the Mountain Region.
5. **THINKING SKILL:** What three questions would you ask a park ranger to find out what you could do to help save the forests of the Mountain Region?

REVIEWING VOCABULARY

acid rain
forestry
orchard
quarry
smog

Number a sheet of paper from 1 to 5. Beside each number write the word or term from the list above that best completes the sentence.

1. The ____, which is a mixture of water and chemicals in the air, killed many plants.
2. Crushed stone is mined from the ____.
3. Exhaust from cars and smoke from factories combine in the air with fog to make ____.
4. Workers picked hundreds of apples from the trees in the ____.
5. The science of managing, developing, and protecting our forests is called ____.

REVIEWING FACTS

1. Name three events or places that help people in the mountains keep their traditions alive.
2. What are the Linville Caverns?
3. Name five products produced in the Mountain Region.
4. What did Carl Schenck do to protect North Carolina's forests?
5. Why are so many trees dying in Mount Mitchell State Park in the Black Mountains?

WRITING ABOUT MAIN IDEAS

1. **Writing a Travel Brochure:** Write a travel brochure that tells tourists about some of the points of interest in the Mountain Region. Briefly describe each attraction in such a way that people would want to visit it.
2. **Writing an Adventure Story:** Mountain climbing can be a very exciting sport. Imagine climbing Grandfather Mountain and getting lost. Write a story about it.
3. **Writing About Perspectives:** Imagine that Gifford Pinchot attended the 75th anniversary celebration of Mount Mitchell State Park. What might he have thought of what he saw there? Write a speech that he might have given to the people gathered in the park.

BUILDING SKILLS: READING CONTOUR MAPS

Use the diagrams on page 291 to answer the following questions.

1. In what ways does a contour map show elevation?
2. How many feet and meters of elevation does the color yellow in the diagrams represent?
3. Which has higher relief—a steep hill or a gently sloping hill?
4. Why is it helpful to know how to read a contour diagram?

REVIEW • UNIT 3

REVIEWING VOCABULARY

acid rain	recreation
census	research
folk art	smog
food processing	suburban
high tech	urban

Number a sheet of paper from 1 to 10. Beside each number write the word or term from the list above that best matches the definition.

1. Work that involves the use of advanced scientific knowledge
2. Having to do with communities on the edges of cities
3. The mixing of smoke and fog
4. Art by people in a community
5. Any activity that is done for fun
6. An official count of population
7. Making different kinds of products from plants and animals
8. The search for new ways of thinking and of doing things
9. A mixture of water and chemicals in the air that can kill plants
10. Having to do with cities

WRITING ABOUT THE UNIT

1. **Completing a Chart:** Make a chart of our regions' economies. On each row, write the name of one region. Label one column "Products" and another column "Ways of Making a Living." Complete the chart.
2. **Writing an Interview:** Interview the owners of a farm that practices mixed farming. Ask them how they choose which crops to grow. Prepare a report that includes the question and the answers.
3. **Writing About Perspectives:** Imagine that you are trying to convince people from outside our state to move to North Carolina. Write an advertisement that might appear in a newspaper describing those things in our state that make it an attractive place. You might mention jobs, schools, recreation, or other things that make North Carolina a great place in which to live.

ACTIVITIES

1. **Researching a Famous Tar Heel:** Research the lives and careers of several famous Tar Heels. They might be artists, educators, athletes, or business leaders. Then prepare a chart that lists where each of these people grew up and went to school. The list should also explain how each came to be well known.
2. **Working Together to Come to a Decision:** Work with several classmates to decide on a project about this unit. The project should help you to review what you have learned. You may wish to put on a show, make a comic book, or mural.

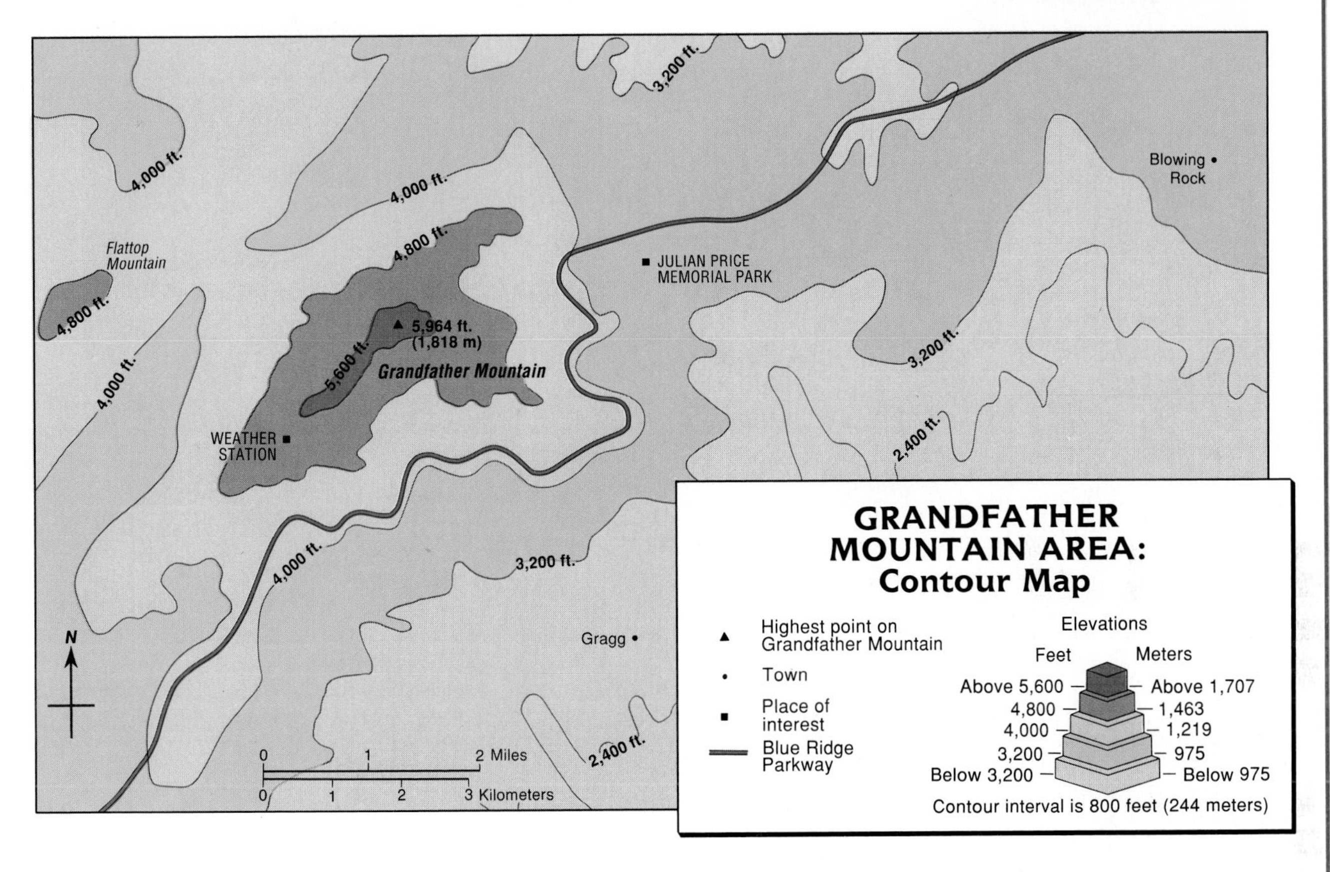

BUILDING SKILLS: READING A CONTOUR MAP

Study the diagrams on page 291 and the map above to answer these questions.

1. What is the contour interval of the area map?
2. How do the diagrams and contour map work together to help you to picture the shape of Grandfather Mountain and of the land around it?

LINKING PAST, PRESENT, AND FUTURE

You have read about the development of public schools in our state. From its beginnings in 1840, our state's education system has grown to include thousands of public schools and many colleges and universities. Find out more about education in North Carolina today. For example, research how much money the state spends on education. What improvements in education would you ask the state to make?

State bird: Cardinal

State mammal: Gray squirrel

State tree: Pine

State flag

State reptile:
Eastern box turtle

CITIZENSHIP IN OUR STATE

TODAY AND TOMORROW

On these pages you will see some of the symbols of North Carolina. These are all things found in our state that make it different from any other. In this unit you will read about our state's leaders and citizens and about what they are doing to keep our state a special place.

State seal

State flower:
Dogwood

CHAPTER 11

GOVERNMENT

FOCUS

I like living in Raleigh, especially in the fall when the State Fair comes to town. It's pretty lively at other times of the year also. When we took our class trip to the building where the legislature meets, we didn't go by school bus. We just walked.

Nathan Katzin lives in Raleigh, the state capital. His uncle works for the state government. He has helped Nathan learn how government works. As you will read, the government provides many services.

LESSON

1 Our State Government

READ TO LEARN

Key Vocabulary

budget
citizen
democracy
governor
elect
executive branch
General Assembly
legislative branch
bill
judicial branch

Key People

Daniel Blue, Jr.
Susie Sharp

Read Aloud

One of the hardest jobs for a state lawmaker is to get people to work together to solve problems.

When Daniel T. Blue, Jr., said these words in January 1991, he had become the Speaker, or leader, of the House of Representatives in North Carolina. In this lesson you will read why being a lawmaker in the state government is an exciting, and often hard, job.

Read for Purpose

1. **WHAT YOU KNOW:** How do you and your friends make decisions about something important to all of you?
2. **WHAT YOU WILL LEARN:** How does the government of our state work?

OUR STATE AND YOU

Supppose that every Saturday you and other classmates bicycle to the local swimming pool for practice. Last week the state government decided to close the bicycle path that you take to the pool. The path is alongside a highway that the state wants to widen. This decision forces you to find a new way to get to swimming practice. As this example shows, acts by our state government affect our lives every day.

Our state government provides many services, such as fixing buildings and roads. To pay for such services, the government collects taxes from people and from businesses.

To decide how much to spend on services, the state government makes a plan for using the taxes called a budget (buj′ it). Look at the circle graph below. It shows how the state spends each dollar of tax money. On what is the largest part of the budget spent?

Will the state government make a good budget? It is the responsibility of the citizens (sit′ ə zənz) to make sure that their government works well. A citizen is a person who is a member of a country by birth or by law. One way that citizens in a democracy can be responsible is to learn how their government works. A democracy is a government that is run by its people, often through leaders that they choose. Citizens should write to these government leaders to tell them they care.

GRAPH SKILL: How much of each tax dollar does North Carolina spend on transportation? On prisons?

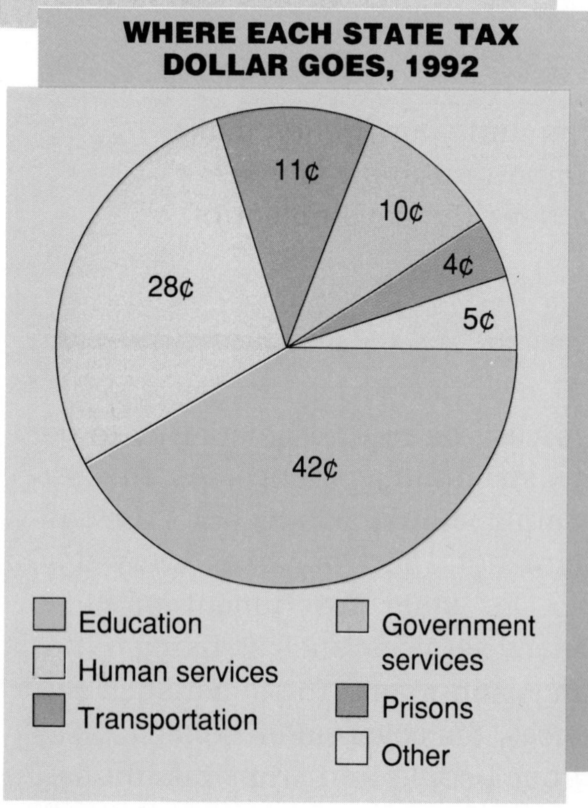

THE EXECUTIVE BRANCH

When North Carolina became a colony, it was ruled by eight Englishmen called Lords Proprietors (prə prī′ i tərz). A proprietor is an owner of land or of a business. The king of England had given the colony's land to these men. Their duty was to choose the colony's governor, or the head of its government.

Today the people of our state elect the governor. To elect means to choose someone for office by voting. Until 1868 governors in North Carolina served for only two years at a time. Since that time governors could serve terms of four years. A term is the number of years a person can hold an office.

Until 1977 our governors could not serve two four-year terms in a row. To give the governor more power, our state's constitution was changed in 1977 to allow a governor to serve up to two terms in a row.

The governor is the head of the executive (eg zek′ yə tiv) branch of our state's government. The executive branch is the part of government that sees to it that our laws are carried out. The offices of the

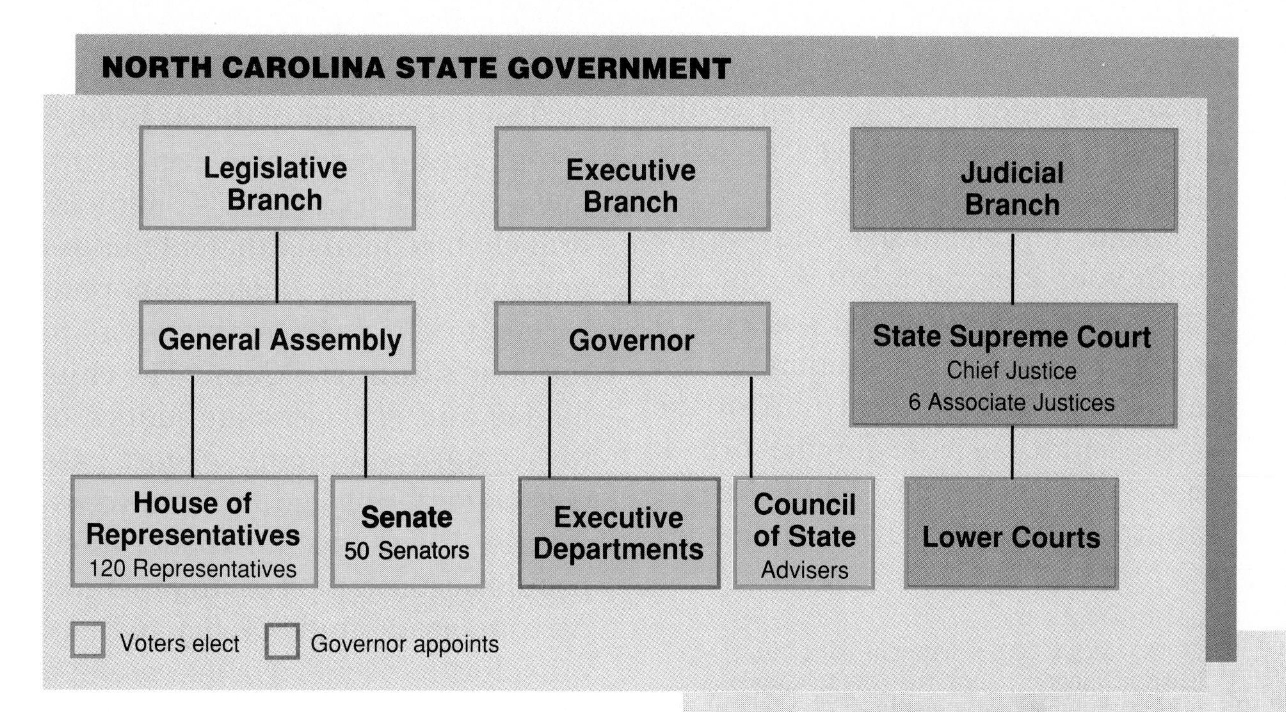

CHART SKILL: How many branches of government does North Carolina have? Which branches are made up of only elected officials?

members of the executive branch are in Raleigh, our state's capital.

The state constitution allows the governor to appoint, or choose, people to help carry out the laws. The chart above shows which part of the executive branch is appointed by the governor and which parts of the executive branch are elected by the voters of our state.

THE LEGISLATIVE BRANCH

One of the most important things that the state government does is to make laws. For example, the state may pass a law to change the number of days you go to school. Laws are passed to meet people's needs.

Our state's laws are made by the **General Assembly**. This body is the **legislative** (lej′ is lā tiv) **branch** of our state government. The Assembly's members meet in Raleigh.

The chart above shows that the General Assembly has two parts. They are the House of Representatives and the Senate. There are 120 representatives and 50 senators. All are elected. Both representatives and senators serve for two-year terms. **Daniel Blue, Jr.**, became the Speaker, or leader, of the House of Representatives in 1991.

Think about some of the problems you face every day. If you have an answer to a community problem, you may have a good idea for a **bill**. A bill is a suggested law.

The flowchart on page 306 shows the steps a bill must go through in order to become a law. Suppose that you have an idea for a bill to start a recycling program. You decide to take your idea to a member of the House of Representatives to write the bill.

Your representative may agree with your idea for a bill. He or she then writes the bill and presents it to the House of Representatives for approval. If more than half of the representatives vote for the bill, it goes to the Senate. If the Senate approves the bill, it becomes a law.

CHART SKILL: What happens to a **bill** if it was changed by the members of the Senate of our state's **General Assembly**?

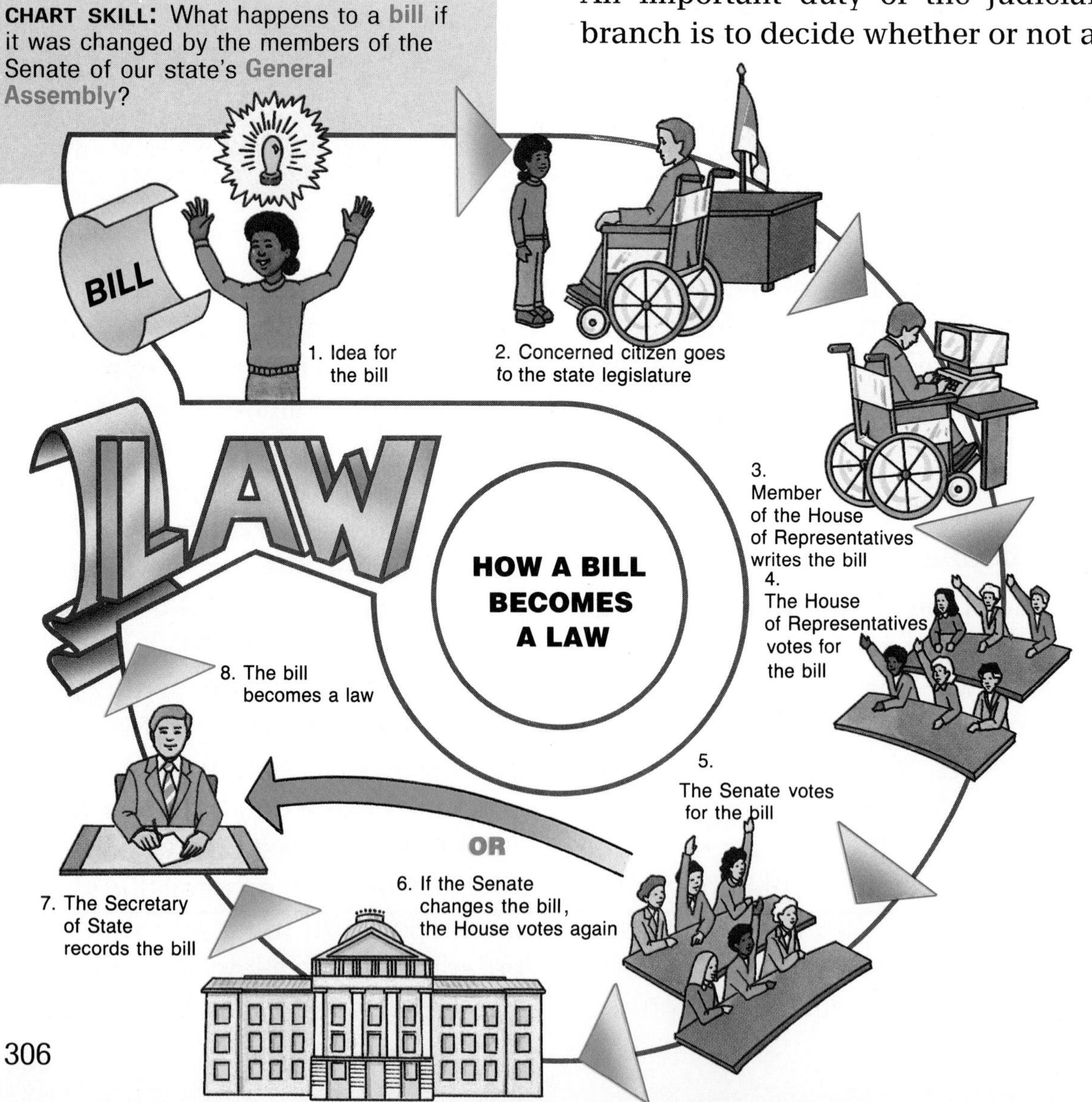

THE JUDICIAL BRANCH

The **judicial** (jü dish′ əl) **branch** of our government also deals with laws. North Carolina's judicial branch has many different judges and courts. The most important judges in our state are members of the state's Supreme Court. The chief justice and six associate judges of the state's Supreme Court are elected for terms lasting eight years.

The judges decide cases about people accused of breaking the law. An important duty of the judicial branch is to decide whether or not a

Susie Sharp was a lawyer and a judge before she was elected to our state's Supreme Court.

law agrees with North Carolina's constitution. The judges make sure that a law does not take away any of the basic rights of the people. If it does, the law is thrown out.

One famous judge from our state is Susie Sharp. Sharp was the only woman in her class at the University of North Carolina Law School. In 1949 Sharp was the first woman to be named a judge in North Carolina. Thirteen years later she was the first woman elected to our state's Supreme Court. In 1974 she became the first female chief justice in North Carolina. Sharp was the second woman to become a chief justice in our country.

RESPONSIBLE CITIZENS

As you have read, our state government collects taxes to pay for services. The three branches of government make the laws and see that they are carried out. Citizens are responsible for our state government. They choose the members of the government by voting for them. Citizens should write to officials to let them know that they care.

Check Your Reading

1. Name the three branches of our state's government. Explain the job that each branch performs.
2. How does our state get the money to pay for services?
3. Which branch of the government would you write to or call if you had an idea for a law?
4. **THINKING SKILL:** Compare the duties of the three branches of state government. How are they alike? How are they different?

Reading Newspapers

Key Vocabulary

news article
feature article
editorial
headline
byline
dateline

In Lesson 1 you read about the government of our state. You learned that we help the government by writing to our representatives about important issues. How do people know what the issues are? One way is by reading newspapers. A newspaper covers stories of local, state, national, and international interest.

The Parts of a Newspaper

Newspapers are divided into several parts. The front part usually contains **news articles**. A news article reports recent events. Most newspapers also have **feature articles**. A feature article reports in detail on a person, subject, or event. For example, a local newspaper in Flat Rock might have a feature article on a summer poetry reading at the Carl Sandburg Home National Historic Site.

Other parts of the newspaper include sports articles, cartoons, and **editorials**. An editorial is an article in which the editor or editors of a newspaper give their opinions about an issue. An editor is the person who runs the paper. Unlike a news article, which includes only statements of fact, an editorial gives opinions about different issues. For example, an editorial might urge readers to support plans to build a new library.

Editorials often appear on the same page with letters to the editor. These letters are written by the paper's readers. In them, readers give their opinions about issues in the news.

The Parts of a News Article

A news article always begins with a **headline**. The headline is printed in large type across the top of the article. Its purpose is to catch the reader's attention. Many news articles have a **byline**. The byline gives the name of the reporter who wrote the article. Some news articles also begin with a **dateline**. A dateline tells where and when the story was written.

A well-written news article begins by answering the following four questions: (1) *Who* is included in the story? (2) *What* happened? (3) *When* did it happen? (4) *Where* did it happen? As you read the news article on page 309, decide whether or not the reporter answered the *Who, What, When,* and *Where* questions.

Leaving Before The Storm

by Sandy Jones

RALEIGH, N.C., Aug. 18, 1991—A powerful storm, Hurricane Bob, passed over Cape Hatteras with winds of 115 miles an hour. The hurricane is the first of the year.

The North Carolina authorities immediately put emergency plans into action. Dare County officials closed a long stretch of the Outer Banks to everyone but the people who live there. The National Park Service closed the park at Ocracoke. The Coast Guard station at Fort Macon said that all but a few needed workers were made to leave Bogue Banks island, where several popular vacation communities are located.

The North Carolina Highway Patrol reported that traffic was backed up for miles, and motorists waited for as long as three hours to cross the bridge from Bodie Island over Currituck Sound. (See photo.)

The state's emergency service said that the hurricane caused less damage than expected. However, about 1,200 people on Ocracoke had no way to get off the island. The storm caused highway 12, the main road, to be flooded.

Police officer directs traffic to the mainland.

Reviewing the Skill

Read the newspaper article above and answer the following questions.

1. Name three different parts of a newspaper.
2. How is an editorial different from a news article?
3. Write another headline for the news article above.
4. Describe the events that were reported in the story.
5. Why is it helpful to know something about the different parts of a newspaper?

LESSON

2 Our Local Governments

READ TO LEARN

Key Vocabulary

board of commissioners
sheriff
county seat
city council
mayor
city council-manager

Read Aloud

You need help—fast! Your home is on fire or someone is breaking into your car. Or there has been an accident and you need to go to the hospital immediately. Whether you live in the city or outside the city limits, you can call . . . for police, fire, or emergency rescue day or night.

Notices such as this one appear in newspapers throughout North Carolina. They mention just three of the services that our local governments provide. In this lesson you will read about the duties and responsibilities of our county, city, and other local governments.

Read for Purpose

1. **WHAT YOU KNOW:** Which services does our state government provide?
2. **WHAT YOU WILL LEARN:** What are some services that local governments provide?

LOCAL GOVERNMENT

In the last lesson you read about the three branches that make up our state government. These three branches work together to keep our state strong and healthy. However, the state government does not make all the important decisions in North Carolina. Some problems, such as the need to build a new school, do not involve everyone in the state. Instead the governments of our counties, cities, and towns decide such local issues.

Suppose you live in the make-believe town of Ventura in North Carolina. Only 100 people live in Ventura. A few people have been hurt in car accidents at the corner of Magnolia and Main streets. The people of the town want to put up a traffic light there. Does the North Carolina General Assembly meet to decide the issue? The answer is no. This decision is made by the leaders of the local government.

The people in a growing city may need a larger police department or may want to add more teachers to its school system. A small town, however, may have different needs. Instead of more police, it may need to add sidewalks along some of its roads. For reasons such as these, different kinds of communities have their own governments.

COUNTY GOVERNMENT

Look at the map of counties below to find the county in which you live. As you read in Chapter 1, North Carolina is divided into 100 counties. No two counties are alike.

MAP SKILL: In which county is the state capital located? Which is the most southern county?

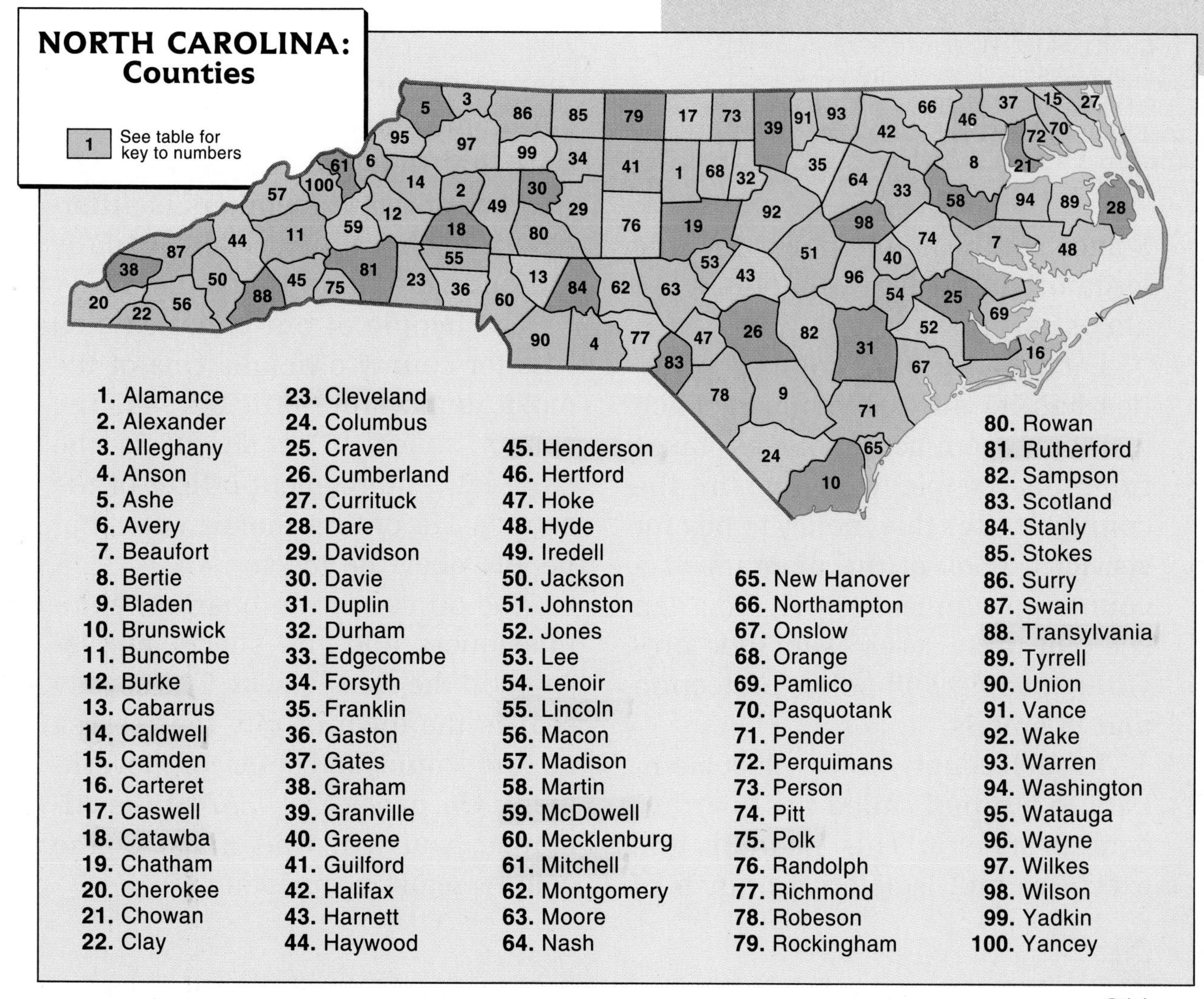

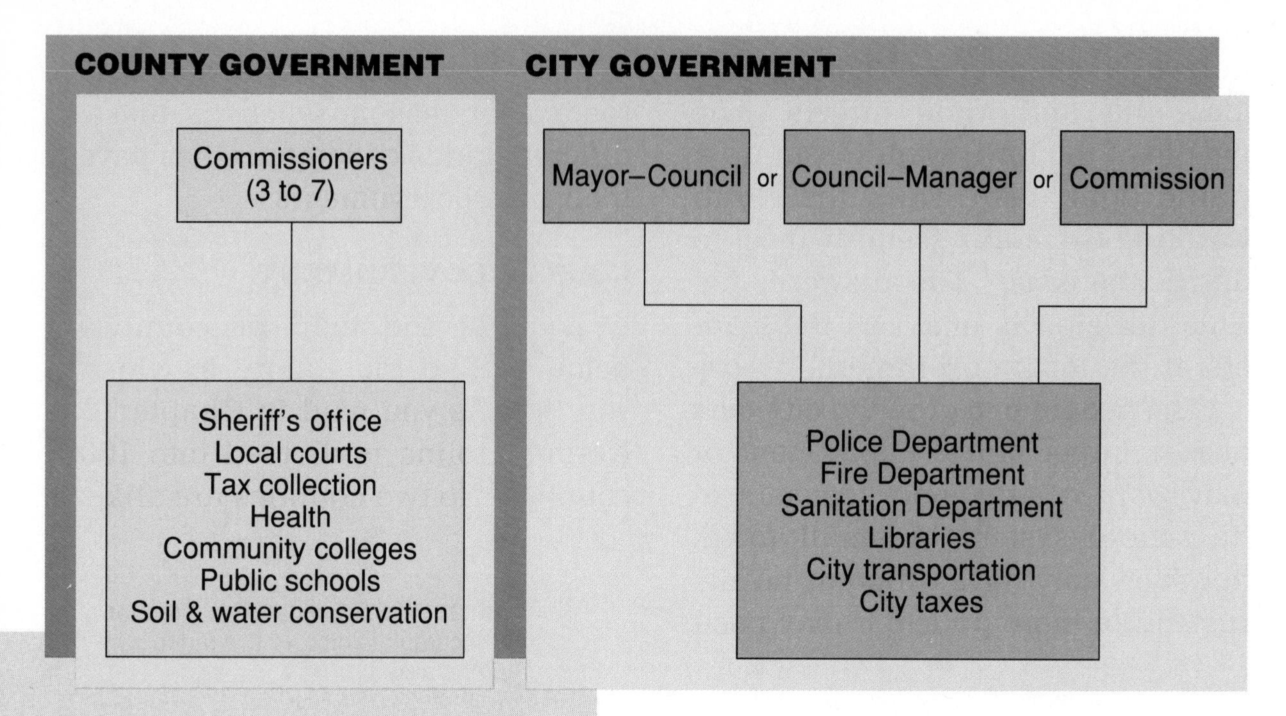

CHART SKILL: Compare the two charts above. Which services do both the county governments and the city governments provide?

Some of these counties include large urban areas, while others are almost all rural.

Each of North Carolina's counties has its own government. Each county government collects taxes from the people who live in the county. It uses this money to pay for services. Look at the diagram of a county government above. You can see that these services include providing people with police protection and hospitals.

In each county, voters elect members to a group called the **board of commissioners**. This board is the executive and legislative branch of the county government. The board of commissioners makes laws and sees that they are carried out. The number of board members is different in each county. There usually are between 3 and 7 members.

The people of our counties also vote for county officials. One of the most important officials is the county **sheriff**. The sheriff is the chief law enforcement officer of the county. He or she makes sure that people obey the laws.

The offices of the board of commissioners and the sheriff are located in the **county seat**. The county seat is the town or city that serves as the county's center of government. On pages 364–367 of the Almanac, you will find a list of the county seats in our state.

John Baker (*left*) is the **sheriff** of Wake County. He and other local officials in our state help their communities run smoothly.

CITIES

Cities and large towns in our state have one of three different kinds of government. Most cities in North Carolina have a governing board called a **city council**. The council is elected by the citizens of a city. The number of people on the city council is different from city to city. Usually there are 3 to 12 members on it. Members of the city council make laws and see that they are carried out. The city council also makes decisions about police protection, taxes, libraries, and other local issues and services.

In some cities the citizens also elect an official called a **mayor**. Often the mayor does not have much power. He or she is in charge of the meetings of the city council. The mayor votes in case of a tie vote by the city council. A tie vote means that each side has ended up with the same number of votes.

Another kind of city government in North Carolina is the **city council-manager** type of government. In this kind of government, the people who live in a city first elect a city council. The city council then hires a city manager, who appoints officials and runs the city.

GOVERNMENTS WORK TOGETHER

The county, city, and other local governments within North Carolina are not completely separate from the state government. Our state and local governments work together to provide important services. These services include libraries, police and fire protection, health care,

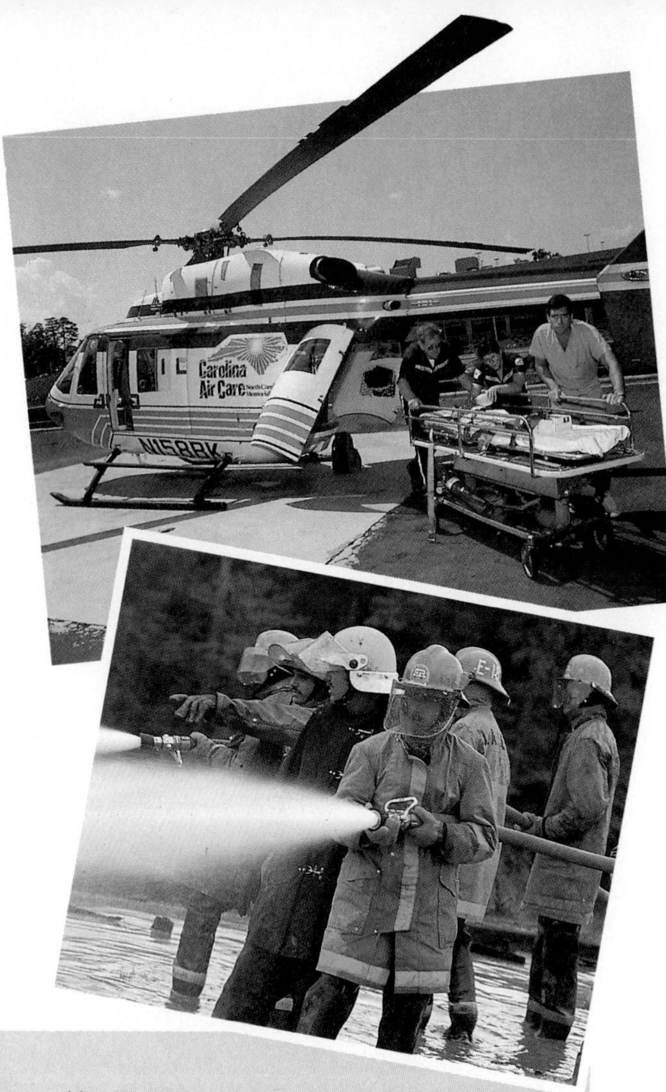

education, and laws that protect the state's environment.

North Carolina's local and state governments also work with our country's government. For example, they work together to protect wildlife and to find the people who break the law. Only by working together can all the governments try to meet the needs of all the people.

LOCAL GOVERNMENTS HELP PEOPLE

Look at the photographs on this page. They show some of the services that city, county, and other local governments provide for their people. How are these services alike? Do they show services that protect us and improve our way of life? Helping people is what government is all about.

Health-care workers, firefighters, and sanitation workers provide services for which our state and local governments are responsible.

Check Your Reading

1. What is the difference between the state government and local governments?
2. What is a county seat? Which government offices are located there?
3. What does a city manager do?
4. What are some of the services that local governments provide for their people?
5. **THINKING SKILL:** What conclusions can you draw from the fact that many people want to lower our state and local taxes?

LESSON

3 Our National Government

READ TO LEARN

Key Vocabulary	Key People	Key Places
national government	Jesse Helms	Washington, D.C.
Congress	Terry Sanford	Fort Bragg
House of Representatives	Sam Ervin, Jr.	Camp Lejeune
Senate	Luther Hodges	
candidate	Elizabeth Dole	
political party		

Read Aloud

After taking my seat in the Senate, I informed North Carolinians by weekly newspaper columns and radio broadcasts exactly how I stood on the issues.

In his book, *Preserving the Constitution,* Senator Sam Ervin, Jr., explained how he saw his job as a lawmaker in the United States government. In this lesson you will read about the responsibilities that North Carolinians have in our country's government.

Read for Purpose

1. WHAT YOU KNOW: What are the three branches of North Carolina's state government?
2. WHAT YOU WILL LEARN: What are the responsibilities of the three branches of our national government?

OUR COUNTRY'S GOVERNMENT

In this chapter you have read that our state and local governments work together with our country's government. The government of our country is called the **national government**

You most likely know something about our national government already. You know that the capital of the United States is **Washington, D.C.** Some of you may have a brother or sister who took a class trip there. From the news you may know that the President often meets with the leaders of other countries. The President also has many other duties and responsibilities.

THREE BRANCHES

The national government, like our state government, has three branches. Their duties are given in the United States Constitution. The Constitution is called the highest law in the land because all our other laws are based on it. You can read the Constitution's Preamble, or opening statement, below.

Like North Carolina's governor, the President of the United States is head of the executive branch of government. The executive branch sees that laws are carried out. The President chooses people to head the many executive offices that provide services. These services include transportation, education, and the defense of our country.

The legislative branch of our national government is called **Congress**. Congress is made up of the **House of Representatives** and the **Senate**. Voters in all states elect people to serve in these two legislative houses.

The judicial branch of the national government is made up of federal courts. *Federal* is a word that is used for describing the national government. The Supreme Court is the most important federal court. It decides whether or not laws are in agreement with the Constitution of the United States.

The United States Constitution set up a government that has kept our country strong and free.

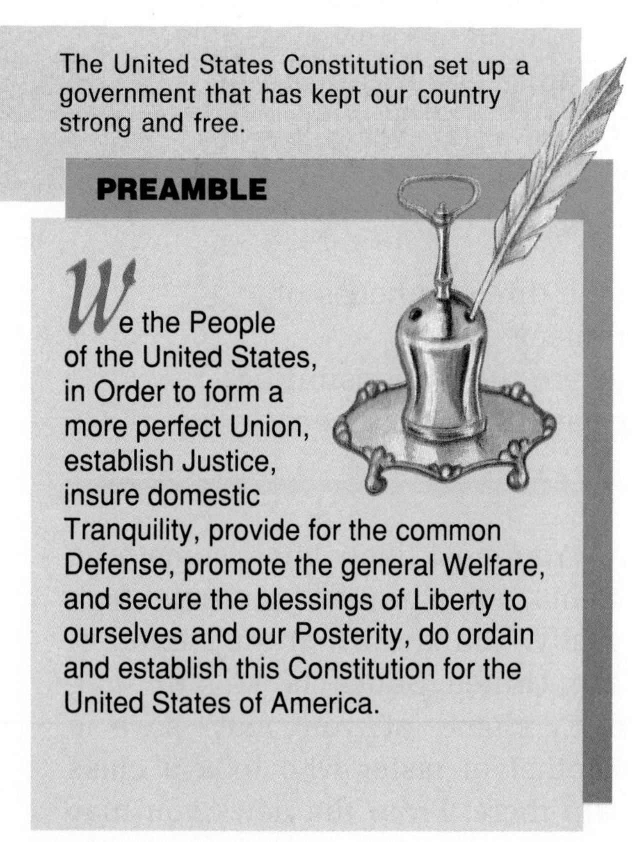

PREAMBLE

We the People of the United States, in Order to form a more perfect Union, establish Justice, insure domestic Tranquility, provide for the common Defense, promote the general Welfare, and secure the blessings of Liberty to ourselves and our Posterity, do ordain and establish this Constitution for the United States of America.

RESPONSIBILITIES

Like our state and local governments, the national government depends on tax money to pay for the services that it provides. But the national government is different from state and local governments in many ways.

The national government handles matters that involve many states. For example, it prints and coins the money that everyone in the country uses. The national government also works with other countries. It has, for instance, signed an agreement with Canada to try and get rid of the pollution caused by the burning of fuels.

The national government is in charge of the armed forces that protect our country. In fact, a few military bases are located in North Carolina. The largest of these bases are **Fort Bragg** in Fayetteville and **Camp Lejeune** (lə jün′) in Jacksonville, both in the east.

ELECTING PRESIDENTS

The voters of North Carolina help to choose the President of the United States. Presidential elections are held every four years during the first week of November. You can vote for the President after you are 18 years old and have registered to vote. To register, you must fill out a voting form.

A national election is an exciting event. Newspapers and radio and television stations carry advertisements for the **candidates**. Candidates are people who are running for office. You might discuss national candidates with your class or prepare a questionnaire, or a list of questions, to ask about them.

Candidates usually belong to a **political party**. A political party is a group of citizens who share some of the same ideas about government and the issues. They work to get these ideas used in government. For example, one political party may want to make the army larger. Another party may want to make the the army smaller. The Democratic and the Republican parties are our two largest political parties.

These North Carolinians are voting for state and local officials. The signs below are advertisements for **candidates** who are running for office.

The citizens of our country have elected three people from our state to be President. They are Andrew Jackson, James K. Polk, and Andrew Johnson. Page 362 of the Almanac tells you about these Presidents.

TAR HEEL REPRESENTATIVES

Congress, our national legislative branch, meets in the Capitol Building in Washington, D.C. Representatives are elected for terms of two years.

The number of people that represent a state depends on the size of that state's population. In the 1980s North Carolina had 11 representatives. In 1990 the national census found that North Carolina was growing faster than some other states were. Our state gained one representative in Congress.

TAR HEEL SENATORS

Like every state, North Carolina elects two senators to represent it in the national Senate. A senator's term lasts six years. Senators can be reelected after their first term.

Jesse Helms has served as United States senator since 1973. **Terry Sanford** was first elected to the country's Senate in 1986. He had been our state's governor from 1961 to 1965.

One of North Carolina's most famous senators was **Sam Ervin, Jr.** He served North Carolina in the United States Senate from 1954 to 1975. You read some words by Ervin in the Read Aloud. They suggest that a senator's job is to let the people in a state know what is happening in the national government. Ervin was known for supporting our country's Constitution. He said:

In my judgment, the greatest and most precious possession of the . . . people is the Constitution.

OTHER TAR HEEL LEADERS

Many other Tar Heels have served in our country's government. As you read in Chapter 9, **Luther Hodges** helped plan Research Triangle Park. He was our state's governor from 1954 to 1961. In 1961 he became the United States secretary of commerce. In this job, Hodges guided our country's trade.

Another Tar Heel who served our national government is **Elizabeth Dole**. She was born in Salisbury

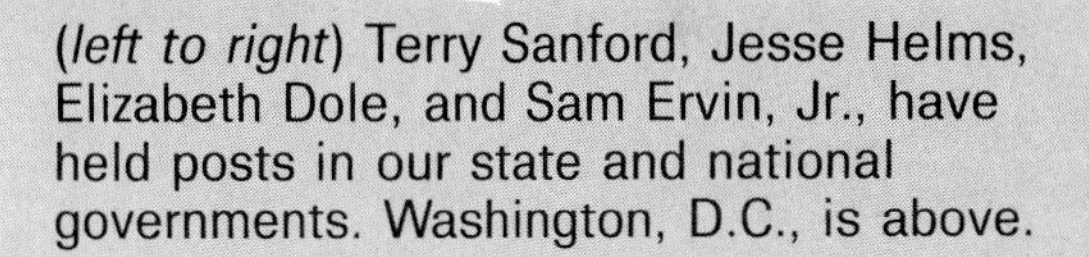

(*left to right*) Terry Sanford, Jesse Helms, Elizabeth Dole, and Sam Ervin, Jr., have held posts in our state and national governments. Washington, D.C., is above.

and went to Duke University. Dole was our country's secretary of transportation from 1983 until 1987. She was the first woman to hold this post. She became our country's secretary of labor in 1989.

Dole no longer works for the government, but she is still serving people. Today she is the head of the American Red Cross. This organization helps victims of disasters all over the world.

SERVING OUR COUNTRY

As you have read, Tar Heels have been important leaders not only in our state but also in our country's government. By voting in elections and working in the national government, citizens help guide North Carolina and the United States toward the future. Citizens in a democracy can also help plan the future by learning about the duties and responsibilities of government.

Check Your Reading

1. What are the duties of the three branches of our national government?
2. How many senators does North Carolina elect to the United States Senate? How many representatives does our state have in the House of Representatives?
3. In what ways can North Carolinians take part in the national government?
4. **THINKING SKILL:** Compare the three branches of our national government with the three branches of North Carolina's state government.

YOU CAN MAKE A DIFFERENCE

In this book you have read about some people who make a difference in North Carolina. By teaching the Cherokee language and Cherokee traditions, Edna Chickelela is keeping alive Cherokee culture. Thanks to the help of L. C. Coonse, a dangerous incinerator was closed down so that people in his community could live in a clean environment.

These are only a few of the many people who have made an effort to help others in our state. Chances are that there is someone who has worked hard to solve a problem in your own community. Perhaps it was an adult. Perhaps it was a young person like you.

You may be too young to know how to close down an incinerator, but there are many other ways in which you can help your community. Is there a park nearby with litter on the ground? Is there a senior citizen in your neighborhood who might enjoy a visit from a young person? Do you have a neighbor who needs help carrying groceries?

You might be able to help out in instances like these, or you might think of other ways in which to help your community. The important thing is to remember that *you*, too, can make a difference.

REVIEWING VOCABULARY

Number a sheet of paper from 1 to 5. Beside each number write **T** if the statement is true. If the statement is false, rewrite it to make it true.

1. The state legislative branch is called Congress and is in charge of carrying out the state laws.
2. The sheriff is the chief law enforcement officer of the county.
3. The budget is all of the annual taxes that the state collects.
4. The General Assembly meets in each county seat to make laws for the county.
5. A political party is a large gathering at which people talk about state programs and have a good time.

REVIEWING FACTS

1. Describe the steps that a bill must go through in North Carolina in order to become a law.
2. Which of these services would be provided by local government? (a) installing a traffic light (b) maintaining a state park (c) running a military base
3. How is the state capital like a county seat?
4. How long are the terms of office in North Carolina for the governor, for a state senator, for a state supreme court judge?
5. Name three jobs done by the national government that are not done by state and local governments.

WRITING ABOUT MAIN IDEAS

1. **Making a List:** Make a list of the key events in Susie Sharp's career. Then write a sentence or two telling what schoolchildren can learn from Sharp's life and work.
2. **Writing About Perspectives:** Suppose that you are a senior citizen writing to the editor of the local newspaper. You are expressing your opinion about the state budget—especially about whether money is being spent on the right things in the right amounts. Give the reasons for your opinion.

BUILDING SKILLS: READING NEWSPAPERS

1. What is the difference between a news article and a feature article?
2. What is an editorial? Who writes the editorials of a newspaper?
3. Write the first paragraph of a news article about an event that took place in school this week.
4. Write a headline for the article.
5. Why is it helpful to understand the different types of articles that appear in a newspaper?

CHAPTER 12

FACING THE FUTURE

FOCUS

When I first came to North Carolina, I just spoke the language of my home country, Cambodia. Television surprised me, but it helped me to learn English. Museums, too, helped me to learn.

Chuom Prak lives in Greensboro. His family is one of many who came to North Carolina from another country. In this chapter you will read about the connections that our state has to the world.

LESSON

1 Equal Rights for All

READ TO LEARN

Key Vocabulary

integration
suffrage
boycott

Key People

Martin Luther King, Jr.

Read Aloud

All of us were afraid. But we went and did it.

David Richmond used these words to talk about the actions that he and three other African-American students took on February 1, 1960. On that day the students walked into a store in Greensboro, sat down at a lunch counter that only served white customers, and ordered coffee. As you will read, their actions were among many in the long fight for equal rights in North Carolina.

Read for Purpose

1. **WHAT YOU KNOW:** How were African Americans denied equal rights after the Civil War?
2. **WHAT YOU WILL LEARN:** How have African Americans and other North Carolinians fought for equality?

AFRICAN AMERICANS FIGHT FOR EQUAL RIGHTS

Tanya and Jennifer are fourth graders. They are in the same class in a public school that has students from the many different groups in our state.

Years ago, Tanya and Jennifer would not have gone to the same public school. Tanya is black, and Jennifer is white. Until the mid-1950s black children were forced to go to segregated schools, or schools that were separate from those of white children. African Americans and other groups fought to open the public schools to all children. The fight to end segregation was known as the civil rights movement. Civil rights, as you know, are the rights of all people to be treated the same.

In 1954 the United States Supreme Court, the highest court in our country, said that segregation in the public schools was against the law. Afterward, black students and white students began to go to the same public schools. However, bringing about **integration** (in ti grā′ shən) was not easy. Integration is making public places open to everyone. It took many years to integrate public places in every state of our country.

BOYCOTTS AND SIT-INS

One method that African Americans used to fight for equal rights was the **boycott**. In a boycott, people refuse to buy, sell, or use certain goods or services. In 1955 blacks in Montgomery, Alabama, began a boycott of the public buses. They wanted to change the laws that made African Americans sit in the back of buses. African Americans refused to ride the buses until the Jim Crow law was changed almost a year later.

In the Read Aloud you read about the students who sat down at a Greensboro lunch counter in 1960. They were refused service because they were black. These students used another method to fight for equal rights. They held a sit-in to peacefully demand equal treatment. In a sit-in, people sit in a place until their demands are met. The students said that they wanted the rights that were given to all Americans by the Constitution.

Over the next few days more African Americans sat at the lunch counter. The sit-in spread to other cities in the state. Finally, six months after the sit-in began, blacks were served at the Greensboro store. The sit-in was a success.

THE CIVIL RIGHTS ACT

Many North Carolinians worked together to bring about integration. They also worked to get new laws

African-American college students held one of the first sit-ins in Greensboro to fight for **integration**.

passed that would protect the rights of African Americans. Leaders like **Martin Luther King, Jr.**, of Georgia led civil rights marches for equal rights in many cities. The largest march took place in Washington, D.C., in 1963. Hundreds of thousands of people from all over the country took part. Finally, the United States Congress passed the Civil Rights Act in 1964. It was now against the law for businesses to treat people differently because of their race, sex, or religion. In 1965 Congress passed the Voting Rights Act. This law ended the practices that were used to keep African Americans from voting.

THE CHALLENGE TODAY

Today the lives of Tanya and other Tar Heel children are better because of the changes brought about by the civil rights movement. However, African Americans and other North Carolinians are still struggling for equal rights in areas such as jobs and housing.

NATIVE AMERICANS FIGHT FOR EQUAL RIGHTS

The Native American groups in North Carolina have also fought for equal rights for many years. As you have read, in 1835 state leaders passed laws that kept Native Americans from voting. Indians were also not allowed to go to the same schools as whites or to own land.

By the 1880s Lumbee leaders persuaded state lawmakers to improve schools for Lumbee children. In 1887 the first public college for the Lumbee was opened near Pembroke. It is now called Pembroke State University.

Martin Luther King, Jr., led the 1963 march on Washington. Pembroke State was our state's first college for Indians.

School segregation began to end for Indians as well as for blacks after 1954. However, the Indians wanted their children to learn about their cultures. The Lumbee started a program in the Robeson County public schools that teaches all students about the Lumbee culture.

WORKING FOR CHANGE

Native American leaders are now working to gain equal rights for all of the Indian groups in our state. Today the Cherokee are the only Indians in our state who are recognized as a group by the United States government. This means that the Cherokee have a right to education and other services that the national government provides some Native American groups. Our state's other Indian groups also want to be recognized by our national government so that they can receive the same services.

WOMEN FIGHT FOR EQUAL RIGHTS

Women in our country also have had to fight for equal rights. This struggle began with women's efforts to gain **suffrage** (suf′ rij), or the right to vote.

Tar Heel women long fought for this important right. In the 1880s some women, such as Helen Morris Lewis, started suffrage groups. They staged marches and held meetings to gain the right to vote.

Support for women's suffrage increased during World War I, when women took over men's jobs in factories and offices. World War I was the war that the United States and other countries fought in Europe, beginning in 1914. In 1920, two years after the war, the Constitution was changed to give women the right to vote.

EQUAL RIGHTS ON THE JOB

Gaining the right to vote was an important step in women's struggle for equality. They also had to fight for equal rights on the job. More women got the chance to work during World War II, the world war that our country fought in the 1940s.

Since World War II ended in 1945, American women have gained more rights. In the 1960s and 1970s large numbers of women began to

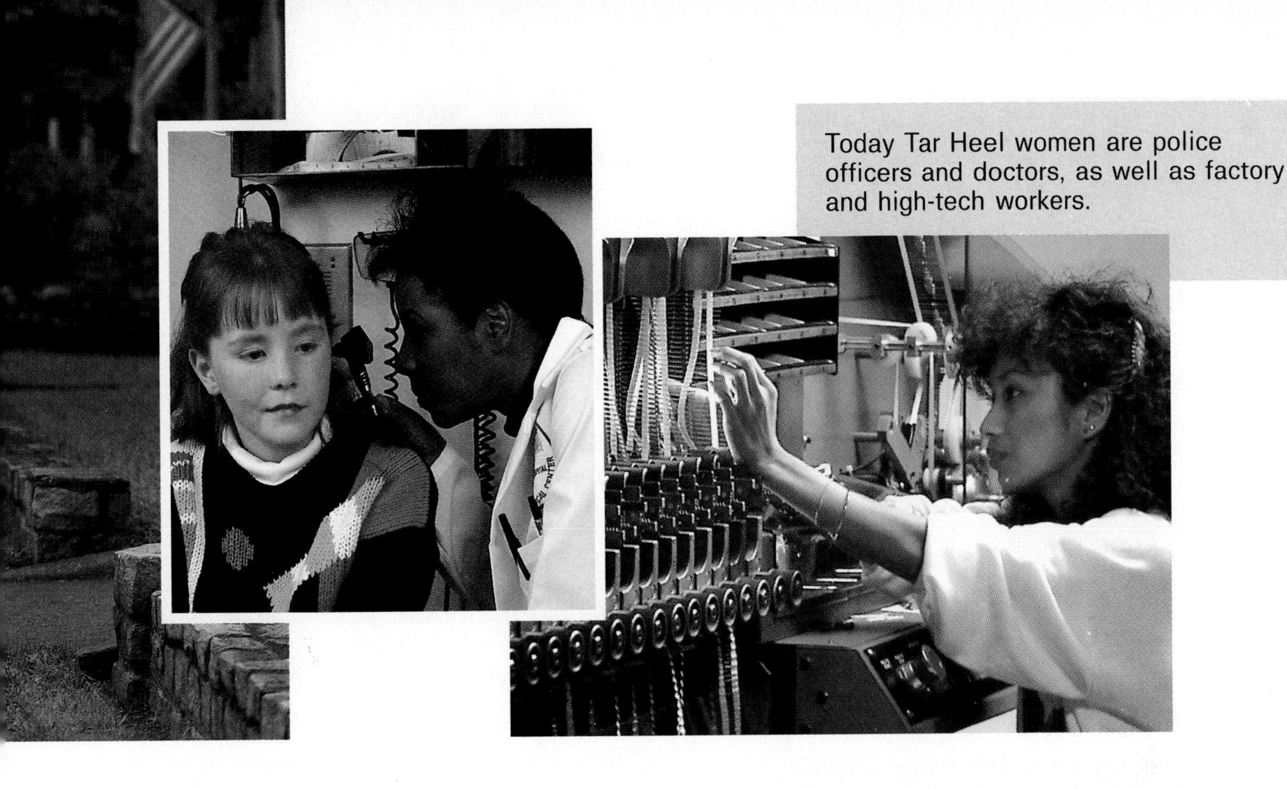

Today Tar Heel women are police officers and doctors, as well as factory and high-tech workers.

work outside the home. Many demanded to be paid the same as men for similar kinds of work.

Today about 6 out of 10 women in our state work outside the home. Some Tar Heel women have top jobs in education and in state and local governments. A few have become mayors of Tar Heel cities.

However, most women in our state still do not earn as much as men do. Sandra Babb is the head of a group working for women's rights. She believes that it is important to help women train for many different kinds of jobs.

> *Being able to move into better jobs means having the skills to do these jobs. As early as elementary school, girls need to know that there are choices and [that] it's okay to do a wide range of things.*

THE STRUGGLE CONTINUES

As you have read, people in North Carolina have joined other people in the United States in an effort to win equal rights for all. By using sit-ins and marches, they have been able to change laws. But more still needs to be done. The fight to gain equal rights for all will continue.

Check Your Reading

1. How have African Americans, women, and Native Americans fought for equal rights?
2. What was the Civil Rights Act?
3. How have the Lumbee fought to gain equal rights?
4. **THINKING SKILL:** Compare the rights that women had before 1914 with those they gained in 1920 and afterward.

Recognizing Point of View

Key Vocabulary

point of view   bias

Read what Kristin and Aaron have to say about skiing.

Kristin: Skiing is fun for both skiers and spectators.

Aaron: Skiing is a dangerous sport. Skiers can get hurt.

Kristin and Aaron each have a different **point of view**. A point of view is the way in which a person looks at something. People often look at the same subject from different points of view. Being able to identify a person's point of view allows you to make up your own mind about a subject.

Trying the Skill

Below are two different points of view about how successful the women's rights movement has been.

Women have made great gains in the area of equal rights. Now they can become firefighters, or run big companies, or become astronauts and go to the moon.

Not enough progress has been made in the area of equal rights for women, because women are still viewed with **bias**. Bias is the favoring of one view or opinion over another. *Men usually get better pay for the same work since some people believe that men do better work.*

How would you describe the two points of view?

HELPING YOURSELF

The steps on the left will help you to recognize a person's point of view. The example on the right shows how to apply these steps to the statements on page 328.

One Way to Determine Point of View	Example
1. Identify the subject.	The subject is the progress made by women in the area of equal rights.
2. Identify the information given.	The statements discuss some changes that have occurred in the position of women and the fact that there is still so much to be done.
3. Identify words that are expressions of opinion. They tell how a person feels about something.	One speaker argues that women have made "great gains." The other speaker says, "Not enough progress has been made."
4. Tell the point of view expressed.	The first speaker thinks women's rights have come a long way; the second speaker focuses on the continuing bias against them.

Applying the Skill

Now apply what you have learned. Identify the point of view expressed by the two speakers below.

The people who took part in the Greensboro sit-in acted bravely. They were trying to bring about civil rights for African Americans.

The people who took part in the Greensboro sit-in broke the law. They should have found some other, lawful way of making their point.

1. What topic are the speakers talking about?
   - **a.** what happened in Greensboro
   - **b.** whether the people who sat-in in Greensboro did the right thing
   - **c.** why people sat-in in Greensboro
2. The first point of view is shown by
   - **a.** the subject identified
   - **b.** the words *acted bravely*
   - **c.** the bias of the speaker
3. Which phrase helped you to determine the second point of view?
   - **a.** *The people who took part*
   - **b.** *broke the law*
   - **c.** *should have found some other way*

Reviewing the Skill

1. Define *point of view.*
2. Describe some of the steps you should take to identify a person's point of view.
3. Why is it important to understand a person's point of view?

LESSON

2 Protecting Our Environment

READ TO LEARN

Key Vocabulary

landfill recycling

Read Aloud

We are trying to get people in North Carolina to change the way they think about garbage.

Mary Beth Powell used these words to describe her job in state government. Powell works with leaders who want to lower the amount of garbage in their communities. In this lesson you will read about some of the ways in which people have improved the environment of our state.

Read for Purpose

1. **WHAT YOU KNOW:** What are some things you can do to protect the environment?
2. **WHAT YOU WILL LEARN:** How can the people of North Carolina continue to improve our state's environment?

POPULATION GROWTH

The natural resources of North Carolina make our state a place in which many people want to live. Our beaches, hills, forests, mountains, rivers, and lakes provide people with beautiful scenery and many places for recreation. Our state's natural beauty is honored in the song "Carolina Calling," which appears on page 331.

North Carolina is a growing state that welcomes people who want to live here. However, a growing population causes new problems for the state. You will read in the Point/Counterpoint on pages 336–337 about the struggle in the Piedmont over whether to build new businesses in the New Hope. The Coastal Plain is another area in which new building is creating problems.

PROTECTING BEACHES

As you have read, more tourists have begun to visit the beaches and communities along our coast.

CAROLINA CALLING

New building in communities along the Outer Banks has led to the loss of some sand dunes and to beach erosion.

Over the years new businesses were built to serve tourists. Resorts, cottages, and restaurants soon took the place of some of the sand dunes. Along the dunes, the plants and grasses that once held the sand and soil in place were also lost. The result was beach erosion.

In 1974 the Coastal Area Management Act, or CAMA, was passed. This law limits the number of buildings in coastal areas. CAMA had two main goals. The first goal was to stop beach erosion. The second one was to stop water pollution along the coast.

THE SCENIC MOUNTAINS

Too much building is also a problem in the Mountain Region. You have read how mountain towns welcome people. Many new businesses have opened. However, some people are worried that the growth of businesses will ruin the natural beauty of the region.

In 1983 some counties in this region passed a law that protects high mountain peaks. The law limits the types of buildings that can be placed on mountains above 3,000 feet (914 m). Many people are in favor of these limits.

Some people in the Mountain Region do not want to limit growth. They believe that enough North Carolina land is already protected in state and national parks and forests. They do not want the government to decide how the state's land should be used.

Others disagree. Chris May, the city manager of Blowing Rock, says,

> *Progress is going to happen. Either you plan for the growth or you end up having it with no controls. It's a lot easier to plan ahead than it is to fix something after it's ruined.*

TOO MUCH TRASH

Yet another problem has been brought about by our state's population growth. It is the question of how to handle the increase in garbage. You read in the Point/Counterpoint feature of Chapter 2 that many people disagree over what should be done to get rid of our growing piles of garbage.

Did you know that each day Americans throw out enough paper trash to fill nearly 10,000 large trucks? If all those trucks were lined up end to end, they would stretch about 120 miles (193 km). That is about the distance between Charlotte and Burlington. How much paper trash do you think that you and your classmates throw away each day?

LANDFILLS

Have you ever wondered where the trash goes after it is picked up from your school and home? For many years most trash was dumped in **landfills**. A landfill is a place where trash is buried.

This **landfill** in Charlotte is one of many that is running out of room in which to bury garbage.

Some people think that we will be able to throw away our trash forever. However, landfills are filling up. North Carolina, like other states, does not have enough room for all of its garbage. Mary Beth Powell, about whom you read in the Read Aloud, explains.

People have to learn that there is no such thing as [getting rid of] garbage. When you throw something away, someone has to deal with it sooner or later.

The recycling of plastic, paper, and other items is helping communities to solve their garbage problems.

During the next 20 years many landfills in our state will have to close. Some will close because they are full. Others will close because they were built long ago and are no longer thought to be safe. Chemicals in products such as motor oil, paint, and nail polish remover can harm the environment. Over time these chemicals can also leak out of a landfill, polluting the soil and underground water. This pollution is a danger to our health.

RECYCLING

People in North Carolina are trying to solve the garbage problem. Our state legislature has passed a law that requires each city and town to cut its waste by one fourth by 1993. By 2001 the law says that communities must cut their waste by close to one half.

What does this law mean for your family? How can you find ways to throw away less garbage? You may have heard about one method called **recycling**. Recycling means collecting and separating trash that can be used again. Newspapers, plastic cups, glass jars, paper boxes, plastic bottles, and aluminum cans can be shredded or melted. Instead of taking up space in landfills, these items are made into new products. Recycling saves our natural resources. For example, recycling 1 ton (.907 metric t) of paper saves 17 trees.

You may live in a city that has a recycling program. One of the first recycling programs in our state was begun in Charlotte. People sort their trash before it is picked up by trucks. Drop-off places for the different kinds of trash are also located throughout the city.

Office workers in Charlotte take part in recycling through the Paper Chase program. Instead of throwing away used paper, workers set it aside for recycling. The recycled paper is then made into newsprint. Newsprint is the paper on which newspapers are printed.

Other Tar Heels also take part in recycling. Restaurants in Orange County, for example, set aside bins for collecting glass bottles and aluminum cans. In Conover people save plastic milk jugs, which they sell to a factory. At the factory the plastic jugs are broken into tiny pieces, or pellets, about the size of a peanut. You may be surprised to learn that these pellets are then made into material for carpets.

FINDING A BALANCE

In the future North Carolinians must find a way to balance the need to grow with the need to protect our environment. The state's beautiful mountains and beaches, its clean air, and its wildlife are important to all of us. Our state must decide how to protect these resources and use them wisely.

After these plastic bottles are shredded at a recycling center, the plastic will be reused.

Check Your Reading

1. What is CAMA and what are its goals?
2. How has population growth affected the environment of the Mountain Region?
3. Name two reasons that many landfills in North Carolina will close during the next 20 years.
4. How can the people of North Carolina continue to improve our state's environment?
5. THINKING SKILL: Reread the quote by the city manager of Blowing Rock on page 333. What is the city manager's point of view on building in the Mountain Region?

BUILDING CITIZENSHIP
POINT/COUNTERPOINT

Should We Develop or Preserve Our Land?

You have just read about how North Carolinians are working to balance the need for growth with the need to protect the environment. Our state is growing quickly. Two of our fast-growing cities are Durham and Chapel Hill. Many people move to them because of their universities and Research Triangle Park. The people moving in need homes, shops, and community services. They also need clean air and water.

Located between Durham and Chapel Hill is the New Hope Creek. This creek and the wooded area that surrounds it is called the New Hope. There are highways all around the New Hope. Many people build homes there. They like to live and shop near the New Hope between Durham and Chapel Hill.

Some people think that the New Hope should be developed, or built up with homes and businesses, to serve the growing population. But others think the New Hope should be preserved, or left as it is. They think our natural resource of land should be saved for our health and enjoyment. What would you decide?

POINT

The New Hope Should Be Preserved

Hildegard Ryals is secretary of the Friends of the New Hope. This group wants to save the New Hope for our health and enjoyment. Read Ryals's argument below.

> The New Hope . . . is not just a place for nature study and recreation. The creek area protects our environment. Creek slopes [*hills*] help protect our home from floods because they [soak] up rainwater. In dry weather, the slopes release water. Saving the New Hope . . . is not just about our water safety. It's about saving our water supply.
>
> Business development there will not add much to our economy. It would create more cars to pollute our air. . . . We would lose trails for nature study, bike paths, and the fresh air of the forests.

- According to Ryals, why should the New Hope be preserved?

COUNTERPOINT

The New Hope Should Be Developed

W. Travis Porter is a Durham lawyer and educator. He believes that the New Hope can have both new businesses and open space. Read Porter's argument below.

> No one ever said that we should not have greenways [*open space and waterways*]. . . .Where is there left for people to operate as a community? The New Hope is already crisscrossed with highways. Traffic is a magnet for business. . . . Business taxes pay for schools, for hospitals, and to keep up our parks. . . . Business creates jobs. For our way of life to survive, we must have economic success. One good business plan would save all the creek slopes and all the white oaks. We can have both parks and economic success if we work together.

- According to Porter, why should the New Hope be developed?

UNDERSTANDING THE POINT/COUNTERPOINT

1. In your opinion, which do you think is the stronger argument? Why?
2. What other opinions might people have about building up or preserving the New Hope?
3. Do you think that an agreement can be reached between the two groups of people? If so, what might it be?

LESSON

3 North Carolina and the World

READ TO LEARN

Key Vocabulary

specialize

Read Aloud

When I first stepped off the plane, I didn't know what I was in for. In the two weeks that followed, I learned more about myself, my country, and my world.

These are the words that Ginny Cox used to describe her visit to Belgium. Twelve-year-old Ginny was visiting Belgium under an exchange program called Citizens for Understanding. In this lesson you will read about other links that North Carolinians have with people in countries all over the world.

Read for Purpose

1. **WHAT YOU KNOW:** Which products does North Carolina send to other states in the United States?
2. **WHAT YOU WILL LEARN:** How is our state connected to other parts of the world?

INTERDEPENDENCE

North Carolina has connections to many other states in our country. You read about the interdependence among states and regions in Chapter 1. Through interdependence the regions of our country make our national economy strong.

Our state cannot produce everything we need. As you know, peanuts, soybeans, and tobacco are crops that are grown in our state. North Carolina **specializes** in these crops. To specialize is to produce more of a certain crop or product than of others. Our state specializes in these crops because they grow well in our climate and soil.

However, North Carolina does not specialize in growing grapefruit or oranges. Other states specialize in these products. Our state depends on other states for scarce resources and for products it needs.

At the busy port of Wilmington, ships bring imports into North Carolina. Trucks from all over our state bring goods for export.

You have read in Chapter 6 about products that are manufactured in North Carolina. In which products do you think our state specializes? If you named textiles or furniture, you chose two of our state's most important manufactured products.

Although North Carolina grows cotton, it cannot grow enough for its many textile mills. Therefore, these mills must buy cotton grown in California. Cotton farmers in California depend on the textile mills in North Carolina to buy their cotton crop. This makes California and North Carolina interdependent.

EXPORTS

North Carolina is also interdependent with other countries. Important crops such as soybeans, peanuts, and tobacco are exported all over the world. Other products that North Carolina specializes in, such as lumber and paper, are mostly exported to countries in Europe and South America.

North Carolina's two most important trading partners are Canada and Japan. In 1990 North Carolina sold over $1 billion in goods to these two countries. Other important trading partners of North Carolina include Great Britain, Germany, the Netherlands, Saudi Arabia, and Hong Kong.

IMPORTS

Many products that cannot be produced in North Carolina come from other countries. For example, salt is not found in North Carolina. The salt we use is imported from Mexico, where it is a plentiful natural resource.

Much of the food that Tar Heels eat comes from other countries. Salt is imported from Mexico, and bananas come from Central America.

Are you wearing anything today that is imported from another country? If you visit the port in Wilmington, you might see ships from other countries unloading boxes of goods for sale in North Carolina.

FOREIGN-OWNED BUSINESSES

Some foreign companies do not transport their goods to North Carolina. Instead they build their factories here. More than 600 businesses in our state are owned by people from other countries.

Our state's leaders work to bring foreign-owned companies to North Carolina. Each new company creates more jobs for Tar Heel workers. One out of every eight people in the state works for a foreign-owned company.

Here are a few examples of the foreign-owned companies in our state. In Charlotte there is a Swiss chocolate factory. A Japanese zipper factory is in Greensboro. Do you know of any others?

SHARING CULTURES

Another way that North Carolina is linked to the world is through the exchange of students. Many students from other countries attend our state's universities. Then they return to work in their own countries. While these students are living here, they share their culture with Tar Heels. For example, each year at North Carolina State University, students from India present an evening of their country's traditional music and dance.

In 1991 Paul McRae, the director of the Greensboro Symphony, toured China as the guest conductor of a Chinese orchestra. In return, a group of Chinese musicians visited North Carolina. Xiao-Lu Li (shou′ lü′ lē′), a Chinese-American musician who traveled with McRae to China, explained why trips like these are important.

> *I believe that it is through cultural exchange . . . that we will achieve an understanding.*

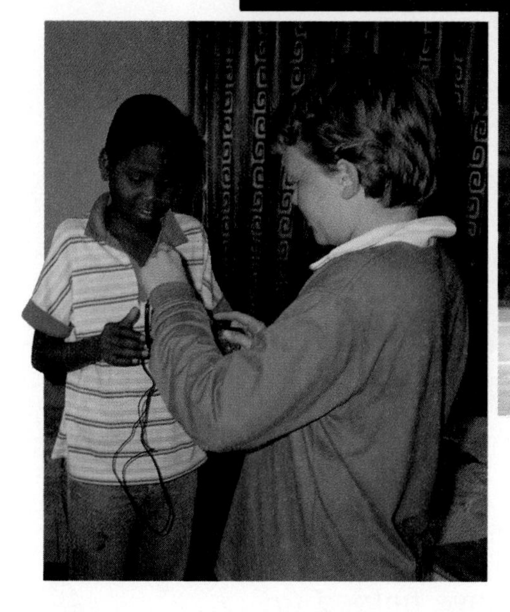

Student dancers from India and Tar Heels in Kenya, Africa, are part of cultural-exchange programs.

Tar Heels share cultures in yet other ways. Visitors to the Folkmoot dance festival near Waynesville can see dancers from all over the world. Every summer a group of our state's teachers tour Japan. Upon return, the teachers share their experiences with their students.

PEOPLE-TO-PEOPLE

In Asheville the Fisher family is packing suitcases for a trip to the city of Espoo (es′ pō), Finland. They are taking part in the Citizens for Understanding program.

Since 1979 thousands of North Carolinians have visited families in other countries through exchange programs. Families from Wilmington have visited Belgium and Finland. People in Charlotte have gone to Brazil, New Zealand, and Korea. In return, thousands of guests from these countries have visited families in North Carolina.

REACHING OUT

North Carolinians have many different connections with people all over the world. Tar Heels exchange products with other countries. Our state also welcomes foreign companies to build businesses here. Through student and cultural exchange programs, Tar Heels reach out to the world's people.

Check Your Reading

1. How is North Carolina connected to other parts of the world?
2. Why are imports important to the people of our state?
3. What is one advantage of having foreign-owned companies in North Carolina?
4. THINKING SKILL: Reread the quote on page 340. Does the quote state a fact or an opinion?

NORTH CAROLINA TRADITIONS

IN THE YEAR 2050

by Eric Kimmel

Our state has gone through many changes as it has made use of new technology. Developments in communications and transportation have helped to link North Carolinians to people in other parts of the world. What will the technology of the future bring? North Carolina has many traditions that help us to remember the past, but it also has a tradition of planning for the future.

This story takes us on an imaginary trip into the future, when North Carolina will have changed even more. As you read, think about how what you have learned from the past helps you to plan for the future.

THE INTERVIEW

"Grandpa, I need your help."

"Sure, Ann. What is it?" Mr. Driscoll switched off the video screen on which he was watching telecasts of his local newspaper.

Ann held up her parents' video camera. "I have to record a report about the changes that have taken place in North Carolina since the old days. We're supposed to talk to someone who remembers. Do you think you're old enough?"

Mr. Driscoll laughed. "I think I'm as old as I need to be. Pull up a chair, Ann. Let's begin."

LIFE IN THE 1990s

"When I was your age, back in the early 1990s, things were a lot different. Every school had some computers, but it wasn't like today. Now you have all your lessons cabled to your own classroom computers directly from the Office of Education. And if my parents wanted to know how I was doing in school, they couldn't just punch in a few numbers. They had to wait for my report card. Back then, when my teacher gave us a report, I had to go to the library. Today you just punch the right numbers on your computer and you are connected with the state library.

"Things moved a lot slower in those days, Ann. We used to spend our summer vacations pretty much in one place. We might go to the Outer Banks, or to the Blue Ridge Mountains, or to Raleigh. Even though we had good highways, it still took my dad a whole day to drive from the Outer Banks to the Blue Ridge Mountains."

A NEW INVENTION

"A whole day?" Ann found that hard to believe.

"You bet. Remember, the HyperRail system wasn't finished until 2035. Now we can spend the morning at Chapel Hill, go to a county fair in the Great Smoky Mountains, and be back home in Hatteras for dinner."

"Mom says that HyperRail was invented in North Carolina," Ann said.

"She's right," Mr. Driscoll said. "The extra-fast electricity and the new kind of cold-water power that run HyperRail were developed by scientists in Research Triangle Park. Without the work of those scientists, life in North Carolina wouldn't be much fun."

"How come, Grandpa?"

"Well, by the end of the twentieth century we were in big trouble. Our cities produced more garbage than they could get rid of. Gasoline fumes were polluting the air. Hydroelectric power was cheap and clean, but we'd run out of places to build dams.

"So we were stuck, until scientists discovered how to make energy by using cold water and copper wire. No waste to worry about. No danger to anyone. North Carolina became a leading producer of energy because we have plenty of water. In the meantime, we learned to recycle our trash. Soon cars and trucks began to run on water and stopped making the air dirty. The smog over our cities gradually disappeared. All around the world people began using the HyperRail system.

"So, Ann, I guess it comes down to this. You had better take care of your environment. People understand that a lot more now than they did when I was a kid."

LOOKING FORWARD

Ann switched off the camera. "Gee, Grandpa! When you were my age, did you ever think you would see so many changes?"

Mr. Driscoll smiled. "Ann, you will probably see more changes during your lifetime than I have seen during mine. Who knows what lies ahead? Someday North Carolinians may be living in a city on the moon. Our best is yet to come."

By talking about the past, how can older people help us to understand the present and plan for the future?

REVIEW - CHAPTER 12

REVIEWING VOCABULARY

boycott
integration
recycling
specialize
suffrage

Number a sheet of paper from 1 to 5. Beside each number write the word or term from the list above that best completes the sentence.

1. Women worked for ___, or the right to vote, for many years.
2. One way we can have less garbage is by ___.
3. The U.S. Supreme Court passed a law requiring school ___ in 1954.
4. During a ___ people stop buying or using something.
5. North Carolinian farmers ___ in growing peanuts and soybeans.

REVIEWING FACTS

1. Describe one successful result of the civil rights movement.
2. Name some of the rights that women have worked to achieve over the years.
3. What are two results of the growing population in our state?
4. Name two products in which North Carolina specializes.
5. How does having foreign-owned companies operate in North Carolina help our state?

WRITING ABOUT MAIN IDEAS

1. **Writing a Newspaper Article:** Choose one of the events discussed in this chapter, such as the Supreme Court decision outlawing school segregation, or passage of the Civil Rights Act. Write a news article about the event.
2. **Writing About the Environment:** Imagine that you were on one of the barrier islands during a storm and saw an empty beach house being washed away. Write a paragraph giving your opinion of the loss of the beach house, and the Coastal Area Management Act.
3. **Writing About Perspectives:** How do you think Helen Morris Lewis would feel about the kinds of jobs women have in the United States today? Write a paragraph that discusses her possible feelings.

BUILDING SKILLS: POINT OF VIEW

1. What are some steps you can take to identify a point of view?
2. Write two sentences about the Greensboro sit-in—the first by a student and the second by the owner of a lunch counter.
3. Why is it important to try to recognize point of view?

REVIEWING VOCABULARY

boycott	legislative
budget	political party
candidate	recycling
county seat	specialize
integration	suffrage

Number a sheet of paper from 1 to 10. Beside each number write the word from the list above that best matches the definition.

1. A person who runs for government office
2. To produce a particular crop or product
3. To refuse to use or buy something
4. Making public places open to all people by law
5. A group of people who share many similar views on political issues
6. Having to do with making laws
7. The government center of a county
8. A plan for how to use taxes to provide services
9. Collecting trash that can be reused or turned into a new product
10. The right to vote

WRITING ABOUT THE UNIT

1. **Writing a Story:** You have read about the local, state, and national governments under which you live. Imagine what your life would be like if there were no government. Write a story about it.
2. **Writing About Perspectives:** You have read about the many foreign companies that have built factories in our state, such as the Japanese-owned zipper factory in Greensboro. Write a paragraph about how an American-owned zipper factory owner might feel about foreign companies doing business in the state.

ACTIVITIES

1. **Surveying Your Trash:** Keep track of the kinds and amounts of trash that your family throws away during one week. Then work out a plan for reducing the amount of trash. Your plan might include different kinds of actions such as buying products with less packaging and the recycling of items.
2. **Working Together to Research Government Leaders:** With a group of classmates, make a chart of the people who represent you in government. List the positions that exist in your local, county, state, and national governments. Then find out who now holds those positions and put these people's names on the chart.

(continued on next page)

REVIEW ▪ UNIT 4

BUILDING SKILLS: RECOGNIZING POINT OF VIEW

Samuel and Rebecca were talking about the mayor of their town, Jane Bickett. Read what they had to say and then answer the questions that follow.

Samuel: Our mayor really cares about our town. She has worked hard to keep the buses running this winter. I will vote for her again.

Rebecca: Bickett has made some bad mistakes in running the town. She has let our parks get run down. I will not vote for her again.

1. What is the subject of Rebecca's and Samuel's conversation?
2. What information does each speaker give about his or her views?
3. Identify some expressions of opinion stated by each speaker.
4. What is Samuel's point of view? What is Rebecca's point of view?

LINKING PAST, PRESENT, AND FUTURE

You have read about the struggles for equal rights by African Americans, by women, and by Native Americans. Which rights have Americans gained since North Carolina became a state? List some of the things that still need to be done to gain equal rights for all.

REFERENCE SECTION

ATLAS

THE WORLD
Political

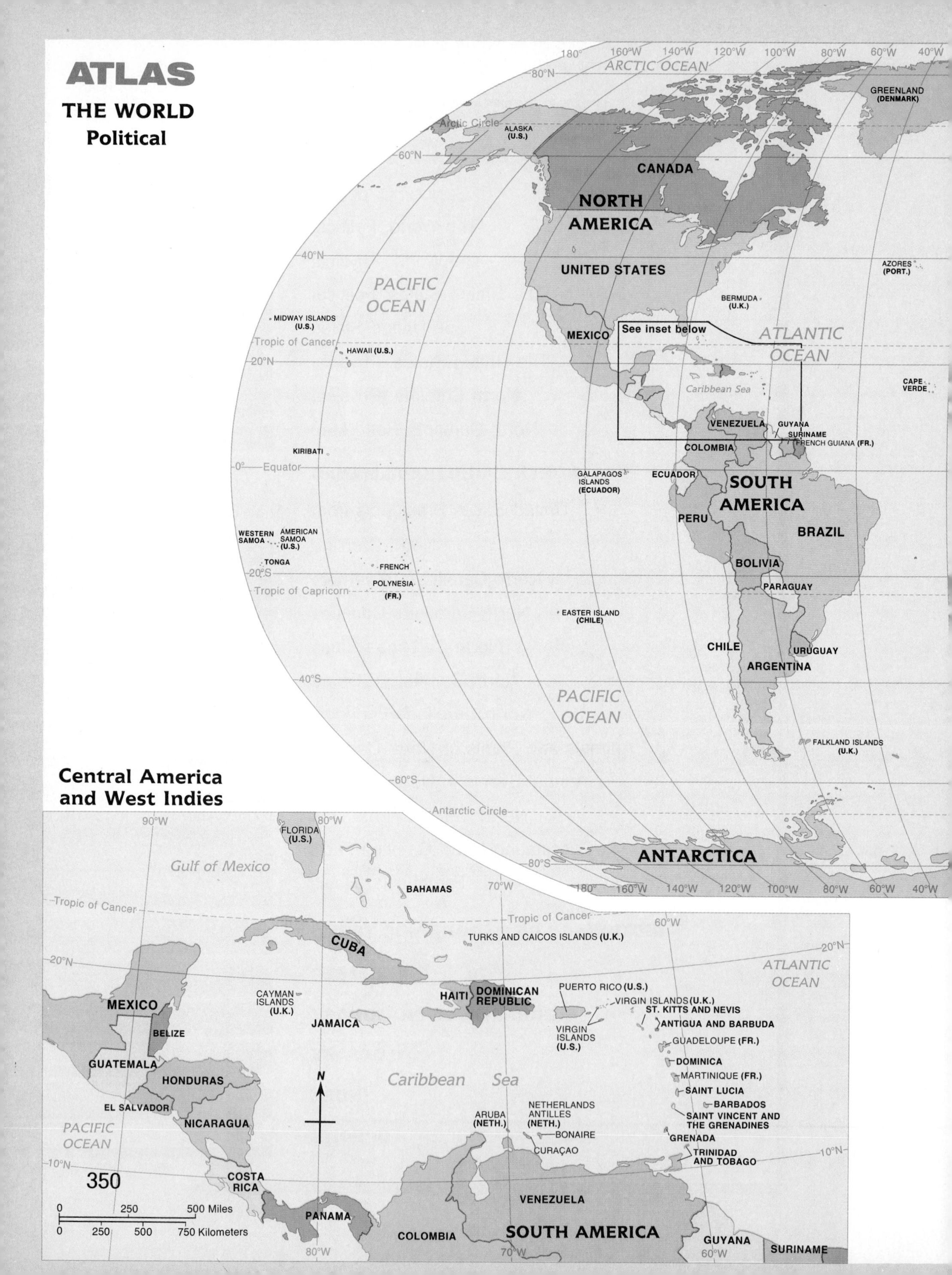

Central America and West Indies

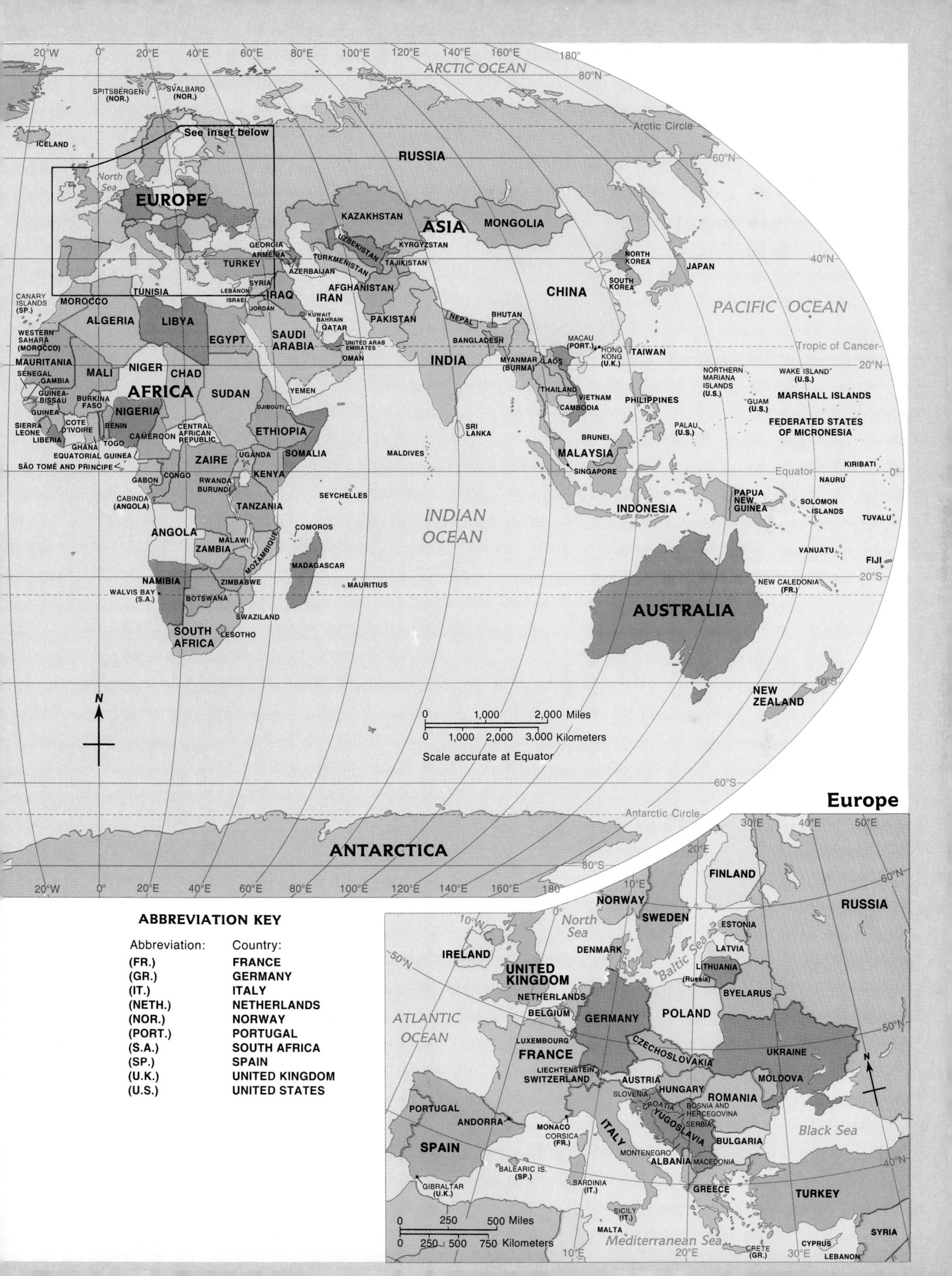
ARCTIC OCEAN
Arctic Circle
See inset below
SPITSBERGEN (NOR.)
SVALBARD (NOR.)
ICELAND
North Sea
EUROPE
RUSSIA
KAZAKHSTAN
ASIA
MONGOLIA
UZBEKISTAN
KYRGYZSTAN
GEORGIA
ARMENIA
AZERBAIJAN
TURKMENISTAN
TAJIKISTAN
TURKEY
SYRIA
LEBANON
ISRAEL
JORDAN
IRAQ
IRAN
AFGHANISTAN
PAKISTAN
NEPAL
BHUTAN
BANGLADESH
INDIA
CHINA
NORTH KOREA
SOUTH KOREA
JAPAN
PACIFIC OCEAN
Tropic of Cancer
MACAU (PORT.)
HONG KONG (U.K.)
TAIWAN
KUWAIT
BAHRAIN
QATAR
UNITED ARAB EMIRATES
OMAN
SAUDI ARABIA
YEMEN
MYANMAR (BURMA)
LAOS
THAILAND
VIETNAM
CAMBODIA
PHILIPPINES
SRI LANKA
MALDIVES
BRUNEI
MALAYSIA
SINGAPORE
INDONESIA
PAPUA NEW GUINEA
NORTHERN MARIANA ISLANDS (U.S.)
GUAM (U.S.)
WAKE ISLAND (U.S.)
MARSHALL ISLANDS
PALAU (U.S.)
FEDERATED STATES OF MICRONESIA
KIRIBATI
NAURU
Equator
SOLOMON ISLANDS
TUVALU
VANUATU
FIJI
NEW CALEDONIA (FR.)
AUSTRALIA
NEW ZEALAND
INDIAN OCEAN
SEYCHELLES
COMOROS
MADAGASCAR
MAURITIUS
CANARY ISLANDS (SP.)
MOROCCO
TUNISIA
ALGERIA
LIBYA
EGYPT
WESTERN SAHARA (MOROCCO)
MAURITANIA
SENEGAL
GAMBIA
GUINEA-BISSAU
GUINEA
SIERRA LEONE
LIBERIA
COTE D'IVOIRE
GHANA
TOGO
BENIN
BURKINA FASO
MALI
NIGER
CHAD
SUDAN
AFRICA
NIGERIA
CAMEROON
CENTRAL AFRICAN REPUBLIC
DJIBOUTI
ETHIOPIA
SOMALIA
EQUATORIAL GUINEA
SÃO TOMÉ AND PRINCIPE
GABON
CONGO
ZAIRE
UGANDA
KENYA
RWANDA
BURUNDI
TANZANIA
CABINDA (ANGOLA)
ANGOLA
ZAMBIA
MALAWI
MOZAMBIQUE
ZIMBABWE
NAMIBIA
WALVIS BAY (S.A.)
BOTSWANA
SWAZILAND
LESOTHO
SOUTH AFRICA
ANTARCTICA
Antarctic Circle
N
0 1,000 2,000 Miles
0 1,000 2,000 3,000 Kilometers
Scale accurate at Equator
20°W 0° 20°E 40°E 60°E 80°E 100°E 120°E 140°E 160°E 180°
80°N 60°N 40°N 20°N 0° 20°S 40°S 60°S 80°S
ABBREVIATION KEY
Abbreviation: Country:
(FR.) FRANCE
(GR.) GERMANY
(IT.) ITALY
(NETH.) NETHERLANDS
(NOR.) NORWAY
(PORT.) PORTUGAL
(S.A.) SOUTH AFRICA
(SP.) SPAIN
(U.K.) UNITED KINGDOM
(U.S.) UNITED STATES
Europe
FINLAND
NORWAY
SWEDEN
RUSSIA
ESTONIA
LATVIA
LITHUANIA
(Russia)
Baltic Sea
North Sea
DENMARK
IRELAND
UNITED KINGDOM
NETHERLANDS
BELGIUM
GERMANY
POLAND
BYELARUS
ATLANTIC OCEAN
LUXEMBOURG
FRANCE
CZECHOSLOVAKIA
UKRAINE
LIECHTENSTEIN
SWITZERLAND
AUSTRIA
HUNGARY
MOLDOVA
SLOVENIA
CROATIA
BOSNIA AND HERCEGOVINA
SERBIA
ROMANIA
YUGOSLAVIA
PORTUGAL
ANDORRA
MONACO
CORSICA (FR.)
ITALY
Black Sea
BULGARIA
SPAIN
MONTENEGRO
ALBANIA
MACEDONIA
BALEARIC IS. (SP.)
SARDINIA (IT.)
GIBRALTAR (U.K.)
GREECE
TURKEY
SICILY (IT.)
MALTA
Mediterranean Sea
CRETE (GR.)
CYPRUS
SYRIA
LEBANON
0 250 500 Miles
0 250 500 750 Kilometers
10°W 0° 10°E 20°E 30°E 40°E 50°E
60°N 50°N 40°N

THE WORLD
Physical

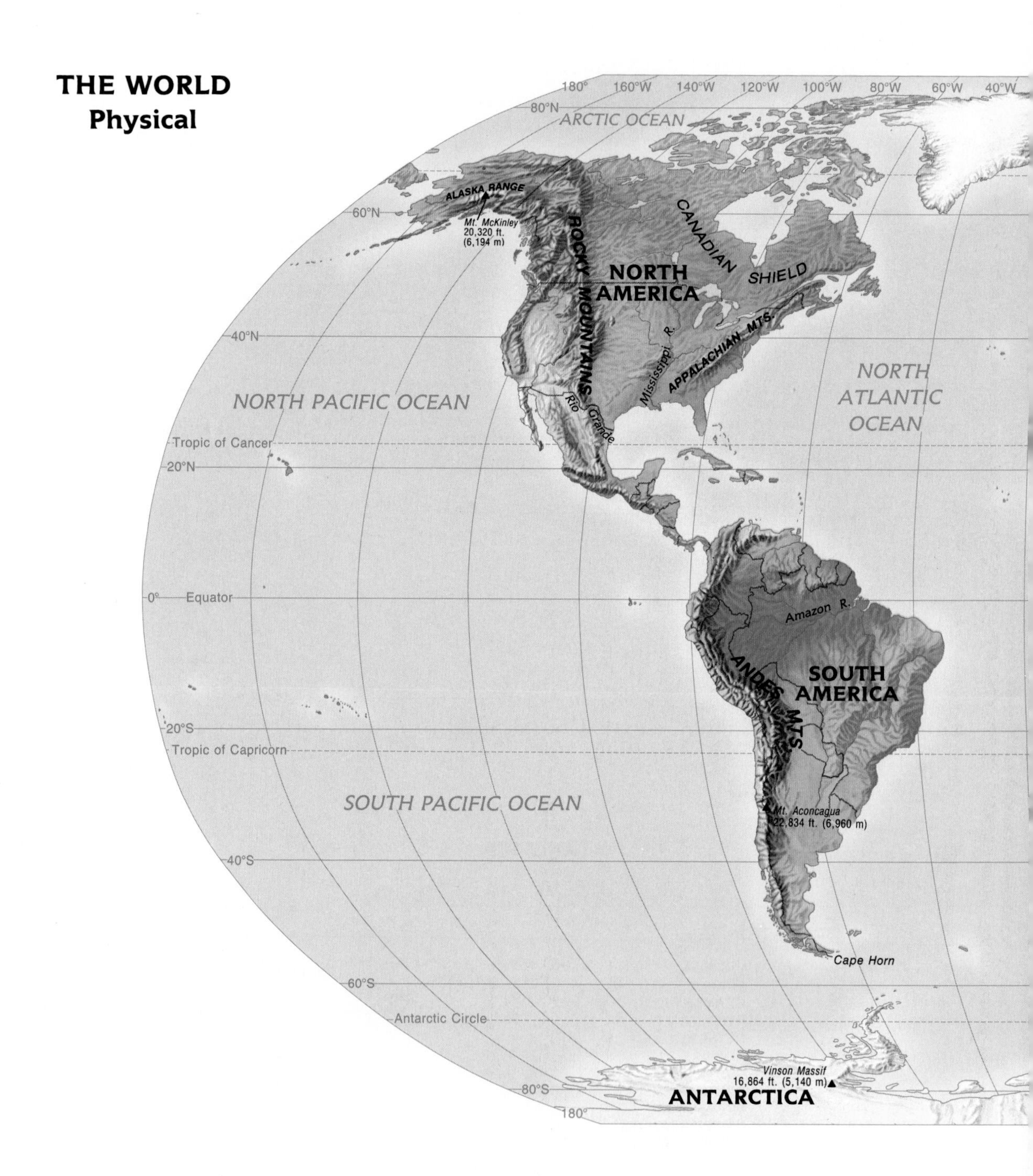

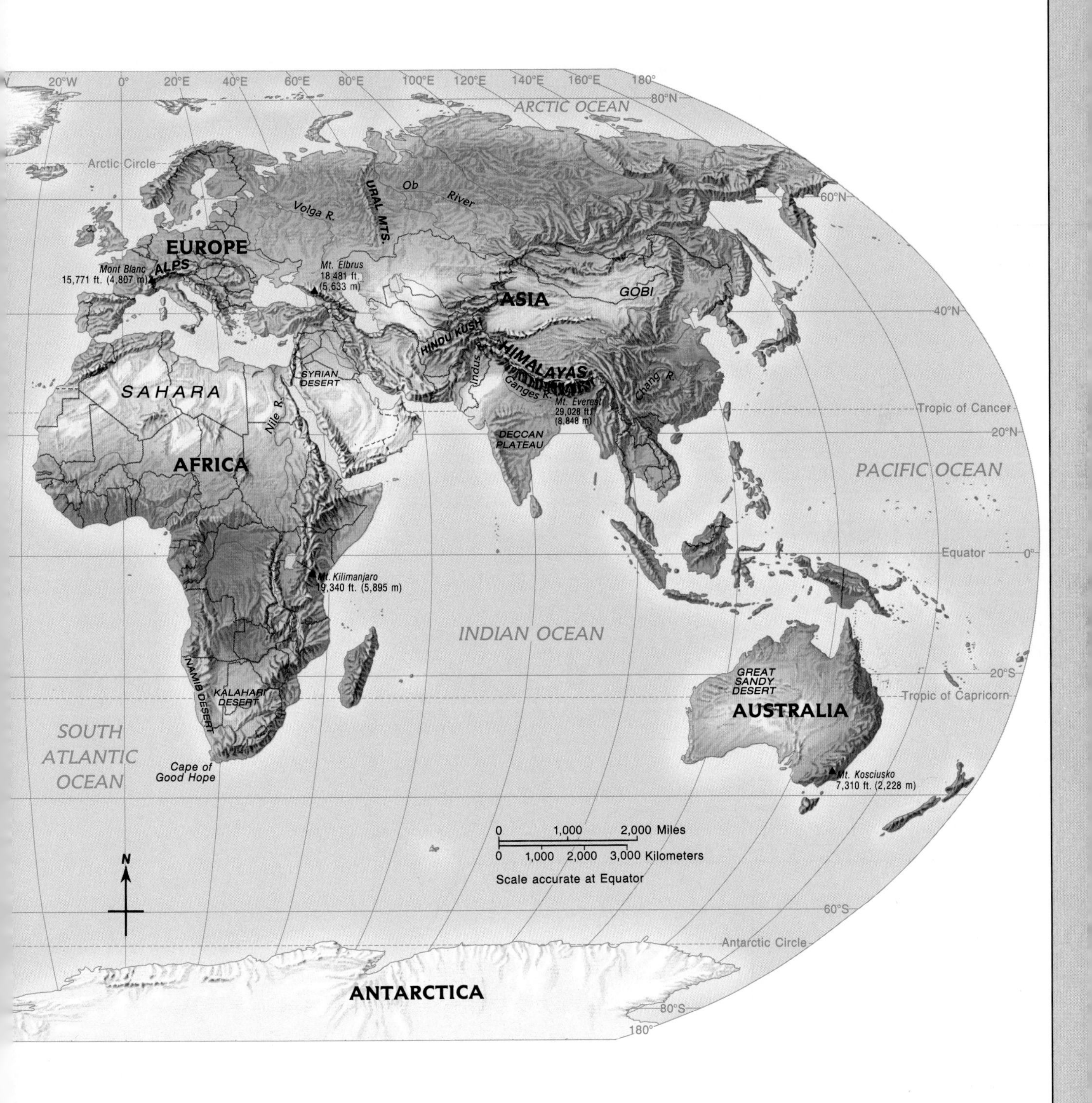

20°W
0°
20°E
40°E
60°E
80°E
100°E
120°E
140°E
160°E
180°
ARCTIC OCEAN
80°N
Arctic Circle
URAL MTS.
Ob
River
Volga R.
60°N
EUROPE
Mont Blanc
15,771 ft. (4,807 m)
ALPS
Mt. Elbrus
18,481 ft.
(5,633 m)
ASIA
GOBI
40°N
HINDU KUSH
HIMALAYAS
Indus R.
Ganges R.
Chang R.
SYRIAN DESERT
SAHARA
Nile R.
Mt. Everest
29,028 ft.
(8,848 m)
Tropic of Cancer
20°N
DECCAN PLATEAU
AFRICA
PACIFIC OCEAN
Equator
0°
Mt. Kilimanjaro
19,340 ft. (5,895 m)
INDIAN OCEAN
GREAT SANDY DESERT
20°S
NAMIB DESERT
KALAHARI DESERT
Tropic of Capricorn
AUSTRALIA
SOUTH ATLANTIC OCEAN
Cape of Good Hope
Mt. Kosciusko
7,310 ft. (2,228 m)
0 1,000 2,000 Miles
0 1,000 2,000 3,000 Kilometers
Scale accurate at Equator
N
60°S
Antarctic Circle
ANTARCTICA
80°S
180°

CANADA
PACIFIC OCEAN
WASHINGTON
Seattle
Olympia
Spokane
Portland
Columbia
River
Salem
Eugene
OREGON
IDAHO
Boise
Snake River
Pocatello
MONTANA
Great Falls
Helena
Billings
NORTH DAKOTA
Grand Forks
Fargo
Bismarck
SOUTH DAKOTA
Pierre
Sioux Falls
WYOMING
Casper
Cheyenne
NEBRASKA
Platte River
Lincoln
NEVADA
Reno
Carson City
Las Vegas
UTAH
Great Salt Lake
Ogden
Salt Lake City
Provo
COLORADO
Denver
Colorado Springs
Pueblo
KANSAS
Arkansas R.
CALIFORNIA
San Francisco
Oakland
San Jose
Sacramento
Los Angeles
Long Beach
San Diego
Colorado River
ARIZONA
Phoenix
Tucson
NEW MEXICO
Santa Fe
Albuquerque
El Paso
OKLAHOMA
Oklahoma City
TEXAS
Dallas
Austin
San Antonio
Rio Grande
MEXICO
50°N
40°N
30°N
120°W
110°W
100°W
HAWAII
Kauai
Oahu
Honolulu
Molokai
Maui
Hilo
Hawaii
PACIFIC OCEAN
20°N
160°W
0 100 Miles
0 100 Kilometers
ARCTIC OCEAN
RUSSIA
170°W
150°W
70°N
ALASKA
Arctic Circle
Nome
Yukon River
Fairbanks
Anchorage
CANADA
60°N
Juneau
Gulf of Alaska
PACIFIC OCEAN
50°N
170°E
170°W
150°W
130°W
100°W
0 250 500 Miles
0 250 500 750 Kilometers

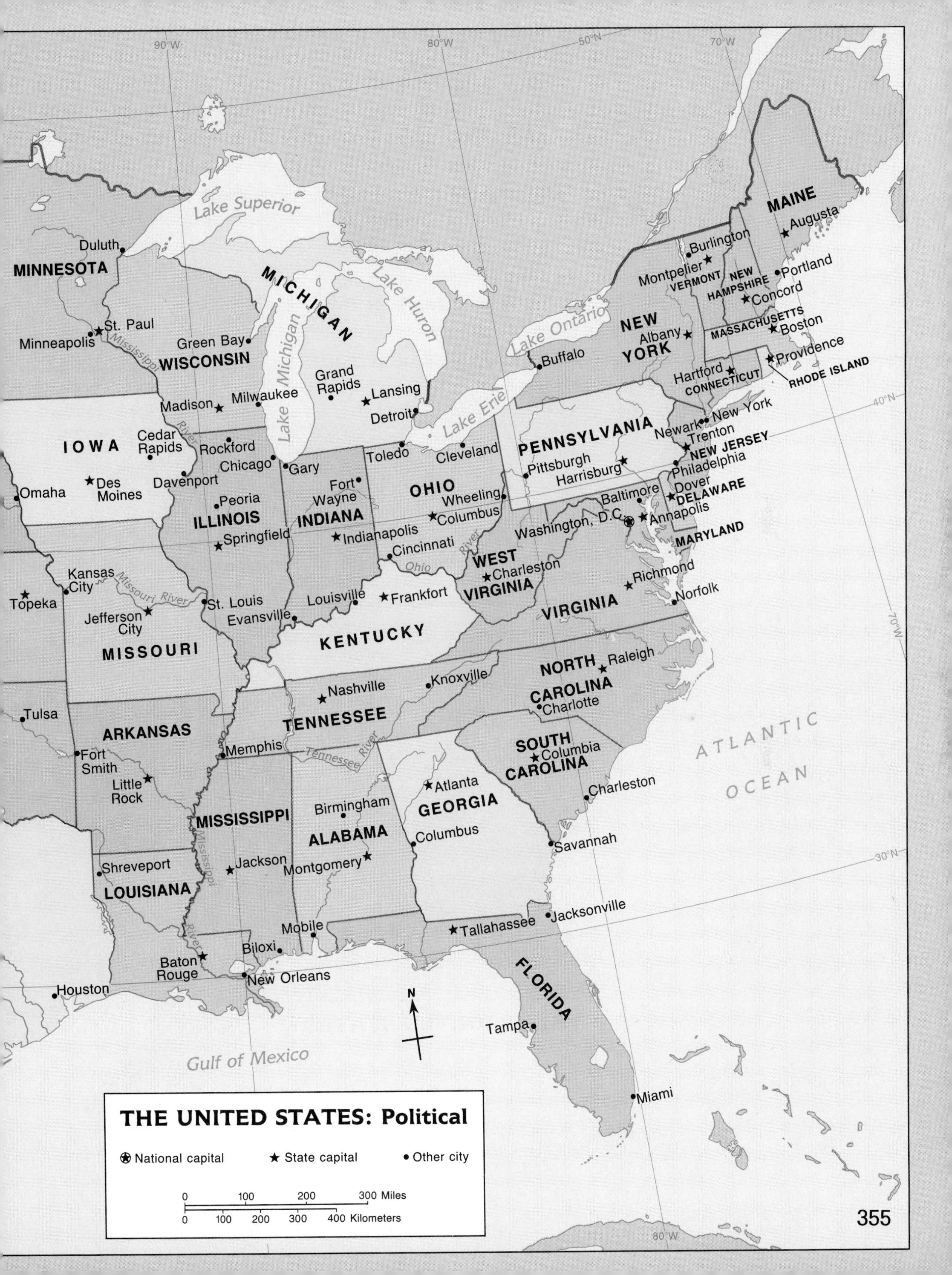
THE UNITED STATES: Political
National capital
State capital
Other city
0
100
200
300 Miles
0
100
200
300
400 Kilometers
90°W
80°W
70°W
50°N
40°N
30°N
Lake Superior
Lake Michigan
Lake Huron
Lake Ontario
Lake Erie
Gulf of Mexico
ATLANTIC
OCEAN
N
MINNESOTA
WISCONSIN
MICHIGAN
IOWA
ILLINOIS
INDIANA
OHIO
PENNSYLVANIA
NEW YORK
VERMONT
NEW HAMPSHIRE
MAINE
MASSACHUSETTS
CONNECTICUT
RHODE ISLAND
NEW JERSEY
DELAWARE
MARYLAND
WEST VIRGINIA
VIRGINIA
KENTUCKY
MISSOURI
TENNESSEE
NORTH CAROLINA
SOUTH CAROLINA
GEORGIA
ALABAMA
MISSISSIPPI
ARKANSAS
LOUISIANA
FLORIDA
Duluth
St. Paul
Minneapolis
Mississippi
Green Bay
Madison
Milwaukee
River
Grand Rapids
Lansing
Detroit
Cedar Rapids
Rockford
Chicago
Gary
Davenport
Des Moines
Omaha
Peoria
Springfield
Fort Wayne
Indianapolis
Toledo
Cleveland
Wheeling
Columbus
Cincinnati
Ohio
River
Buffalo
Pittsburgh
Harrisburg
Philadelphia
Albany
Burlington
Montpelier
Augusta
Portland
Concord
Boston
Providence
Hartford
Newark
New York
Trenton
Dover
Baltimore
Washington, D.C.
Annapolis
Charleston
Richmond
Norfolk
Kansas City
Topeka
Missouri River
Jefferson City
St. Louis
Evansville
Louisville
Frankfort
Knoxville
Nashville
Raleigh
Charlotte
Tulsa
Fort Smith
Little Rock
Memphis
Tennessee
River
Columbia
Atlanta
Charleston
Birmingham
Columbus
Savannah
Montgomery
Jackson
Shreveport
Mississippi
River
Mobile
Biloxi
Tallahassee
Jacksonville
Baton Rouge
New Orleans
Houston
Tampa
Miami

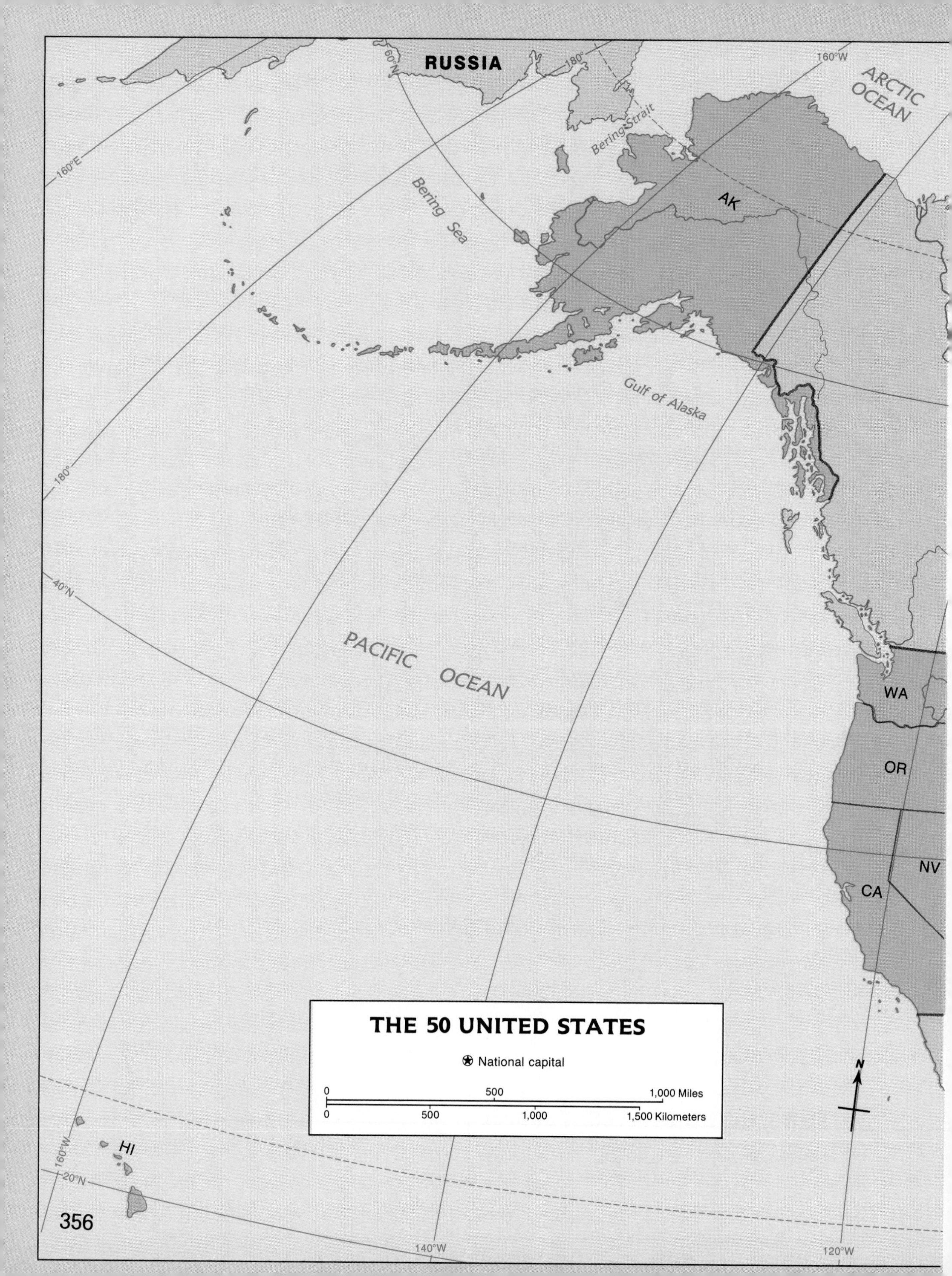
RUSSIA
ARCTIC OCEAN
Bering Strait
Bering Sea
AK
Gulf of Alaska
PACIFIC OCEAN
WA
OR
NV
CA
HI
60°N
180°
160°W
160°E
40°N
20°N
140°W
120°W
THE 50 UNITED STATES
National capital
0
500
1,000 Miles
0
500
1,000
1,500 Kilometers
N

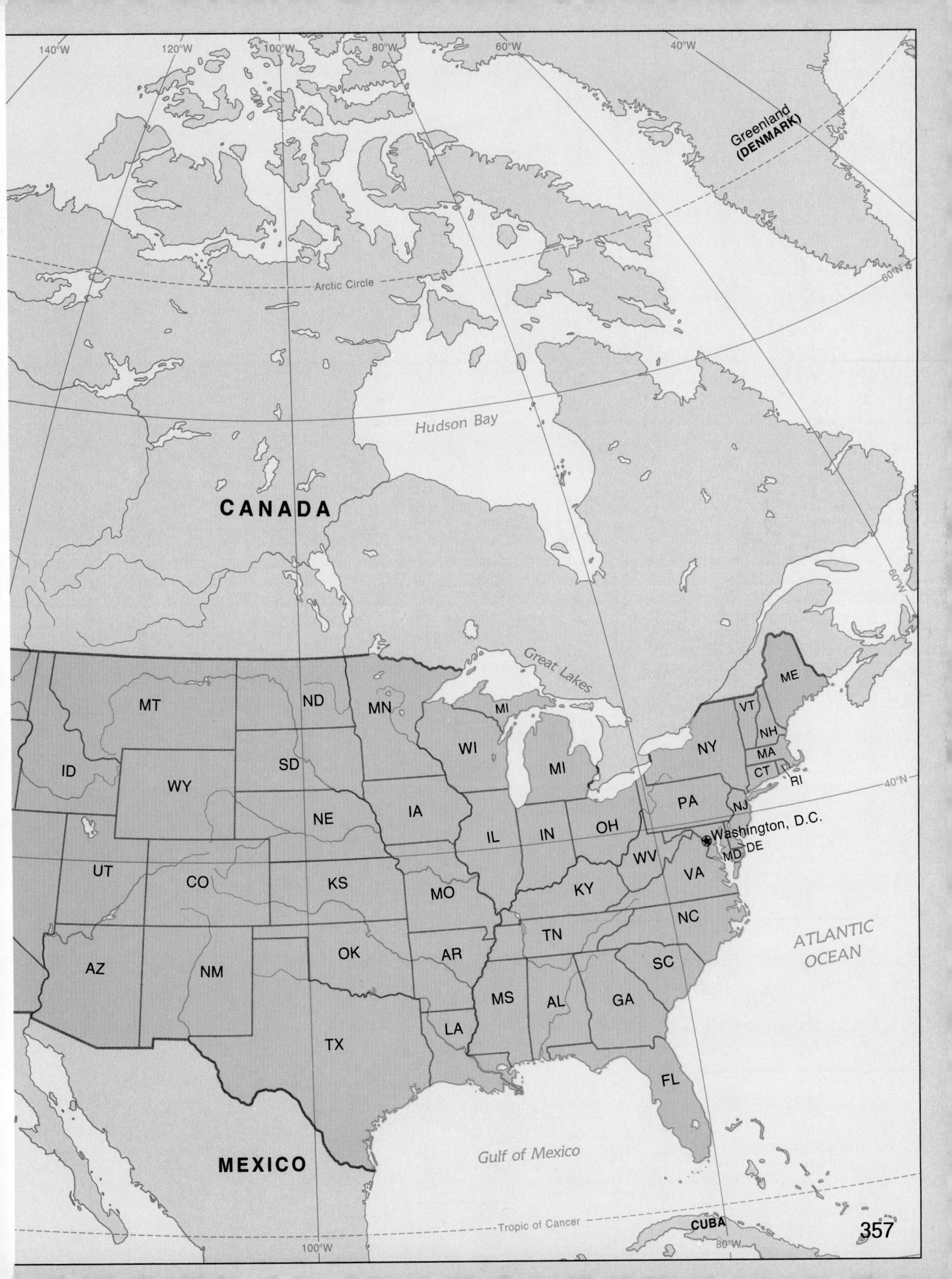
140°W
120°W
100°W
80°W
60°W
40°W
Greenland
(DENMARK)
Arctic Circle
60°N
Hudson Bay
CANADA
60°W
Great Lakes
MT
ND
MN
MI
ME
VT
NH
MA
CT
RI
NY
WI
MI
ID
SD
WY
40°N
PA
NJ
IA
NE
IL
IN
OH
Washington, D.C.
MD
DE
WV
UT
CO
KS
MO
KY
VA
NC
TN
ATLANTIC
OCEAN
AZ
NM
OK
AR
SC
MS
AL
GA
LA
TX
FL
Gulf of Mexico
MEXICO
Tropic of Cancer
CUBA
100°W
80°W

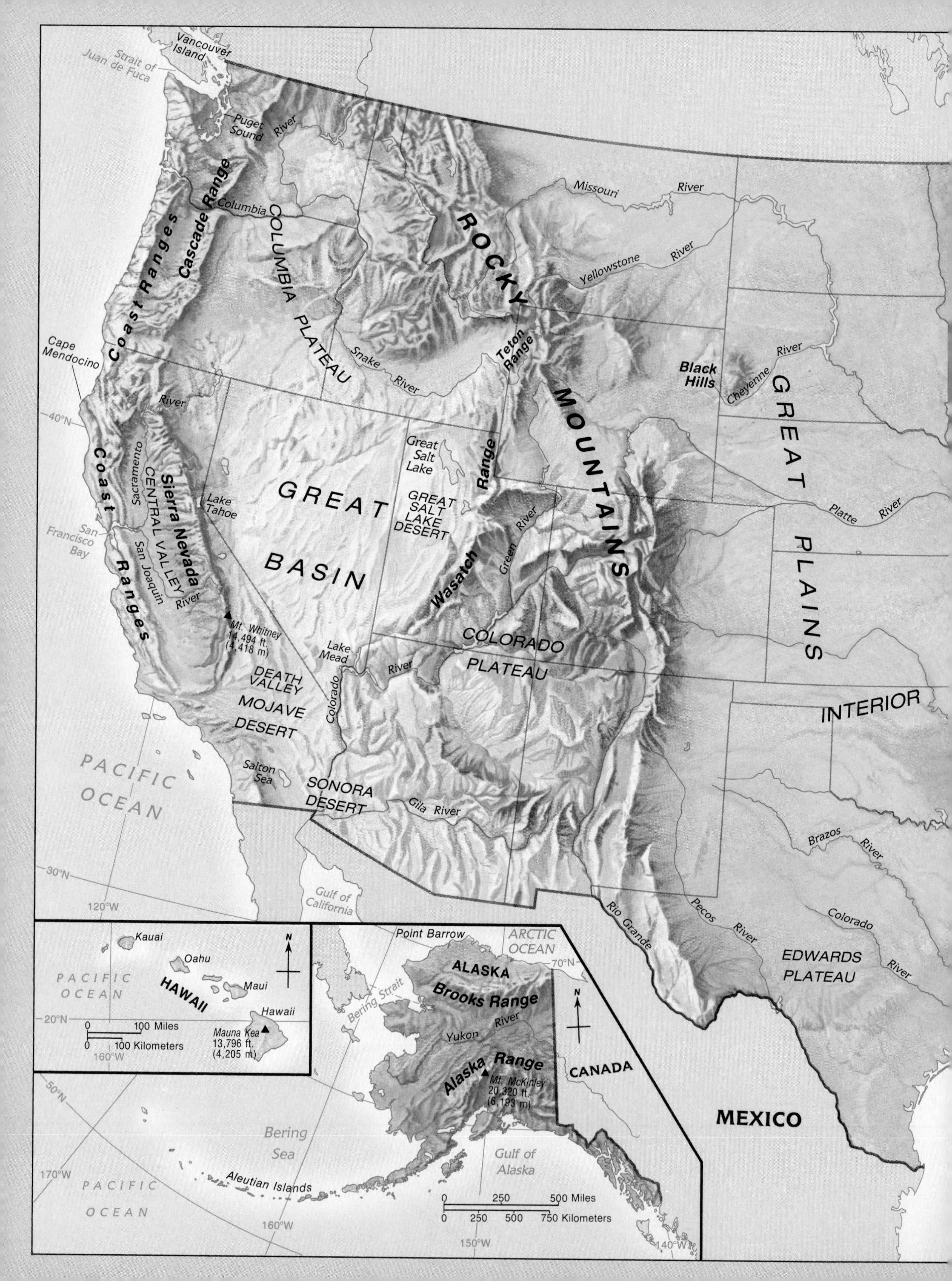

Vancouver Island
Strait of Juan de Fuca
Puget Sound
River
Cascade Range
Coast Ranges
Columbia
COLUMBIA PLATEAU
ROCKY MOUNTAINS
Missouri River
Yellowstone River
Snake River
Teton Range
Black Hills
Cheyenne River
GREAT PLAINS
Cape Mendocino
River
40°N
Sacramento
CENTRAL VALLEY
Sierra Nevada
Coast Ranges
Lake Tahoe
San Francisco Bay
San Joaquin River
Great Salt Lake
GREAT SALT LAKE DESERT
Range
GREAT BASIN
Wasatch
Green River
Platte River
Mt. Whitney 14,494 ft. (4,418 m)
Lake Mead
River
COLORADO PLATEAU
DEATH VALLEY
MOJAVE DESERT
Colorado
INTERIOR
PACIFIC OCEAN
Salton Sea
SONORA DESERT
Gila River
Brazos River
30°N
Gulf of California
120°W
Rio Grande
Pecos River
Colorado River
EDWARDS PLATEAU
Kauai
Oahu
PACIFIC OCEAN
HAWAII
Maui
Hawaii
20°N
0 100 Miles
0 100 Kilometers
Mauna Kea 13,796 ft. (4,205 m)
160°W
N
Point Barrow
ARCTIC OCEAN
70°N
ALASKA
Brooks Range
Bering Strait
Yukon River
Alaska Range
Mt. McKinley 20,320 ft. (6,193 m)
CANADA
MEXICO
50°N
Bering Sea
Gulf of Alaska
170°W
PACIFIC OCEAN
Aleutian Islands
160°W
0 250 500 Miles
0 250 500 750 Kilometers
150°W
140°W

THE UNITED STATES
Physical
CANADA
Lake of the Woods
Mesabi Range
Lake Superior
GREAT LAKES
St. Lawrence River
White Mts.
Bay of Fundy
Lake Huron
Lake Michigan
Lake Ontario
Adirondack Mts.
Green Mts.
Hudson River
Cape Cod
Mississippi River
CENTRAL PLAINS
Lake Erie
Long Island
ALLEGHENY PLATEAU
Susquehanna River
Delaware R.
APPALACHIAN MOUNTAINS
Potomac R.
Delaware Bay
Wabash River
Allegheny Mountains
Missouri River
Ohio River
Chesapeake Bay
PIEDMONT
ATLANTIC COASTAL PLAIN
Cape Hatteras
PLAINS
OZARK PLATEAU
Arkansas River
Ouachita Mountains
Kentucky Lake
Tennessee River
ATLANTIC OCEAN
Savannah River
Alabama River
Chattahoochee River
Red River
GULF COASTAL PLAIN
Mobile Bay
Mississippi Delta
Galveston Bay
Gulf of Mexico
Lake Okeechobee
Florida Keys
Straits of Florida
WEST INDIES
40°N
30°N
70°W
80°W
90°W
N
0 100 200 300 Miles
0 100 200 300 400 Kilometers

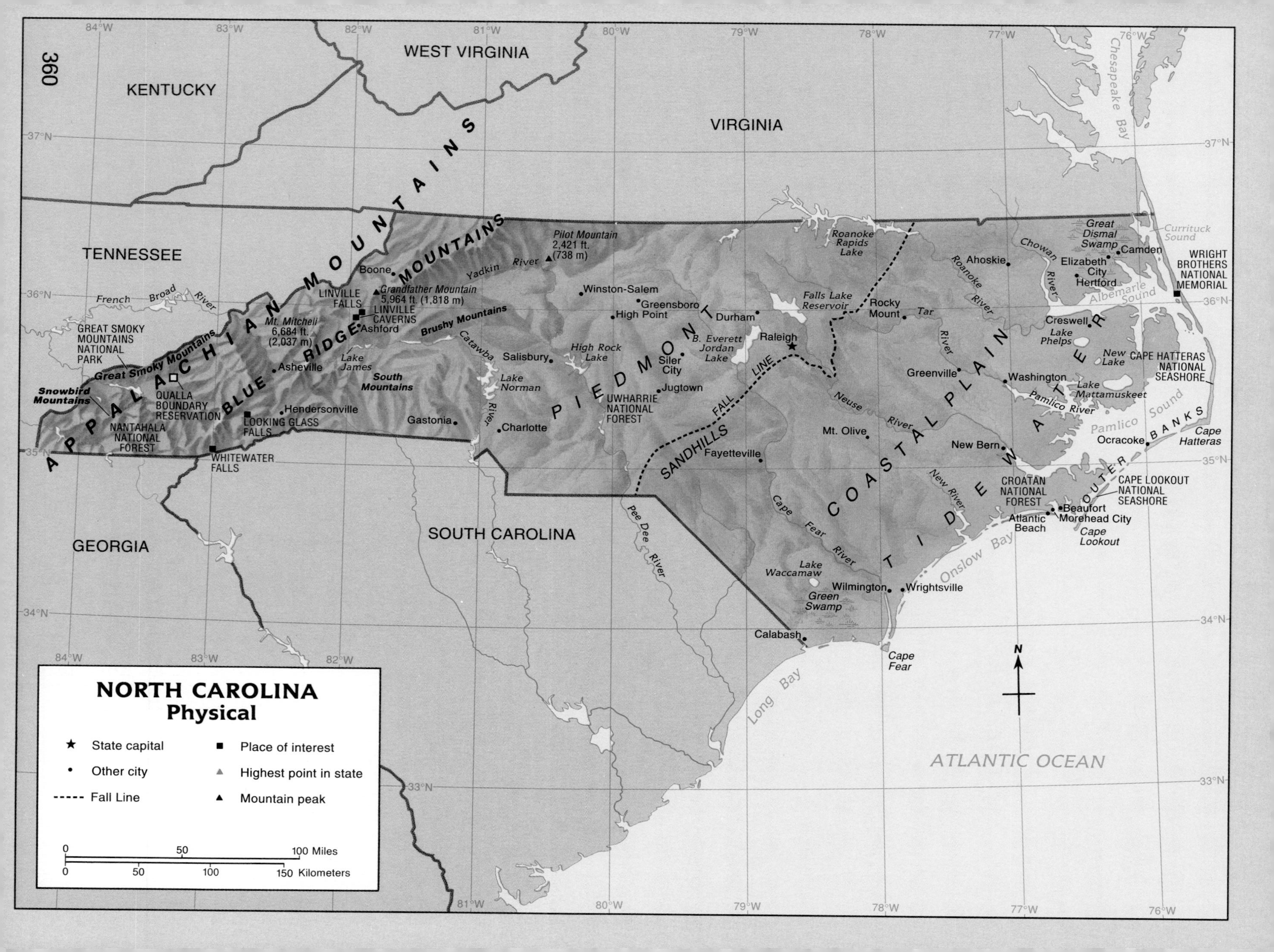
NORTH CAROLINA
Physical
State capital
Other city
Fall Line
Place of interest
Highest point in state
Mountain peak
0
50
100 Miles
0
50
100
150 Kilometers
KENTUCKY
WEST VIRGINIA
VIRGINIA
TENNESSEE
GEORGIA
SOUTH CAROLINA
ATLANTIC OCEAN
APPALACHIAN MOUNTAINS
BLUE RIDGE
MOUNTAINS
PIEDMONT
COASTAL PLAIN
TIDEWATER
OUTER BANKS
SANDHILLS
FALL LINE
Great Smoky Mountains
Snowbird Mountains
Brushy Mountains
South Mountains
GREAT SMOKY MOUNTAINS NATIONAL PARK
QUALLA BOUNDARY RESERVATION
NANTAHALA NATIONAL FOREST
WHITEWATER FALLS
LOOKING GLASS FALLS
Hendersonville
Asheville
Mt. Mitchell 6,684 ft. (2,037 m)
Lake James
Ashford
LINVILLE CAVERNS
LINVILLE FALLS
Grandfather Mountain 5,964 ft. (1,818 m)
Boone
French Broad River
Yadkin River
Pilot Mountain 2,421 ft. (738 m)
Catawba River
Gastonia
Charlotte
Lake Norman
Salisbury
High Rock Lake
UWHARRIE NATIONAL FOREST
Winston-Salem
Greensboro
High Point
Jugtown
Siler City
B. Everett Jordan Lake
Durham
Raleigh
Falls Lake Reservoir
Roanoke Rapids Lake
Rocky Mount
Tar River
Roanoke River
Ahoskie
Chowan River
Great Dismal Swamp
Elizabeth City
Hertford
Camden
Currituck Sound
Chesapeake Bay
Albemarle Sound
WRIGHT BROTHERS NATIONAL MEMORIAL
Creswell
Lake Phelps
New Lake
CAPE HATTERAS NATIONAL SEASHORE
Lake Mattamuskeet
Washington
Pamlico River
Greenville
Pamlico Sound
Ocracoke
Cape Hatteras
Neuse River
Mt. Olive
New Bern
New River
Fayetteville
Pee Dee River
Cape Fear River
CROATAN NATIONAL FOREST
Beaufort
Morehead City
Atlantic Beach
CAPE LOOKOUT NATIONAL SEASHORE
Cape Lookout
Onslow Bay
Lake Waccamaw
Green Swamp
Wilmington
Wrightsville
Calabash
Cape Fear
Long Bay
N
84°W
83°W
82°W
81°W
80°W
79°W
78°W
77°W
76°W
37°N
36°N
35°N
34°N
33°N

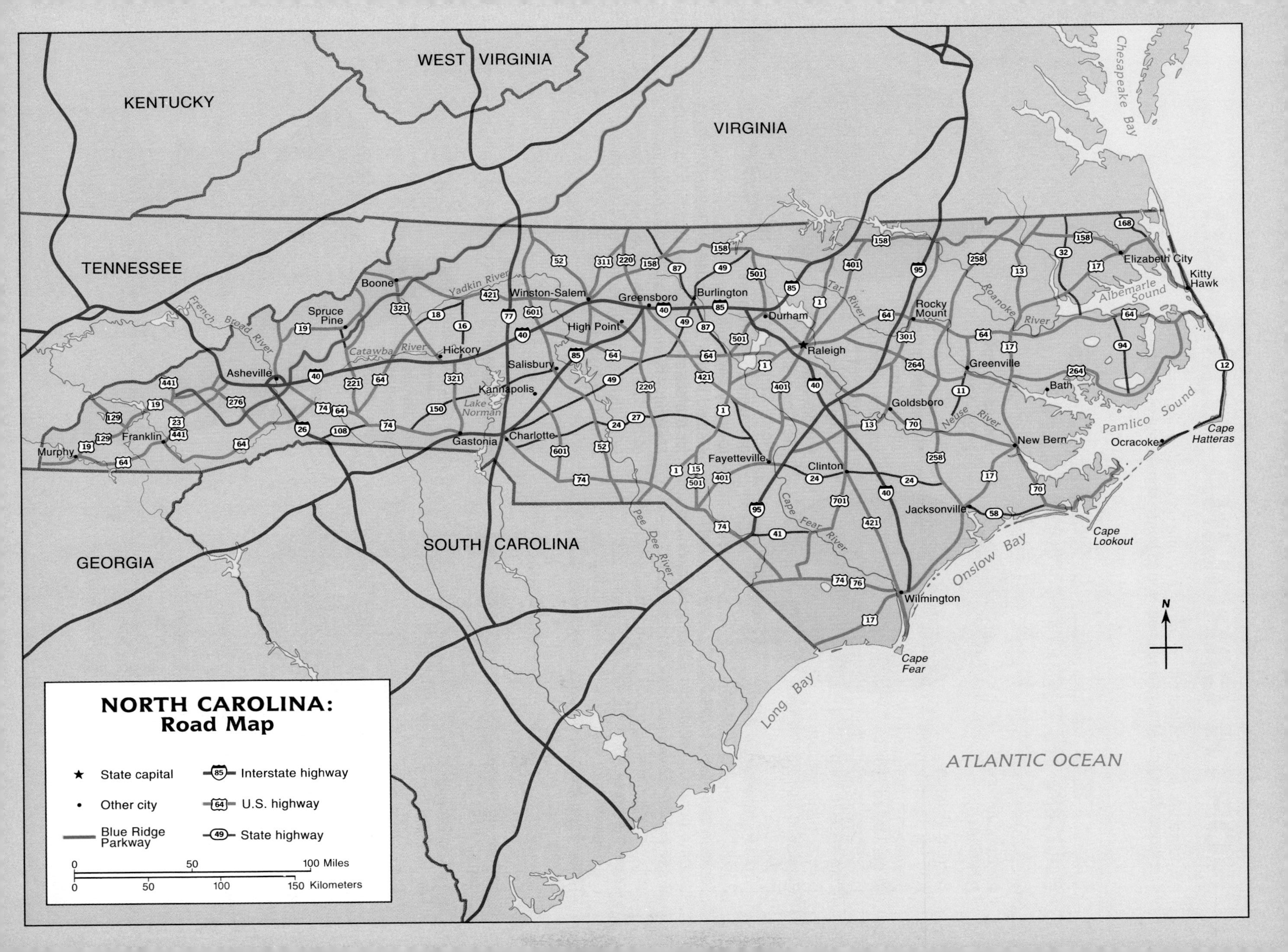

NORTH CAROLINA:
Road Map
State capital
Other city
Blue Ridge Parkway
Interstate highway
U.S. highway
State highway
0
50
100 Miles
0
50
100
150 Kilometers
KENTUCKY
WEST VIRGINIA
VIRGINIA
TENNESSEE
GEORGIA
SOUTH CAROLINA
ATLANTIC OCEAN
Chesapeake Bay
Albemarle Sound
Pamlico Sound
Onslow Bay
Long Bay
Cape Hatteras
Cape Lookout
Cape Fear
Elizabeth City
Kitty Hawk
Ocracoke
Bath
Greenville
Rocky Mount
Raleigh
Durham
Burlington
Greensboro
High Point
Winston-Salem
Boone
Spruce Pine
Hickory
Asheville
Salisbury
Kannapolis
Lake Norman
Charlotte
Gastonia
Franklin
Murphy
Goldsboro
New Bern
Fayetteville
Clinton
Jacksonville
Wilmington
Yadkin River
French Broad River
Catawba River
Tar River
Roanoke River
Neuse River
Cape Fear River
Pee Dee River
N

NORTH CAROLINA ALMANAC

An almanac is a collection of important and interesting information. The North Carolina Almanac will help you to learn more about your state.

UNITED STATES PRESIDENTS BORN IN NORTH CAROLINA

Andrew Jackson (1767–1845)

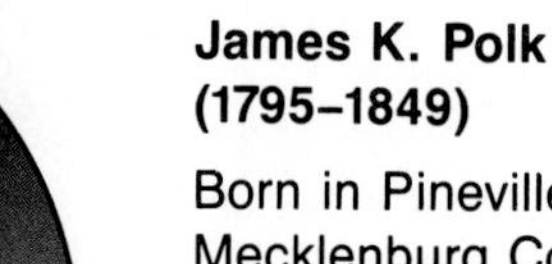

Born in Waxhaw, Andrew Jackson was the seventh President of the United States. He served in this office from 1829 to 1837. Before being elected President, Jackson served in the U.S. House of Representatives and the Senate for the state of Tennessee. Jackson believed in states' rights and believed that the poor as well as the wealthy should have a say in their government. Demands from farmers who wanted more land led Jackson to enforce the Indian Removal Act of 1830, which forced the Cherokee to take the "Trail of Tears" to the West. Today there is an Andrew Jackson Museum in Waxhaw.

James K. Polk (1795–1849)

Born in Pineville, Mecklenburg County, James Knox Polk was the eleventh President of the United States. He graduated from the University of North Carolina in 1818 and went to Tennessee to study law. Polk was elected to the U.S. House of Representatives for the state of Tennessee in 1824. During the Mexican-American War, he was commander of the U.S. Army. Polk served as President from 1845 to 1849. Today Polk's birthplace is a state historic site.

Andrew Johnson (1808–1875)

Born in Raleigh, Andrew Johnson moved with his family to Tennessee when he was 17 years old. Vice President Johnson became the seventeenth President of the United States following the death of Abraham Lincoln in 1865. Johnson served as President from 1865 to 1869. During this time, slavery was ended by the U.S. government. In 1875 Johnson became a U.S. senator, the only person ever to hold this office after having been President. Today Johnson's birthplace is a state historic site.

In 1948 President Harry Truman dedicated this statue, *Three Presidents North Carolina Gave the Nation,* by the sculptor Charles Keely.

NORTH CAROLINA'S GOVERNORS

Governor	Term
Richard Caswell	1776–1780
Abner Nash	1780–1781
Thomas Burke	1781–1782
Alexander Martin	1782–1784
Richard Caswell	1784–1787
Samuel Johnston	1787–1789
Alexander Martin	1789–1792
Richard D. Spaight, Sr.	1792–1795
Samuel Ashe	1795–1798
William R. Davie	1798–1799
Benjamin Williams	1799–1802
James Turner	1802–1805
Nathaniel Alexander	1805–1807
Benjamin Williams	1807–1808
David Stone	1808–1810
Benjamin Smith	1810–1811
William Hawkins	1811–1814
William Miller	1814–1817
John Branch	1817–1820
Jesse Franklin	1820–1821
Gabriel Holmes	1821–1824
Hutchins G. Burton	1824–1827
James Iredell, Jr.	1827–1828
John Owen	1828–1830
Montfort Stokes	1830–1832
David L. Swain	1832–1835
Richard D. Spaight, Jr.	1835–1836
Edward B. Dudley	1836–1841
John M. Morehead	1841–1845
William A. Graham	1845–1849
Charles Manly	1849–1851
David S. Reid	1851–1854
Warren Winslow	1854–1855
Thomas Bragg	1855–1859
John W. Ellis	1859–1861
Henry T. Clark	1861–1862
Zebulon B. Vance	1862–1865
William W. Holden	1865–1865
Jonathan Worth	1865–1868
William W. Holden	1868–1871
Tod R. Caldwell	1871–1874
Curtis H. Brogden	1874–1877
Zebulon B. Vance	1877–1879
Thomas J. Jarvis	1879–1885
Alfred M. Scales	1885–1889
Daniel G. Fowle	1889–1891
Thomas M. Holt	1891–1893
Elias Carr	1893–1897
Daniel L. Russell	1897–1901
Charles B. Aycock	1901–1905
Robert B. Glenn	1905–1909
William W. Kitchin	1909–1913
Locke Craig	1913–1917
Thomas W. Bickett	1917–1921
Cameron Morrison	1921–1925
Angus W. McLean	1925–1929
O. Max Gardner	1929–1933
J.C.B. Ehringhaus	1933–1937
Clyde R. Hoey	1937–1941
J. Melville Broughton	1941–1945
R. Gregg Cherry	1945–1949
W. Kerr Scott	1949–1953
William B. Umstead	1953–1954
Luther H. Hodges	1954–1961
Terry Sanford	1961–1965
Daniel K. Moore	1965–1969
Robert W. Scott	1969–1973
James E. Holshouser, Jr.	1973–1977
James B. Hunt, Jr.	1977–1985
James G. Martin	1985–1992

The Governor's Mansion, home to North Carolina's governors since 1891, is located at 200 North Blount Street, in Raleigh.

NORTH CAROLINA'S COUNTIES

County Name	County Seat	County Population (1990)*	Area in Sq. Miles	Named for	Year Formed
Alamance	Graham	108,213	428	Siouan word meaning "noisy stream"	1728
Alexander	Taylorsville	27,544	259	the local Alexander family	1847
Alleghany	Sparta	9,590	230	Algonquian word meaning "best stream"	1859
Anson	Wadesboro	23,474	533	Lord George Anson, British admiral	1750
Ashe	Jefferson	22,209	427	Colonel Samuel Ashe, superior court judge	1799
Avery	Newland	14,867	300	Waighstill Avery, N.C. attorney general	1911
Beaufort	Washington	42,283	828	the Duke of Beaufort	1705
Bertie	Windsor	20,388	701	James Bertie, a lords proprietor	1722
Bladen	Elizabethtown	28,663	879	Martin Bladen, member of the board of trade	1734
Brunswick	Bolivia	50,985	860	King George I, Duke of Brunswick	1764
Buncombe	Asheville	174,821	659	Edward Buncombe, officer in the American Revolution	1791
Burke	Morganton	75,744	504	Dr. Thomas Burke, governor	1777
Cabarrus	Concord	98,935	364	Stephen Cabarrus, member of the General Assembly	1792
Caldwell	Lenoir	70,709	471	Joseph Caldwell, first president of the University of North Carolina	1841
Camden	Camden	5,904	240	Charles Pratt, Earl of Camden	1777
Carteret	Beaufort	52,556	526	John Carteret, Earl of Granville	1722
Caswell	Yanceyville	20,693	428	Richard Caswell, governor	1777
Catawba	Newton	118,412	396	the Catawba people of the area	1842
Chatham	Pittsboro	38,758	708	William Pitt, Earl of Chatham	1771
Cherokee	Murphy	20,170	452	the Cherokee people of the area	1839
Chowan	Edenton	13,506	182	the Chowanoc people of the area	1668
Clay	Hayesville	7,155	214	Henry Clay, cofounder of the U.S. Whig party	1861
Cleveland	Shelby	84,714	468	Benjamin Cleaveland, officer in the American Revolution	1841
Columbus	Whiteville	49,587	938	Christopher Columbus	1808
Craven	New Bern	81,613	701	William Craven, Earl of Craven	1705
Cumberland	Fayetteville	274,566	657	William Augustus, Duke of Cumberland	1754
Currituck	Currituck	13,736	256	the Currituck people of the area	1668
Dare	Manteo	22,746	391	Virginia Dare, first English child born in North America	1870
Davidson	Lexington	126,677	548	William Davidson, soldier in the American Revolution	1836

County Name	County Seat	County Population (1990)*	Area in Sq. Miles	Named for	Year Formed
Davie	Mocksville	27,859	267	William R. Davie, governor	1836
Duplin	Kenansville	39,995	819	Thomas Hay, Lord Duplin, English nobleman	1750
Durham	Durham	181,835	298	Bartlett Snipes Durham, local doctor	1881
Edgecombe	Tarboro	56,558	506	Baron Richard Edgecumbe, lord of the treasury	1741
Forsyth	Winston-Salem	265,878	412	Benjamin Forsyth, soldier in the War of 1812	1849
Franklin	Louisburg	36,414	494	Benjamin Franklin	1779
Gaston	Gastonia	175,093	357	William Gaston, U.S. congressman	1846
Gates	Gatesville	9,305	338	Horatio Gates, officer in the American Revolution	1779
Graham	Robbinsville	7,196	269	William A. Graham, governor	1872
Granville	Oxford	38,345	534	John Carteret, Earl of Granville	1746
Greene	Snow Hill	15,384	266	Nathanael Greene, general in the American Revolution	1799
Guilford	Greensboro	347,420	651	Francis North, Earl of Guilford	1771
Halifax	Halifax	55,516	724	George Montagu, Earl of Halifax	1758
Harnett	Lillington	67,822	601	Cornelius Harnett, delegate to the Continental Congress	1855
Haywood	Waynesville	46,942	555	John Haywood, state treasurer	1808
Henderson	Hendersonville	69,285	374	Leonard Henderson, chief justice to the Supreme Court of N.C.	1838
Hertford	Winton	22,523	356	Francis S. Conway, Earl of Hertford	1759
Hoke	Raeford	22,856	391	Robert F. Hoke, general in the Civil War	1911
Hyde	Swan Quarter	5,411	624	Edward Hyde, appointed governor by the Lords Proprietors	1705
Iredell	Statesville	92,931	574	James Iredell, supporter of N.C.'s adoption of the U.S. Constitution	1788
Jackson	Sylva	26,846	491	President Andrew Jackson	1851
Johnston	Smithfield	81,306	795	Gabriel Johnston, royal governor of N.C.	1746
Jones	Trenton	9,414	470	Willie Jones, officer in the American Revolution	1779

*Population figures are based on the 1990 census

County Name	County Seat	County Population (1990)*	Area in Sq. Miles	Named for	Year Formed
Lee	Sanford	41,374	259	General Robert E. Lee, Southern commander in the Civil War	1907
Lenoir	Kinston	57,274	402	William Lenoir, hero of the American Revolution	1791
Lincoln	Lincolnton	50,319	298	General Benjamin Lincoln, officer in the American Revolution	1779
Macon	Franklin	23,499	517	Nathaniel Macon, U.S. senator	1828
Madison	Marshall	16,953	451	President James Madison	1851
Martin	Williamston	25,078	461	Josiah Martin, royal governor	1774
McDowell	Marion	35,681	437	Joseph McDowell, officer in the American Revolution	1842
Mecklenburg	Charlotte	511,433	528	Princess Charlotte of Mecklenburg	1762
Mitchell	Bakersville	14,433	222	Dr. Elisha Mitchell, professor	1861
Montgomery	Troy	23,346	490	Richard Montgomery, soldier in the American Revolution	1779
Moore	Carthage	59,013	701	Alfred Moore, associate justice of the U.S. Supreme Court	1784
Nash	Nashville	76,677	540	Francis Nash, soldier in the American Revolution	1777
New Hanover	Wilmington	120,284	185	the royal family of Great Britain	1729
Northampton	Jackson	20,798	538	James of Compton, Earl of Northampton	1741
Onslow	Jacksonville	149,838	763	Arthur Onslow, member of the British House of Commons	1734
Orange	Hillsborough	93,851	400	William V of Orange, British royalty	1752
Pamlico	Bayboro	11,372	341	the Pamlico people of the area	1872
Pasquotank	Elizabeth City	31,298	228	the Pasquotank people of the area	1668
Pender	Burgaw	28,855	875	General William D. Pender, officer in the Civil War	1875
Perquimans	Hertford	10,447	246	the Perquimans people of the area	1668
Person	Roxboro	30,180	398	General Thomas Person, officer in the American Revolution	1791
Pitt	Greenville	107,924	657	William Pitt, Earl of Chatham	1760
Polk	Columbus	14,416	238	William Polk, officer in the American Revolution	1855
Randolph	Asheboro	106,546	789	Peyton Randolph, president of the Continental Congress	1779
Richmond	Rockingham	44,518	477	Charles Lennox, Duke of Richmond	1779

County Name	County Seat	County Population (1990)*	Area in Sq. Miles	Named for	Year Formed
Robeson	Lumberton	105,179	949	Colonel Thomas Robeson, officer in the American Revolution	1787
Rockingham	Wentworth	86,064	569	Marquis of Rockingham, English supporter of American independence	1785
Rowan	Salisbury	110,605	519	Matthew Rowan, acting governor	1753
Rutherford	Rutherfordton	56,918	568	General Griffith Rutherford, officer in the American Revolution	1779
Sampson	Clinton	47,297	947	John Sampson, member of the governor's council	1784
Scotland	Laurinburg	33,754	319	the country of Scotland	1899
Stanly	Albemarle	51,765	396	John Stanly, speaker of the House of Commons	1841
Stokes	Danbury	37,223	452	John Stokes, district court judge	1789
Surry	Dobson	61,704	539	Surry County, England	1771
Swain	Bryson City	11,268	526	David L. Swain, governor	1871
Transylvania	Brevard	25,520	378	Latin words meaning "across" and "woods"	1861
Tyrrell	Columbia	3,856	407	Sir John Tyrrell, a Lords Proprietor	1729
Union	Monroe	84,211	639	an agreement between two groups	1842
Vance	Henderson	38,892	249	Zebulon Baird Vance, governor	1881
Wake	Raleigh	423,380	854	Margaret Wake, wife of governor	1771
Warren	Warrenton	17,265	427	Joseph Warren, officer in the American Revolution	1779
Washington	Plymouth	13,997	332	President George Washington	1799
Watauga	Boone	36,952	314	a Cherokee town	1849
Wayne	Goldsboro	104,666	554	General "Mad Anthony" Wayne, officer in the American Revolution	1779
Wilkes	Wilkesboro	59,393	752	John Wilkes, English opponent of Tories	1777
Wilson	Wilson	66,061	374	Louis D. Wilson, state legislator	1855
Yadkin	Yadkinville	30,488	336	Yadkin River	1833
Yancey	Burnsville	15,419	314	Barlett Yancey, state legislator	1850

*Population figures are based on the 1990 census

NORTH CAROLINA'S CITIES

City Name	City Population	County	Population Rank	Year Formed
Albemarle	14,939	Stanly	37	1841
Archdale	6,913	Guilford	69	1786
Asheboro	16,362	Randolph	29	1796
Asheville	61,607	Buncombe	8	1797
Belmont	8,434	Gaston	57	1895
Boone	12,915	Watauga	43	1872
Burlington	39,498	Alamance	15	1893
Carrboro	11,553	Orange	47	1882
Cary	43,858	Wake	13	1871
Chapel Hill	38,719	Orange	16	1793
Charlotte	395,934	Mecklenburg	1	1768
Clinton	8,204	Sampson	59	1818
Concord	27,347	Cabarrus	21	1798
Dunn	8,336	Harnett	58	1887
Durham	136,611	Durham	5	1856
Eden	15,238	Rockingham	34	1967
Elizabeth City	14,292	Pasquotank	40	1800
Fayetteville	75,695	Cumberland	6	1783
Forest City	7,475	Rutherford	65	1877
Garner	14,967	Wake	36	1905
Gastonia	34,732	Gaston	10	1909
Goldsboro	40,709	Wayne	14	1850
Graham	10,426	Alamance	50	1851
Greensboro	183,521	Guilford	3	1808
Greenville	44,972	Pitt	12	1774
Havelock	20,268	Craven	24	1857
Henderson	15,655	Vance	33	1841
Hendersonville	7,284	Henderson	67	1840
Hickory	28,301	Catawba	20	1873
High Point	69,496	Davidson	7	1859
Hope Mills	8,184	Cumberland	60	1891
Jacksonville	30,013	Onslow	18	1842
Kannapolis	29,696	Cabarrus	19	1906
Kernersville	10,836	Forsyth	49	1871

City Name	City Population	County	Population Rank	Year Formed
Kings Mountain	8,763	Cleveland	56	1874
Kinston	25,295	Lenoir	22	1762
Laurinburg	11,643	Scotland	45	1877
Lenoir	14,192	Caldwell	41	1851
Lexington	16,581	Davidson	28	1827
Lumberton	18,601	Robeson	25	1788
Matthews	13,651	Mecklenburg	42	1879
Mint Hill	11,567	Mecklenburg	46	1971
Monroe	16,127	Union	30	1844
Mooresville	9,317	Iredell	52	1873
Morganton	15,085	Burke	35	1777
Mount Airy	7,156	Surry	68	1885
Mount Holly	7,710	Gaston	62	1879
New Bern	17,363	Craven	27	1710
Newton	9,304	Catawba	53	1843
Oxford	7,913	Granville	61	1811
Raleigh	207,951	Wake	2	1792
Reidsville	12,183	Rockingham	44	1873
Roanoke Rapids	15,722	Halifax	32	1893
Rockingham	9,399	Richmond	51	1784
Rocky Mount	48,997	Edgecombe	11	1867
Roxboro	7,332	Person	66	1793
Salisbury	23,087	Rowan	23	1753
Sanford	14,475	Lee	39	1872
Shelby	14,669	Cleveland	38	1843
Smithfield	7,540	Johnston	63	1777
Southern Pines	9,129	Moore	54	1887
Spring Lake	7,524	Cumberland	64	1951
Statesville	17,567	Iredell	26	1789
Tarboro	11,037	Edgecombe	48	1764
Thomasville	15,915	Davidson	31	1957
Washington	9,075	Beaufort	55	1783
Wilmington	55,530	New Hanover	9	1733
Wilson	36,930	Wilson	17	1849
Winston-Salem	143,485	Forsyth	4	1913

All cities with a population greater than 6,900 in the 1990 Census have been listed.

-34° F.

(−37° Celsius)

The lowest temperature ever recorded in North Carolina was on January 21, 1985 at Mount Mitchell.

60 inches

(152 centimeters)

The largest annual snowfall ever recorded in North Carolina was in April of 1987 at Newfound Gap in the Great Smoky Mountains National Park.

110° F.

(43° Celsius)

The highest temperature ever recorded in North Carolina was on August 21, 1983 at Fayetteville.

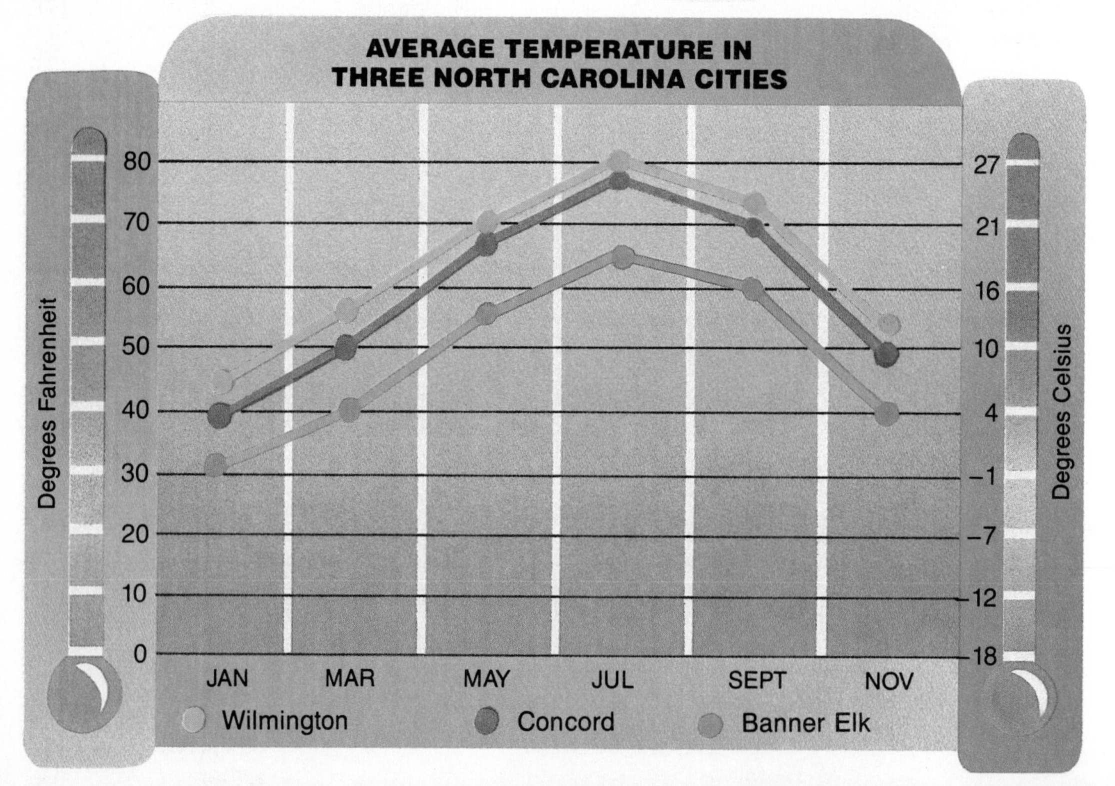

NORTH CAROLINA'S ECONOMY

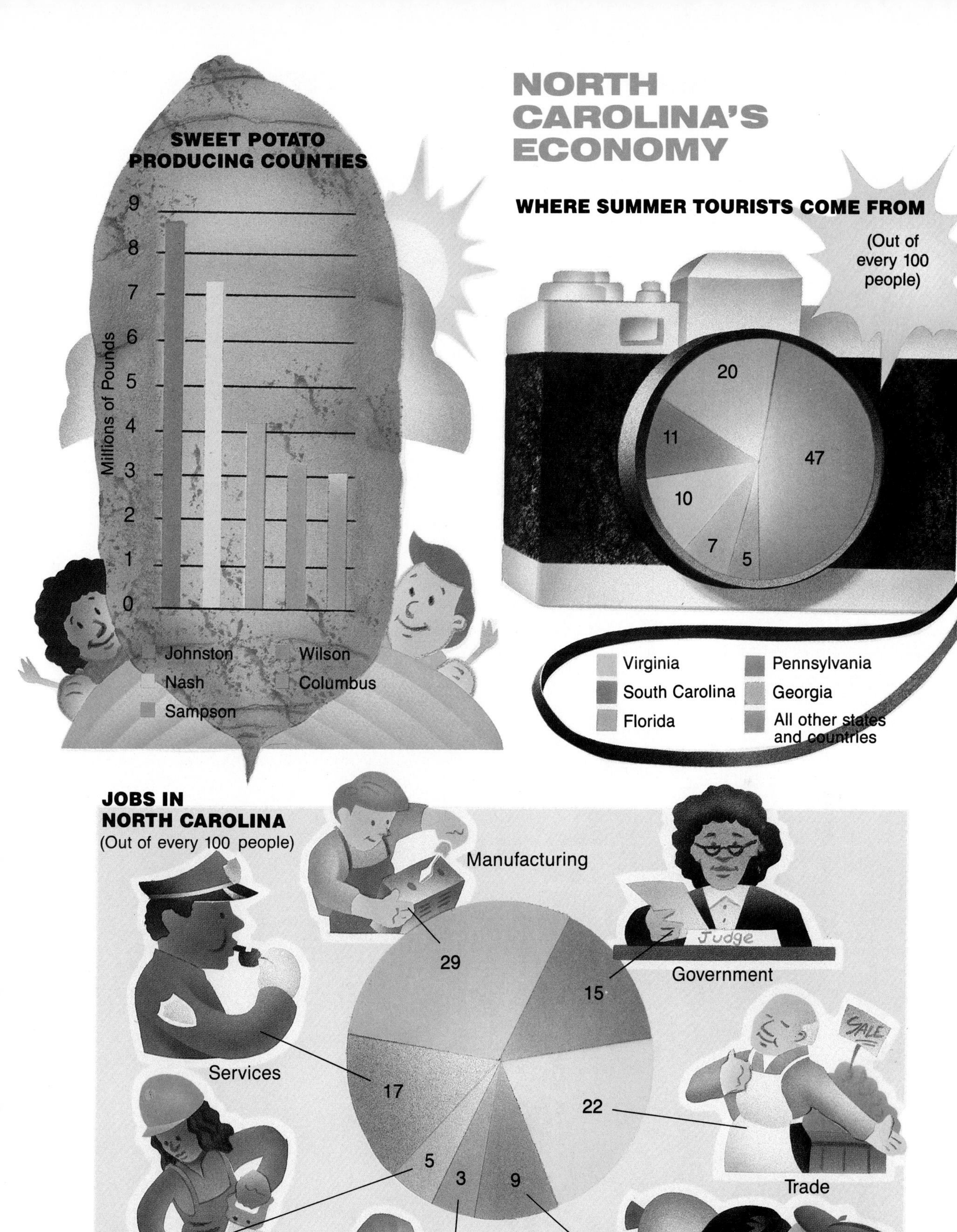

ANIMALS AND PLANTS OF NORTH CAROLINA

1. Cardinal
2. Spanish moss
3. Longleaf pine
4. Willow oak
5. Starling
6. Flowering dogwood
7. Umbrella magnolia
8. Bald cypress
9. Rhododendron
10. River otter
11. Venus's–flytrap
12. Wood duck
13. Box turtle
14. Honeysuckle
15. Black rat snake
16. Bluestem grass
17. Bluebird
18. Yaupon shrub
19. Holly
20. Black bear
21. River birch
22. Fox
23. Opossum
24. Robin (in nest)
25. Great horned owl
26. White oak
27. Soft maple
28. Pond pine
29. Loblolly pine
30. Marsh hawk
31. White tailed deer
32. Pheasant
33. American beach grass
34. Laughing gull
35. Eastern Cottontail rabbit
36. Blue crab
37. Bluefish
38. Largemouth bass
39. Gar
40. Horseshoe crab
41. Oyster catcher
42. Sea oats
43. Skimmer
44. Gulls
45. Wild banker ponies
28
29
45
44
30
31
43
42
32
35
41
40
34
36
39
33
37
38

NORTH CAROLINA ALMANAC

ANNUAL EVENTS IN NORTH CAROLINA

WINTER

DECEMBER
Christmastown, USA, McAdenville
Menorah Candlelighting, Charlotte
Old Salem Christmas, Winston-Salem
Kwanzaa Cultural Arts Celebration, Durham
Tryon Palace Christmas Celebration, New Bern

JANUARY
Southeast Regional Special Olympics, Blowing Rock
North Carolina Young People's Concert, Raleigh

FEBRUARY
Battle of Moores Creek Bridge, Currie
African-American Arts Festival, Greensboro

SPRING

MARCH
Annual Gemboree, Morganton
Easter Bonnet Parade and Egg Hunt, Marion
Purim Carnival, Charlotte

APRIL
Zoo Fling, Asheboro
Earth Day, Rocky Mount
Annual Pig-Cookin' Contest, Newport
Carolina Dogwood Festival, Statesville
National Whistler's Convention, Louisburg
"Message of Easter" Outdoor Drama, Williamston
Autofair, Charlotte Motor Speedway, Concord
Haliwa-Saponi Annual Pow-wow, Hollister
Carolina Model Railroaders Swap Meet, Greensboro

MAY
World Gee Haw Whimmy Diddle Competition, Asheville
Hacky Sack and Frisbee Festival, Raleigh
Children's Walking Tour, Salisbury
White Lake Water Festival, White Lake
Strawberry Festival, Conover
Duke Children's Classic, Durham
Pleasure Island Spring Festival, Carolina/Kure Beaches
Alamance Balloon Festival, Burlington

SUMMER

JUNE

African American Heritage Festival, Sedalia
National Hollerin' Contest, Spivey's Corner
Heroes Comic Book Convention, Charlotte
Beech Mountain Storytelling Festival, Beech Mountain
Lake Michie Children's Day Fishing Tournament, Durham
"Unto These Hills" Cherokee Drama, Cherokee
"Lost Colony" Outdoor Drama, Manteo

JULY

"First For Freedom" Drama, Halifax
Grandfather Mountain Highland Games, Linville
Land Hermit Crab Race, Nags Head
"Strike at the Wind" Lumbee Drama, Pembroke
4th of July Festival, Southport
Wright Kite Festival, Kill Devil Hills
Junior Rodeo, Love Valley
Sand Sculpture Contest, Ocracoke

AUGUST

Ashe County Fiddler's Convention, Jefferson
North Carolina's Apple Festival, Hendersonville
Mineral and Gem Festival, Spruce Pine
Shrimp Festival, Sneads Ferry

FALL

SEPTEMBER

Country Heritage Festival, Kenly
Andrews Founders Day, Andrews
Everybody's Day Festival, Thomasville
Fall Jamboree, Millbridge
Collard Festival, Ayden
Confederate Reenactment, Flat Rock
Jones County Youth Livestock Show, Trenton

OCTOBER

Peanut Festival, Edenton
Statewide American Indian Cultural Festival, Fayetteville
Textile Olympics, Gastonia
Annual Leaflookers Clogging Jamboree, Franklin

NOVEMBER

Molasses Festival, Snow Camp
Wooly Worm Festival, Banner Elk

NORTH CAROLINA TIME LINE

10,000 years ago Native Americans begin to settle in North Carolina

1400s Algonquians, Iroquoians, and Siouans live in North Carolina

1524 Giovanni da Verrazano explores the coast of North Carolina

1526 Spanish and Africans under L. Vásquez de Ayllón try to start a colony

1540 Hernando De Soto explores southwestern North Carolina

1663 The eight Lords Proprietors claim land in North Carolina

1705 English colonists settle Bath

1711 Tuscarora War

1729 North Carolina becomes a royal colony of England

1776 Halifax Resolves; Declaration of Independence; battle of Moores Creek Bridge

1789 North Carolina becomes the twelfth state of the U.S.

1792 Raleigh becomes the state capital

1829 Andrew Jackson becomes the seventh U.S. President

1838 The Cherokee are forced west along the "Trail of Tears"

1840 The first passenger railroad in North Carolina is built

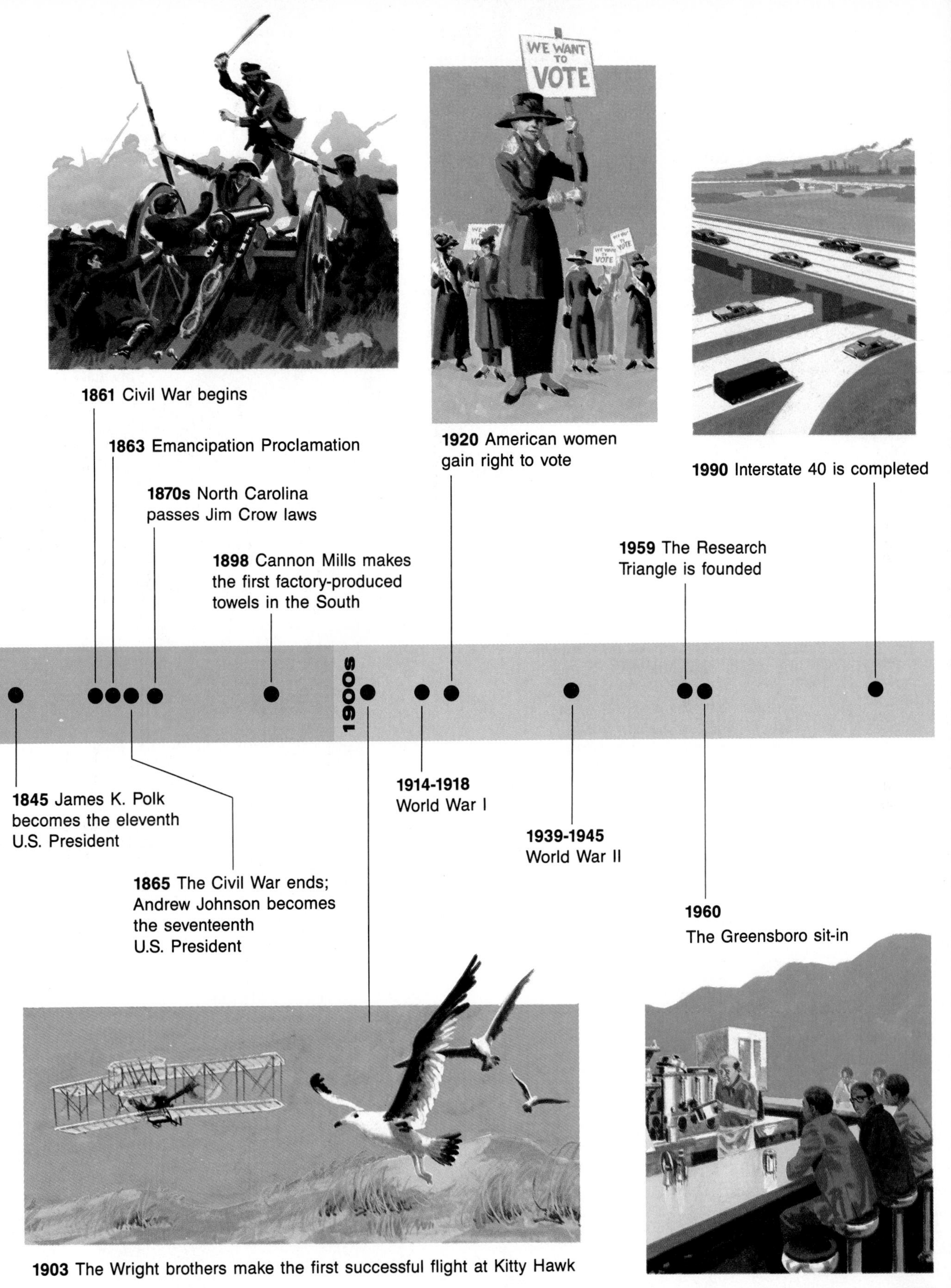
WE WANT TO VOTE
1845 James K. Polk becomes the eleventh U.S. President
1861 Civil War begins
1863 Emancipation Proclamation
1865 The Civil War ends; Andrew Johnson becomes the seventeenth U.S. President
1870s North Carolina passes Jim Crow laws
1898 Cannon Mills makes the first factory-produced towels in the South
1900s
1903 The Wright brothers make the first successful flight at Kitty Hawk
1914-1918 World War I
1920 American women gain right to vote
1939-1945 World War II
1959 The Research Triangle is founded
1960 The Greensboro sit-in
1990 Interstate 40 is completed

FASCINATING NORTH CAROLINA FACTS

The largest collard ever grown was 35 feet (10.7 m) tall and 59¼ inches (150.5 cm) wide. It was grown by Bobby Rackley of Rocky Mount in 1980.

Durham is home to the world's largest refuge for lemurs. These animals come from the island of Madagascar, off the east coast of Africa. As the forests in Madagascar are being cut down, these animals are becoming extinct or are dying off, just as the dinosaurs became extinct.

In 1954 Don Clayton started the first Putt-Putt Miniature Golf Course in the world in Fayetteville. The first manager of that golf course, J.L. Dawkins, became the mayor of Fayetteville. When you play putt-putt in North Carolina, you will hear Dawkins's famous saying: "The first person scoring the hole-in-one with the red or yellow ball will get a free game of putt-putt golf."

Thomasville, known as "The Chair City," has "The World's Most Famous Chair" in the center of town. The "Big Chair" is 18 feet (5.5 m) tall, is built on top of a 12-foot-high (3.7 m) block of Indiana limestone, and is made of metal and cement.

The largest fraser fir tree in North America is in Cashiers which is in Jackson County. It is 87 feet (26.52 m) tall and its trunk is 9 feet (2.7 m) around.

In 1973 John T. Capps III formed Bald-Headed Men of America at 102 Bald Drive, Morehead City. The organization's goal is to help bald people to be proud of the way they look. Mr. Capps says, "We believe that bald is beautiful."

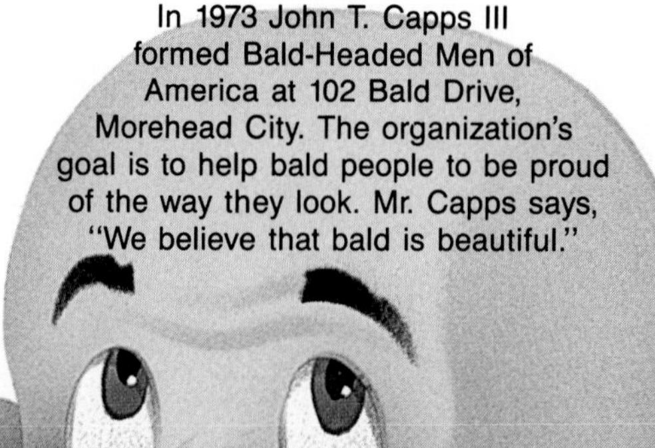

FAMOUS TAR HEELS

David Brinkley
Born in Wilmington in 1920; television reporter; has won ten Emmy Awards and two Peabody Awards; best known for *This Week with David Brinkley* on ABC

Andy Griffith
Born in Mount Airy in 1926; actor; best known for his television programs *The Andy Griffith Show* and *Matlock*

William (Billy) E. Taylor Born in Greenville in 1926; jazz pianist, author, television jazz reporter; won an Emmy award (1984)

Elizabeth Duncan Koontz Born in Salisbury in 1919; educator, government director; first African-American president of the NEA (National Education Association); died in 1989

Doug Marlette Born in Greensboro in 1949; creator of "Kudzu" comic strip; editorial cartoonist

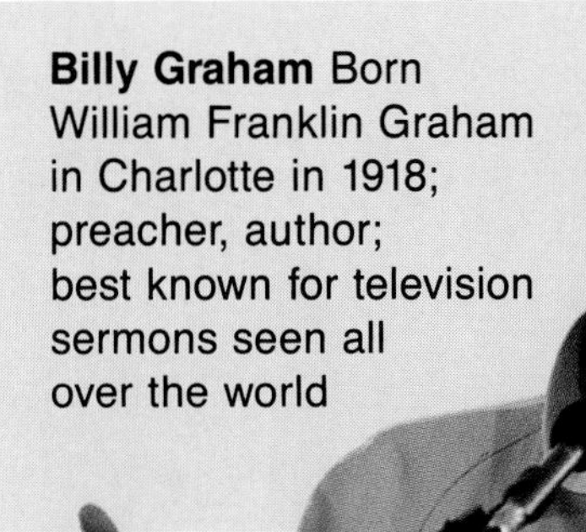

Billy Graham Born William Franklin Graham in Charlotte in 1918; preacher, author; best known for television sermons seen all over the world

Barbara D. Howar Born in Raleigh in 1934; television reporter, writer; best known for her appearances on *Entertainment Tonight*

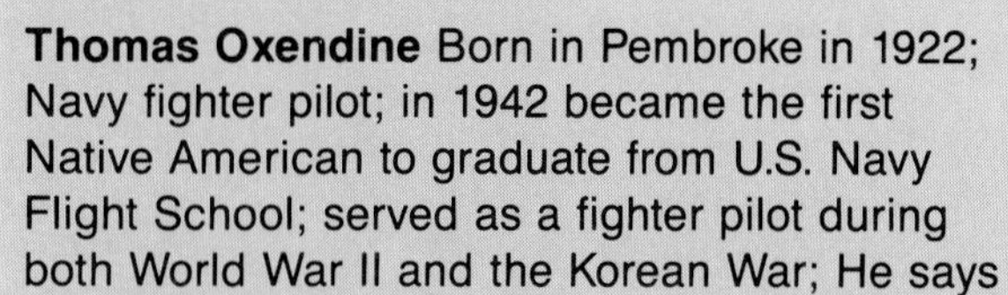

Thomas Oxendine Born in Pembroke in 1922; Navy fighter pilot; in 1942 became the first Native American to graduate from U.S. Navy Flight School; served as a fighter pilot during both World War II and the Korean War; He says that "Whatever you conceive [think of], you can achieve. And never be afraid of the truth."

Roberta Flack Born in Asheville in 1940; pop singer, recording star; won Grammy Awards (1972-73)

Ava Gardner Born Lucy Johnson in Smithfield in 1922; actress; best known for the films *On the Beach* (1959), *Night of the Iguana* (1964), and *Earthquake* (1974); died in 1990

Randy Travis Born in Marshville in 1959; country music singer; won People's Choice Award (1989)

Amanda Crowe Born in Murphy in 1922; Cherokee woodcarver; started carving when she was four years old; her art sells all over the world

Elizabeth Dole Born in Salisbury in 1936; former secretary of transportation; now heads the Red Cross

Susie M. Sharp Born in Rocky Mount in 1907; government official; became the first female chief justice of the state supreme court in 1974

Thomas Wolfe Born in Asheville in 1900; author; died in 1938

Ernest Eugene Barnes, Jr. Born in Durham in 1938; artist; former football player with the Denver Broncos (1964-65); official artist for the American Football League (1966); best known today for his art that is exhibited around the country

Charles Kuralt Born in Wilmington in 1934; writer, television reporter; wrote: *North Carolina Is My Home* in 1986

Sam Ervin Born in Morganton in 1896; U.S. senator (1954-74); best known for his role during the Watergate hearings; died 1985

Anne Tyler Born in Minnesota in 1941; Anne Tyler grew up in Raleigh; author; graduated from Duke University at age 19; best known for her book *The Accidental Tourist*

John Coltrane Born in Hamlet in 1926; jazz tenor saxophonist; toured with Dizzy Gillespie and Miles Davis; died in 1967

Eileen Fulton Born in Asheville; actress; best known for her work on the television series *As the World Turns*

Richard Petty Born in Level Cross in 1937; race-car driver; has won 200 of 1,127 National Association of Stock Car Auto Racing (NASCAR) Winston Cup races entered; received NASCAR's Award of Excellence (1987); celebrated his two-hundredth victory on July 4, 1984, at the Daytona International Speedway

Maya Angelou Born Marguerite Johnson in St. Louis in 1924; now lives in Winston-Salem; author, singer, playwright, editor, actress, and civil rights worker; first African-American woman to become a director in Hollywood; now the Reynolds Professor of American Studies at Wake Forest University

Harvey B. Gantt Born in South Carolina in 1943; architect, government official; mayor of Charlotte (1983-87); known for his role in the growth of Charlotte while mayor

Elizabeth Cotten Born in Chapel Hill in 1892; folk singer, composer; won Grammy Award (1984); best known for her style of guitar playing called "cotten pickin'"; died in 1987

Ronnie Milsap Born in Robbinsville in 1943; country music singer, pianist; won a Country Music Award (1977)

Shirley Caesar Born in Durham in 1938; gospel singer, preacher; has won five Grammy Awards; head of a foundation in Durham that helps needy families

Sugar Ray Leonard Born Ray Charles Leonard in Wilmington in 1956; World Boxing Light Heavyweight Champion (1988)

DICTIONARY OF GEOGRAPHIC TERMS

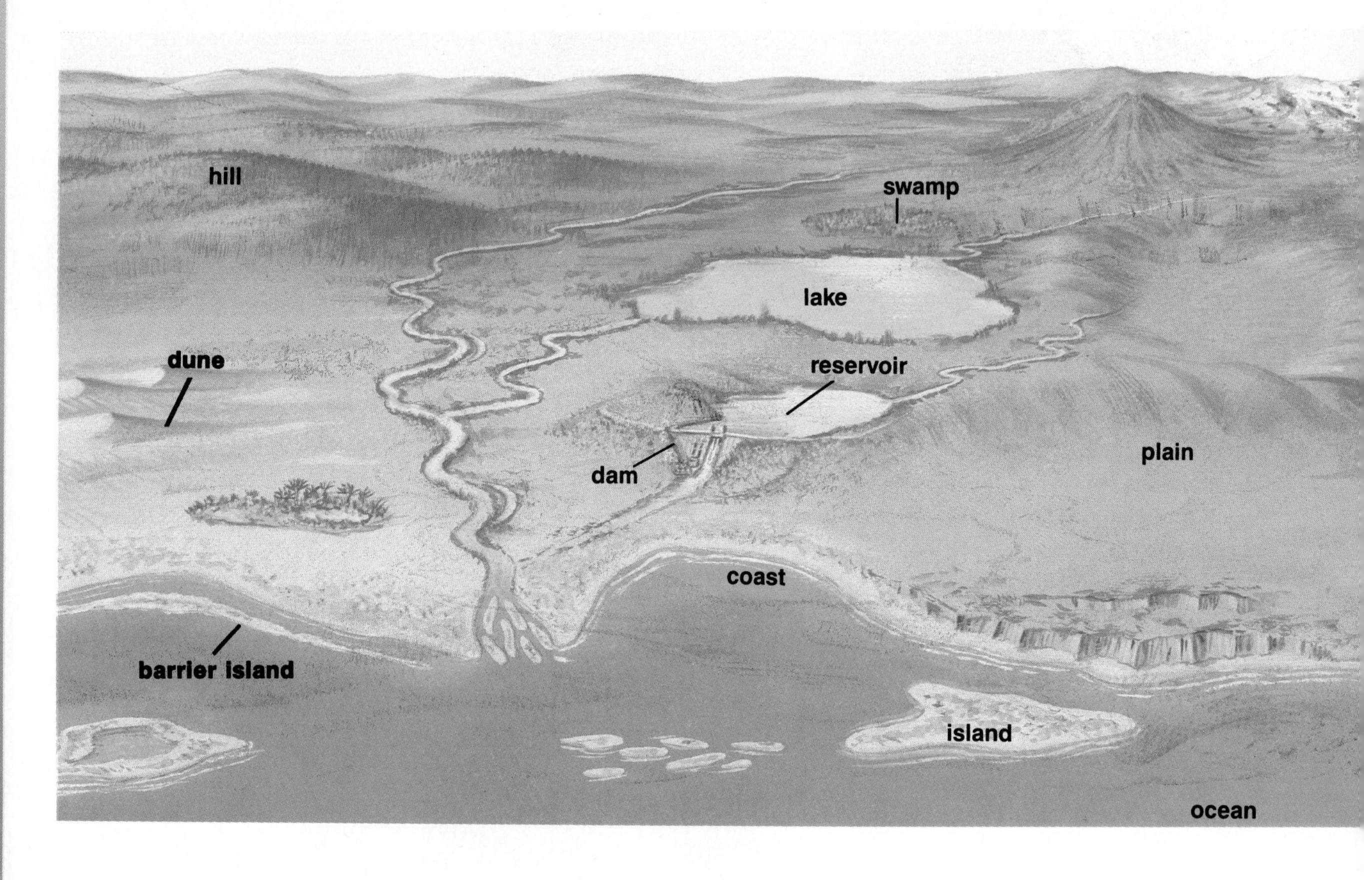

barrier island (bar 'ē ər ī' lənd) An island that separates the mainland from the ocean.

bay (bā) A part of an ocean or lake that reaches into the land.

canal (kə nal') A waterway for ships dug across the land.

cavern (kav' ərn) A large underground cave.

coast (kōst) The land along an ocean or sea.

coastal plain (kōs' təl plān) The flat area of land near a coast.

dam (dam) A wall built across a stream or river to hold back the water and form a lake or pond.

dune (dün) A mound or ridge of sand that has been piled up by the wind and water.

gap (gap) A narrow passage through a mountain range.

glacier (glā' shər) A huge sheet of ice that moves slowly over the land.

gorge (gôrj) A deep, narrow valley that has steep, rocky walls.

harbor (här' bər) A safe place along a coast where ships can dock.

hill (hil) A rounded, raised landform, not as high as a mountain.

inlet (in' let) A narrow opening flowing between islands.

island (ī' lənd) A body of land that is completely surrounded by water.

lake (lāk) A body of water completely or almost completely surrounded by land.

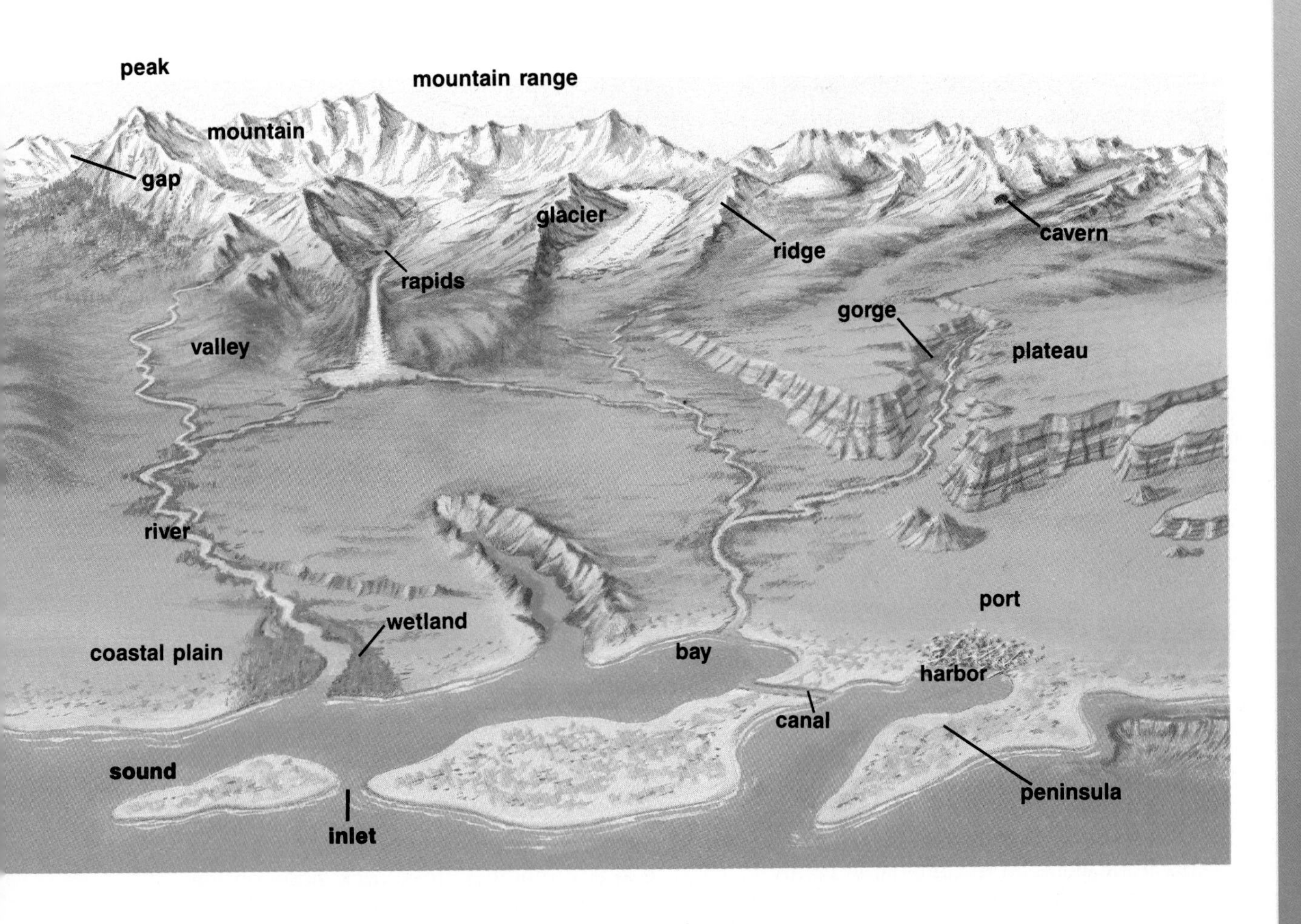

mountain (moun′ tən) A mass of land that rises very high above the surrounding area.

mountain range (moun′ tən rānj) A group or chain of mountains.

ocean (ō′ shən) The body of salt water that covers nearly three fourths of the earth's surface.

peak (pēk) A high mountain, or the pointed top of a high mountain.

peninsula (pə nin′ sə lə) A body of land surrounded almost entirely by water.

plain (plān) An area of flat or almost flat land.

plateau (pla tō′) An area of flat land that is raised above the surrounding country.

port (pôrt) A place where ships can dock safely to load and unload goods.

rapids (rap′ idz) A part of a river where the water flows swiftly and roughly.

reservoir (rez′ ər vwär) A place where water is collected and stored.

ridge (rij) A long and narrow chain of hills or mountains.

river (riv′ ər) A large stream of water that flows in a natural channel and empties into a lake, ocean, or other river.

sound (sound) A large body of water between the mainland and an island.

swamp (swomp) An area of wet land.

valley (val′ ē) An area of low land between hills or mountains.

wetland (wet′ land) An area of swamp, marsh, or other wet surface.

GAZETTEER

This Gazetteer is a geographical dictionary that will help you to pronounce and locate the places discussed in this book. Latitude and longitude are given for cities and some other places. The page number tells you where each place appears on a map.

PRONUNCIATION KEY

a	cap	hw	**wh**ere	oi	c**oi**n	ü	m**oo**n
ā	cake	i	bib	ôr	f**or**k	ū	c**u**te
ä	father	ī	kite	ou	c**ow**	ûr	t**er**m
är	c**ar**	îr	p**ier**ce	sh	**sh**ow	ə	**a**bout, tak**e**n, penc**i**l, apr**o**n, helpf**u**l
âr	d**ar**e	ng	so**ng**	th	**th**in	ər	lett**er**, doll**ar**, doct**or**
ch	**ch**ain	o	t**o**p	th̲	**th**ose		
e	h**e**n	ō	r**o**pe	u	s**u**n		
ē	m**e**	ô	s**aw**	u̇	b**oo**k		

Appalachian Mountains (ap ə lā′ chē ən moun′ tənz) The low, rounded mountains that run through most of the eastern United States from Alabama to Canada. In North Carolina they are located in the western part of the state. (p. 27)

Asheville (ash′ vil) A city in the southern part of the Mountain Region in North Carolina. It is located on the French Broad River; 36°N, 83°W. (p. 89)

Atlantic Ocean (at lan′ tik ō′ shən) The ocean that borders the eastern coast of the United States. (p. 12)

Bath (bath) A town on the Pamlico River in the Coastal Plain. It was the first European town in North Carolina; 35°N, 77°W. (p. 123)

Beaufort (bū′ fərt) A coastal town in southeastern North Carolina; 35°N, 77°W. (p. 360)

Bethabara (be tha′ bə rə) A town in the northern Piedmont, the first to be built by the Moravians in North Carolina. It was established in 1753; 36°N, 80°W. (p. 130)

Black Mountains (blak moun′ tənz) A high mountain range in the center of the Mountain Region of North Carolina. (p. 89)

Blue Ridge Escarpment (blü rij e skärp′ mənt) A steep rock slope on the western edge of the Piedmont that forms the beginning of the Blue Ridge Mountains. (p. 89)

Blue Ridge Mountains (blü rij moun′ tənz) The most eastern of the mountain ranges that make up the Appalachian Mountains; it is in western North Carolina. (p. 67)

Blue Ridge Parkway (blü rij pärk wā) A scenic road that winds along the top of the Blue Ridge Mountains. Over 250 miles (402 km) are in North Carolina. (p. 15)

Brushy Mountains (brush′ ē moun′ tənz) A group of low mountains in the western part of the Piedmont Region. (p. 81)

C

Cape Fear River (kāp fîr riv′ ər) It begins in the Piedmont Region and is the deepest river in North Carolina; it is the only major river in North Carolina to flow directly into the Atlantic Ocean. (p. 130)

Cape Hatteras (kāp hat′ ər əs) A point of land on the southern tip of Hatteras Island that stretches into the Atlantic Ocean. (p. 55)

Cape Hatteras National Seashore (kāp hat′ ər əs nash′ ə nəl sē′ shôr) A national seashore on Hatteras and Ocracoke islands off the coast of North Carolina. (p. 55)

Cape Lookout National Seashore (kāp lu̇k′ out nash′ ə nəl sē′ shôr) A national seashore on the Core Banks off the coast of North Carolina. (p. 55)

Chapel Hill (chap′ əl hil) A town in the central Piedmont Region known for its university; 36°N, 79°W. (p. 271)

Charlotte (shär′ lət) Located in the south-central Piedmont, it is the largest city in North Carolina; 35°N, 81°W. (p. 13)

Cherokee (cher′ ə kē) A town on the Qualla Boundary Reservation, located in the Smoky Mountains. The Oconaluftee River runs through it; 35°N, 83°W. (p. 22)

Chesapeake Bay (ches′ ə pēk bā) A bay of the Atlantic Ocean, off the coast of Maryland and Virginia. (p. 118)

Coastal Plain Region (kōs′ təl plān rē′ jən) The eastern region of North Carolina. It is a lowland plain bordered by the Atlantic Ocean on the east and the Fall Line on the west. (p. 66)

D

Durham (dər′ əm) A city in the Piedmont that is known for its work in research and medicine; 36°N, 79°W. (p. 360)

E

Edenton (e′ dən tun) A town started by the colonists along the coast; 36°N, 77°W. (p. 123)

F

Fayetteville (fā′ ət vil) A city in eastern North Carolina on the Cape Fear River. Fort Bragg military base is nearby; 35°N, 79°W. (p. 360)

G

Gastonia (ga stō′ nē ə) A center of textile manufacturing in the southern Piedmont Region; 35°N, 81°W. (p. 179)

Grandfather Mountain (grand′ fä t͟hər moun′ tən) A mountain in the Blue Ridge Mountains known for its unusual shape; 36°N, 82°W. (p. 360)

Great Dismal Swamp (grāt diz′ məl swomp) A 600-square-mile (1,550-sq-km) swamp located in northeastern North Carolina and southeastern Virginia. (p. 360)

Great Smoky Mountains (grāt smō′ kē moun′ tənz) A mountain range in the Appalachian Mountains that forms part of the western boundary of North Carolina with Tennessee. (p. 22)

Great Smoky Mountains National Park (grāt smō′ kē moun′ tənz nash′ ən əl pärk) A large national park located in western North Carolina and eastern Tennessee. (p. 293)

Great Wagon Road (grāt wag′ ən rōd) The major Indian trail used by European settlers of the early 1800s to get from Pennsylvania to North and South Carolina. (p. 130)

Greensboro (grēnz′ bûr ō) A city located in the north-central Piedmont Region; 36°N, 80°W. (p. 66)

Greenville (grēn′ vil) A city in the center of the Coastal Plain Region; 36°N, 77°W. (p. 43)

Guilford Courthouse (gil′ fərd kôrt′ hous) In the central Piedmont Region, the place where an important battle of the American Revolution was fought in 1781; 36°N, 80°W. (p. 147)

Gulf of Mexico (gulf əv mek′ si kō) A large gulf to the south of the United States that is connected with the Atlantic Ocean. (p. 27)

H

Hatteras Island (hat′ ər as ī lənd) One of the Outer Banks off the northern coast of North Carolina. (p. 55)

Hendersonville (hen′ dər sən vil) A town in the southern Mountain Region; 35°N, 82°W. (p. 360)

High Point (hī point) A city in the northern Piedmont that is an important furniture center; 36°N, 80°W. (p. 81)

I

Inner Coastal Plain (in′ ər kōs′ təl plān) Lowlands that are located in North Carolina between the western edge of the Tidewater and the Fall Line. (p. 73)

Intracoastal Waterway (in trə kōs′ təl wô′ tər wā) The water highway made up of many bays, inlets, sounds, rivers, and canals along the coast of North Carolina. (p. 172)

J

Jacksonville (jak′ sən vil) A southern Coastal Plain city on the New River. Camp Lejeune military base is nearby; 35°N, 77°W. (p. 43)

Jamestown (jāmz′ toun) The first permanent English settlement in North America. It is located on the James River in what is now Virginia; 37°N, 77°W. (p. 123)

Jockey's Ridge (jok′ ēz rij) A long sand dune on Bodie Island off the east coast of North Carolina. It is the highest sand dune in North Carolina; 36°N, 76°W. (p. 55)

K

Kings Mountain (kingz moun′ tən) A mountain in North Carolina near the South Carolina border. It is the place where an important battle of the American Revolution was fought in 1780; 35°N, 81°W. (p. 147)

L

Lake Mattamuskeet (lāk mat ə mə skēt′) The largest natural lake in North Carolina; it is located in the eastern Coastal Region near Pamlico Sound. (p. 55)

Lake Norman (lāk nôr′ mən) The largest lake in North Carolina; it is in the south-central Piedmont Region, and was made by damming the Catawba River. (p. 360)

Lincolnton (ling′ kən tən) A center of textile manufacturing in the central Piedmont; 35°N, 81°W. (p. 179)

Linville Caverns (lind′ vil kav′ ərnz) A large cave in the central Mountain Region of North Carolina known for its stalactites and stalagmites; 36°N, 82°W. (p. 360)

Lost Cove (lôst kōv) An area in the Mountain Region where the "Brown Mountain lights" can sometimes be seen at night; 36°N, 82°W. (p. 89)

M

Metrolina (met′ rō līn ä) A large urban area in the Piedmont that surrounds Charlotte and extends into South Carolina. (p. 254)

Moore's Creek (mürz krēk) A small creek in the southern Coastal Region. It is the place where the first battle of the American Revolution in North Carolina was fought in 1776; 34°N, 78°W. (p. 147)

Mountain Region (moun′ tən rē′ jən) The western region of North Carolina, it is bordered by the Piedmont Plateau on the east and Tennessee on the west. (p. 66)

Mount Mitchell (mount mich′ əl) Located in the central Mountain Region of North Carolina, it is the tallest mountain in the eastern United States. Its elevation is 6,684 feet (2,037 m); 36°N, 82°W. (p. 360)

Mount Mitchell State Park (mount mich′ əl stāt pärk) A state park in the central Mountain Region of North Carolina. (p. 293)

N

Neuse River (nūs riv′ ər) A river that begins in the central Piedmont Region and flows into Pamlico Sound. (p. 73)

New Bern (nü bûrn) The second-oldest European town in North Carolina, it was settled in 1710; 35°N, 77°W. (p. 123)

O

Occaneechi Village (äk ə nē′ chē vil′ ij) A 1,000-year-old village and one of the earliest Indian settlements in the Piedmont Region of North Carolina; 36°N, 79°W. (p. 103)

Ocracoke (ō′ krə kōk) A town on Ocracoke Island off the coast of North Carolina; 35°N, 76°W. (p. 22)

Ocracoke Island (ō′ krə kōk ī′ lənd) One of the Outer Banks off the northern coast of North Carolina. (p. 22)

Outer Banks (ou′ tər bangkz) A long string of barrier islands off the northern coast of North Carolina. (p. 55)

P

Pamlico River (pam′ li kō riv′ ər) A river in the Coastal Region that flows into Pamlico Sound. (p. 73)

Pamlico Sound (pam′ li kō sound) The largest sound on the eastern coast of North Carolina. It is between the mainland and the barrier islands; 35°N, 76°W. (p. 55)

Piedmont Region (pēd′ mont rē′ jən) The central region of North Carolina. It is a hilly plateau bordered by the Coastal Plain Region on the east and the Mountain Region on the west. (p. 66)

Piedmont Urban Crescent (pēd′ mont ûr′ bən kres′ ənt) An area of densely populated cities in the central Piedmont between Raleigh and Charlotte. (p. 254)

Pilot Mountain (pī′ lət moun′ tən) A mountain peak north of Winston-Salem. It is 2,421 feet (738 m) in elevation; 36°N, 80°W. (p. 360)

Pinehurst (pīn′ hûrst) A retirement community in the Sandhills of southern North Carolina; 35°N, 79°W. (p. 81)

Pisgah National Forest (piz′ gə nash′ ə nəl fôr′ ist) A national forest in the western part of the Mountain Region of North Carolina. (p. 293)

Q

Qualla Boundary Reservation (kwäl′ ə boun′ də rē rez ər vā′ shən) Land in southwestern North Carolina on which the Cherokee and Oconaluftee Indians live; 35°N, 83°W. (p. 149)

R

Raleigh (rô′ lē) A city located in the center of the state and the capital of North Carolina; 36°N, 79°W. (p. 360)

Research Triangle Park (ri sûrch′ trī′ ang gəl pärk) A research center located in the central Piedmont between Raleigh, Durham, and Chapel Hill. (p. 271)

Roanoke Island (rō′ ə nōk ī′ lənd) An island between North Carolina's mainland and the northern part of the barrier islands; 36°N, 76°W. (p. 118)

S

Salem (sā′ ləm) The second-oldest Moravian town in North Carolina, built in 1766. It became part of Winston-Salem; 36°N, 80°W. (p. 130)

Sandhills (sand′ hilz) Rolling hills of rough, sandy soil in the southwestern part of the Coastal Plain Region. (p. 67)

Sauratown Mountains (sôr′ ä ten moun′ tənz) A group of low mountains in the northwestern part of the Piedmont Region. (p. 81)

Seagrove (sē′ grōv) A town in the Piedmont Region known for its pottery; 36°N, 80°W. (p. 269)

Southern Pines (su_th_′ ərn pīnz) A retirement community in the Sandhills of southern North Carolina; 35°N, 79°W. (p. 81)

South Mountains (south moun′ tənz) A group of low mountains in the western part of the Piedmont Region. (p. 81)

T

Tidewater (tīd′ wô tər) The low-lying coastal land in eastern North Carolina that is washed by the tides. (p. 73)

Town Creek Indian Mound (toun krēk in′ dē ən mound) A ceremonial mound that was made by the Pee Dee Indians. It is near Mt. Gilead in the south-central Piedmont Region; 35°N, 80°W. (p. 103)

Triad (trī′ ad) A large metropolitan area formed by the cities of High Point, Greensboro, and and Winston-Salem. (p. 254)

Tusquittee Valley (tus kēt′ ē val′ ē) A river valley in southwestern North Carolina; 35°N, 84°W. (p. 89)

W

Washington, D.C. (wô′ shing tən dē sē) The capital of the United States, located on the Potomac River between Maryland and Virginia; 39°N, 77°W. (p. 35)

Wilderness Road (wil′ dər nis rōd) The Native American trail that was used by Daniel Boone to cross the mountains. It ran from land that is present-day Virginia through the Cumberland Gap. (p. 147)

Wilmington (wil′ ming tən) A city in the Coastal Plain Region, and the largest deepwater port in North Carolina; 34°N, 78°W. (p. 360)

Winston-Salem (win′ stən sā′ ləm) A city in the northern Piedmont Region of North Carolina; 36°N, 80°W. (p. 360)

a cap; ā cake; ä father; är car; âr dare; ch chain; e hen; ē me; hw where; i bib; ī kite; îr pierce; ng song; o top; ō rope; ô saw; oi coin; ôr fork; ou cow; sh show; th thin; _th_ those; u sun; ů book; ü moon; ū cute; ûr term; ə about, taken, pencil, apron, helpful; ər letter, dollar, doctor

BIOGRAPHICAL DICTIONARY

The Biographical Dictionary will help you to pronounce the names of and to identify the Key People in this book. The page number tells you where each name first appears in the text.

PRONUNCIATION KEY

a	cap	hw	**wh**ere	oi	c**oi**n	ü	m**oo**n
ā	cake	i	bib	ôr	f**or**k	ū	c**u**te
ä	f**a**ther	ī	kite	ou	c**ow**	ûr	t**er**m
är	c**ar**	îr	p**ier**ce	sh	**sh**ow	ə	**a**bout, tak**e**n, penc**i**l, apr**o**n, helpf**u**l
âr	d**ar**e	ng	so**ng**	th	**th**in	ər	lett**er**, doll**ar**, doct**or**
ch	**ch**ain	o	t**o**p	t͟h	**th**ose		
e	h**e**n	ō	r**o**pe	u	s**u**n		
ē	m**e**	ô	s**aw**	u̇	b**oo**k		

A

Aycock, Charles B. (ā′ kok), 1859–1912 Governor in the early 1900s who improved North Carolina's public schools by building more schools and lengthening the school year. (p. 207)

Ayllón, Lucas Vásquez de (īl yôn′, lü′ käs väs′ kās dā), 1475–1526 Spanish explorer who started the first European settlement in North Carolina in 1526. (p. 117)

B

Baker, John (bā′ kər), 1935– Sheriff of Wake County; former professional football player. (p. 255)

Barker, Penelope (bär′ kər), 1728–1796 Colonist who organized the Edenton "tea party" in 1774 to protest the British tax on tea. (p. 141)

Batts, Nathaniel (batz), 1620?–1679? In 1660, the first Virginian to settle in Carolina. (p. 123)

Berry, Harriet Moorehead (ber′ ē), 1877–1940 State official born in Hillsborough, fought to set up North Carolina's state highway system in 1918. (p. 172)

Betts, Doris (betz), 1932– North Carolina author and journalist. Many of her stories are set in North Carolina. (p. 215)

Blue, Jr., Daniel (blü) 1949– Became the speaker of the House of Representatives of North Carolina in 1991. (p. 305)

Boone, Daniel (bün), 1734–1820 Frontier scout who led pioneers west across the Appalachian Mountains through the Cumberland Gap. (p. 147)

C

Cannon, James W. (kan′ ən), 1852–1921 Founder of the textile mill that produced the first manufactured towels in the South in 1898. (p. 179)

Chavis, John (cha′ vis), 1763–1838 African-American minister who set up schools for both blacks and whites in Raleigh in the early 1800s. (p. 207)

Chesnutt, Charles W. (ches′ nut) 1858–1932 Author from Fayetteville who wrote about African Americans who lived under segregation. (p. 214)

Coffin, Levi (kôf′ ən), 1789–1877 Quaker leader of the Underground Railroad; known as the "President of the Underground Railroad." (p. 153)

Coleman, Warren C. (kōl′ mən), 1849–1903 Born in Cabarrus County, he was the first African American to own a textile mill in North Carolina. (p. 179)

Coltrane, John (kōl′ trān), 1926–1967 Famous jazz saxophonist, born in the town of Hamlet. (p. 215)

D

Dare, Virginia (dâr), 1587–? John White's granddaughter, the first child born in America to English parents, and one of the colonists to disappear from Roanoke. (p. 119)

Davis, Archie (dā′ vis), 1911– North Carolina leader who helped, with Governor Luther Hodges, to develop the Research Triangle Park in 1959; he was born in Winston-Salem. (p. 271)

Day, Thomas (dā), 1800?–1860? African-American furniture maker whose furniture became popular throughout the Southeast in the 1850s. (p. 263)

De Soto, Hernando (də sō′ tō, er nän′ dō), 1500?–1542 Spanish explorer who marched from Florida through North Carolina looking for gold in 1539. He died when he reached the Mississippi River in 1542. (p. 118)

Dole, Elizabeth (dōl), 1936– Born in Salisbury, she was United States secretary of transportation and secretary of labor in the 1980s; became head of the American Red Cross in 1991. (p. 318)

Duke, James Buchanan (dük), 1856–1925 Head of the American Tobacco Company in the 1890s; donated large sums of money to Trinity College, which, in his honor, changed its name to Duke University. (p. 265)

Duke, Washington (dük), 1820–1905 In 1884, started the cigarette company that became the American Tobacco Company; father of James Buchanan Duke. (p. 265)

E

Ervin, Sam, Jr. (ûr′ vin), 1896–1985 Born in Morganton, he was United States senator from North Carolina from 1954 to 1975. He was well-known for his beliefs about the United States Constitution. (p. 318)

G

Greene, Nathanael (grēn), 1742–1786 American commander at the Battle of Guilford Courthouse in 1781 during the American Revolution. (p. 142)

H

Helms, Jesse (helmz), 1921– United States senator from North Carolina, first elected in 1972. (p. 318)

Henry, O. (hen′ rē), 1862–1910 Pen name for William Sydney Porter, who was born near Greensboro and wrote many short stories, often with surprise endings. (p. 214)

Hodges, Luther (hoj′ əz), 1898–1974 North Carolina governor in the 1950s, who helped to develop the Research Triangle Park. (p. 271)

J

Jordan, Michael (jôr′ dən), 1963– Star basketball player who played for the Tarheels, the U.S. Olympic team, and is now with the Chicago Bulls. (p. 224)

K

King, Martin Luther, Jr. (king), 1929–1968 From Georgia, a national civil rights leader during the 1950s and 1960s. (p. 325)

L

Lincoln, Abraham (ling′ kən), 1809–1865 Sixteenth President of the United States (1861–1865); he served during the Civil War and issued the Emancipation Proclamation. (p. 153)

Lowry, Henry Berry (lôr′ ē), 1800s Lumbee leader who fought for the Union cause in the Civil War; he also helped the poor. (p. 231)

M

Merrick, John (mâr′ ik) 1859–1919 One of the founders of the North Carolina Mutual Life Insurance Company. (p. 192)

Moore, Aaron (môr) 1863–1923 One of the founders of the North Carolina Mutual Life Insurance Company. (p. 192)

Murphey, Archibald (mûr′ fē), 1777–1832 State legislator in the early 1800s who favored setting up public schools. (p. 207)

P

Pearson, James Larkin (pir′ sun), 1879–1981 Born in Wilkes County, was poet laureate of North Carolina from 1953 until his death at the age of 101. (p. 215)

Petty, Richard (pet′ ē) 1937– Well-known stock-car racer, lives in Randleman. (p. 225)

Pinchot, Gifford (pin′ shō), 1865–1946 Conservationist who was manager of the forestlands on the Biltmore Estate in the 1890s. With Carl Schenck, he started the first forestry school in the United States in 1898. (p. 293)

R

Raleigh, Walter (rô′ lē), 1552?–1618 Englishman who planned and supplied the English colony at Roanoke in the 1580s. The capital is named after him. (p. 118)

Reed, Conrad (rēd), late 1700s A youngster who discovered gold in Charlotte in 1799. (p. 254)

Reynolds, Richard Joshua (ren′ əldz), 1906–1964 Founder of the R. J. Reynolds Company. (p. 265)

S

Sandburg, Carl (sand′ bûrg), 1878–1967 Poet and historian from the Midwest, who lived in Flat Rock, North Carolina, for the last 20 years of his life. (p. 214)

Sanford, Terry (san′ fərd), 1917– United States senator from North Carolina, first elected in 1986. (p. 318)

Sequoyah (si kwoi′ ə) 1770?–1843 A Cherokee leader who created the Cherokee alphabet and taught his people how to read and write. (p. 148)

Schenck, Carl (shenk), 1868–1955 Manager of the forest on the Biltmore Estate; set up the first forestry school in the United States, near Mount Pisgah in 1898. (p. 293)

Schenck, Michael (shenk) 1771–1849 Built first textile mill in North Carolina in 1813. (p. 178)

Scruggs, Earl (skrugz), 1924– Born in Flint Hill, well-known bluegrass music star. (p. 215)

Sharp, Susie (shärp), 1907– Born in Rocky Mount, first woman judge in North Carolina; first woman elected to North Carolina Supreme Court in 1962 and first woman chief justice in 1974. (p. 307)

Spaulding, Charles C. (spôl′ ding), 1874–1952 African-American business leader who was manager of North Carolina Mutual Life Insurance Company. (p. 192)

V

Vanderbilt, George (van′ dər bilt), 1862–1914 A millionaire who built the Biltmore Estate in the 1890s. (p. 289)

Verrazano, Giovanni da (ver ə zän′ ō, jō vän′ nē dā), 1485?–1528 Italian explorer for France who explored the area around the Cape Fear River and Pamlico Sound in 1524. (p. 117)

W

Watson, Arthel "Doc" (wät′ sən) 1923– World-famous country music star, born in Deep Gap. (p. 215)

White, John (hwīt), 1500s Leader of the second Roanoke colony. (p. 119)

Wolfe, Thomas (wůlf), 1900–1938 Novelist from Asheville. (p. 214)

a cap; ā cake; ä father; är car; âr dare; ch chain; e hen; ē me; hw where; i bib; ī kite; îr pierce; ng song; o top; ō rope; ô saw; oi coin; ôr fork; ou cow; sh show; th thin; th̲ those; u sun; ů book; ü moon; ū cute; ûr term; ə about, taken, pencil, apron, helpful; ər letter, dollar, doctor

GLOSSARY

This Glossary will help you to pronounce and understand the meanings of the Key Vocabulary in this book. The page number at the end of the definition tells where the word or term first appears.

PRONUNCIATION KEY

a	cap	hw	**wh**ere	oi	c**oi**n	ü	m**oo**n
ā	cake	i	bib	ôr	f**or**k	ū	c**u**te
ä	f**a**ther	ī	k**i**te	ou	c**ow**	ûr	t**er**m
är	c**ar**	îr	p**ier**ce	sh	**sh**ow	ə	about, tak**e**n, pencil, apr**o**n, helpf**u**l
âr	d**ar**e	ng	so**ng**	th	**th**in		
ch	**ch**ain	o	top	<u>th</u>	**th**ose		
e	h**e**n	ō	r**o**pe	u	s**u**n	ər	lett**er**, doll**ar**, doct**or**
ē	m**e**	ô	s**aw**	u̇	b**oo**k		

A

acid rain (as′ id rān) Rain, sleet, or other water vapor that mixes with gases given off by burning coal, gas, and oil. Acid rain pollutes waterways and kills plants. (p. 295)

agriculture (ag′ ri kul chər) Farming, or the business of raising crops and farm animals. (p. 163)

almanac (ôl′ mə nak) A reference book that is published every year and has up-to-date facts on many subjects. (p. 211)

amateur team (am′ ə chər tēm) Athletes who play in sports mainly for fun. (p. 225)

American Revolution (ə mer′ i kən rev′ ə lü′ shən) The war fought between the 13 colonies and Great Britain from 1775 to 1783. It led to the forming of the United States. (p. 141)

ancestor (an′ ses tər) A relative who lived long before you. (p. 131)

archaeologist (är kē ol′ ə jist) A scientist who digs up artifacts and uses them to help piece together a picture of the past. (p. 101)

art (ärt) Any creative activity, such as painting, writing, or music. (p. 213)

artifact (är′ tə fakt) Something made by people long ago that often provides clues to past ways of life. (p. 101)

atlas (at′ ləs) A reference book that contains many maps. (p. 211)

auction (ôk′ shən) A public sale at which goods are sold to the highest bidder. (p. 233)

automate (ô′ tə māt) To run machines by other machines, instead of by people. (p. 181)

B

backcountry (bak′ kun trē) Name used by the colonists for the Piedmont Region, which is "in back of" the Coastal Plain. (p. 131)

barrier island (bar′ e ər ī′ lənd) A string of islands that separates the mainland from the ocean, made up mostly of sand. (p. 54)

bartering (bär′ tər ing) A system of trading goods without using money. (p. 148)

bias (bi′ əs) The favoring of one view or opinion over another. (p. 328)

bill (bil) A suggested law. (p. 305)

board of commissioners (bôrd əv kə mish′ ən rz) In North Carolina, the legislative and executive branch of the county government. (p. 312)

boycott (boi′ kot) To refuse to buy, sell, or use certain goods or services. (p. 324)

budget (buj′ it) A plan for spending money. (p. 304)

byline (bī′ līn) The line at the beginning of a newspaper article that tells who wrote it. (p. 308)

C

call number (kôl num′ bər) The number used in a library to classify a book so that it can be located. (p. 211)

candidate (kan′ di dāt) A person who is running for office. (p. 317)

cape (kāp) A point of land that stretches into a large body of water. (p. 57)

capital resources (kap′ i təl rē sôr səz) The tools and machines used to produce goods and services. (p. 264)

cardinal directions (kar də nəl di rek′ shənz) The four main directions: north, east, south, and west. (p. 12)

cash crop (kash krop) A crop that is grown for sale. (p. 136)

cause (kôz) Something that makes something else happen. (p. 182)

census (sen′ səs) An official count of the population of an area or country. (p. 246)

circle graph (sër′ kəl graf) A graph that uses a circle to show how something can be divided into parts. (p. 205)

citizen (sit′ ə zən) A member of a country by birth or by law. (p. 304)

city council (sit′ ē koun′ səl) The legislative and executive body of a city. (p. 313)

city council-manager (sit′ ē koun′ səl man′ i jər) A city government in which an elected city council hires a manager to run the city and to appoint its officials. (p. 313)

civil rights (siv′ əl rīts) The rights of all people to be treated equally under the law. (p. 156)

Civil Rights Act (siv′ əl rīts akt) A law passed in 1964 that made it unlawful for businesses to treat people differently because of their race, sex, or religion. (p. 325)

Civil War (siv′ əl wôr) The war fought between the Confederacy and the Union, from 1861 to 1865. (p. 154)

climate (klī′ mit) The type of weather in an area over a long period of time. (p. 41)

colony (kol′ ə nē) A place that is ruled by another country. (p. 116)

commercial fishing (kə mur′ shəl fish′ ing) The business of catching fish. (p. 243)

communication (kə mū ni kā′ shən) The exchange of information. (p. 36)

compass rose (kum′ pəs rōz) A small drawing on a map that shows directions. (p. 12)

conclusion (kən klü′ zhən) A final opinion about information. (p. 234)

Confederacy (kən fed′ ər ə sē) The 11 states that broke away from the United States in 1861 and joined to fight the Union. (p. 153)

Congress (kong′ gris) The legislative branch of the United States government. (p. 316)

conservation (kon′ sər vā shən) The protection of natural resources. (p. 51)

Constitution (kon sti tü′ shən) A plan of government. (p. 142)

continent (kon′ tə nənt) A very large body of land. (p. 10)

contour interval (kon tůr in′ tər vəl) The difference in elevation between two contour lines. (p. 290)

contour line (kon′ tůr līn) A line on a contour map that connects areas that have the same elevation. (p. 290)

contour map (kon′ tůr map) A map that shows the shape of the earth's surface. (p. 290)

contract grower (kon′ trakt grō′ ər) A farmer who signs an agreement to raise crops or animals. (p. 242)

corduroy road (kôr′ də roi rōd) A type of road built by placing logs side by side. (p. 171)

council (koun′ səl) A group that governs or gives advice to a community. (p. 110)

county (koun′ tē) One of the sections into which a state is divided. (p. 24)

county seat (koun′ tē sēt) The city or town that serves as a county's center of government. (p. 312)

craftsworker (krafts′ wûr kər) A person who makes products that require a special skill. (p. 137)

culture (kul′ chər) The way of life of a group of people. (p. 28)

current (kur′ ənt) Part of a body of water flowing in the same path, like a river flowing in an ocean. (p. 57)

custom (kus′ təm) The special way a group of people does something. (p. 28)

D

dam (dam) A wall built across a river to hold back the flowing water. (p. 50)

dateline (dāt′ līn) The line at the beginning of a newspaper article that tells when and where the article was written. (p. 308)

decision (di sizh′ ən) A choice. (p. 46)

Declaration of Independence (dek lə rā′ shən əv in di pen′ dəns) A statement made by the 13 colonies in 1776 that explained why they wanted to be independent, or free, of Great Britain. (p. 142)

demand (di mand′) The desire for a product along with the willingness to buy it. (p. 166)

democracy (di mok′ rə sē) A government that is run by the people it governs. (p. 304)

dictionary (dik′ shə ner ē) A reference book that has the pronunciations and definitions of words listed in alphabetical order. (p. 211)

dune (dün) A large pile of sand made by action of the wind and the ocean. (p. 55)

E

economy (i kon′ ə mē) The way in which resources are used to meet people's needs and wants. (p. 34)

editorial (ed i tôr′ ē əl) A newspaper article in which an editor gives an opinion about something. (p. 308)

effect (i fekt′) What happens as a result of something else. (p. 182)

elect (i lekt′) To choose someone for office by voting. (p. 304)

elevation (el ə vā′ shən) The height of a place above sea level. (p. 42)

Emancipation Proclamation (i man sə pā′ shən prok lə mā′ shən) The announcement by President Lincoln in 1863 that said that enslaved people in the Confederacy were free. (p. 154)

encyclopedia (en sī klə pē′ dē ə) A reference book or set of books that has information on many different kinds of subjects. (p. 210)

environment (en vī′ rən mənt) The surroundings in which people, plants, and animals live. (p. 9)

equator (i kwā′ tər) An imaginary line that lies midway between the North Pole and the South Pole. (p. 11)

erosion (i rō′ zhən) The wearing away of sand, rock, and soil by water, wind, or ice. (p. 57)

executive branch (eg zek′ yə tiv branch) The part of government that carries out the laws. (p. 304)

export (eks′ pôrt) Something that is sold or traded to another country. (p. 123)

F

fact (fakt) A statement that can be proved true. (p. 144)

Fall Line (fôl līn) The eastern edge of the Piedmont, at which the streams flowing east across the Piedmont plateau fall onto the lower Coastal Plain. (p. 83)

feature article (fē′ chər är′ ti kəl) An article in a newspaper that reports in detail on a person, subject, or event. (p. 308)

fertile (fûr′ təl) Good for growing crops. (p. 49)

festival (fes′ tə vəl) A celebration that takes place regularly, usually every year. (p. 232)

finished goods (fin′ isht gůdz) Products that are made from raw materials. (p. 263)

folk art (fōk ärt) A traditional form of art or craft, such as quilting or pottery making, of a community. (p. 213)

food processing (füd pros′ es ing) The turning of raw foods into different kinds of products, such as peanuts into peanut butter. (p. 241)

forestry (fôr′ ə strē) The science of managing, developing, and protecting forests. (p. 293)

free enterprise (frē en′ tər prīz) A type of economy in which people are free to own and run businesses. (p. 36)

a cap; ā cake; ä father; är car; âr dare; ch chain; e hen; ē me; hw where; i bib; ī kite; îr pierce; ng song; o top; ō rope; ô saw; oi coin; ôr fork; ou cow; sh show; th thin; th those; u sun; ů book; ü moon; ū cute; ûr term; ə about, taken, pencil, apron, helpful; ər letter, dollar, doctor

frontier (frun tîr′) The word used by colonists to describe the edge of settlement. (p. 146)

G

gap (gap) A natural opening between mountain peaks. (p. 147)

General Assembly (jen′ rəl ə sem′ blē) The state legislature of North Carolina, which is the part of the government that makes the state's laws. (p. 305)

geography (jē og′ rə fē) The study of the earth's land, water, plants, animals, and people. (p. 8)

global grid (glō′ bəl grid) A set of crisscrossing lines, made up of lines of latitude and lines of longitude, on a map or globe. (p. 32)

gorge (gôrj) A deep passage cut into a rock, usually by a river. (p. 89)

governor (guv′ ər nər) The head of the executive branch of our state's government or the head of a colony. (p. 304)

graph (graf) A diagram that allows you to compare facts and figures. (p. 204)

grid map (grid map) A map on which two sets of lines cross each other to form a grid that is used to locate places on the map. (p. 15)

growing season (grō′ ing se′ zən) The time of the year during which it is warm enough for crops to grow. (p. 44)

H

headline (hed′ līn) The lines at the top of a newspaper article that are its title. (p. 308)

hemisphere (hem′ i sfir) A half of a sphere or globe. (p. 10)

high tech (hī tek) Work that involves the use of advanced scientific learning or equipment. (p. 272)

history (his′ tə rē) The story of the past. (p. 120)

House of Representatives (hous əv rep ri zen′ tə tivz) The part of Congress, along with the Senate, that makes up the legislative branch of our national government. (p. 316)

hurricane (hur′ i kān′) A violent storm with high winds and heavy rains. (p. 57)

hydroelectric (hī drō i lek′ trik) Electricity formed by using the force of falling water. (p. 186)

I

immigrant (im′ i grənt) A person who moves to a new country to live. (p. 130)

import (im′ pôrt) A good that is brought in from another country for sale or trade. (p. 123)

indentured servant (in den′ chərd sûr′ vənt) A person who agreed to work for someone for a certain number of years in exchange for passage to the colonies and food, clothing, and housing. (p. 135)

industry (in′ də strē) All the businesses that produce the same kind of goods or service for sale. (p. 178)

inlet (in′ let) A narrow body of water between two islands. (p. 55)

insurance (in shur′ əns) Protection that people buy to make sure that they will have money in case of an accident or illness. (p. 191)

integration (in ti grā′ shən) Making public places open to all people. (p. 324)

interdependence (in tər di pen′ dəns) The dependence of people, regions, or countries on others to meet their needs and wants. (p. 36)

intermediate directions (in tər mē′ dē it di rek′ shənz) The directions that lie halfway between two cardinal directions. (p. 12)

interstate highway (in′ tər stāt hī′ wā) A wide road or highway that runs between two or more states. (p. 175)

J

Jim Crow laws (jim crō lôz) Laws passed in the southern states in the late 1800s requiring that blacks and whites be segregated in public places. (p. 155)

judicial branch (jü dish′ əl branch) The part of government made up of courts. (p. 306)

L

labor (lā′ bər) Workers; also work. (p. 179)

land use map (land ūs map) A map that shows the different ways in which people in an area use the land. (p. 268)

landfill (land′ fil) A place where trash is buried. (p. 333)

landform (land′ fôrm) One of the shapes that makes up the earth's surface. (p. 66)

latitude (lat′ i tüd) An imaginary line on a map that measures distance in degrees north or south of the equator. (p. 30)

legislative branch (lej′ is lā tiv branch) The lawmaking part of government. (p. 305)

line graph (līn graf) A type of graph that uses a line to show changes that took place over a period of time. (p. 204)

livestock (līv′ stok) Farm animals raised for profit, such as hogs or turkeys. (p. 242)

longitude (lon′ ji tüd) An imaginary line on a map that measures distance in degrees east or west of the prime meridian. (p. 31)

lowlands (lō′ landz) Lands with an elevation at or slightly above sea level. (p. 72)

M

manufacturing (man yə fak′ chər ing) The making of many goods by machine. (p. 177)

map key (map kē) The box or area on a map that explains the meaning of the symbols used on the map. (p. 13)

marsh (märsh) An area of low, wet land that is covered mostly with tall grasses. (p. 73)

mayor (mā′ ər) The leading official in the executive branch of a city government. (p. 313)

meridian (mə rid′ ē ən) A line of longitude. (p. 31)

metropolitan area (met rə pol′ i tən âr′ ē ə) A large city or group of cities and their nearby suburbs. (p. 185)

migrant worker (mi′ grənt wûr′ kər) A farm worker who moves from place to place in search of work. (p. 232)

migrate (mī′ grāt) To move from one place to another. (p. 104)

mileage chart (mī′ lij chärt) A table that shows the distances between places. (p. 176)

mineral (min′ ər əl) A natural substance found in the earth. (p. 50)

mixed farming (mikst fär′ ming) A farm on which several cash crops are grown. (p. 241)

N

national government (nash′ ə nəl guv′ ərn mənt) A country's central government. (p. 315)

natural resource (nach′ ər əl rē′ sôrs) Something found in nature that is useful to people. (p. 48)

naval stores (nā′ vəl stôrz) Products made from the sap of pine trees. (p. 136)

news article (nüz är′ ti kəl) A newspaper article that reports recent events. (p. 308)

nonrenewable resource (non ri nü′ ə bəl rē′ sôrs) Something found in nature that is useful and that cannot be replaced. (p. 51)

O

opinion (ə pin′ yən) A belief or feeling that a person has about something. (p. 144)

orchard (ôr′ chərd) Land on which fruit trees are grown. (p. 287)

outline (out′ l īn) A written plan that organizes information about a subject. (p. 86)

P

parallel (par′ ə lel) A line of latitude. (p. 30)

peak (pēk) Pointed top of a mountain. (p. 81)

peninsula (pə nin′ sə lə) A body of land that is almost entirely surrounded by water. (p. 73)

pioneers (pī ə nîr′z) Those who lead the way into an area unknown to them. (p. 146)

plain (plān) A large area of flat or almost flat land. (p. 66)

plank road (plangk rōd) A road made of long, flat pieces of wood placed over a thick layer of wood and covered with dirt. (p. 171)

plantation (plan tā′ shən) A large farm on which cash crops are grown. (p. 135)

plateau (pla tō′) A large area of land that is raised above the surrounding country. (p. 66)

point of view (point əv vū) The way in which a person looks at or thinks about something. (p. 328)

a cap; ā cake; ä father; är car; âr dare; ch chain; e hen; ē me; hw where; i bib; ī kite; îr pierce; ng song; o top; ō rope; ô saw; oi coin; ôr fork; ou cow; sh show; th thin; th those; u sun; ů book; ü moon; ū cute; ûr term; ə about, taken, pencil, apron, helpful; ər letter, dollar, doctor

political party (pə lit′ i kəl pär′ tē) A group of citizens who share ideas about government and public issues. (p. 317)

pollution (pə lü′ shən) The dirtying of the air, land, and water. (p. 51)

population (pop yə lā′ shən) The total number of people living in a place. (p. 84)

population density (pop yə lā′ shən den′ si tē) The number of people living in a square mile or square kilometer of an area. (p. 185)

population density map (pop yə lā′ shən den′ si tē map) A map that shows the number of people living in a square mile or a square kilometer. (p. 268)

precipitation (pri sip i tā′ shən) Any form of water that falls to the earth, such as rain or snow. (p. 42)

prime meridian (prīm mə rid′ ē ən) The imaginary line from which other meridians are measured. (p. 31)

private college (prī′ vit kol′ ij) A privately run school of higher education that students must pay to attend. (p. 209)

productive (prə duk′ tiv) Able to produce abundantly; fertile. (p. 165)

product map (prod′ ukt map) A map that shows the kinds of things that are made or grown in an area. (p. 17)

professional team (prə fesh′ ə nəl tēm) Athletes who have special training and earn money from sports. (p. 224)

profile (prō′ fīl) A diagram that shows a side view of a part of the earth. (p. 71)

public school (pub′ lik skül) An elementary or high school that is supported by the local government. (p. 207)

pulpwood (pulp′ wu̇d) The raw material from which paper is made. (p. 242)

Q

quarry (kwôr′ ē) A place where stone is cut or blasted out of the ground. (p. 288)

R

rain shadow (rān shad′ ō) An area that gets little rain because it is protected from rain-bearing winds. (p. 45)

range (rānj) A row of mountains. (p. 89)

rapids (rap′ idz) A place at which water in a stream or river flows quickly and roughly. (p. 83)

raw material (rô mə tîr′ ē əl) A natural resource that has not been changed or prepared in any way. (p. 178)

recreation (rek rē ā′ shən) The way in which people relax and enjoy themselves. (p. 222)

recycling (rē sī′ kling) Separating trash so that it can be turned into new products. (p. 334)

reference book (ref′ ər əns bu̇k) A book, such as an encyclopedia or an atlas, that contains facts about many different subjects. (p. 210)

region (re′ jən) An area with common features that set it apart from other areas. (p. 9)

relief (ri lēf′) Variation in elevation. (p. 291)

religion (ri lij′ ən) The way that people worship the God or gods in which they believe. (p. 104)

renewable resource (ri nü′ ə bəl rē′ sôrs) Something found in nature that is useful to people and that renews itself. (p. 51)

research (ri sûrch′) To search for new ideas or new ways of doing things. (p. 270)

reservation (rez ər vā′ shən) Land set aside for Native Americans to live on. (p. 150)

retire (rē tīr′) To stop working, usually later in life after working many years. (p. 190)

road map (rōd map) A map that shows cities and towns and the roads that connect them. (p. 174)

rural (ru̇r′ əl) Area relating to country areas with few houses or people. (p. 201)

S

scale (skāl) The relationship between distances shown on a map and the actual distances on the earth. (p. 14)

scarce (skârs) A smaller amount of something than is needed or wanted. (p. 255)

segregate (seg′ ri gā′t) To separate groups of people, such as blacks and whites, in public places. (p. 155)

self-sufficient (self′ sə fish′ ənt) Able to provide for one's own needs. (p. 148)

Senate (sen′ it) A part of Congress, along with the House of Representatives, that makes up the legislative branch of our national government. (p. 316)

service industries (sûr′ vis in′ də strēz) Businesses in which workers do useful things that people need and will pay for. (p. 189)

sharecropping (shâr′ krop ing) A way of farming in which farmers rent farmland and pay with part of the crop they grow. (p. 165)

sheriff (sher′ if) The chief law enforcement officer of a county. (p. 312)

slavery (slā′ və rē) The practice of owning people and forcing them to work without pay. (p. 134)

smog (smog) A mixture of smoke and fog. (p. 295)

sound (sound) A body of water between the mainland and an island. (p. 55)

specialize (spesh′ ə līz) To produce a particular crop or product. (p. 338)

spectator (spek′ tā tər) A person who watches an event. (p. 224)

suburban (səb ûr′ bən) Communities just outside a city. (p. 201)

suffrage (suf′ rij) The right to vote. (p. 326)

Sunbelt (sun′ belt) Part of the United States in which the weather is mild year-round. (p. 29)

surplus (sûr′ plus) An amount greater than what is used or needed. (p. 123)

swamp (swomp) An area of low, wet land that is covered with tall grasses, trees, and shrubs. (p. 74)

symbol (sim′ bəl) Something that stands for something else. (p. 13)

synthetic (sin thet′ ik) Made in laboratories from chemicals. (p. 180)

T

tax (taks) Money paid by people to support their government. (p. 141)

technology (tek nol′ ə jē) The use of scientific knowledge for practical purposes. (p. 164)

temperature (tem′ pər ə chər) The measure of how hot or cold something is. (p. 42)

temple (tem′ pəl) A place of worship. (p. 104)

textile (teks′ tīl) Cloth or other materials made by knitting or weaving. (p. 178)

tide (tīd) The regular rise and fall of the ocean and the bodies of water connected to it. (p. 73)

time line (tīm līn) A diagram that shows when events took place. (p. 120)

tourism (tůr′ iz əm) The business of providing services for people on vacation. (p. 190)

trade (trād) The business of buying, selling, and exchanging goods. (p. 37)

tradition (trə dish′ ən) A custom or belief that has been handed down from the past. (p. 59)

Trail of Tears (trāl əv tîrz) The forced journey made by the Cherokee to what is now Oklahoma. (p. 149)

transportation (trans pər tā′ shən) The way in which goods and people are moved from one place to another. (p. 36)

transportation map (trans pər tā′ shən map) A map that shows different ways to travel from one place to another. (p. 16)

treaty (trē′ tē) A written agreement between countries. (p. 148)

U

Underground Railroad (un′ dər ground rāl′ rōd) The network of hiding places that were used by African Americans escaping from slavery. (p. 153)

Union (ūn′ yən) 23 states that stayed in the United States and fought against the Confederacy in the Civil War. (p. 153)

urban (ûr′ bən) Area made by a city and the communities surrounding it. (p. 201)

a cap; ā cake; ä father; är car; âr dare; ch chain; e hen; ē me; hw where; i bib; ī kite; îr pierce; ng song; o top; ō rope; ô saw; oi coin; ôr fork; ou cow; sh show; th thin; th̲ those; u sun; ů book; ü moon; ū cute; ûr term; ə about, taken, pencil, apron, helpful; ər letter, dollar, doctor

INDEX

CREDITS

MAPS: R.R. Donnelly and Sons Company Cartographic Services
CHARTS AND GRAPHS: Tom Cardamone Associates, Inc.
ILLUSTRATION AND CREDITS: Cheryl Arnemann: pp. 112–115. **Alex Bloch:** pp. 157–159. **Gary Ciccarelli:** p. 24, Traditions Medallion. **Len Ebert:** pp. 98–99, 258, 260–261. **Allan Eitzen:** p. 167. **Malcolm Farley:** pp. 59–62. **Joe Forte:** pp. 376–377. **Linda Graver:** pp. 218–221. **Meryl Henderson:** pp. 182, 210, 234, 348. **Dave Joly:** pp. 332–335, 370–372. **James McConnell:** pp. 77–79. **Stephen Marchesi:** pp. 236–238. **Monks of New Skete:** p. 68. **Ann Neumann:** pp. 4–5, 372–373, 374–375. **Hima Pamoedjo:** pp. 49, 86. **Margaret Sanfilippo:** p. 95. **Joel Synder:** pp. 104–105, 133. **Arvis Stewart:** pp. 107–111. **Gary Torrisi:** pp. 18–19, 96–97. **Carolyn Vibbert:** pp. 108, 331. **Sarah Woodward:** pp. 45, 46. **Lane Yerkes:** p. 216.

PHOTOGRAPHY CREDITS
All photographs are by Macmillan/McGraw-Hill School Division (MMSD) except as indicated below.
Table of Contents: iii-ix: Jim Stratford for MMSD. **Introduction:** 8: Mike Booher. 10: David Phillips. **Chapter 1:** 20: Jim Stratford for MMSD. 22, 23: Chip Henderson for MMSD. 25: M.E. Warren/Photo Researchers. 28: Scott Harvey for MMSD. 29: l. Martin Fox/Picturesque; r. Will McIntyre/Photo Researchers. 35: David Phillips. 36: Chip Henderson. 37: Charles Gupton for MMSD. 38: Drew C. Wilson For MMSD. **Chapter 2:** 40: Jim Stratford for MMSD. 44: l. Howard Walker for MMSD; m. Al Stephenson/Woodfin Camp & Assoc.; r. Tim Barnwell/Picturesque. 49: Wayne Lankinen/DRK. 51: Chip Henderson. 52: Art Gentile, KPC/MMSD. 56: l. Michael Dick/Animals Animals; r. Jack Dermid; l. insert, Terry Livington/Picturesque. 57: t.l. Keith Longiotti/Picturesque; t.r. Jack Dermid; m. Steve Murray/Picturesque; b. Billy E. Barnes. 59: t. Smithsonian Institution, Photo # A4441; b. Courtesy of Wright State University. 60, 62: Courtesy of Wright State University. **Chapter 3:** 64: Jim Stratford for MMSD. 67: t. Jack Dermid; b. Stephen J. Krasemann/DRK. 69: l Sandra Fox for MMSD; r. Steve Murray/Picturesque. 73: Stephen J. Krasemann/DRK. 74: l. Patti Murray/Animals Animals; r. Jack Dermid. 75: t.l. J.L. Lepore/Photo Researchers; t.r. Michael Male/Photo Researchers; b.l. Mike & Carol Warner/Comstock; b.r. Jack K. Clark/Comstock. 76: r. Jonathan Wallen; l. Mark E. Barnett. 81: 2 Mark Wagoner/ Picturesque. 82–83: t. Frederica Georgia/Photo Researchers; l. Courtesy of Hiddenite Gem Co./Scott Harvey for MMSD. 83: l. Randy Trine/DRK; r. Mike Booher. 84–85: b. Donald Johnson/The Stock Market; t. insert, Nancy Pierce for MMSD. 89: Susan McCartney/Photo Researchers. 90–91: Tim Barnwell. 92: l. Lowell Georgia/Photo Researchers; r. Geoff Gilbert/Photo Researchers. **Chapter 4:** 100: Jim Stratford for MMSD. 102: t. Research Laboratories of Anthropology, University of North Carolina, Chapel Hill; b. Field Museum of Natural History. 105: Jonathan Wallen. 118: Mike Booher. 119: t., b. Courtesy of The Lost Colony. 124: Culver Pictures. 125: l. New York Public Library; r. Courtesy of NCDA & H (North Carolina Division of Archives and History). 126: Courtesy of Old Salem. **Chapter 5:** 128: Jim Stratford for MMSD. 130–131: b. Courtesy of NCDA & H. 131: t. Clyde H. Smith/Peter Arnold. 132–133: inset, Will & Demi McIntyre/Photo Researchers. 132: Jonathan Wallen. 136: Library of Congress. 137: l. Culver Pictures; r. Courtesy of NCC (North Carolina Collection, University of North Carolina, Chapel Hill.). 139: Tom McCarthy/The Picture Cube. 141: Edenton Historical Commission, Cupola House/Glenn Tucker of MMSD. 143: Culver Pictures. 148: l., r. Courtesy of the American Museum of Natural History. 150: Woolaroc Museum, Bartlesville, OK. 151: Jim Stratford for MMSD. 153: l. Courtesy of NCDA & H.; m., r. Culver Pictures. 154–155: Courtesy of NCDA & H. 156: The Bettmann Archive. 157, 158: Courtesy of NCDA & H. 159: t. Glenn Tucker for MMSD; b. Jim Stratford for MMSD. 160: Jim Stratford for MMSD. **Chapter 6:** 162: Jim Stratford for MMSD. 164: l. NCDA & H; r. Mike Booher. 165: Courtesy of NCC. 166–167: Steve Dunwell/The Image Bank. 168: Sissie Brimburg/Woodfin Camp & Assoc. 171: l. Courtesy of NCDA & H; r. Library of Congress. 173: Roger Ball/Picturesque. 178–179: Courtesy of NCC. 180: l. Abe Rezny/The Image Works; r. Chip Henderson/Picturesque. 181: t. Abe Rezny/The Image Works. 186: Audrey Gibson. 188: t., insert, Courtesy of Winston-Salem School of the Arts. 190: l. Roger Ball/Picturesque; m. Billy E. Barnes. 190–191: Tim Barnwell. 191: l. inset, Mark E. Gibson; r. inset, Eric N. Blevins. 192: Spike Nannarello/Shooting Star. **Chapter 7:** 198: Jim Stratford for MMSD. 200: Will & Demi McIntyre/Picturesque. 201: l. Mike Booher; r. Eric N. Blevins. 202: Mike Booher. 203: Jim Stratford for MMSD. 207: Culver Pictures. 208: l. Will & Demi McIntyre/Picturesque. 208–209: r. Billy E. Barnes. 213. t.l. Bill Weems/Woodfin Camp & Assoc.; t.r. Arthur Tress/Photo Researchers; b. inset, Bill Ballenberg/Ross Ehlert. 214: t. The Bettmann Archive; m.t. Courtesy of Cleveland Public Library; m.b. The Bettman Archive; b. Laura Alderson. 215: t., m. The Bettman Archive; b. Courtesy of Sugar Hill Records. 217: Chip Henderson/Picturesque. 223: t. Henderson/Muir/Picturesque; l. inset, Steve Murray/Picturesque; r. inset, Will & Demi McIntyre/Picturesque. 224: l. Mitchell B. Reibel/Sportschrome East/West; r. Martin Fox. 225: l. Wide World of Photos; m. Melanie Carr/Picturesque; r. Crisp Images/Sportschrome East/West. 226: t. Gary M. Jensen/Picturesque; b. Charles Gupton/Picturesque. **Chapter 8:** 228: Jim Stratford for MMSD. 230: Henderson/Muir/Picturesque. 231: Courtesy of Lumbee Regional Development Assn. 232: Will McIntyre/Photo Researchers. 233: l. Courtesy of N.C. Maritme Museum; r. Ira Block/The Image Bank. 236, 239: Scott Taylor for MMSD. 241: Jim Stratford for MMSD. 242: Mark E. Gibson. 243: Karen Kasmanski/Woodfin Camp & Assoc. 244: Scott Taylor for MMSD. 248: l. Courtey N.C. Maritime Museum; r. Mark E. Gibson. 249: t. Mark E. Gibson; b. Fridmar Damm/Leo de Wys. 250: Joel Gordon/DPI. **Chapter 9:** 252: Jim Stratford for MMSD. 255: l. Roger Ball/Picturesque; r. Chip Henderson/Picturesque. 256: t. Mark Wagoner; b. Jonathan Wallen. 257: l. Tony Freeman/PhotoEdit; r. Steve Murray/The Stock Market. 258: t. Scott Harvey for MMSD; b. Jim Stratford for MMSD. 259: Jim Stratford for MMSD. 260: t. Scott Harvey for MMSD; b. Courtesy Sarah Parrish. 260–261: m. Mark Weinke, Greg Plachta/North Carolina Quilt Project. 261: t.r. Paul Arnold, Craftsman/Folk Art Center, Ashville, NC. 263: North Carolina Museum of History. 264: Chip Henderson/Picturesque. 265: l., r. Courtesy of NCDA & H. 267: Courtesy, Ed Spence. 266: Charles Gupton/The Stock Market. 272: t., b. Billy E. Barnes; m. Courtesy of Glaxo, Inc. 273: t. Charles Gupton/Picturesque; b. inset, Courtesy of IBM. 274: Courtesy of Burroughs-Wellcome. **Chapter 10:** 276: Jim Stratford for MMSD. 278: Joyce Ravid. 279: t. William Bake/Picturesque. 279: b. Billy E. Barnes. 280: Steve Murray/Picturesque; r. Edward Bower/The Image Bank; l. Comstock. 281: Courtesy of L.C. Coonse. 282–285: boarder, Scott Harvey for MMSD. 282: Hugh Morton/Grandfather Mountain, Inc. 283: t. DPI; b. Hugh Morton/Grandfather Mountain, Inc. 284: Kay Chernush/The Image Bank. 285: t. Chip Henderson for MMSD; b. Hugh Morton/Grandfather Mountain, Inc. 287: t. David Young-Wolff/PhotoEdit; b. Myrleen Ferguson/PhotoEdit. 288: t. Steve Murray/Picturesque; b.r. insert, Mike Booher; b.l. Roger Ball/Picturesque. 289: Clive G. House/Uniphoto. 293: Gabe Palmer/The Stock Market. 294: t.l. Kelly Culpepper/Transparencies; t.r. William Bake/Picturesque; t.r. inset, Johnny Johnson/ Animals Animals. 295: t.r. insert; Mark E. Gipson/The Stock Market; t.l. insert; Mark E. Gipson/The Stock Market. 296: Tim Barnwell/Picturesque. **Unit 4:** 300: t.l. L. West/Photo Researchers; t.r. John Dommers/Photo Researchers; m.l. MMSD; b.r. R.F. Head/Earth Scenes. 301: t. Joe B. Blossom/Photo Researchers; m. Courtesy of Office of the Governor; b. Narinder Sall. **Chapter 11:** 302: Jim Stratford for MMSD. 307: Courtesy of NCDA & H. 309: AP/Wide World Photos. 313: Billy E. Barnes. 314: t. Billy E. Barnes; m. Kelly Culpepper/Transparencies; b. Eric N. Blevins. 317: Billy E. Barnes. 318: l. Wide World Photos; r. Courtesy of the Office of Senator Helms. 318–319: t. Comstock. 319: t.r. inset, The Bettmann Archive; b. inset, R. Perry/SYGMA. 320: Richard Haynes. **Chapter 12:** 322: Jim Stratford for MMSD. 324: The Bettman Archive. 325: b.l. Francis Miller/life Magazine, Time Warner; b.r. Billy E. Barnes. 326–327: Steve Murray/Picturesque; t.l. The Bettman Archive. 327: t.l. inset, Joe Viesti; t.r. Gabe Palmer/The Stock Market. 332: t. Dick Meseroll/Picturesque; m., b. Mike Booher. 333: b. Pam Bracker/Transparencies; b.l. inset, Frank Pedrick/The Image Works. 334: t. Bill Bachmann/Picturesque; b. Joe Sohm/Uniphoto. 335: Tim O'Dell/Transparencies. 336: l., r. Billy E. Barnes. 339: t. Steve Murray/Picturesque; b.l., b.r. Jane Faircloth/Transparencies. 340: t. Jane Faircloth/Transparencies; b. Billy E. Barnes. 341: l. Courtesy of North Carolina Center for International Understanding; r. Steve Murray/Picturesque. **Epilogue:** 362: t.l. National Portrait Gallery/Smithsonian Institution; t.r. The National Portrait Gallery/Smithsonian Institution, Gift of the James Polk Memorial Assn. of Nashville & the James Polk Auxiliary of Columbia, TN; b.l. The National Portrait Gallery/Smithsonian Institution; b.r. Kenneth D. Holt. 363: Billy E. Barnes. 374: t. Nancy Pierce for MMSD; m. Henderson/Muir Picturesque; m.r. Mike Booher; b. Jane Faircloth/Transparencies. 375: t.l. Carol Shanks/Transparencies; t.r. Charles Gupton/Picturesque; b.l. Courtesy of the James Polk Memorial; b.r. Mike Booher. 379: t.l. ABC News; t.r. Frank Carrol/NBC; m.l. AP/Wide World Photos; m.r. Courtesy of Dr. Billy E. Taylor; b.l. Jaakko Avikainen/Woodfin Camp & Assoc.; b.r. Permission of Creators Syndicate & Doug Marlette. 380: t.l. AP/Wide World Photos; t.r. Courtesy of Gene Warren, Pembroke State University; m.l. Bernard Gotfryd/Woodfin Camp & Assoc.; m.r. AP/Wide World Photos; b.l. M. Grecco/Stock Boston; b.r. Eddie Adams/SYGMA. 381: t.l. Courtesy of Amanda Crowe; t.r. Arthur Grace/SYGMA; m.l. AP/Wide World Photos; m.r. The Bettman Archive; b.r. NFL Photos. 382: t.l. AP Photocolor; t.r. Kay Chernush/NYT Pictures; m.l. Chuck Stewart; m.r. CBS; b.l. George Rose/Gamma-Liaison; b.r. John Sotomayor/NYT Pictures. 383: t.l. The Raleigh News & Observer; t.r. Joshel Namkung/Traditional Arts Services; m.r. Courtesy of Evelyn Crawford; m.l. Courtesy of Shirley Caeser; b.r. Wide World Photos.